T0260038

Data Structure Using C

Theory and Program

Data Structure Using C

Theory and Program

Ahmad Talha Siddiqui
Asst. Professor
Dept. of Computer Science & IT
Maulana Azad National Urdu University, Hyderabad

Shoeb Ahad Siddiqui
Sr. Instructor
Computer Science & Engineering
Integral University, Lucknow

CRC Press is an imprint of the
Taylor & Francis Group, an **informa** business

First published 2024
by CRC Press
4 Park Square, Milton Park, Abingdon, Oxon, OX14 4RN

and by CRC Press
2385 NW Executive Center Drive, Suite 320, Boca Raton FL 33431

CRC Press is an imprint of Informa UK Limited

ISBN: 9781032591636 (hbk)
ISBN: 9781032591643 (pbk)
ISBN: 9781003453291 (ebk)

DOI: 10.4324/9781003453291

Typeset in Times New Roman
by Manakin Press, Delhi

Brief Contents

Detailed Contents

1

Introduction to Data Structures

1.1 INTRODUCTION

In computer science, a data structure is a particular way of storing data in a computer so that it can be used efficiently. Different kinds of data structures are suited to various kinds of applications, and some are highly specialized to certain tasks. For Example, B-Trees are well suited for implementation of databases, while compiler implementations usually use hash tables to look up for identifiers.

Data structures are used almost in every program or software. Data structures are generally based on the ability of a computer to fetch and store data at any place in its memory, specified by an address- a bit string that can be itself stored in memory and manipulated by the program. Thus, the record and array data structure are based on computing the address of data items with arithmetic's operation; while the linked list data structures are based on storing address of data items within the structure itself.

Definition

- A data structure is a method of representing data; it not only deals with raw data but also involves the relationship between the data.
- A data structure is defined as a way of representing data in computer memory.
- Data structure is the structural representation of logical relationships between elements of data.

1.2 CLASSIFICATION OF DATA STRUCTURE

1. Linear data structure
2. Non-linear data structure

3. Primitive and non-primitive data structure
4. Homogeneous and non-homogeneous data structure

Linear data structure: In linear data structure, data is stored in consecutive memory locations *i.e.*, array, linked list, stack and queue.

Non-linear data structure: In non-linear data structure, data is stored in non consecutive memory location. A non-linear data structure is mainly used to represent data containing a hierarchical relationship between data elements *i.e.*, tree, graph.

Primitive data structures: are the basic data structures and are directly operated upon by the machine instructions, which is in a primitive level. These have different representations on different computers. They are integer, floating point numbers, characters, string constants, etc.

Non-primitive data structures: Is the more complicated data structure on structuring of a group of homogeneous or heterogeneous data items. These are derived from the primitive data structures. They are array, linked-list, stack, queue, graph, tree, files, etc.

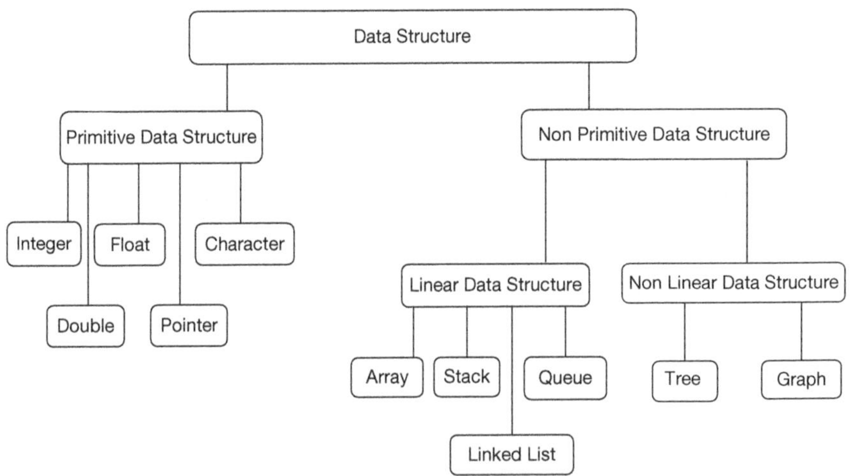

Figure 1 Classification of Data Structure

In homogeneous data structures, the data elements are of same type like array. In non-homogeneous data structures, the data elements may not be of same type.

1.3 OPERATION ON DATA STRUCTURE

Create: this is the first operation to create a data.

Inserting: adding new record from the data structure.

Deleting: remove a record from the data structure.

Updating: it changes values of the data structure.

Traversing: access each record exactly once so that certain items in the record may be processed.

Searching: finding the location of the record with a given key value, or finding the locations of all records, which satisfy one or more condition in the data.

Sorting: arranging the data elements in some logical order *i.e.* in ascending and descending order.

Merging: combine the two different data elements into a single set of data element.

1.4 OVERVIEW OF VARIOUS DATA STRUCTURE

Array

The simplest type of data structure is a linear array and most often it is the only data structure that is provided in any programming language. An array can be defined as a collection of homogenous elements, in the form of index or value, stored in consecutive memory locations. An array always has a predefine size and the elements of an array are referenced by means of an index or value. Thus an array is a collection of variables of the same data type that share a common name. The general syntax of an array is as type variable-name [SIZE].

a [0]	a [1]	a [2]	a [3]	a [4]

Stack

A stack is an ordered list elements. Insertion in a stack is done using PUSH function and removal from a stack is done using POP function. There are only two basic operations possible on a stack.

(*i*) PUSH: Insert an element or value into a stack.

(*ii*) POP: Retrieve an element or value into the stack.

Stack is also called as LIFO (Last-in First-Out).

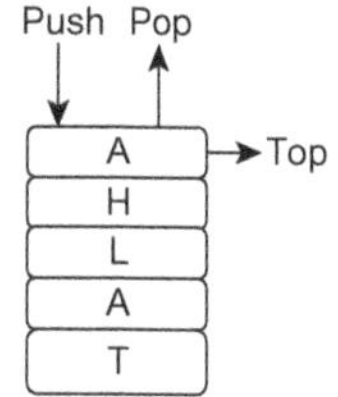

Figure 2: Schematic Diagram of Stack

Queue

A queue is an ordered list in which all insertions can take place at one end called the REAR and all deletions take place at the other end called the FRONT. The two operations that are possible in a queue are insertion and deletion. Queue is also called FIFO (First-In-First-Out).

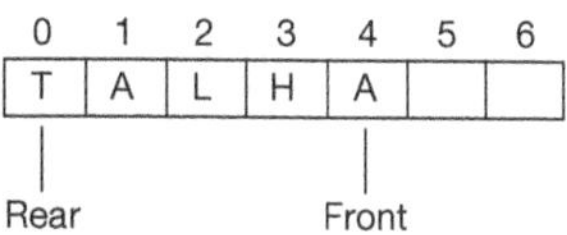

Figure 3: Representation of Queue

Linked list

A linked list is a linear collection of data elements called nodes, where the linear order is given by means of pointers. The key here is that every node will have two parts: first part contains the information/data and the second part contains the link/address of the next node in the list. Memory is allocated for every node when it is actually required and will be free when not required.

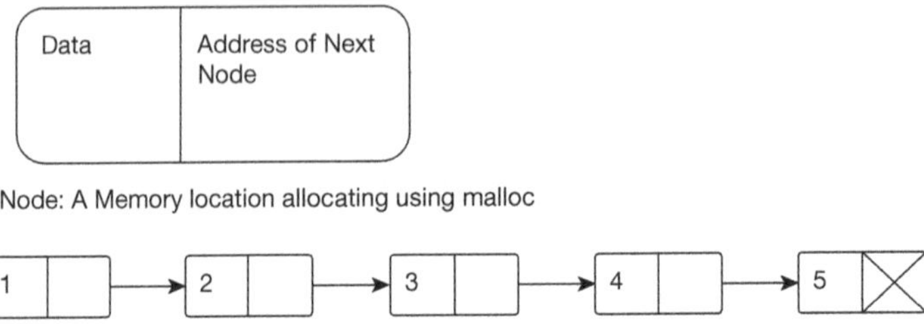

Figure 4 Representation of Linked List

Tree

A tree is a non linear data structure. A tree is a finite set of one or more nodes such that:

There is a specially designated node called the root.

The remaining nodes are partitioned into n>=0 disjoint sets T_1.......T_n where each of these sets is a tree. T_1..... T_n are called sub-tree of the root.

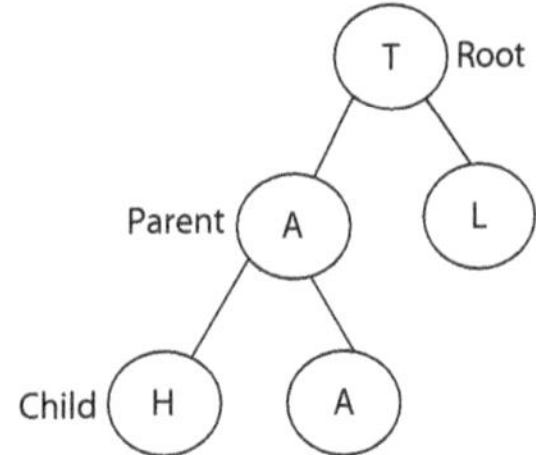

Figure 5: Representation of Tree

Graphs

Graph is a general tree with no parent child relationship. In general, a graph G may be defined as a finite set V of vertices and a set E of edge pair of connected vertices. The notation used is as follows: graph G = (V, E).

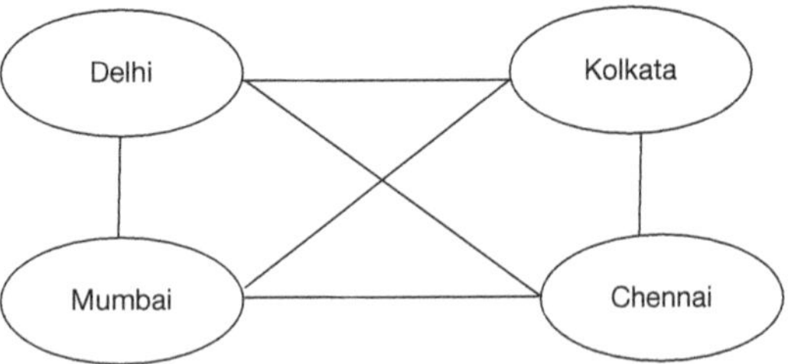

Figure 6: Representation of Graph

Advantages and Disadvantages

Data Structure	Advantages	Disadvantages
array	Quick insertion, very fast access if index is known.	Slow search, slow deletion, fixed size
Ordered array	Quicker search than unsorted array	Slow insertion and deletion, fixed size.

Data Structure	Advantages	Disadvantages
Stack	Provides last-in-first-out access	Slow access to other items
Queue	Provides first-in-first-out access	Slow access to other items
Linked list	Quick insertion and deletion	Slow search
Binary tree	Quick search, insertion, deletion (if tree remains balanced)	Deletion algorithm is complex
Red-Black tree	Quick search, insertion, deletion. Tree always balanced	Complex
2-3-4 tree	Quick search, insertion, deletion. Tree always balanced. Similar trees good for disk storage	Complex
Hash	Table very fast access if key known. Fast insertion	Slow deletion, access slow if key not known, inefficient memory usage
Heap	Fast insertion, deletion, access to large item	Slow access to other items
Graph	Models real world situations	Some algorithms are slow and complex

1.5 ALGORITHM

An algorithm is a step-by-step finite sequence of instructions to solve a problem. Every algorithm must satisfy the following condition:

Input: zero or more quantities.

Output: at least one quantity is produced.

Definiteness: each instruction is clear and unambiguous.

Finiteness: if we trace out the instructions of an algorithm, then for all cases the algorithm will terminate after a finite number of steps.

Effectiveness: every instruction must be sufficiently basic that it can in principle be carried out by a person using only pencil and paper.

1.6 APPROACH FOR ALGORITHM DESIGN

There are two basic approaches for designing an algorithm; they are Top-Down Approach and Bottom-Up Approach.

Top-Down Approach: A top-down approach (also known as *stepwise design* and in some cases used as a synonym of *decomposition*) is essentially the breaking down of a system to gain insight into its compositional sub-systems in a reverse engineering fashion. In a top-down approach an overview of the system is formulated, specifying but not detailing any first-level subsystems. Each subsystem is then refined in yet greater detail, sometimes in many additional subsystem levels, until the entire specification is reduced to base elements. A top-down model is often specified with the assistance of "black boxes", these make it easier to manipulate. However, black boxes may fail to elucidate elementary mechanisms or be detailed enough to realistically validate the model. Top down approach starts with the big picture. It breaks down from there into smaller segments

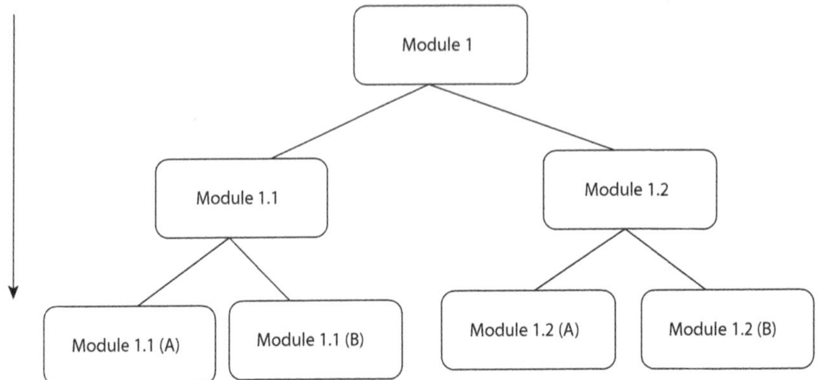

Figure 7: Representation of Top down Approach

Bottom-Up Approach: A bottom-up approach is the piecing together of systems to give rise to more complex systems, thus making the original systems sub-systems of the emergent system. Bottom-up processing is a type of information processing based on incoming data from the environment to form a perception. From a Cognitive Psychology perspective, information enters the eyes in one direction (sensory input, or the "bottom"), and is then turned into an image by the brain that can be interpreted and recognized as a perception (output that is "built up" from processing to final cognition). In a bottom-up approach the individual base elements of the system are first specified in great detail. These elements are then linked together to form larger subsystems, which then in turn are linked, sometimes in many levels, until a complete top-level system is formed. This strategy often resembles a "seed" model, by which the beginnings are small but eventually grow in complexity and completeness. However, "organic strategies" may result in a tangle of elements and subsystems, developed in isolation and subject to local optimization as opposed to meeting a global purpose

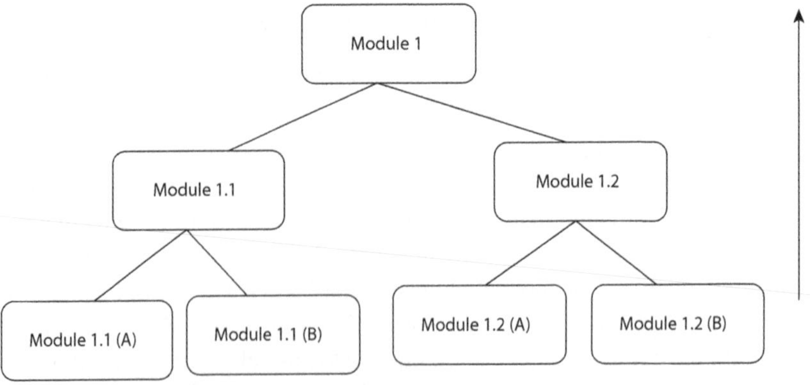

Figure 8: Representation of Bottom-up Approach

There are another popular design approaches

1. Incremental Approach
2. Divide and Conquer Approach
3. Greedy Approach
4. Dynamic Programming Approach
5. Backtracking Approach
6. Branch and Bound Approach

1. **Incremental Approach:** In this approach every time we increase the index to insert the element at proper position. Insertion sort uses an incremental approach. Having sorted the sub-array [1.....j-1], insert the single element A[j] into its proper place, yielding the sorted sub-array A[1....j].
2. **Divide and Conquer Approach:** Divide the original problem into a set of sub-problems. Solve every sub-problem individually, recursively. Combine the solutions of the sub-problems (top level) into a solution of the whole original problem.
3. **Greedy Approach:** A greedy algorithm is a mathematical process that looks for simple, easy-to-implement solutions to complex, multi-step problems by deciding which next step will provide the most obvious benefit. Such algorithms are called greedy because while the optimal solution to each smaller instance will provide an immediate output, the algorithm doesn't consider the larger problem as a whole. Once a decision has been made, it is never reconsidered. Greedy algorithms work by recursively constructing a set of objects from the smallest possible constituent parts. Recursion is an approach to problem solving in which the solution to a particular problem depends on solutions to smaller instances of the same problem. The advantage to using a greedy algorithm is that solutions to smaller instances of the problem can be straightforward and easy to understand. The disadvantage is that it is entirely possible that the most optimal short-term solutions may lead to the worst possible long-term outcome. Greedy algorithms are often used in mobile networking to efficiently route packets with the fewest number of hops and the shortest delay possible. They are also used in machine learning, business intelligence (BI), artificial intelligence (AI) and programming.
4. **Dynamic Approach:** Dynamic programming is a technique for efficiently computing recurrences by storing partial result. It is a method of solving problems exhibiting the properties of overlapping sub-problems and optimal sub-structure that takes much less time than naïve methods.
5. **Backtracking Approach:** Backtracking is a form of recursion. The usual scenario is that you are faced with a number of options, and you must choose one of these. After you make your choice you will get a new set of options; just what set of options you get depends on what choice you made. This procedure is repeated over and over until you reach a final state. If you made

a good sequence of choices, your final state is a *goal state;* if you didn't, it isn't. Conceptually, you start at the root of a tree; the tree probably has some good leaves and some bad leaves, though it may be that the leaves are all good or all bad. You want to get to a good leaf. At each node, beginning with the root, you choose one of its children to move to, and you keep this up until you get to a leaf.

6. **Branch and Bound:** In a branch and bound algorithm a given sub-problem, which cannot be bounded, has to be divided into at least two new restricted sub-problems. Branch and bound algorithms are methods for global optimization in non-convex problems.

Analysis of algorithm

The algorithm can be analysed by tracing all step-by-step instructions, reading the algorithm for logical correctness, and testing it on some data using mathematical techniques to prove it correct. After designing an algorithm, it has to be checked and its correctness needs to be predicted; this is done by analysing the algorithm. thus, an algorithm analysis measures the efficiency of the algorithm. The efficiency of an algorithm can be checked by (i) correctness of an algorithm, (ii) implementation of an algorithm, (iii) simplicity of an algorithm (iv) execution time and memory requirements of an algorithm.

Types of Analysis

Best Case: The best case complexity of the algorithm is the function defined by the minimum number of steps taken on any instance of size n.

Average Case: The average case complexity of the algorithm is the function defined by an average number of steps taken on any instance of size n.

Worst Case: The worst case complexity of an algorithm is the function defined by the maximum number of steps taken on any instance of size n.

1.7 TIME-SPACE TRADE OFF

For many natural problems, such as sorting or matrix-multiplication, there are many choices of algorithms to use, some of which are extremely space-efficient and others of which are extremely time-efficient. This is an instance of a general phenomenon where one can often save space by recomputing intermediate results. Research in time-space trade off lower bounds seeks to prove that, for certain problems, no algorithms exist that achieve small space and small time simultaneously. In computer science, a space-time or time-memory trade off is a way of solving a problem or calculation in less time by using more storage space (or memory), or by solving a problem in very little space by spending a long time. Most computers have a large amount of space, but not infinite space. Also, most people are willing to wait a little while for a big calculation, but not forever. So if your problem is taking a long time but not much memory, a space-time trade off would let you use more memory and solve the problem more quickly. Or, if it could be solved very quickly but requires more memory than you have, you can try to spend more time solving the problem in the limited memory.

Time Complexity

In computer science, the **time complexity** of an algorithm quantifies the amount of time taken by an algorithm to run as a function of the length of the string representing the input. The time complexity of an algorithm is commonly expressed using big oh notation, which excludes coefficients and lower order terms. When expressed this way, the time complexity is said to be described *asymptotically*, *i.e.*, as the input size goes to infinity. Time complexity is commonly estimated by counting the number of elementary operations performed by the algorithm, where an elementary operation takes a fixed amount of time to perform. Thus the amount of time taken and the number of elementary operations performed by the algorithm differ by at most a constant factor.

"The time complexity of an algorithm is the amount of time it needs to run to completion". Some of the reasons for studying time complexity are

1. We may be interested to know in advance that whether the program will provide a satisfactory real time response.
2. There may be several possible solutions with different time requirements or with different time complexity.

Space Complexity

Space complexity is a measure of the amount of working storage an algorithm needs. That means how much memory, in the worst case, is needed at any point in the algorithm. As with time complexity, we're mostly concerned with how the space needs grow, in big-Oh terms, as the size N of the input problem grows. *Space Complexity* of an algorithm is total space taken by the algorithm with respect to the input size. Space complexity includes both Auxiliary space and space used by input.

"The space complexity of an algorithm is the amount of memory it needs to run to completion". The space needed by a program consists of following components-

1. **Instructions space** - to store executable version of program
2. **Data space** - to store all constants, variables etc.
3. **Environment stack space** - it is used in case of recursive program

The total space needed by a program can be divided in two parts- A fixed part that is independent of particular problem, and includes instructions space for constants, variables and fixed size structure variables A variable part that includes structure variables whose size depends on the particular problem being solved dynamically allocated space and the recursion stack space.

1.8 ASYMPTOTIC NOTATION

Big-Oh Notation

We use 0-Notation to give an upper bound on a function, to within constant factor. For a given function g(n), we denote by O(g(n)),

O(g(n)) = {f(n): there exit positive constant c and n_0 such that: $O \leq f(n) \leq cg(n)$ for all $n \geq n_0$ }

Example

Suppose $f(n) = 2n^2 + 3n + 5$. We want to express f(n) as the upper bound of some other function.

We can proceed as follows.

$f(n) = 2n^2 + 3n + 5$

$\leq 2n^2 + 3n^2 + 5n^2$

$\leq 10n^2$

Thus, $f(n) = 0(n^2)$, here $g(n) = n^2$ where c = 10 and $n \geq 1$

Note:

$f(n) = 0(n^2)$ implies that $f(n) = 0(n^x)$ for all $x \geq 2$

f(n) = c where c is a positive constant, then f(n) can be expressed with 0-notation as f(n) = 0(1)

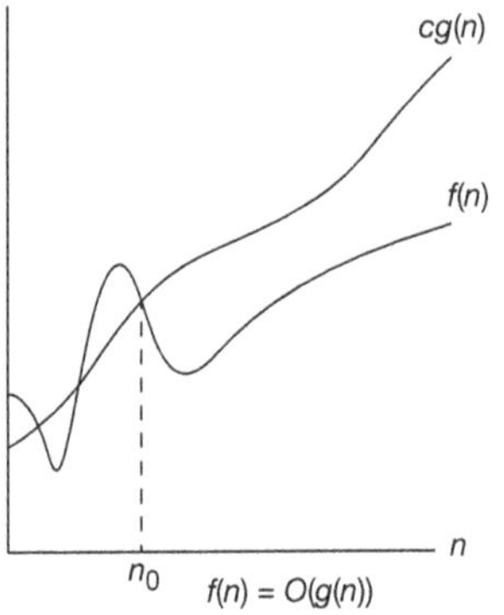

Figure 9: Graphically Representation of Big-Oh Notation

Omega (Ω) Notation

This is almost the same definition as Big-Oh except that "$f(n) \geq g(n)$". This makes g(n) a lower bound function instead of an upper bound function. For a given function g(n), Ω(g(n)) = {f(n): there exit positive constants c and n_0 such that: $O \leq cg(n) \leq f(n)$ for all $n \geq n_0$ }

Example

$f(n) = n^3 + n^2 + n + 1$ and $g(n) = 3n^2 + 2n + 1$

since, $f(n) \geq g(n)$ for all $n \geq 3$

hence, we have f(n) = Ω(g(n)

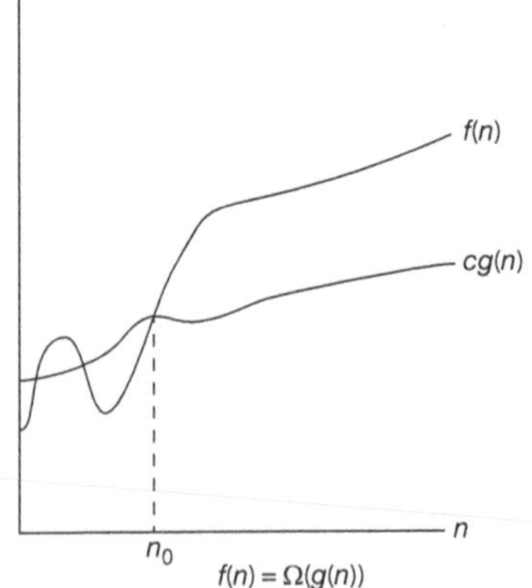

Figure 10 Graphically Representation of Omega (Ω) Notation

f(n) = 5 log n + 3 log (log n). Let us find the Ω-notation of f(n)

now, f(n) = 5 log n + 3 log (log n)

≥ 5 log n for n ≥ 2

Hence, f(n) = Ω (log n)

Theta (θ) Notation

The lower and upper bound for the function T is provided by the theta notation. For a given function g(n), we denote by θ(g(n)) the set of functions as: θ(g(n)) = {f(n): it exit positive constants c_1, c_2 and n_0 such that: $0 \le c_1 g(n) \le f(n) \le c_2 g(n)$ for all $n \ge n_0$}

Example

Suppose $f(n) = 1/2n^2 - 3n$. we can show that $f(n) = \theta(n^2)$

Here,we have to find c_1, c_2 and n_0 such that $c_1.n^2 \le f(n) \le c_2.n^2$

Let $c_1 . n^2 \le 1/2n^2 - 3n \le c_2 . n^2$

Or $c_1 \le ½ - 3/n \le c^2$ (dividing both side by n^2)

We see that the above inequality holds for $n \ge 7$ (thus $n_0 = 7$) and $c_1 = 1/14$, $c_2 = 1/2$

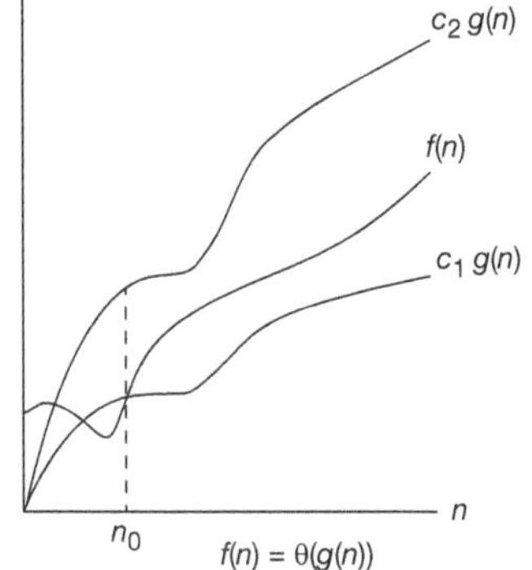

Figure 11: Graphically Representation of Theta (θ) Notation

1.9 DYNAMIC MEMORY ALLOCATION

The process of allocating memory at runtime is known as **dynamic memory allocation**. Library routines known as "memory management functions" are used for allocating and freeing memory during execution of a program. These functions are defined in **stdlib.h**.

Function	Description
malloc()	allocates requested size of bytes and returns a void pointer pointing to the first byte of the allocated space
calloc()	allocates space for an array of elements, initialize them to zero and then return a void pointer to the memory
free	releases previously allocated memory
realloc	modify the size of previously allocated space

Memory Allocation Process

Global variables, static variables and program instructions get their memory in permanent storage area whereas local variables are stored in area called Stack.

The memory space between these two regions is known as Heap area. This region is used for dynamic memory allocation during execution of the program. The size of heap keeps changing.

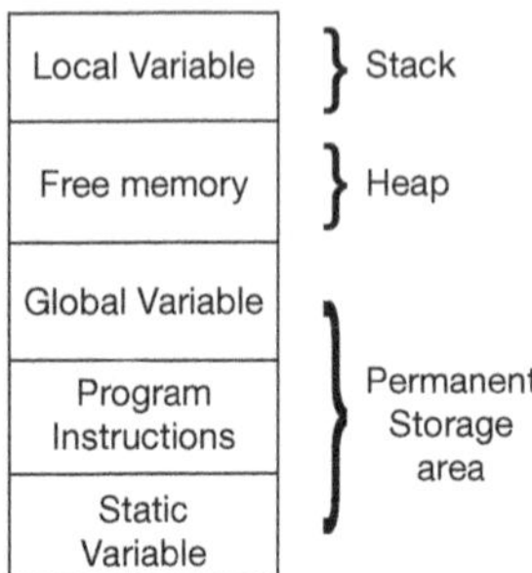

Allocating block of Memory

malloc ():

malloc () function is used for allocating block of memory at runtime. This function reserves a block of memory of given size and returns a pointer of type void. This means that we can assign it to any type of pointer using typecasting. If it fails to locate enough space it returns a NULL pointer.

Example using malloc ():

```
int *x;
x = (int*) malloc (50 * sizeof (int));      //memory space allocated to variable x
free (x);                 //releases the memory allocated to variable x
```

calloc():

calloc() is another memory allocation function that is used for allocating memory at runtime. **calloc** function is normally used for allocating memory to derived data types such as **arrays** and **structures**. If it fails to locate enough space it returns a NULL pointer.

Example using calloc () :

```
struct employee
{
char *name;
int salary;
};
typedef struct employee emp;
emp *e1;
e1 = (emp*)calloc(30,sizeof(emp));
```

realloc ():

realloc () changes memory size that is already allocated to a variable.

Example using realloc () :

int *x;

x = (int*)malloc(50 * sizeof(int));

x = (int*)realloc(x,100); *//allocated a new memory to variable **x***

Diffrence between malloc() and calloc()

calloc()	malloc()
calloc() initializes the allocated memory with 0 value.	malloc() initializes the allocated memory with garbage values.
Number of arguments is 2	Number of argument is 1
Syntax : (cast_type *)calloc(blocks, size_of_block);	**Syntax :** (cast_type *)malloc(Size_in_bytes);

POINTS TO REMEMBER

1. A data structure is a particular way of sorting and organizing data either in computer's memory or on the disk storage so that it can be used efficiently.
2. There are two types of data structure: primitive and non-primitive data structure.
3. Primitive data structures are the fundamental data types which are supported by a programming language.
4. Non-primitive data structures are those data structures which are created using primitive data structure.
5. Non-primitive data structures can further be classified into two categories: linear and non-linear data structure.
6. In the elements of a data structures are stored in a linear or sequential order, then it is a linear data structure. However, if the elements of a data structure are not stored in sequential order, then it is a non-linear data structure.
7. An array is a collection of similar data elements which are stored in consecutive memory locations.
8. A linked list is a linear data structure consisting of a group of elements called nodes which together represent a sequence.
9. A stack is a last-in-first-out (LIFO) data structure in which insertion and deletion of elements are done at only one end, which is known as the top of the stack.
10. A queue is a first-in-first-out (FIFO) data structure in which the element that is inserted first is the first to be taken out. The elements in a queue are added at one end called the rear and removed from the other end called the front.

11. A tree is a non-linear data structure which consists of a collection of nodes arranged in a hierarchical tree structure. The simplest form of a tree is a binary tree. A binary tree consists of a root node and left and right sub-tree, where both sub-trees are also binary trees.
12. A graph is often viewed as a generalization of the tree structure.
13. An algorithm is basically a set of instructions that solve a problem.
14. The time complexity of an algorithm is basically the running time of the program as a function of the input size.
15. The space complexity of an algorithm is the amount of computer memory required during the program execution as a function of the input size.
16. The worst-case running time of an algorithm is an upper bound on the running time for any input.
17. The average-case running time specifies the expected behavior of the algorithm when the input is randomly drawn from a given distribution.
18. The efficiently of an algorithm is expressed in terms of the number of elements that has to be processed and the type of the loop that is being used.

EXERCISES

1. Define Data Structure and also write down the difference between primitive data structure and non-primitive data structure?
2. Name various Data Structures. Explain them briefly?
3. What are the various operations to be performed on Data Structures?
4. What is an algorithm? Explain with the help of suitable example the time and space analysis of an algorithm?
5. Explain the different ways of analysis of algorithm?
6. Distinguish between time and space complexity?
7. What do you understand by best, worst and average case analysis of an algorithm?
8. What do you understand by time-space trade off?
9. Explain the concept of Big-Oh Notation, Omega (Ω) Notation and Theta (θ) Notation?

MULTIPLE CHOICE QUESTION

1. Which data structure is defined as a collection of similar data elements?

   (*a*) Arrays (*b*) Linked list
   (*c*) Trees (*d*) Graphs

2. The data structure used in hierarchical data model is

   (*a*) Array (*b*) Linked list
   (*c*) Tree (*d*) graph

3. In a stack, insertion is done at
   (*a*) Top (*b*) Front
   (*c*) Rear (*d*) mid
4. The position in a queue from which an element is deleted is called as
   (*a*) Top (*b*) Front
   (*c*) Rear (*d*) mid
5. Which data structure has fixed size?
   (*a*) Arrays (*b*) Linked lists
   (*c*) Trees (*d*) graphs
6. If top=max-1, then that the stack is
   (*a*) Empty (*b*) Full
   (*c*) Contains some data (*d*) None of these
7. Which among the following is a LIFO data structure?
   (*a*) Stacks (*b*) Linked list
   (*c*) Queues (*d*) graphs
8. Which data structure is used to represent complex relationships between the nodes?
   (*a*) Arrays (*b*) Linked lists
   (*c*) Trees (*d*) graphs
9. Examples of linear data structures include
   (*a*) Arrays (*b*) Stacks
   (*c*) Queue (*d*) All of these
10. Th running time complexity of a linear algorithm is given as
   (*a*) O(1) (*b*) O(n)
   (*c*) O(n log n) (*d*) $O(n^2)$
11. Which notation provides a strict upper bound for f(n)?
   (*a*) Omega notation (*b*) Big O notation
   (*c*) Small o notation (*d*) Theta notation
12. Which notation comprises a set of all functions h(n) that are greater than or equal to cg(n) for all values of $n \geq n_0$
   (*a*) Omega notation (*b*) Big O notation
   (*c*) Small o notation (*d*) Theta notation
13. Function in o(n) notation is
   (*a*) $10\ n^2$ (*b*) $N^{1.9}$
   (*c*) $N^2/100$ (*d*) N^2

TRUE OR FALSE

1. Trees and graphs are the examples of linear data structures.
2. Queues is a FIFO data structure.
3. Trees can represent any kind of complex relationship between the nodes.
4. The average-case running time of an algorithm is an upper bound on the running time for any input.
5. Array is an abstract data types.
6. Array elements are stored in consecutive memory locations.
7. The pop operation adds an element to the top of a stack.
8. Graphs have a purely parent-to-child relationship between their nodes.
9. The worst-case running time of an algorithm is a lower bound on the running time for any input.
10. In top-down approach, we start with designing the most basic or concrete modules and then proceed towards designing higher-level modules.

FILL IN THE BLANKS

1. __________ is an arrangement of data either in the computer's memory or on the disk storage.
2. __________ are used to manipulate the data contained in various data structures.
3. In ____________, the elements of a data structure are stored sequentially.
4. __________ of a variable specifies the set of values that the variable can take.
5. A tree is empty if ______________
6. Abstract means __________
7. The time complexity of an algorithm is the running time given as a function of ________
8. _______ analysis guarantees the average performance of each operation in the worst case.
9. The elements of an array are referenced by an ___________.
10. __________ is used to store the address of the topmost element of a stack.
11. The _________ operation returns the value of the topmost element of a stack.
12. An overflow occurs when____________.
13. __________ is a FIFO data structure.
14. The elements in a queue are added at __________ and remove from __________.
15. If the elements of a data structure are stored sequentially, then it is a __________.

REFERENCES

1. Gotlieb, C.C. and L.R. Gotlieb, Data Types and Structures, Prentice Hall, Englewood Cliffs, New Jersey, 1986.
2. Horowitz, Ellis, and Sartaj Sahni, Fundamentals of Data Structure, Computer Science Press, Rockville, Maryland, 1985.
3. Kruse, Robert L., Bruce P. Leung and L. Clovis Tondo, Data Structures and Program Design in C, Prentice Hall of India, New Delhi, 1995.
4. Tremblay, Jean Paul, and Paul G. Sorenson, An Introduction to Data Structures with Applications, McGraw-Hill, New York, 1987.
5. J. Cohoon and J. Davidson, An Introduction to Programming and Object Oriented Design, 3rd Edition, McGraw-Hill, New York.
6. H. Deitel and P. Deitel, C++ how to Program, 4th Edition, Prentice Hall, Englewood Cliffs, New Jersey, 2002.

2

Introduction to Array

2.1 ARRAY

Arrays are most frequently used in programming. Mathematical problems like matrix, algebra, etc can be easily handled by arrays. An array is a collection of similar/homogenous data elements described by a single name. Each element of an array is referenced by a variable or value, called index. If an element of an array is referenced by single subscript, then the array is known as one-dimensional array or linear array. If an element of an array is referenced by two subscripts, then the array is known as two-dimensional array. The arrays whose elements are referenced by two or more subscripts are called multi-dimensional arrays.

Definition

An array can be defined as the combination of homogenous elements with consecutive index numbers and successive memory locations. The values of an array are called elements of that array. The general syntax of an array is

<<Data type >> variable name [size];

Example of one-dimensional array

Int arr [5] = {11, 22, 33, 44, 55};

Char arr [5] = “Talha”;

Float arr [5] = {10.5, 20.5, 30.5, 40.5, 50.5}

The data type contained in the array could be int, char, float etc and the size indicates the maximum number of elements that can be stored inside the array. So, when we declare an array, we will have to assign a type as well as size. For example, when we want to store 5 integer values, then we can use the following declaration.

int arr [5]

By this declaration we are declaring arr to be an array, which is supposed to contain in all 5 integer values.

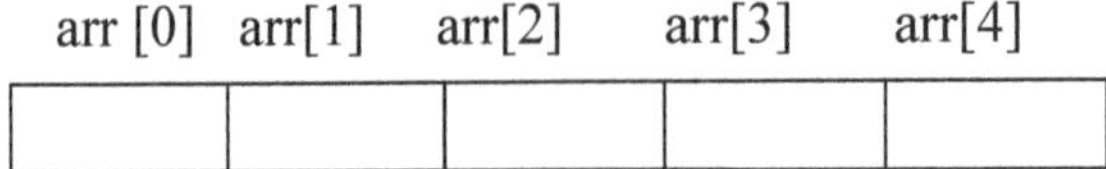

2.2 ONE-DIMENSIONAL ARRAY

This type of array represents and store data in linear form. It is also called single dimensional array. One-dimensional array is a set of ‘n’ finite number of similar/homogenous data elements. The elements of the array are referenced respectively by an index set consisting of ‘n’ consecutive memory locations. The elements of the array are stored respectively in successive memory locations. Sets of ‘n’ numbers are called the length or size of an array. The elements of an array “arr” can be denoted in C Programming language as: A[0], A[1], A[2], A[3],. ......A[n-1]. The number ‘n ’in A [n] is called a subscript or an index and A[n] is called a subscript variable. If ‘n’ is 8, then the array elements are stored in memory A[0], A[1], A[2], A[3], A[4], A[5], A[6], A[7].

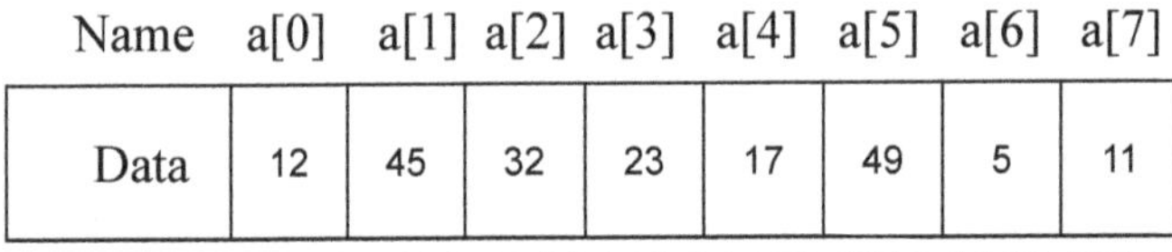

Name	a[0]	a[1]	a[2]	a[3]	a[4]	a[5]	a[6]	a[7]
Data	12	45	32	23	17	49	5	11
Address	1000	1002	1004	1006	1008	1010	1012	1014

Figure 1: I-D int Array memory arrangement

Write a program to insert element in a Single Dimensional Array

```
#include<stdio.h>
void main()
{
int a[4],i,pos,data;
printf (“Enter the number”);
for(i=0;i<=3;i++)
{
scanf(“%d”,&a[i]);
}
printf(“Enter the position”);
scanf(“%d”,&pos);
printf(“Enter the Data”);
scanf(“%d”,&data);
for(i=2;i>=pos;i--)
{
```

```
a[i+1]=a[i];
}
a[pos]=data;
printf("The Final Array is\n");
for(i=0;i<4;i++)
{
printf("%d\t",a[i]);
}
}
```

Output

```
Enter the number 5
3
5
Enter the position2
Enter the Data12
The Final Array is
  5     3     12     5
```

Write a program to Delete element in a Single Dimension Array

```
#include<stdio.h>
void main()
{
int a[5],i,pos,data;
printf("Enter the number");
for(i=0;i<4;i++)
{
scanf("%d",&a[i]);
}
printf("Enter the position");
scanf("%d",&pos);
for(i=pos;i<4;i++)
{
a[i]=a[i+1];
}
printf("The Final Array is\n");
for(i=0;i<3;i++)
{
```

```
printf("%d\t",a[i]);
}
}
```

Output

```
Enter the number6
3
12
4
Enter the position2
The Final Array is
 6     3      4
```

Write a program to find out Maximum and Minimum value in single dimension array

```
#include<stdio.h>
void main()
{
int a[10],i,max,min;
printf("Enter the number of Array\n");
for(i=0;i<10;i++)
{
scanf("%d",&a[i]);
}
printf("The Array Elements Is:-\n");
for(i=0;i<10;i++)
{
printf("%d\t",a[i]);
}
max=a[0];
for(i=1;i<10;i++)
{
if(a[i]>max)
max=a[i];
}
min=a[0];
for(i=1;i<10;i++)
{
```

```
if(a[i]<min)
min=a[i];
}
printf("\n The Maximum Value is:- %d", max);
printf("\n The Minimum Value is:- %d", min);
}
```

Output

```
Enter the number of Array
12
3
21
33
40
-10
5
8
2
45
The Array Elements Is:-
12	3	21	33	40	-10	5	8	2	45
The Maximum Value is:- 45
The Minimum Value is:- -10
```

2.3 OPERATIONS ON ARRAY

Various operations that can be performed on an array are:

1. Traversing.
2. Sorting.
3. Searching.
4. Insertion.
5. Deletion
6. Merging.

Traversing

Traversing is the process of visiting each element of the array exactly once, starting from first element upto the last element. A simple algorithm is below.

Algorithm

Steps:

1. i = L
2. while i ≤ U do
3. process (A[i])
4. i = i + 1
5. end while
6. stop

Sorting

This operation is performed on an array in a specified order (ascending or descending). The given algorithm is used to store the element of an integer array in ascending order.

Algorithm

Steps:

1. i = U
2. while i ≥ L do
3. j = L
4. while j > i do
5. if (A[j], A[j+1]) = FALSE
6. swap (A[j], A[j+1])
7. end if
8. j = j + 1
9. end while
10. i = i - 1
11. end while
12. stop

Searching

This operation is applied to search an element in an array. A simple algorithm is as below.

Algorithm

Steps:

1. i = L, found = 0, location = 0 //found=0 means data is not found in the list
2. while (i ≤ U) and (found = 0) do
3. if Compare (A[i], Key) = TRUE then

4. found = 1
5. location = i
6. else
7. i = i + 1
8. end if
9. end while
10. if found = 0 then
11. print “search is unsuccessful”
12. else
13. print “Search is successful”
14. end if
15. Return
16. stop

Insertion

This operation is used to insert an element into an array into a particular location. A simple algorithm is given below.

Algorithm

Steps:

1. if A[U] ≠ NULL then
2. print “array is full”
3. exit
4. else
5. i = U
6. while i > location do
7. A[i] = A[i - 1]
8. i = i - 1
9. End while
10. A[location] = Key
11. End if
12. Stop

Deletion

This operation is used to delete a particular element from an array. The element will be deleted by overwriting it with its subsequent element. A simple algorithm is as shown.

Algorithm

Steps:

1. if n=0 then array is underflow and stop
2. read data as element to be deleted
3. read location at where deletion will be made
4. k=LB
5. repeat step 6 while a(k) $\neq$ data
6. k=k+1
7. repeat step 8 while k< UB
8. a(k)=a(k+1)
9. k=k+1
10. a(UB)=NULL
11. UB=UB-1
12. Stop

Merging

This operation is use to merge two sorted array and create a third array in the sorted order. A simple algorithm is as given.

Note:

LBA: lower bound of array_1

UBA: upper bound of array_1

LBB: lower bound of array_2

UBB: upper bound of array_2

Algorithm

Steps:

1. i=LBA, J=LBB, K=0
2. repeat step 3 to 4 while I $\leq$ UBA and I $\leq$ UBB
3. if A(i) < B(j) then
4. c(k)=A(i)
5. i=i+1
6. else
7. c(k) = A(i)
8. j=j+1
9. k=k+1

10. repeat step 11 while i $\leq$ UBA
11. c(k)=A(i)
12. i=i+1
13. k=k+1
14. repeat step 15 while j $\leq$ UBB
15. c(k) = B(j)
16. j=j+1
17. k=k+1
18. Stop

2.4 REPRESENTATION OF ONE-DIMENSION IN MEMORY

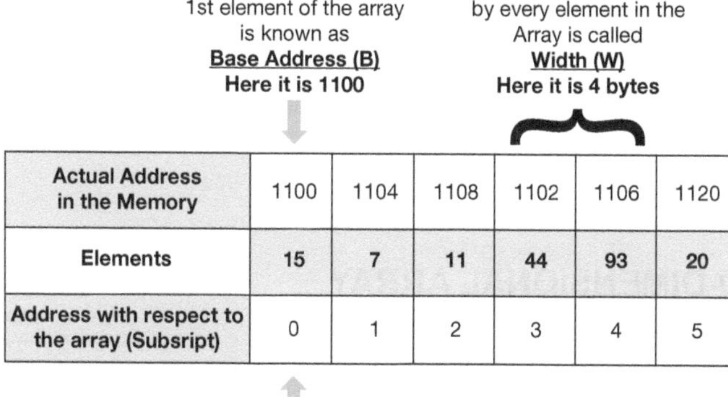
Actual Address of the 1st element of the array is known as
Base Address (B)
Here it is 1100
Memory space acquired by every element in the Array is called
Width (W)
Here it is 4 bytes
Lower Limit/Bound of Subscript (LB)

Actual Address in the Memory	1100	1104	1108	1102	1106	1120
Elements	15	7	11	44	93	20
Address with respect to the array (Subsript)	0	1	2	3	4	5

Calculation in single (one Address) Dimension Array

Let A be a 1-D array with n elements. As array are stored in consecutive memory location, the system need not keep track of the address of every element of A, but needs to keep track of the address of 1st element only, denoted by: base address (A). The address of a particular element in a 1-D array is given below:

Address of element a[k]=B+W*K

Where B=base address

W= size of each element of the array

K= address of the element.

Q1. Suppose the base address of the 1st element of the array is 5000 and each element of the array occupies 2 bytes in the memory, then address of 5th element of a 1-D array a[20] will be given as:

Solution: apply the formula

Address of element a[k] = B + W * K

Base address=5000

W=2

K=5

A [5] = 5000 + 2 * 5

=5000 + 10

=5010

Q2. Suppose the base address of the 1st element of the array is 200 and each element of the array occupies 4 bytes in the memory, then address of 6th element of a 1-D array a[20] will be given as:

Solution: Apply the formula

Address of element a[k] = B + W * K

Base address=200

W=4

K=6

A [6] = 200 + 4 * 6

=200 + 24

=224

2.5 TWO-DIMENSIONAL ARRAY

While storing the elements of a 2-D array in memory, these are allocated in contiguous memory locations. Therefore, a 2-D array must be linearized so as to enable their storage. There are two alternatives to achieve linearization: Row-Major and Column-Major.

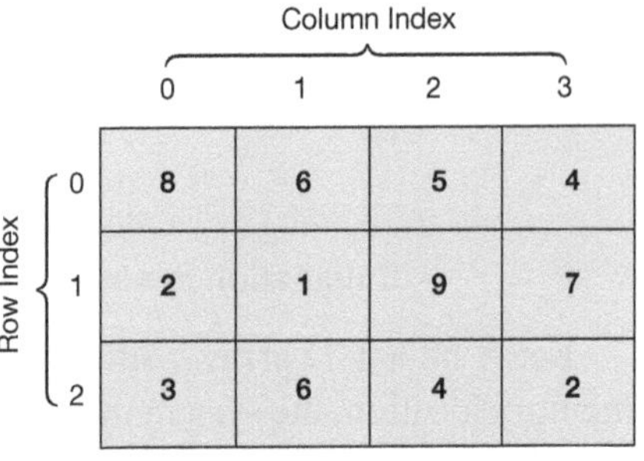

Two-Dimensional Array

The general syntax of two-dimensional array is:

<<Data_type>> array-name [size1][size2];

2.6 IMPLEMENTATION OF 2-D (DIMENSION) ARRAY IN MEMORY

The elements of a 2-D array are stored in computer's memory row-by-row or column-by-column. If the array is stored as row-by-row, it is called row-major order. If the array is stored as column-by-column, it is called column-major order. A 2-D array can be implemented in a computer programming language in two ways:

1. Row-Major Implementation
2. Column-Major Implementation

Row-Major Implementation

Row major ordering assigns successive elements moving across the rows and then down the columns to successive memory locations. The mapping is best described by the diagram.

Row major ordering is the method employed by most high level programming languages including Pascal, C, Ada Modula-2 etc. It is very easy to implement and easy to use in machine language (especially within a debugger such as CodeView). The conversion from a two-dimensional structure to a linear array is very intuitive.

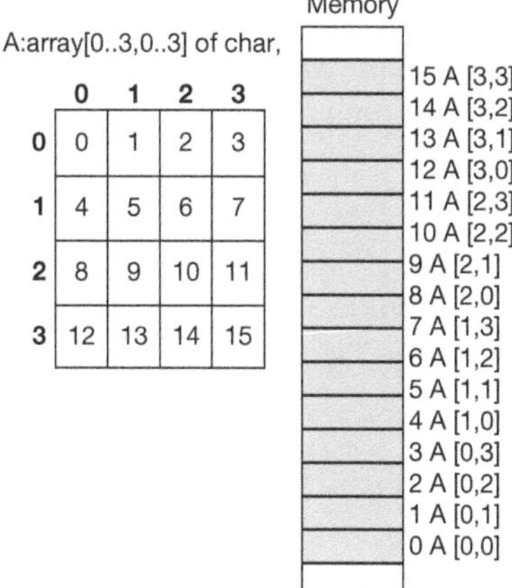

1. **Address of element in Row-Major Implementation**

   Address of element a[i] [j]=B + W (n (i - L1) + (j - L2))

   Where B=base address

   W=size of each array element

   n=number of column (i.e., U2 - L2 + 1)

   L1=lower bound of row

   L2=lower bound of column

   U2=upper bound of a column

Q1. A 2-D array defined as A [4.....6, 1.....4] required 4 bytes of storage space for each element. If the array is stored in row major, then calculate the address of element at location A [5, 2]. Base address is 100.

Solution: Apply the formula

Address of element a[i][j]=B + W (n (i - L1) + (j - L2))

B=100, W=4, i=5, j=2, L1=4, L2=1, U2=4

Calculate n=U2 – L2 +1

=4-1+1

=4

Address of A[5,2]=100 + 4 (4 (5 - 4) + (2 - 1))

=100 + 4 (4 * 1 + 1)

=100 + 20

=120

Q2. Calculate the address of Y [4,3] in a 2-D array Y[-1....6, -1....5] stored in row major order in the main memory. Suppose the base address to be 200 and that each element required 4 bytes of storage.

Solution: Apply the formula

Address of element a[i][j]=B + W (n (i - L1) + (j - L2))

B=200, w=4,i=4,j=3,L1=-1,L2=-1, U2=5

Calculate n=U2 - L2 + 1

=5- (-1) + 1

=7

Address of Y [4,3]=200 + 4(7 (4 - (-1) + (3 - (-1))

=200+4(7 * 5 + 4)

=200+4 * 39

=200 + 156

=356

Q3. Each element of an array ABC [15][45] requires 4 bytes of storage. Suppose base address of ABC is 2000, calculate the location of ABC [5][5] when the array is stored in row major order?

Solution: Apply the formula

Address of element a[i][j]=B + W (n (i - L1) + (j - L2))

B=2000, w=4, n=45, i=5, L1=0, j=5, L2=0

n=number of column, therefore n=45

Address of ABC [5][5]=2000+4 (45(5-0)+(5-0))

=2000+4(225+5)

=2000+920

=2920

Q4. Give an array X [6][6] whose base address is 100. Calculate the location X [2][5] if each element occupies 4 bytes and array is stored row-wise?

Solution: Apply the formula

Address of element a[i][j]=B + W (n (i - L1) + (j - L2))

B=100, w=4, n=6, i=2, j=5, L1=0, L2=0

n=number of column, therefore n=6

Address of X [2][5]=100+4(6(2-0)+(5-0))

=100+4(12+5)

=100+68

=168

1. Address of element in Column-Major Implementation

Column major ordering is the other function frequently used to compute the address of an array element. FORTRAN and various dialects of BASIC (e.g. Microsoft) use this method to index arrays. In row major ordering the right most index increased fast as you moved through consecutive memory locations. In column major ordering the left most index increases the fastest.

Address of element a[i][j]=B + W (m (j - L2)+(i-L1))

Where B=base address

W=size of each array element

m=number of row (i.e., U1 – L1 + 1)

L1=lower bound of row

L2=lower bound of column

U1=upper bound of a row

Q1. A 2-D array defined as A[4.....6, 1.....4] required 4 bytes of storage space for each element. If the array is stored in column major, then calculate the address of element at location A[5,2]. Base address is 100.

Solution: Apply the formula

Address of element a[i][j]=B + W (m (j - L2)+(i-L1))

B=100, w=4, m=3, i=5, j=2, L1=4, L2=1

m=U1-L1+1

=6-4+1

=3

Address of element A [5][2] = 100 + 4 (3 (2 - 1) + (5 - 4)

=100 + 4 * 4

=100 + 16

=116

Q2. Calculate the address of Y [4,3] in a 2-D array Y[-1....6, -1....5] stored in column major order in the main memory. Suppose the base address to be 200 and that each element required 4 bytes of storage.

Solution: Apply the formula

Address of element Y[i][j]=B + W (m (j - L2)+(i-L1))

B=200, w=4, m=7, i=4, j=3, L1=-1, L2=-1

m=U1-L1+1

=6-(-1)+1

=7

Address of element Y [4][3] = 200 + 4 (7 (3 - (-1) + (4 - (-1))

=200 + 4 * 33

=200 + 132

332

Q3. Each element of an array ABC [15][45] requires 4 bytes of storage. Suppose base address of ABC is 2000, calculate the location of ABC [5][5] when the array is stored in column major order?

Solution: Apply the formula

Address of element Y[i][j]=B + W (m (j - L2)+(i-L1))

B=2000, w=4, m=15, i=5, j=5, L1=0, L2=0

m=number of row, therefore m=15

Address of ABC [5][5] = 2000 + 4 (15 (5 – 0) + (5 - 0))

=2000 + 4 *80

=2000 + 320

=2320

Q4. Give an array X [6][6] whose base address is 100. Calculate the location X[2][5] if each element occupies 4 bytes and array is stored column-wise?

Solution: Apply the formula

Address of element Y[i][j]=B + W (m (j - L2)+(i-L1))

B=100, w=4, m=6, i=2,j=5, L1=0, L2=0

m=number of row, therefore m=6

Address of ABC [2][5] = 100 + 4 (6 (5 – 0) + (2 - 0))

=100 + 4 * 32

=100 + 128

=228

2.7 SPARSE MATRICES

There are special types of matrices in which most of the elements are "0s" (Zeros). That is, if lot of elements from a matrix have a value 0 then the matrix is known as a sparse matrix.

There is no clear definition of when a matrix is sparse and when it is not, but it is a concept, which we can all recognise intuitively. If the matrix is sparse, we must consider an alternate way of representing it rather than the normal row-major or column-major arrangement. This is because a sparse matrix is a matrix containing very few non-zero elements. If the user stores the entire matrix including zero elements then there is wastage of storage space.

Consider a 1000 × 1000 matrix have 5 non-zero elements per row then the non-zero percentage of the matrix can be calculated as:

$$\left(\left\{\frac{\left[\frac{5 \times \text{non-zero element}}{\text{Row}}\right]}{\left[1000 \times 1000 \text{ element}\right]}\right\} \times 1000 \text{ rows}\right) \times 100\%$$

$$= 0.005\% \text{ non-zero elements}$$

Thus, to represent this 1000 x 1000 matrix in memory only 0.005% of the memory is required. So, significant storage and computational saving can be realised by using sparse storage and solution techniques.

There are two types of representing sparse matrices.

1. Array Representation.
2. Linked List Representation.

2.8 ARRAY REPRESENTATION OF A SPARSE MATRIX

In the array representation of a sparse matrix, only the non-zero elements are stored so that storage space can be reduced. Each non-zero element in the sparse matrix is represented as Row, Column, and Value. For this, a two-dimension array containing 3 columns can be used. The first column is for storing the row numbers, the second column is for storing the column numbers and the third column represents the value corresponding to the non-zero element at row, column in the first two columns. For example, consider the following sparse matrix.

$$\begin{pmatrix} 2 & 0 & 0 & 0 \\ 0 & 1 & 0 & 0 \\ 0 & 4 & 3 & 0 \\ 0 & 0 & 6 & 0 \end{pmatrix}$$

The above matrix can be represented as

Row	Column	Value
0	0	2
1	1	1
2	1	4
2	2	3
3	2	6

The structure declaration for array is as:

```
#define MAX 50;
struct triplet {
int row;
int column;
int element;
} sparse_matrix[MAX];
```

The maximum number of non-zero elements in sparse matrix is defined by constant MAX. The array representation will use [2 * (n + 1) * size of (int) + n * size of (T)] bytes of memory where n is the number of non-zero bytes and T is the data type of elements.

Linked List Representation of a Sparse Matrix

Representing a sparse matrix as an array of 3-tuples. When carry out addition or multiplication, we need to know the number of non-zero terms in each of the sparse matrices. As a result, it is not possible to predict the size of the resultant matrix before hand. So instead of an array, we can represent the sparse matrix in the form of a linked list. In the linked list representation a separate list is maintained for each column as well as each row of the matrix, i.e., if the matrix is of size 4 x 4, then there would be 4 lists for 4 columns and 4 lists for 4 rows. A node in a list stores the information about the non-zero element of the sparse matrix. The head node for a column list stores the column number, a pointer to the node which comes first in the column and a pointer to the next column head node. A head node for a row list stores, a pointer to the node, which comes first in the row list, and a pointer to the next row head node.

Example: Show through appropriate data structure representation of the following 4 x 4 sparse matrix.

$$\begin{pmatrix} 0 & 0 & 11 & 0 \\ 12 & 0 & 0 & 0 \\ 0 & -4 & 0 & 0 \\ 0 & 0 & 0 & -25 \end{pmatrix}$$

Solution: The given 4 x 4 sparse matrix can be represented in array is:

Row	Column	Value
0	2	11
1	0	12
2	1	-4
3	3	-25

And the linked list representation is:

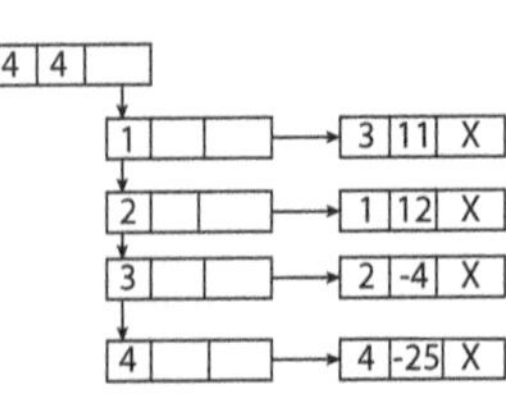

Example: Let A be N x N sparse matrix array. Write algorithm for the following:

(*i*) Find the number NUM of non-zero element in A.

(*ii*) Find the product PROD of the diagonal elements (a11, a22,. ......, ann)

Solution:

(*i*) The algorithm finds the number of non-zero elements in Matrix A.

Steps:

1. Set k=0
2. Repeat for i = 0 to N – 1
3. Repeat for j = 0 to N – 1
4. if A[i,j] ≠ 0
5. then k = k+1
6. print " number of non-zero elements", k
7. stop

(*ii*) The algorithm finds the product of diagonal elements.

Steps:

1. PROD = 1
2. Repeat for i = 0 to N – 1
3. Repeat for j = 0 to N – 1
4. if (i ≠ j)
5. then PROD = PROD * A[i,j]
6. print "PROD"
7. stop

2.9 ADVANTAGES AND DISADVANTAGES OF ARRAYS

Advantages of Arrays

1. It is used to represent multiple data items of same type by using only single name.
2. It can be used to implement other data structures like linked lists, stacks, queues, trees, graphs etc.
3. 2D arrays are used to represent matrices.

Disadvantages of Arrays

1. The dimension of an array is determined at the moment the array is created, and cannot be changed later on.
2. The array occupies an amount of memory that is proportional to its size, independently of the number of elements that are actually of interest.
3. If we want to keep the elements of the collection ordered, and insert a new value in its correct position, or remove it, then, for each such operation we may need to move many elements (on the average, half of the elements of the array); this is very inefficient.

POINTS TO REMEMBER

1. An array is a collection of elements of the same data type.
2. The elements of an array are stored in consecutive memory locations and are referenced by an index.
3. The index specifies an offset from the beginning of the array to the element being referenced.
4. Declaring an array means specifying three parameters: data type, name, and its size.
5. The length of an array is given by the number of elements stored in it.
6. The name of an array is a symbolic reference to the address of the first byte of the array. Therefore, whenever we use the array name, we are actually referring to the first byte of that array.
7. A two-dimensional array is specified using two subscripts where the first subscript denotes the row and the second subscript denotes the column of the array.
8. Using two-dimensional arrays, we can perform the different operations on matrices: transpose, addition, subtraction, multiplication.
9. A multi-dimensional array is an array of arrays.
10. Multi-dimensional arrays can be stored in either row major order or column major order.

EXERCISES

1. What is an array? How is it represented in memory?
2. What are the uses of an array? What is an ordered array?
3. Write short notes on (i) Row-Major Implementation (ii) Column-Major Implementation?
4. Write a C function to insert an element in order stored in an array?
5. How address calculation is done in the array? Derive the formula for two-dimensional, three-dimensional and N-dimensional array?
6. What do you understand by multi-dimensional array? How they are represented in memory?
7. For a single-dimensional array if the base address is 1500. Find 5th index elements address. If a data stored in this array needs only 2 byte?

MULTIPLE CHOICE QUESTION

1. If an array is declared as arr[] = {1,3,5,7,9}; then what is the value of sizeof (arr[3])?

   (*a*) 1 (*b*) 2

   (*c*) 3 (*d*) 8

2. If an array is declared as arr[] = {1,3,5,7,9}; then what is the value of arr[3]?
   (*a*) 1 (*b*) 7
   (*c*) 9 (*d*) 5
3. If an array is declared as double arr[50]; how many bytes will be allocated to it?
   (*a*) 50 (*b*) 100
   (*c*) 200 (*d*) 400
4. If an array is declared as int arr[50], how many elements can it hold?
   (*a*) 49 (*b*) 50
   (*c*) 51 (*d*) 0
5. If an array is declared as int arr[5][5], how many elements can it store?
   (*a*) 5 (*b*) 25
   (*c*) 10 (*d*) 0
6. Given an integer array arr[]; the ith element can be accessed by writing
   (*a*) *(arr+i) (*b*) *(i+arr)
   (*c*) arr[i] (*d*) all of these

TRUE OR FALSE

1. An array is used to refer multiple memory locations having the same name.
2. An array name can be used as a pointer.
3. A loop is used to access all the elements of an array.
4. An array stores all its data elements in non-consecutive memory locations.
5. Lower bound is the index of the last element in an array.
6. Merger array contains contents of the first array followed by the contents of the second array.
7. It is possible to pass an entire array as a function argument.
8. arr[i] is equivalent to writing *(arr+i)
9. Array name is equivalent to the address of its last element.
10. mat[i][j] is equivalent to *(*mat + i)+j).
11. An array contains elements of the same data type.
12. When an array is passed to a function, C passes the value for each element.
13. A two-dimensional array contains data of two different types.
14. The maximum number of dimensional that an array can have is 4.
15. By default, the first subscript of the array is zero.

FILL IN THE BLANKS

1. Each array element is assessed using a ___________.
2. The elements of an array are stored in ____________ memory locations.
3. An n-dimensional array contains ___________ subscripts.
4. Name of the array acts as a _____________
5. Declaring an array means specifying the ___________, _______ and __________
6. _______ is the address of the first element in the array.
7. Length of an array is given by the number of ___________
8. A multi-dimensional array, in simple terms, is an _____________
9. An expression that evaluates to an ___________ value may be used as an index.
10. arr[3] = 10; initializes the __________ element of the array with value 10.

REFERENCES

1. Gotlieb, C.C. and L.R. Gotlieb, Data Types and Structures, Prentice Hall, Englewood Cliffs, New Jersey, 1986.
2. Horowitz, Ellis, and Sartaj Sahni, Fundamentals of Data Structure, Computer Science Press, Rockville, Maryland, 1985.
3. Kruse, Robert L., Bruce P. Leung and L. Clovis Tondo, Data Structures and Program Design in C, Prentice Hall of India, New Delhi, 1995.
4. Tremblay, Jean Paul, and Paul G. Sorenson, An Introduction to Data Structures with Applications, McGraw-Hill, New York, 1987.

3

Linked List

3.1 INTRODUCTION

An array is a very useful data structure provided in programming languages. However, it has some limitations.

1. Memory storage space is wasted, as the memory remains allocated to the array throughout the program execution even few nodes are stored. Because additional nodes are still reserved and their storage can't be used for any purpose.
2. The size of array can't be changed after its declaration *i.e.*, its size has to be known at compilation time.

These limitations can be overcomed by using linked list data structure. Linked list is the most commonly used data structure used to store similar type of data in memory. The elements of a linked list are not stored in adjacent locations as in arrays. In array, once memory space is allocated it cannot be extended. That is why this type of data structure is called static data structure. In Linked list memory space allocated for the elements of the list can be extended at any time. That is why this type of data structure is called dynamic data structure.

A linked list is an ordered collection of finite homogeneous data elements called nodes where the linear order is maintained by means of links or pointers. That is, each node is divided into two parts: the first part contains the information of the node and the second part contains the link to the next node.

Information	Link to the next node

Figure: structure of a node

3.2 REPRESENTATION OF LINKED LIST IN MEMORY

There are two ways to represent a linked list in memory:

1. Static representation using array.
2. Dynamic representation using free pool of storage

1. Static Representation

In static representation of a single linked list, two arrays are maintained: one array for information and other for links. Two parallel arrays of equal size are allocated which should be sufficient to store the entire linked list. The static representation of the linked list is shown in figure:

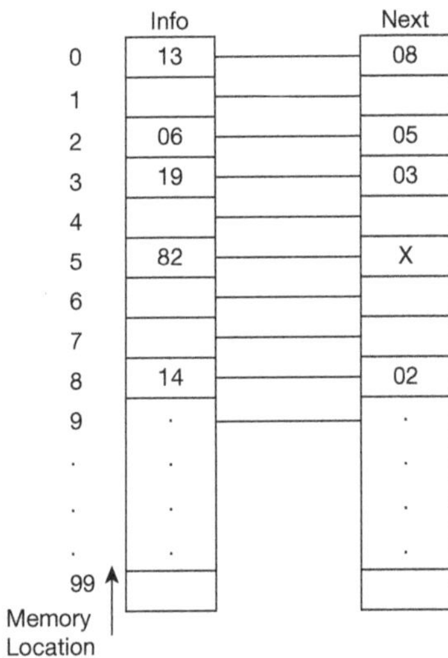

Figure Static Representation of a Single Linked List using Arrays

2. Dynamic Representation

The efficient way of representing a linked list is using free pool of storage. In this method, there is a memory, which is nothing but a collection of free memory spaces, and a memory manager (a program). During the creation of linked list, whenever a node is required, the request is placed to the memory manager; memory manager will then search the memory for the block requested and if found grants a desired block to the caller. Again, there is also another program called garbage collection, whenever a node is no more in use; it returns the unused node to the memory. Such a memory management is known as dynamic memory management.

In this section, we will study the following:

1. Single Linked List.
2. Circular Linked List.
3. Double Linked List.
4. Circular Double Linked List.

3.3 SINGLE LINKED LIST

In a single linked list each node contains only one link which points to the next subsequent node in the list. In other words, each node has a single pointer to the next node and in the last node a NULL pointer representing that there are no more nodes in the linked list.

3.4 OPERATIONS ON A SINGLE LINKED LIST

There are various operations possible on a single linked list.

(*a*) Traversing the linked list.

(*b*) Inserting a node into the linked list.

- Insert at beginning.
- Insert at end
- Insert at particular location

(*c*) Deleting a node into the linked list.

- Delete at beginning.
- Delete at end.
- Delete at particular location.

(*d*) Merging of two linked list into a single linked list.

(*e*) Searching for an element in the linked list.

(*f*) Sorting the node in the linked list

(*g*) Reverse a linked list.

a. Traversing the Linked List

Suppose a single linked list is in memory and we want to traverse the list in order to process each node at least once. Our approach is to traverse the list starting from the first node to the last node of the list.

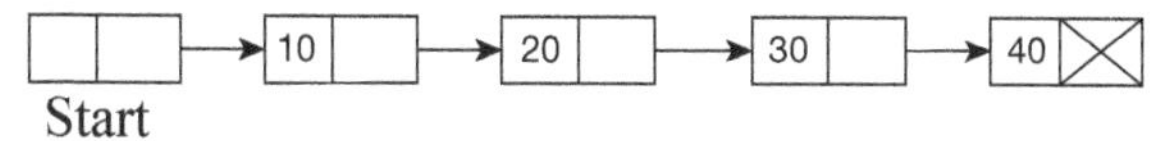

Figure Traversing a Single Linked List

Algorithm

Steps

1. Start
2. Hold the address of the first node.
3. Set node = start // initialize pointer variable called node
4. While node ≠ NULL

5. Repeat steps 6 and 7
6. Process info [node] // apply process to info [node]
7. Set node = next [node] // move pointer to next node
8. Stop

Program: Create a Single Linked List and Display all Nodes

```
#include<stdio.h>
#include<stdlib.h>
struct node
{
int info;
struct node *next;
};
void create (struct node*);
void display (struct node*);
void main ()
{
struct node *next;
node=(struct node*)malloc(sizeof(struct node));
if(node==NULL)
{
printf("\n out of memory space");
exit(0);
}
create ()
display ();
}
void create (struct node * next)
{
char ch;
int i=1;
printf("\n enter the value of %d node", i);
scanf ("%d", &node->info);
node->next=NULL;
i=i+1;
printf (\n Press 'E' key to exit and Press 'Y' key to continue: ");
ch=getchar ();
```

```
while (ch!='N')
{
node->next=(struct node*)malloc(sizeof (struct node));
if(node->next==NULL)
{
printf ("\n out of memory space");
exit(0);
}
node=node->next;
printf ("\n enter the value %d node", i);
scanf(%d", &node->info)
node->next=NULL;
i=i+1;
printf (\n Press 'E' key to exit and Press 'Y' key to continue");
ch=getchar ();
}
}
void display (struct node *next)
{
printf("\n value of nodes in the list are as follows:\n");
while(node!=NULL)
{
printf("%d", node->info);
node=node->next;
}
}
```

Output

```
Enter the value node: 10
Press 'E' key to exit and Press 'Y' key to continue: Y
Enter the value node: 20
Press 'E' key to exit and Press 'Y' key to continue: Y
Enter the value node: 30
Press 'E' key to exit and Press 'Y' key to continue: Y
Enter the value node: 40
Press 'E' key to exit and Press 'Y' key to continue: E
```

value of nodes in the list are as follows:

10 20 30 40

b. Insert a node into the linked list

The insertion operation is used to add an element in an existing linked list. The list may be ordered or unordered. For ordered linked list, the ordering may be in increasing or decreasing order of the information field. An attempt to insert an element at appropriate place in an ordered list requires us to compare the information filed of each node till the end of the list and insert at that place.

b. (i) Insert at Beginning

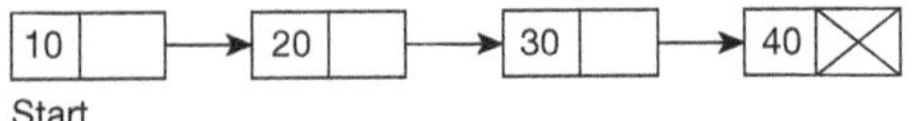

Figure Before Insertion

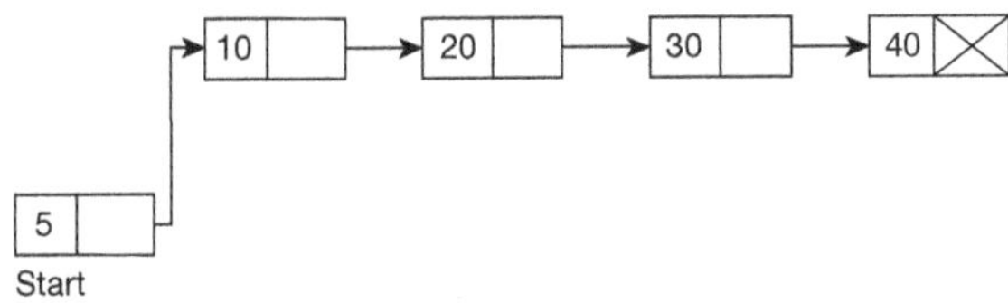

Figure After Insertion (x = 5)

Algorithm

Steps

1. Start
2. Holds the address of the first node.
3. Create a new node named as temp/node
4. If node = NULL then
5. write “out of memory space” and
6. exit
7. set info [node] = x //copies new data into new node
8. set next [node] = start // new node now points to first node
9. set start = node
10. stop

Program: Insert a node at the beginning

```
#include<stdio.h>
#include<stdlib.h>
struct node
```

```
{
int info;
struct node *next;
};
struct node *start;
void insert (struct node *);
void create (struct node*);
void display (struct node*);
void main ()
{
char ch='1';
struct node *next;
node=(struct node*)malloc(sizeof(struct node));
if(node==NULL)
{
printf("\n out of memory space");
exit(0);
}
printf("\n Creation of a Linked List\n");
create (node)
while (ch!='3')
{
printf (\n 1. Insert at Beg");
printf("\n 2. Display");
printf("\n 3. Exit");
printf("\n Enter your choice");
ch=getchar();
switch(ch)
{
case '1':
insert(node);
node=start;
start=NULL;
break;
case '2':
display (node);
```

```
break;
case '3':
break;
default:
printf("\n Wrong Choice");
}
}
}
void create (struct node * next)
{
char ch;
int i=1;
printf("\n enter the value of %d node", i);
scanf ("%d", &node->info);
node->next=NULL;
i=i+1;
printf (\n Press 'E' key to exit and Press 'Y' key to continue: ");
ch=getchar ();
while (ch!='N')
{
node->next=(struct node*)malloc(sizeof (struct node));
if(node->next==NULL)
{
printf ("\n out of memory space");
exit(0);
}
node=node->next;
printf ("\n enter the value %d node", i);
scanf(%d", &node->info)
node->next=NULL;
i=i+1;
printf (\n Press 'E' key to exit and Press 'Y' key to continue");
ch=getchar ();
}
}
void insert (struct node *next)
```

```
{
struct node *curr;
curr=(struct node*)malloc(sizeof(struct node));
if(curr==NULL)
{
printf("\n Out of memory");
exit(0);
}
curr->next=node;
printf("\n Input the First Node Information:");
scanf("%d", &curr->info);
start=curr;
}
void display (struct node *next)
{
printf("\n value of nodes in the list are as follows:\n");
while(node!=NULL)
{
printf("%d", node->info);
node=node->next;
}
}
```

Output

Enter the value node: 10
Press 'E' key to exit and Press 'Y' key to continue: Y
Enter the value node: 20
Press 'E' key to exit and Press 'Y' key to continue: Y
Enter the value node: 30
Press 'E' key to exit and Press 'Y' key to continue: Y
Enter the value node: 40
Press 'E' key to exit and Press 'Y' key to continue: E

1. Insert at Beg
2. Display
3. Exit

Enter your choice: 2

value of nodes in the list are as follows:

10 20 30 40

1. Insert at Beg
2. Display
3. Exit

Enter your choice: 1

Input the First Node Information: 50

1. Insert at Beg
2. Display
3. Exit

Enter your choice: 2

value of nodes in the list are as follows:

50 10 20 30 40

1. Insert at Beg
2. Display
3. Exit

Enter your choice: 3

b. (ii) Insert at End

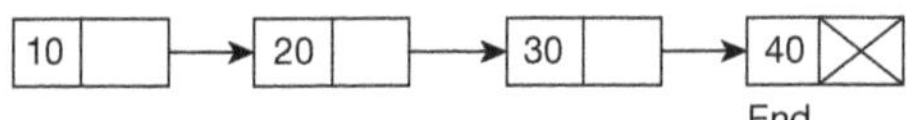

Figure Before Insertion

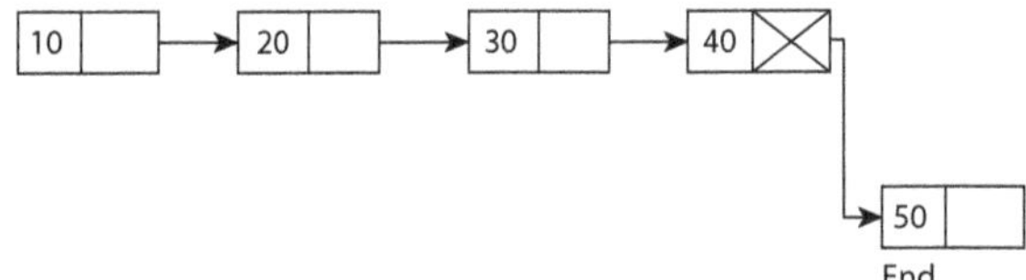

Figure After Insertion

Algorithm

Steps

1. Start
2. Holds the address of the first node.
3. Create a new node named as temp/node
4. If node = NULL then
5. Write "out of memory space" and
6. Exit
7. Set info [node] = x // copies new data into new node

8. Set next [node] = NULL
9. Set curr = start
10. Repeat step 11 and 12 while curr ≠ NULL
11. Set prev = curr
12. Set curr = next[curr]
13. End of step 10 loop
14. Set next [prev] = node
15. Stop

Program: Insert a node at the End

```
#include<stdio.h>
#include<stdlib.h>
struct node
{
int info;
struct node *next;
};
void insert (struct node *);
void create (struct node*);
void display (struct node*);
void main ()
{
char ch='1';
struct node *next;
node=(struct node*)malloc(sizeof(struct node));
if(node==NULL)
{
printf("\n out of memory space");
exit(0);
}
printf("\n Creation of a Linked List\n");
create (node)
while (ch!='3')
{
printf (\n 1. Insert at End");
printf("\n 2. Display");
printf("\n 3. Exit");
```

```
printf("\n Enter your choice");
ch=getchar();
switch(ch)
{
case '1':
insert(node);
break;
case '2':
display (node);
break;
case '3':
break;
default:
printf("\n Wrong Choice");
}
}
}
void create (struct node * next)
{
char ch;
int i=1;
printf("\n enter the value of %d node", i);
scanf ("%d", &node->info);
node->next=NULL;
i=i+1;
printf (\Press 'E' key to exit and Press 'Y' key to continue: ");
ch=getchar ();
while (ch!='N')
{
node->next=(struct node*)malloc(sizeof (struct node));
if(node->next==NULL)
{
printf ("\n out of memory space");
exit(0);
}
node=node->next;
```

```
printf ("\n enter the value %d node", i);
scanf(%d", &node->info)
node->next=NULL;
i=i+1;
printf (\n Press 'E' key to exit and Press 'Y' key to continue");
ch=getchar ();
}
}
void insert (struct node *next)
{
struct node *curr;
while (node->next!=NULL)
node=node->next;
curr=(struct node*)malloc(sizeof(struct node));
if(curr==NULL)
{
printf("\n Out of memory");
exit(0);
}
curr->next=NULL;
node->next=curr;
printf("\n Input the Last Node Information:");
scanf("%d", &curr->info);
}
void display (struct node *next)
{
printf("\n value of nodes in the list are as follows:\n");
while(node!=NULL)
{
printf("%d", node->info);
node=node->next;
}
}
```

Output

```
Enter the value node: 10
Press 'E' key to exit and Press 'Y' key to continue: Y
```

Enter the value node: 20

Press 'E' key to exit and Press 'Y' key to continue: Y

Enter the value node: 30

Press 'E' key to exit and Press 'Y' key to continue: Y

Enter the value node: 40

Press 'E' key to exit and Press 'Y' key to continue: E

1. Insert at End
2. Display
3. Exit

Enter your choice: 2

value of nodes in the list are as follows:

10 20 30 40

1. Insert at End
2. Display
3. Exit

Enter your choice: 1

Input the Last Node Information: 50

1. Insert at End
2. Display
3. Exit

Enter your choice: 2

value of nodes in the list are as follows:

10 20 30 40 50

1. Insert at End
2. Display
3. Exit

Enter your choice: 3

b. (iii) Insert at particular location

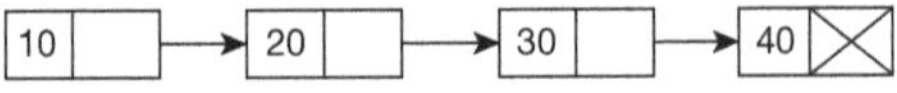

Figure Before Insertion

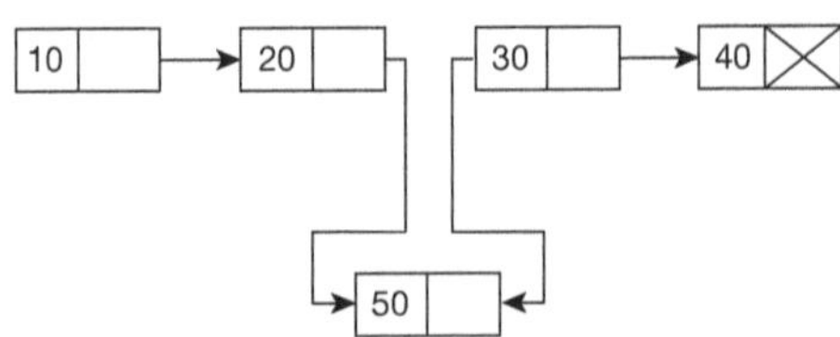

Figure After Insertion (loc = 3, x = 50)

Algorithm

Steps

1. Start
2. Holds the address of the first node
3. Set curr = start
4. Create a new node named as temp/node
5. If node = NULL then
6. Write "out of memory space" and
7. Exit
8. Set info [node] = x // copies new data into new node
9. Set next [node] = Curr
10. Read loc
11. Set i = 1
12. Repeat steps 13 to 15 while curr ≠ NULL and i < loc
13. Set prev = curr
14. Set curr = next[curr]
15. Set i = i+1
16. End of step 11 loop
17. If curr = NULL then
18. Write "position not found" and
19. Exit
20. Set next [prev] = node
21. Set next [node] =curr
22. Stop

Program: Insert a node at particular location

```
#include<stdio.h>
#include<stdlib.h>

struct node
{
int info;

struct node *next;
};
struct node *start;
void insert (struct node *);
void create (struct node*);
void count(struct node*);
```

```
void display (struct node*);
void main ()
{
char ch='1';
struct node *next;
node=(struct node*)malloc(sizeof(struct node));
if(node==NULL)
{
printf("\n out of memory space");
exit(0);
}
start=node;
printf("\n Creation of a Linked List\n");
create (node)
while (ch!='3')
{
printf (\n 1. Insert at Particular Location");
printf("\n 2. Display");
printf("\n 3. Exit");
printf("\n Enter your choice");
ch=getchar();
switch(ch)
{
case '1':
insert(node);
node=start;
break;
case '2':
display (node);
break;
case '3':
break;
default:
printf("\n Wrong Choice");
}
}
```

```
}
void create (struct node * next)
{
char ch;
int i=1;
printf("\n enter the value of %d node", i);
scanf ("%d", &node->info);
node->next=NULL;
i=i+1;
printf (\n Press 'E' key to exit and Press 'Y' key to continue: ");
ch=getchar ();
while (ch!='N')
{
node->next=(struct node*)malloc(sizeof (struct node));
if(node->next==NULL)
{
printf ("\n out of memory space");
exit(0);
}
node=node->next;
printf ("\n enter the value %d node", i);
scanf(%d", &node->info)
node->next=NULL;
i=i+1;
printf (\n Press 'E' key to exit and Press 'Y' key to continue");
ch=getchar ();
}
}
void insert (struct node *next)
{
int loc, c=0,i=1;
struct node *curr, *prev;
printf("\n Enter the location at which node will be Insert");
scanf("%d", &loc);
c=count(node);
if(loc>c)
```

```
{
printf("\n Enter the location exceed the number of node");
return;
}
curr=(struct node*)malloc(sizeof(struct node));
if(curr==NULL)
{
printf("\n Out of memory space");
exit(0);
}
while(i<loc)
{
prev=node;
node=node->;
i=i+1;
}
printf("\n Input the Node Information at %d Location:", loc);
scanf("%d", &curr->info);
if(loc==1)
start=curr;
else
prev->next=curr;
curr->next=node;
}
int count(struct node *next)
{
int i=0;
while(node!=NULL)
{
i=i+1;
node=node->next;
}
return i;
}
void display (struct node *next)
{
```

```
printf("\n value of nodes in the list are as follows:\n");
while(node!=NULL)
{
printf("%d", node->info);
node=node->next;
}
}
```

Output

```
Enter the value node: 10
Press 'E' key to exit and Press 'Y' key to continue: Y
Enter the value node: 20
Press 'E' key to exit and Press 'Y' key to continue: Y
Enter the value node: 30
Press 'E' key to exit and Press 'Y' key to continue: Y
Enter the value node: 40
Press 'E' key to exit and Press 'Y' key to continue: E
   1. Insert at Particular Location
   2. Display
   3. Exit
Enter your choice: 2
value of nodes in the list are as follows:
10 20 30 40
   1. Insert at Particular Location
   2. Display
   3. Exit
Enter your choice: 1
Enter the location at which node will be Insert: 3
Input the Node Information at 3 Location: 50
   1. Insert at Particular Location
   2. Display
   3. Exit
Enter your choice: 2
value of nodes in the list are as follows:
10 20 50 30 40
   1. Insert at Particular Location
   2. Display
```

3. Exit

Enter your choice: 3

c. Deleting a node into the linked list

The deletion operation is used to delete an element from a single linked list, one should remember the following points.

- If the list is empty, deletion is not possible.
- If the list contains only one node, after deletion the list will be empty.
- If the node is deleted, the memory space for the deleted node is de-allocated.
- If beginning node is deleted start should point to the next node automatically.

c. (i) Deletion at beginning

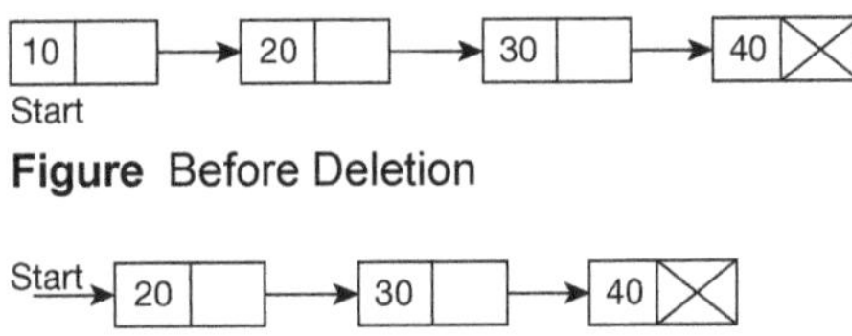

Figure Before Deletion

Figure After Deletion

Algorithm

Steps

1. Start
2. Holds the address of the first node.
3. Set temp = start
4. If start = NULL then
5. Write "UNDERFLOW" and
6. Exit
7. Set start = next [start]
8. Free the space associated with temp
9. Stop

Program: Delete a node at the beginning

```
#include<stdio.h>
#include<stdlib.h>
struct node
{
```

```
int info;
struct node *next;
};
struct node *start;
void delete (struct node *);
void create (struct node*);
void display (struct node*);
void main ()
{
char ch='1';
struct node *next;
node=(struct node*)malloc(sizeof(struct node));
if(node==NULL)
{
printf("\n out of memory space");
exit(0);
}
printf("\n Creation of a Linked List\n");
create (node)
while (ch!='3')
{
printf (\n 1. Delete at Beg");
printf("\n 2. Display");
printf("\n 3. Exit");
printf("\n Enter your choice");
ch=getchar();
switch(ch)
{
case '1':
delete(node);
node=start;
start=NULL;
break;
case '2':
display (node);
break;
```

```
case ‘3’:
break;
default:
printf(“\n Wrong Choice”);
}
}
}
void create (Struct node *next)
{
char ch;
int i=1;
printf(“\n enter the value of %d node”, i);
scanf (“%d”, &node->info);
node->next=NULL;
i=i+1;
printf (\n Press ‘E’ key to exit and Press ‘Y’ key to continue:”);
ch=getchar ();
while (ch!=’N’)
{
node->next=(struct node*)malloc(sizeof (struct node));
if(node->next==NULL)
{
printf (“\n out of memory space”);
exit(0);
}
node=node->next;
printf (“\n enter the value %d node”, i);
scanf(%d”, &node->info)
node->next=NULL;
i=i+1;
printf (\n Press ‘E’ key to exit and Press ‘Y’ key to continue”);
ch=getchar ();
}
}
void delete(struct node *next)
{
```

```
struct node *temp;
temp=node;
node=node->next;
free(temp);
start=node;
}
void display (struct node *next)
{
if(node==NULL)
{
printf("\n List is Empty");
return;
}
printf("\n value of nodes in the list are as follows:\n");
while(node!=NULL)
{
printf("%d", node->info);
node=node->next;
}
}
```

Output

```
Enter the value node: 10
Press 'E' key to exit and Press 'Y' key to continue: Y
Enter the value node: 20
Press 'E' key to exit and Press 'Y' key to continue: Y
Enter the value node: 30
Press 'E' key to exit and Press 'Y' key to continue: Y
Enter the value node: 40
Press 'E' key to exit and Press 'Y' key to continue: E
   1. Delete at Beg
   2. Display
   3. Exit
Enter your choice: 2
value of nodes in the list are as follows:
10 20 30 40
```

1. Delete at Beg
2. Display
3. Exit

Enter your choice: 1

1. Delete at Beg
2. Display
3. Exit

Enter your choice: 2

value of nodes in the list are as follows:

20 30 40

1. Delete at Beg
2. Display
3. Exit

Enter your choice: 3

c. (ii) Deletion at end

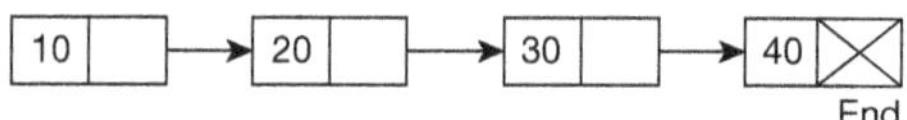

Figure Before Deletion

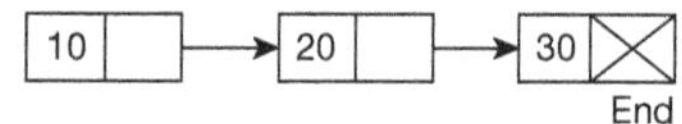

Figure After Deletion

Algorithm

Steps

1. Start
2. Holds the address of the first node
3. Set node = start
4. Set temp = start
5. If node = NULL then
6. Write "UNDERFLOW" and
7. Exit
8. Repeat steps 9 and 10 while next [node] ≠ NULL
9. Set temp = node
10. Set node = next [node]
11. End of step 8 loop
12. Set next [temp] = NULL

13. Free the apace associated with node
14. Stop

Program: Delete a node at the End

```
#include<stdio.h>
#include<stdlib.h>
struct node
{
int info;
struct node *next;
};
struct node *start;
void delete (struct node *);
void create (struct node*);
void display (struct node*);
void main ()
{
char ch='1';
struct node *next;
node=(struct node*)malloc(sizeof(struct node));
if(node==NULL)
{
printf("\n out of memory space");
exit(0);
}
printf("\n Creation of a Linked List\n");
create (node)
while (ch!='3')
{
printf (\n 1. Delete at End");
printf("\n 2. Display");
printf("\n 3. Exit");
printf("\n Enter your choice");
ch=getchar();
switch(ch)
{
```

```
case '1':
start=node
delete(node);
node=start;
break;
case '2':
display (node);
break;
case '3':
break;
default:
printf("\n Wrong Choice");
}
}
}
void create (struct node * next)
{
char ch;
int i=1;
printf("\n enter the value of %d node", i);
scanf ("%d", &node->info);
node->next=NULL;
i=i+1;
printf (\n Press 'E' key to exit and Press 'Y' key to continue: ");
ch=getchar ();
while (ch!='N')
{
node->next=(struct node*)malloc(sizeof (struct node));
if(node->next==NULL)
{
printf ("\n out of memory space");
exit(0);
}
node=node->next;
printf ("\n enter the value %d node", i);
scanf(%d", &node->info)
```

```
node->next=NULL;
i=i+1;
printf (\n Press 'E' key to exit and Press 'Y' key to continue");
ch=getchar ();
}
}
void delete(struct node *next)
{
struct node *prev;
if(node->next==NULL)
{
free(node);
start=NULL;
return;
}
while(node->next!=NULL)
{
prev=node;
node=node->next;
}
prev->next=NULL;
free(node);
void display (struct node *next)
{
if(node==NULL)
{
printf("\n n List is Empty");
return;
}
printf("\n value of nodes in the list are as follows:\n");
while(node!=NULL)
{
printf("%d", node->info);
node=node->next;
}
}
```

Output

Enter the value node: 10
Press 'E' key to exit and Press 'Y' key to continue: Y
Enter the value node: 20
Press 'E' key to exit and Press 'Y' key to continue: Y
Enter the value node: 30
Press 'E' key to exit and Press 'Y' key to continue: Y
Enter the value node: 40
Press 'E' key to exit and Press 'Y' key to continue: E

1. Delete at End
2. Display
3. Exit

Enter your choice: 2

value of nodes in the list are as follows:
10 20 30 40

1. Delete at End
2. Display
3. Exit

Enter your choice: 1

1. Insert at End
2. Display
3. Exit

Enter your choice: 2

value of nodes in the list are as follows:
10 20 30

1. Delete at End
2. Display
3. Exit

Enter your choice: 3

c. (iii) Deletion at particular location

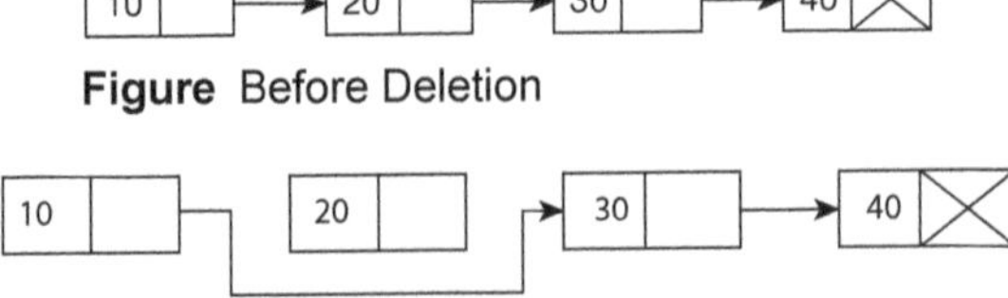

Figure Before Deletion

Figure After Deletion (loc = 2, value=20)

Algorithm

Steps

1. Start
2. Holds the address of the first node.
3. Set node = start
4. Set temp = start
5. If node = NULL then
6. Write "UNDERFLOW" and
7. Exit
8. Set i = 1
9. Read loc
10. Repeat steps 11 to 13 while node ≠ NULL and i < loc
11. Set temp = node
12. Set node = next [node]
13. Set i = i +1
14. End of step 10 loop
15. If node = NULL then
16. Write "position not found" and
17. Exit
18. Set next [temp] = next [node]
19. Free the space associated with node
20. Stop

Program: Delete a node at particular location

```
#include<stdio.h>
#include<stdlib.h>
struct node
{
int info;
struct node *next;
};
struct node *start;
void delete (struct node *);
void create (struct node*);
void count(struct node*);
void display (struct node*);
void main ()
```

```
{
char ch='1';
struct node *next;
node=(struct node*)malloc(sizeof(struct node));
if(node==NULL)
{
printf("\n out of memory space");
exit(0);
}
start=node;
printf("\n Creation of a Linked List\n");
create (node)
while (ch!='3')
{
printf (\n 1. Delete at Particular Location");
printf("\n 2. Display");
printf("\n 3. Exit");
printf("\n Enter your choice");
ch=getchar();
switch(ch)
{
case '1':
delete(node);
node=start;
break;
case '2':
display (node);
break;
case '3':
break;
default:
printf("\n Wrong Choice");
}
}
}
void create (struct node * next)
```

```
{
char ch;
int i=1;
printf("\n enter the value of %d node", i);
scanf ("%d", &node->info);
node->next=NULL;
i=i+1;
printf (\n Press 'E' key to exit and Press 'Y' key to continue: ");
ch=getchar ();
while (ch!='N')
{
node->next=(struct node*)malloc(sizeof (struct node));
if(node->next==NULL)
{
printf ("\n out of memory space");
exit(0);
}
node=node->next;
printf ("\n enter the value %d node", i);
scanf(%d", &node->info)
node->next=NULL;
i=i+1;
printf (\n Press 'E' key to exit and Press 'Y' key to continue");
ch=getchar ();
}
}
void delete (struct node *next)
{
int loc, c=0,i=1;
struct node *prev;
printf("\n Enter the location at which node will be Delete");
scanf("%d", &loc);
c=count(node);
if(loc>c)
{
printf("\n Enter the location exceed the number of node");
```

```
return;
}
while (i<loc)
{
prev=node;
node=node->next;
i=i+1;
}
if(loc==1)
start=node->next;
else
prev->next=node->next;
free(node);
}
int count(struct node *next)
{
int i=0;
while(node!=NULL)
{
i=i+1;
node=node->next;
}
return i;
}
void display (struct node *next)
{
if(node==NULL)
{
printf("\n n List is Empty");
return;
}
printf("\n value of nodes in the list are as follows:\n");
while(node!=NULL)
{
printf("%d", node->info);
node=node->next;
```

```
}
}
```

Output

```
Enter the value node: 10
Press 'E' key to exit and Press 'Y' key to continue: Y
Enter the value node: 20
Press 'E' key to exit and Press 'Y' key to continue: Y
Enter the value node: 30
Press 'E' key to exit and Press 'Y' key to continue: Y
Enter the value node: 40
Press 'E' key to exit and Press 'Y' key to continue: E
  1. Delete at Particular Location
  2. Display
  3. Exit
Enter your choice: 2
value of nodes in the list are as follows:
10 20 30 40
  1. Insert at Particular Location
  2. Display
  3. Exit
Enter your choice: 1
Enter the location at which node will be Insert: 2
  1. Delete at Particular Location
  2. Display
  3. Exit
Enter your choice: 2
value of nodes in the list are as follows:
10 30 40
  1. Insert at Particular Location
  2. Display
  3. Exit
Enter your choice: 3
```

d. Merging of two linked list into a single linked list

Two linked lists are available in memory, it is required to merge two linked list into a single linked list. To obtain the merged linked list, it is necessary to link the last node of the first linked list to the first node of the second linked list.

List_1

List_2

Figure Before Merge

List

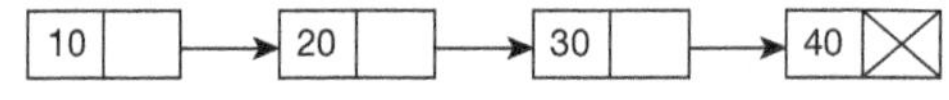

Figure After Merge

Algorithm

Steps

1. Set node_1 = list_1
2. Create a new node named as list
3. If list = NULL then
4. Write "out of memory space" and
5. Exit
6. Set info [list] = info [node_1]
7. Set next [list] = NULL
8. Set node_1 = next [node_1]
9. Set node = list
10. Repeat steps 11 to 19 while node_1 ≠ NULL
11. Create a new node named as curr
12. If curr = NULL then
13. Write "out of memory space" and
14. Exit
15. Set info [curr] = info [node_1]
16. Set next [curr] = NULL
17. Set node_1 = next [node_1]
18. Set next [node] = curr
19. Set node = curr
20. End of step 10 loop
21. Set node_2 = list_2
22. Repeat steps 23 to 29 while node_2 ≠ NULL
23. If curr = NULL then
24. Write "out of memory space" and

25. Exit
26. Set info [curr] = info [node_2]
27. Set next _2 = next [node_2]
28. Set next [node] = curr
29. Set node = curr
30. End of step 22 loop
31. Stop

Program: Merging of two single linked list

```
#include<stdio.h>
#include<stdlib.h>
struct node
{
int info;
struct node *next;
};
struct node *start;
void create (struct node *);
void merge (struct node*, struct node*, struct node*);
void display (struct node*);
void main ()
{
char ch='1';
struct next *node1, *node2, node3;
node1=(struct node*)malloc(sizeof(struct node));
if(node1==NULL)
{
printf("\n out of memory space");
exit(0);
}
node2=(struct node*)malloc(sizeof(struct node));
if(node2==NULL)
{
printf("\n out of memory space");
exit(0);
}
node3=(struct node*)malloc(sizeof(struct node));
```

```
if(node3==NULL)
{
printf("\n out of memory space");
exit(0);
}
Printf("\n Create of First Linked List");
Create(node1);
Printf("\n Create of Second Linked List");
Create(node2);
Merge(node1, node2, node3);
Printf("\n Value of Nodes in First Linked List is:");
Display(node1);
Printf("\n Value of Nodes in Second Linked List is:");
Display(node2);
Printf("\n Value of Nodes in Merged Linked List is:");
Display(node3);
void create (struct node * next)
{
char ch;
int i=1;
printf("\n enter the value of %d node", i);
scanf ("%d", &node->info);
node->next=NULL;
i=i+1;
printf (\n Press 'E' key to exit and Press 'Y' key to continue: ");
ch=getchar ();
while (ch!='N')
{
node->next=(struct node*)malloc(sizeof (struct node));
if(node->next==NULL)
{
printf ("\n out of memory space");
exit(0);
}
node=node->next;
printf ("\n enter the value %d node", i);
```

```
scanf(%d", &node->info)
node->next=NULL;
i=i+1;
printf (\n Press 'E' key to exit and Press 'Y' key to continue");
ch=getchar ();
}
}
void merge (struct node node1*, struct node node2*, struct node node3*);
{
node3->info=node1->info;
node3->next=NULL;
node1=node1->next;
while(node1!=NULL)
{
node3->next=(struct node*)malloc(sizeof(struct node));
if(node3->==NULL)
{
printf("\n out of memory space");
exit(0);
}
node3=node3->next;
node3->info=node1->info;
node1=node1->next;
node3->next=NULL;
}
while(node2!=NULL)
{
node3->next=(struct node*)malloc(sizeof(struct node));
if(node3->next==NULL)
{
printf("\n out of memory space");
exit(0);
}
node3=node3->next;
node3->info=node2->info;
node2=node2->next;
```

```
node3->next=NULL;
}
}
void display (struct node *next)
{
while(node!=NULL)
{
printf("%d", node->info);
node=node->next;
}
}
```

Output

```
Create First Linked List
Enter the value node: 10
Press 'E' key to exit and Press 'Y' key to continue: Y
Enter the value node: 20
Press 'E' key to exit and Press 'Y' key to continue: E
Create Second Linked List
Enter the value node: 30
Press 'E' key to exit and Press 'Y' key to continue: Y
Enter the value node: 40
Press 'E' key to exit and Press 'Y' key to continue: E
Value of Nodes in First Linked List is:
10 20
Value of Nodes in Second Linked List is:
30 40
Value of Nodes in Merged Linked List is:
10 20 30 40
```

e. Searching for an element in the linked list

Searching means finding a value in a given linked list. Suppose we have a linked list and we want to search for a value, say 30. If the value is present in the linked list, it will return the location otherwise it will display a message "element not found in the linked list"

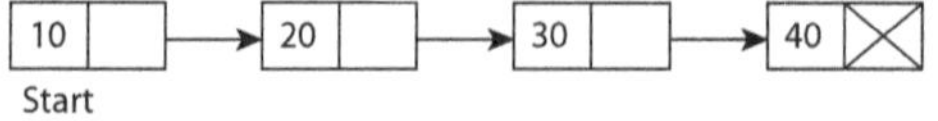

Figure searching an element (say 30)

Algorithm

Steps

1. Start
2. Holds the address of the first element
3. Set node = start
4. Set count = 1
5. Read item
6. Repeat steps 7 to 11 while node ≠ NULL
7. If item = info [node] then
8. Write "element found at position", count and then exit
9. End of step 7 if structure
10. Set count = count + 1
11. Set node = next [node]
12. End of step 6 loop
13. Write "element not found"
14. Stop

Program: Searching a Node in a Single Linked List

```
#include<stdio.h>
#include<stdlib.h>
struct node
{
int info;
struct node *next;
};
void create (struct node *);
void search (struct node*);
void display (struct node*);
void main ()
{
struct node *next;
char ch='1';
node=(struct node*)malloc(sizeof(struct node));
if(node==NULL)
{
printf("\n out of memory space");
```

```
exit(0);
}
create(node);
while (ch!='3')
{
printf (\n 1. Search");
printf("\n 2. Display");
printf("\n 3. Exit");
printf("\n Enter your choice");
ch=getchar();
switch(ch)
{
case '1':
search(node);
break;
case '2':
display (node);
break;
case '3':
break;
default:
printf("\n Wrong Choice");
}
}
}
void create (struct node * next)
{
char ch;
int i=1;
printf("\n enter the value of %d node", i);
scanf ("%d", &node->info);
node->next=NULL;
i=i+1;
printf (\n Press 'E' key to exit and Press 'Y' key to continue: ");
ch=getchar ();
while (ch!='N')
```

```
{
node->next=(struct node*)malloc(sizeof (struct node));
if(node->next==NULL)
{
printf ("\n out of memory space");
exit(0);
node=node->next;
printf ("\n enter the value %d node", i);
scanf(%d", &node->info)
node->next=NULL;
i=i+1;
printf (\n Press 'E' key to exit and Press 'Y' key to continue");
ch=getchar ();
}
}
void search(struct node *next)
{
int x, i=1;
printf("\n enter the value of a node to be search");
scanf(%d", &x);
while(node!=NULL)
{
if(node->info==x)
{
printf("\n Searched element %d is at location:", x,i);
return;
}
i=i+1;
printf("\n Searched element %d is not found in the list", x);
}
void display (struct node *next)
{
printf("\n value of nodes in the list are as follows:\n");
while(node!=NULL)
{
printf("%d", node->info);
```

```
node=node->next;
}
}
```

Output

Enter the value node: 10

Press 'E' key to exit and Press 'Y' key to continue: Y

Enter the value node: 20

Press 'E' key to exit and Press 'Y' key to continue: Y

Enter the value node: 30

Press 'E' key to exit and Press 'Y' key to continue: Y

Enter the value node: 40

Press 'E' key to exit and Press 'Y' key to continue: E

1. Search
2. Display
3. Exit

Enter your choice: 2

10 20 30 40

1. Search
2. Display
3. Exit

Enter your choice: 1

Enter the value of a node to be searched: 30

Searched element 30 is at location: 3

1. Search
2. Display
3. Exit

Enter your choice: 1

Enter the value of a node to be searched: 15

Searched element 15 is not found in the list

1. Search
2. Display
3. Exit

Enter your choice: 3

f. Sorting the node in the linked list

Sorting is arranging the linked list in ascending or descending order.

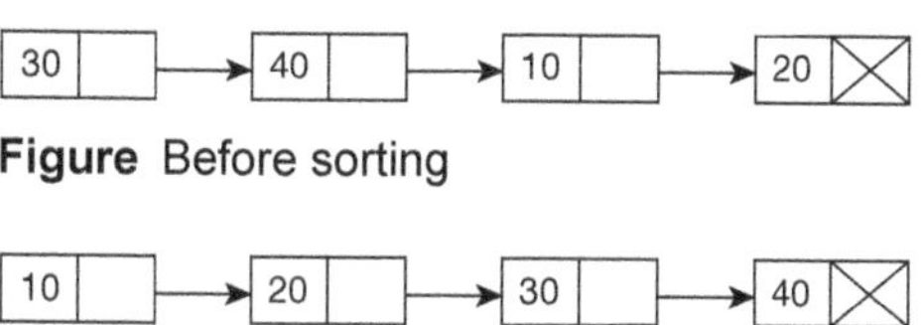

Figure Before sorting

Figure After sorting (sorting of node values in ascending order)

Algorithm

Steps

1. Start
2. Holds the address of the first node
3. Set node = start
4. Repeat steps 5 to 14 while next [node] ≠ NULL
5. Set ptr = next [node]
6. Repeat steps 7 to 12 while ptr ≠ NULL
7. If info [node] > info [ptr] then
8. Set temp = info [node]
9. Set info [node] = info [ptr]
10. Set info [ptr] = temp
11. End of step 7 if structure
12. Set ptr = next [ptr]
13. End of step 6 loop
14. Set node = next [node]
15. End of step 4 loop
16. Stop

Program: Sorting the values in a Single Linked List

```
#include<stdio.h>
#include<stdlib.h>
struct node
{
int info;
struct node *next;
};
void create (struct node *);
void sort (struct node*);
void display (struct node*);
void main ()
```

```
{
struct node *next;
node=(struct node*)malloc(sizeof(struct node));
if(node==NULL)
{
printf("\n out of memory space");
exit(0);
}
create(node);
printf("\n Values of nodes in the list is:");
display(node);
sort(node);
printf("value of nodes in the list after sorting is:");
display(node);
}
void create (struct node * next)
{
char ch;
int i=1;
printf("\n enter the value of %d node", i);
scanf ("%d", &node->info);
node->next=NULL;
i=i+1;
printf (\n Press 'E' key to exit and Press 'Y' key to continue: ");
ch=getchar ();
while (ch!='N')
{
node->next=(struct node*)malloc(sizeof (struct node));
if(node->next==NULL)
{
printf ("\n out of memory space");
exit(0);
}
node=node->next;
printf ("\n enter the value %d node", i);
scanf(%d", &node->info)
```

```
node->next=NULL;
i=i+1;
printf (\n Press 'E' key to exit and Press 'Y' key to continue");
ch=getchar ();
}
}
void sort (struct node *next)
{
struct node *index1, *index2;
int temp;
for(index1=node; index1->next!=NULL;index1=index1->next)
{
for(index2=index1->next;index2!=NULL;index2=index2->next)
{
if(index1->info>index2->info)
{
temp=index1->info;
index1->info=index2->info;
index2->info=temp;
}
}
}
}
void display (struct node *next)
{
while(node!=NULL)
{
printf("%d", node->info);
node=node->next;
}
}
```

Output

```
Enter the value node: 30
Press 'E' key to exit and Press 'Y' key to continue: Y
Enter the value node: 40
Press 'E' key to exit and Press 'Y' key to continue: Y
```

Enter the value node: 10

Press 'E' key to exit and Press 'Y' key to continue: Y

Enter the value node: 20

Press 'E' key to exit and Press 'Y' key to continue: E

Values of nodes in the list is:

30 40 10 20

value of nodes in the list after sorting is:

10 20 30 40

g. Reverse a linked list

Reverse of the linked list will do the following things:

1. First node will become the last node of linked list.
2. Last node will become the first node of linked list and now start will point to it.
3. Link of 2nd node will point to 1st node, link of 3rd node will point to second node and so on.
4. Link of last node will point to the previous node of last node in linked list.

Figure Before Reverse a Linked List (Original)

Figure After Reverse a Linked List

Algorithm

Steps

1. Start
2. Holds the address of the first node
3. Set curr = start
4. If next [curr] = NULL then
5. Exit
6. Set prev = next [curr]
7. Set next [curr] = NULL
8. Repeat steps 9 to 12 while next [prev] ≠ NULL
9. Set ptr = next [prev]
10. Set next [prev] = curr
11. Set curr = prev

12. Set prev = ptr
13. End of step 8 loop
14. Set next [prev] = curr
15. Set start = prev
16. Stop

Program: Reverse a Linked List

```
#include<stdio.h>
#include<stdlib.h>
struct node
{
  int data;
  struct node *next;
}*head;
void insert_data(int value)
{
   struct node *var,*temp;
   temp=head;
   var=(struct node *)malloc(sizeof(struct node));
   var->data=value;
   if(head==NULL)
   {
      head=var;
      head->next=NULL;
   }
   else
   {
      while(temp->next!=NULL)
      {
          temp=temp->next;
      }
      var->next=NULL;
      temp->next=var;
   }
}
void reverse_list()
```

```
{
   struct node *temp,*temp1,*var;
   temp=head;
   var=NULL;
   while(temp!=NULL)
   {
      temp1=var;
      var=temp;
      temp=temp->next;
      var->next=temp1;
   }
   head=var;
}
void display()
{
   struct node *var;
   var=head;
   printf("\nlist of elments are \n");
   while(var!=NULL)
   {
      printf("%d-> ",var->data);
      var=var->next;
   }
   printf("NULL");
}
int main()
{
   int i,value;
   char ch='y';
   head=NULL;
   printf("\n 1.)  Insert node");
   printf("\n 2.)  display the list");
   printf("\n 3.)  reverse the nodes");
   printf("\n 4.)  exit");
   while(ch=='y')
   {
```

```
printf("\nChoose to do operation :");
scanf("%d",&i);
switch(i)
{
  case 1 :
  {
  printf("\nEnter the data to be inserted in node ");
  scanf("%d",&value);
  insert_data(value);
  display();
  break;
  }
  case 2 :
  {
  display();
  break;
  }
  case 3 :
  {
  reverse_list();
  display();
  break;
  }
  case 4 :
  {
  exit(0);
  break;
  }
}
}
}
```

Output

1. Insert node
2. display the list
3. reverse the nodes
4. exit

```
Choose to do operation :1
Enter the data to be inserted in node 10
list of elments are
10-> NULL
Choose to do operation :1
Enter the data to be inserted in node 20
list of elements are
10-> 20-> NULL
Choose to do operation :1
Enter the data to be inserted in node 30
list of elments are
10-> 20-> 30-> NULL
Choose to do operation :1
Enter the data to be inserted in node 40
list of elments are
10-> 20-> 30-> 40-> NULL
Choose to do operation :2
list of elments are
10-> 20-> 30-> 40-> NULL
Choose to do operation :3
list of elments are
40-> 30-> 20-> 10-> NULL
Choose to do operation :4
```

3.5 CIRCULAR LINKED LIST

Circular Linked List is little more complicated linked data structure. In the circular linked list we can insert elements anywhere in the list whereas in the array we cannot insert element anywhere in the list because it is in the contiguous memory. In the circular linked list the previous element stores the address of the next element and the last element stores the address of the starting element. The elements points to each other in a circular way which forms a circular chain. The circular linked list has a dynamic size which means the memory can be allocated when it is required. Circular linked list is a linked list where all nodes are connected to form a circle. There is no NULL at the end. A circular linked list can be a singly circular linked list or doubly circular linked list.

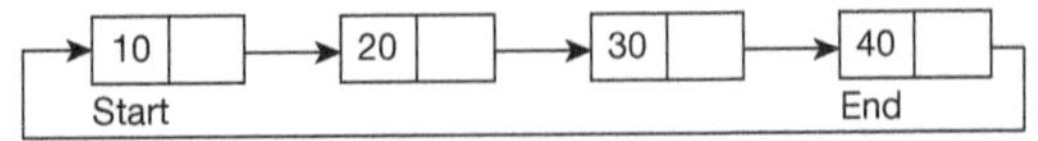

Figure Circular Linked List

3.6 OPERATIONS IN A CIRCULAR LINKED LIST

There are various operations possible on a Circular Linked List.

(*a*) Creation of a circular linked list.

(*b*) Insertion of a node

(*c*) Deletion of a node

a. Creation of Circular Linked List

Creation of Circular Linked List is same as Single Linked List. Only one thing is needed that here last node will always point to first node instead of NULL.

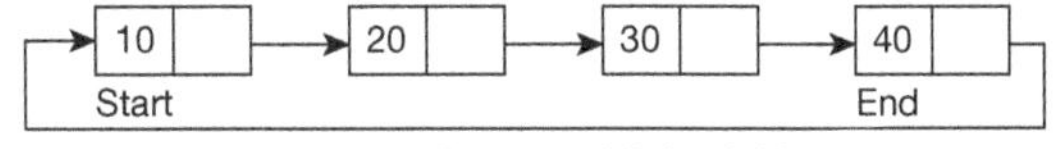

Figure: Circular Linked List

Algorithm

Steps

1. start
2. ptr = ptr->start
3. start=start->link
4. read info
5. first=first->ptr
6. ch='Y'
7. repeat steps 8 to 13 while ch='Y'
8. curr=curr->link
9. start=start->link
10. read info
11. ptr=ptr->curr
12. ptr=ptr->curr
13. press<Y/N> for more node information
14. link=link->first
15. stop

```
void create()
{
struct node *ptr, *curr;
char ch;
ptr=(struct node *) malloc (sizeof (struct node));
printf(" Input First Node Information");
scanf("%d", &ptr->info);
```

```
first=ptr;
do
{
curr= (struct node *) malloc (sizeof (struct node));
printf("Input Second Node Information");
scanf("%d", &curr->info);
ptr->link=curr;
ptr=curr;
printf("Press <Y/N>for more Node Information");
ch=getchar();
}
while (ch='Y');
ptr->link=first;
}
```

b. (i) Insertion of a Node (At Beg)

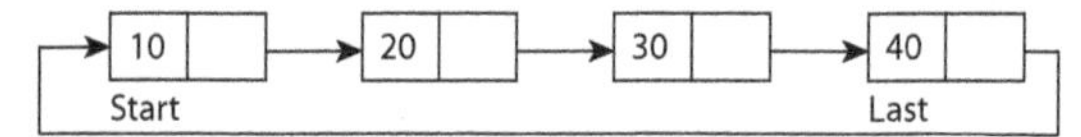

Figure Before Insert

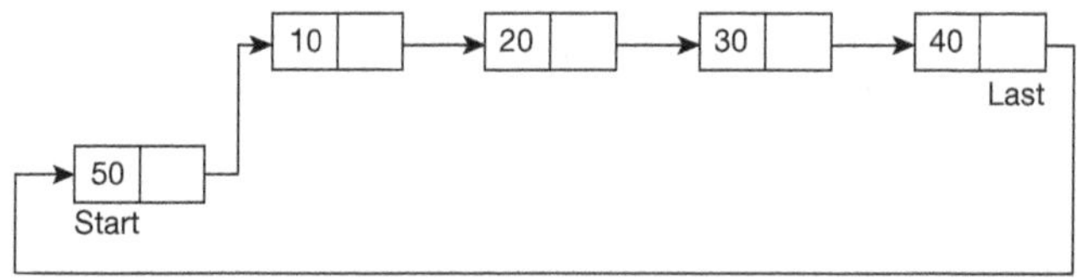

Figure After Insert value = 50

Algorithm

Steps

1. start
2. if start=NULL then
3. print "OVERFLOW" and then
4. stop
5. ptr=ptr->start
6. start=start->link
7. read info
8. curr=curr->first

9. repeat steps 10 while curr->link!=first
10. curr=curr->link
11. ptr->link=first
12. first=ptr
13. curr->link=first
14. stop

```
void insertatbeg()
{
struct node *ptr;
ptr=(struct node *) malloc (sizeof (struct node));
if(ptr==NULL)
{
printf("OVERFLOW\n");
return;
}
printf ("Input New Node Information");
scanf("%d", &ptr->info);
curr=first;
while(curr->link!=first)
{
curr=curr->link;
}
ptr->link=first;
first=ptr;
curr->link=first;
}
```

b. (ii) Insertion of a Node (At End)

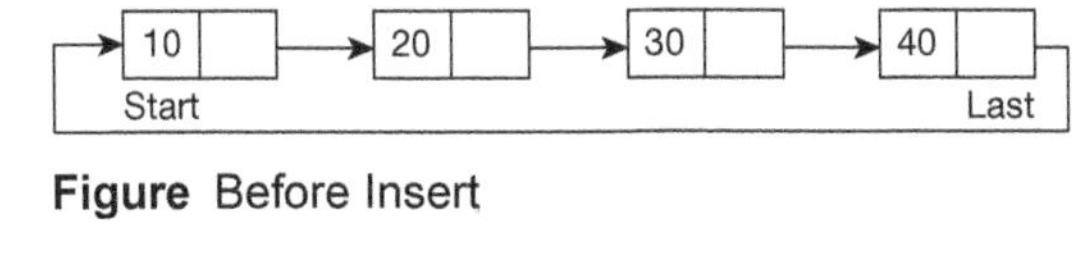

Figure Before Insert

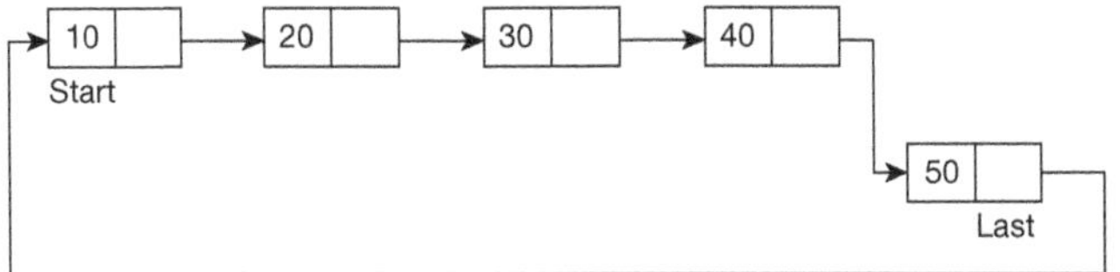

Figure After Insert value = 50

Algorithm

Steps

1. start
2. if start=NULL then
3. print "OVERFLOW" and then
4. stop
5. ptr=ptr->start
6. start=start->link
7. read info
8. curr=curr->link
9. repeat step 10 while curr->link!=first
10. curr=curr->link
11. curr->link=ptr
12. ptr->link=first
13. stop

```
void insertatend()
{
struct node *ptr, *curr;
ptr=(struct node *) malloc (sizeof (struct node));
if(ptr==NULL)
{
printf("OVERFLOW\n");
return;
}
printf ("Input New Node Information");
scanf("%d", &ptr->info);
curr=first;
while(curr->link!=first)
curr=curr->link;
curr->link=ptr;
ptr->link=first;
}
```

c. Deletion from Circular Linked List

Deletion from circular linked list is little bit different from single linked list.

c. (i) Deletion of a Node (At Beg)

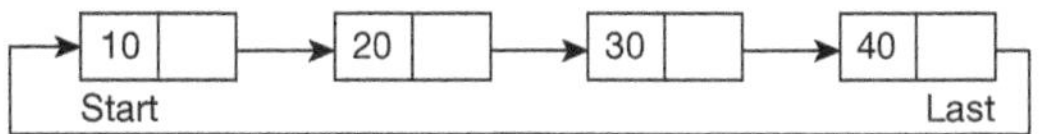

Figure Before Deletion

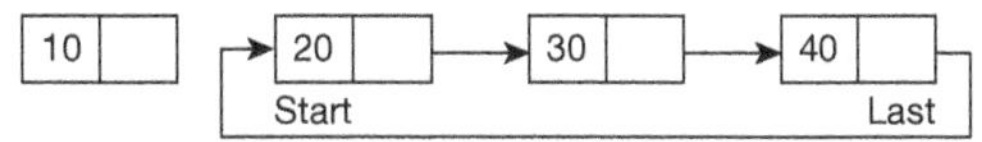

Figure After Deletion node whose value is 10

Algorithm

Steps

1. start
2. if first=NULL then
3. print "UNDERFLOW" and then
4. stop
5. curr=curr->first
6. repeat step 7 while curr->link!=first
7. curr=curr->link
8. ptr=ptr->first
9. first=ptr->link
10. curr->link=first
11. ptr->link=avail
12. avail=avail->ptr
13. stop

```
void deleteatbeg()
{
struct node *ptr, *curr;
if (first==NULL)
{
printf("\n UNDERFLOW");
return;
}
curr=first
while(curr->link!=first)
curr=curr->link
ptr=first;
```

```
first=ptr->link
curr->link=first;
free(ptr);
}
```

c. (ii) Deletion of a Node (At End)

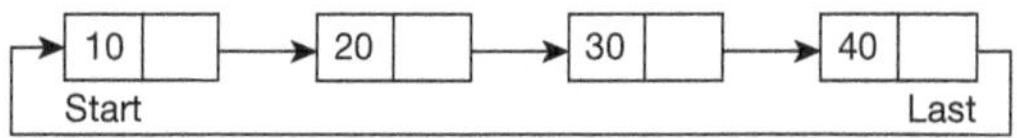

Figure Before Deletion

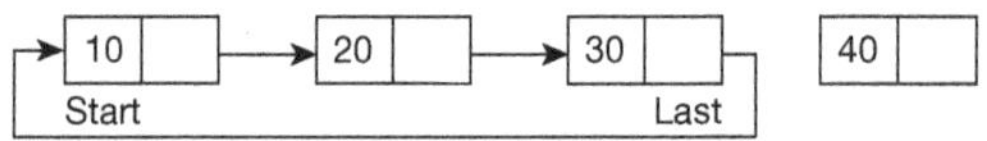

Figure After Deletion node whose value = 40

Algorithm

Steps

1. start
2. if first=NULL then
3. print "UNDERFLOW" and then
4. stop
5. curr->link=first
6. repeat step 4 while curr->link!=first
7. ptr=curr
8. curr=curr->link
9. ptr->link=first
10. curr->link=avail
11. stop

```
void deleteatend()
{
struct node *ptr, *curr;
if (first==NULL)
{
printf("\n UNDERFLOW");
return;
}
curr=first
```

```
while(curr->link!=first)
{
ptr=curr;
curr=curr->link;
}
ptr->link=first;
free(ptr);
}
```

Program: Implement Circular Linked List

```
#include<stdio.h>
#include<stdlib.h>
typedef struct Node
{
        int data;
        struct Node *next;
}node;
void insert(node *pointer, int data)
{
        node *start = pointer;
        while(pointer->next!=start)
        {
        pointer = pointer -> next;
        }
        pointer->next = (node *)malloc(sizeof(node));
        pointer = pointer->next;
        pointer->data = data;
        pointer->next = start;
}
int find(node *pointer, int key)
{
        node *start = pointer;
        pointer = pointer -> next;
        while(pointer!=start)
        {
            if(pointer->data == key)
```

```
            {
            return 1;
            }
            pointer = pointer -> next;
        }
        return 0;
}
void delete(node *pointer, int data)
{
        node *start = pointer;
          while(pointer->next!=start && (pointer->next)->data != data)
        {
            pointer = pointer -> next;
        }
        if(pointer->next==start)
        {
            printf("Element %d is not present in the list\n",data);
            return;
        }
        node *temp;
        temp = pointer -> next;
        pointer->next = temp->next;
        free(temp);
        return;
}
void print(node *start,node *pointer)
{
        if(pointer==start)
        {
            return;
        }
        printf("%d-> ",pointer->data);
          print(start,pointer->next);
}
int main()
{
```

```
node *start,*temp;
int query;
start = (node *)malloc(sizeof(node));
temp = start;
temp -> next = start;
while(1)
{
printf("1. Insert\n");
printf("2. Delete\n");
printf("3. Print\n");
printf("4. Find\n");
printf("5. Exit\n");
scanf("%d",&query);
        if(query==1)
        {
                int data;
                        printf("\nEnter the data:-");
                scanf("%d",&data);
                insert(start,data);
        }
        else if(query==2)
        {
            int data;
                    printf("\nEnter the data:-");
            scanf("%d",&data);
            delete(start,data);
        }
        else if(query==3)
        {
            printf("The list is ");
            print(start,start->next);
            printf("\n");
        }
        else if(query==4)
        {
            int data;
```

```
                printf("\nEnter the data:-");
            scanf("%d",&data);
            int status = find(start,data);
            if(status)
            {
                printf("Element Found\n");
            }
            else
            {
                printf("Element Not Found\n");
            }
        }
            if(query==5)
            {
                exit(0);
            }
    }
}
```

Output

```
    1. Insert
    2. Delete
    3. Print
    4. Find
    5. Exit
    1
 Enter the data:-2
    1. Insert
    2. Delete
    3. Print
    4. Find
    5. Exit
    1
 Enter the data:-3
    1. Insert
    2. Delete
```

3. Print
4. Find
5. Exit

1

Enter the data:-4

1. Insert
2. Delete
3. Print
4. Find
5. Exit

1

Enter the data:-5

1. Insert
2. Delete
3. Print
4. Find
5. Exit

3

The list is 2-> 3-> 4-> 5->

1. Insert
2. Delete
3. Print
4. Find
5. Exit

2

Enter the data:-4

1. Insert
2. Delete
3. Print
4. Find
5. Exit

3

The list is 2-> 3-> 5->

1. Insert
2. Delete
3. Print

4. Find
5. Exit

5

3.7 DOUBLE LINKED LIST

In a single linked list one can move starting from the first node to any node in one direction from left-to-right. This is why, a single linked list is also called as a one way linked list. On the other hand, a double linked list is a two way linked list because one can move in both direction (left-to-right or right-to-left). A two way linked list is a linear collection of data elements called nodes, where each node is divided into three parts:

(*a*) A pointer field prev which contains the location of the preceding node in the list.

(*b*) An information field info which contains the data.

(*c*) A pointer field next which contains the location of the next node in the list.

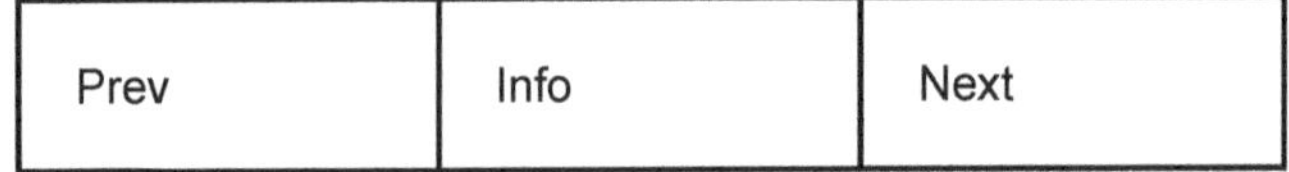

Figure Double linked list

The pointer prev of the first node and next of the last node contain the value NULL *i.e.* they do not store the address of any other node. This indicates the beginning and end of the list respectively. The advantage of a double linked list over a single linked list is that traversal is possible in both directions. This makes it an ideal data structure for applications like database and word processors in which moving in both directions is necessary.

3.8 OPERATIONS IN A DOUBLE LINKED LIST

There are a various operations possible on a Doubly Linked List.

1. Traversing a double linked list.
2. Insertion of a node
   (*a*) Insert at Beginning
   (*b*) Insert at End
   (*c*) Insert at a particular location
3. Deletion of a node
   (*a*) Delete at Beginning
   (*b*) Delete at End
   (*c*) Delete at a particular location

1. Traversing a double linked list

We want to traverse the list in order to process each node exactly once. Our aim is to traverse the list starting from the first node to the end of the list. Consider a pointer type variable curr that points to the node currently being processed next [curr] points to the next node.

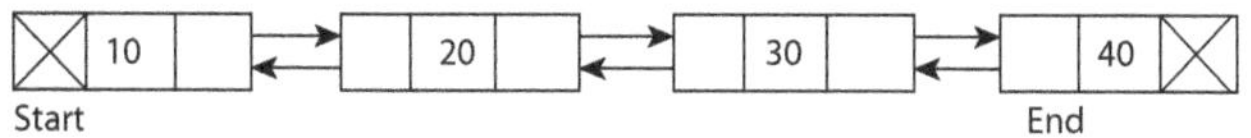

Figure Traversing a Double Linked List

Algorithm

Steps

1. Start
2. Holds the address of the first node
3. Set node = start //initialize pointer variable node
4. Repeat steps 5 and 6 while node ≠ NULL
5. Process info [node] // apply process to info [node]
6. Set node = next [node] // move pointer to next node
7. End of step 4 loop
8. Stop

Program: Create a Double Linked List

```
#include<stdio.h>
#include<stdlib.h>
struct dllnode
{
int info;
struct dllnode *prev;
struct dll *next;
};
void create (struct dllnode *);
void display(struct dllnode *);
void main()
{
struct dllnode *node;
node=(struct dllnode *)malloc(sizeof(struct dllnode));
if(node==NULL)
```

```
{
printf("\n out of memory");
exit(0);
}
create(node);
display(node);
}
void create (struct dllnode *node)
{
struct dllnode *curr;
char ch;
int i=1;
printf("\n Enter the value of %d node:", i);
scanf("%d", &node->info);
node->prev=NULL;
node->next=NULL;
i=i+1;
printf("\n Press 'E' key to exit and Press 'Y' key to continue:");
ch=getchar();
while(ch!='N')
{
curr=(struct dllnode *)malloc(sizeof(struct dllnode));
if(curr==NULL)
{
printf("\n Out of memory");
exit(0);
}
node->next=curr;
curr->prev=node;
node=node->next;
printf("\n Enter the value of %d node:", i);
scanf("%d", &node->info);
node->next=NULL;
printf("\n Press 'E' key to exit and Press 'Y' key to continue:");
ch=getchar();
```

```
i=i+1;
}
}
void display(struct dllnode*node)
{
struct dllnode *temp;
printf("\n Value of Nodes in the List is Forward Direction");
while(node!=NULL)
{
temp=node;
printf("%d", node->info);
node=node->next;
}
printf("\n Value of Nodes in the List is Reverse Direction");
node=temp;
while(node!=NULL)
{
printf("%d", node->info);
node=node->prev;
}
}
```

Output

```
Enter the value node: 10
Press 'E' key to exit and Press 'Y' key to continue: Y
Enter the value node: 20
Press 'E' key to exit and Press 'Y' key to continue: Y
Enter the value node: 30
Press 'E' key to exit and Press 'Y' key to continue: Y
Enter the value node: 40
Press 'E' key to exit and Press 'Y' key to continue: Y
Press 'E' key to exit and Press 'Y' key to continue: E
Value of Nodes in the List in Forward Direction:
10 20 30 40
Value of Nodes in the List in Reverse Direction:
40 30 20 10
```

2. Insertion of a node in a double linked list

The insertion is used to add an element in a double linked list. The following points should be remembered before making insert operation.

(*a*) Create a new node.

(*b*) If the list is empty, insert the node in the list and update the previous and next pointer field of the node

(*c*) If the node is to be inserted at the beginning, insert the node and adjust the previous and next pointer field of the node.

a. Insert at Beginning

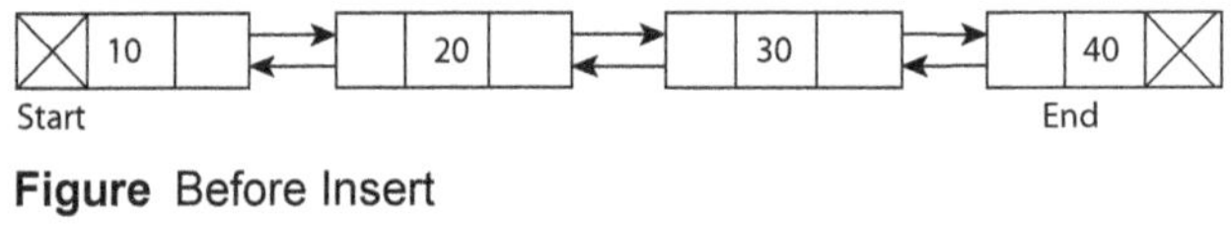

Figure Before Insert

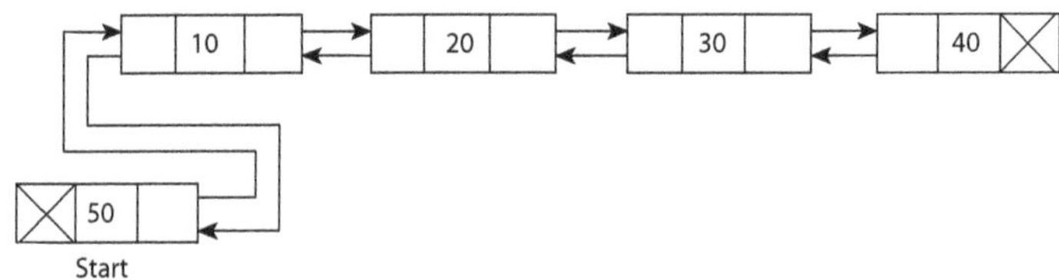

Figure After Insert (x= 50)

Algorithm

Steps

1. Start
2. Holds the address of the first node
3. Create a new node name as temp/node
4. If node = NULL then
5. Write "out of memory space" and
6. Exit
7. Set info [node] = x //copies new data into new node
8. Set next [node] = start // new node now points to original first node
9. Set prev [node] = NULL
10. Set prev [start] = node
11. Set start = node
12. Stop

Program: Insert a Node at the Beginning of a Double Linked List

```
#include<stdio.h>
```

```
#include<stdlib.h>
struct dllnode
{
int info;
struct dllnode *prev;
struct dll *next;
};
struct dllnode *start;
void create (struct dllnode *);
void insert(struct dllnode *);
void display(struct dllnode *);
void main()
{
struct dllnode *node;
char ch='1';
node=(struct dllnode *)malloc(sizeof(struct dllnode));
if(node==NULL)
{
printf("\n out of memory");
exit(0);
}
start=node;
create(node);
while(ch!='3')
{
printf("\n 1. Insert at Beg");
printf("\n 2. Display");
printf("\n 3. Exit");
printf("\n Enter your choice:");
ch=getchar();
switch(ch)
{
case '1':
insert(node);
node=start;
break;
```

```
case '2':
display(node);
break;
case '3':
break;
default:
printf("Wrong Choice");
}
}
}
void create (struct dllnode *node)
{
struct dllnode *curr;
char ch;
int i=1;
printf("\n Enter the value of %d node:", i);
scanf("%d", &node->info);
node->prev=NULL;
node->next=NULL;
i=i+1;
printf("\n Press 'E' key to exit and Press 'Y' key to continue:");
ch=getchar();
while(ch!='N')
{
curr=(struct dllnode *)malloc(sizeof(struct dllnode));
if(curr==NULL)
{
printf("\n Out of memory");
exit(0);
}
node->next=curr;
curr->prev=node;
node=node->next;
printf("\n Enter the value of %d node:", i);
scanf("%d", &node->info);
node->next=NULL;
```

```
printf("\n Press 'E' key to exit and Press 'Y' key to continue:");
ch=getchar();
i=i+1;
}
}
void insert (struct dllnode *node)
{
struct dllnode *curr;
curr=(struct dllnode *)malloc(sizeof(struct dllnode));
if(curr==NULL)
{
printf("\n Out of Memory");
exit(0);
}
printf("\n Enter the Value to be Insert:");
scanf("%d", &curr->info);
curr->prev=NULL;
curr->next=node;
node->prev=curr;
node=curr;
start=node;
}
void display(struct dllnode*node)
{
struct dllnode *temp;
printf("\n Value of Nodes in the List is Forward Direction");
while(node!=NULL)
{
temp=node;
printf("%d", node->info);
node=node->next;
}
printf("\n Value of Nodes in the List is Reverse Direction");
node=temp;
while(node!=NULL)
{
```

```
printf("%d", node->info);
node=node->prev;
}
}
```

Output

```
Enter the value node: 10
Press 'E' key to exit and Press 'Y' key to continue: Y
Enter the value node: 20
Press 'E' key to exit and Press 'Y' key to continue: Y
Enter the value node: 30
Press 'E' key to exit and Press 'Y' key to continue: Y
Enter the value node: 40
Press 'E' key to exit and Press 'Y' key to continue: Y
Press 'E' key to exit and Press 'Y' key to continue: E
   1. Insert at Beg
   2. Display
   3. Exit
Enter Your Choice: 2
10 20 30 40
Value of Nodes in the List is Forward Direction:
10 20 30 40
Value of Nodes in the List is Reverse Direction:
40 30 20 10
   1. Insert at Beg
   2. Display
   3. Exit
Enter Your Choice:1
50
   1. Insert at Beg
   2. Display
   3. Exit
Value of Nodes in the List is Forward Direction:
50 10 20 30 40
Value of Nodes in the List is Reverse Direction:
40 30 20 10 50
Enter Your Choice: 3
```

b. Insert at End

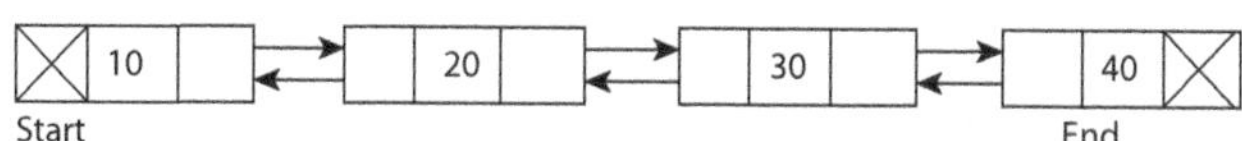

Figure Before Insert

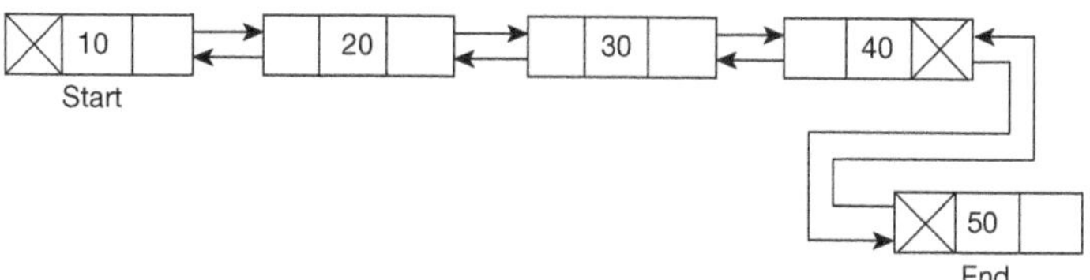

Figure After Insert (x = 50)

Algorithm

Steps

1. Start
2. Holds the address of the first node
3. Create a new node named as temp/node
4. If node = NULL then
5. Write "out of memory space" and
6. Exit
7. Set info [node] = x //copies new data into new node
8. Set next [node] = NULL
9. Set curr = start
10. Repeat steps 11 and 12 while curr ≠ NULL
11. Set prev = curr
12. Set curr = next [curr]
13. End of step 10 loop
14. Set next [prev] = node
15. Set prev [node] = prev
16. Stop

Program: Insert a Node at the End of a Double Linked List

```
#include<stdio.h>
#include<stdlib.h>
struct dllnode
{
int info;
struct dllnode *prev;
```

```
struct dll *next;
};
void create (struct dllnode *);
void insert(struct dllnode *);
void display(struct dllnode *);
void main()
{
struct dllnode *node;
char ch='1';
node=(struct dllnode *)malloc(sizeof(struct dllnode));
if(node==NULL)
{
printf("\n out of memory");
exit(0);
}
create(node);
while(ch!='3')
{
printf("\n 1. Insert at End");
printf("\n 2. Display");
printf("\n 3. Exit");
printf("\n Enter your choice:");
ch=getchar();
switch(ch)
{
case '1':
insert(node);
break;
case '2':
display(node);
break;
case '3':
break;
default:
printf("Wrong Choice");
}
```

```
}
}
void create (struct dllnode *node)
{
struct dllnode *curr;
char ch;
int i=1;
printf("\n Enter the value of %d node:", i);
scanf("%d", &node->info);
node->prev=NULL;
node->next=NULL;
i=i+1;
printf("\n Press 'E' key to exit and Press 'Y' key to continue:");
ch=getchar();
while(ch!='N')
{
curr=(struct dllnode *)malloc(sizeof(struct dllnode));
if(curr==NULL)
{
printf("\n Out of memory");
exit(0);
}
node->next=curr;
curr->prev=node;
node=node->next;
printf("\n Enter the value of %d node:", i);
scanf("%d", &node->info);
node->next=NULL;
printf("\n Press 'E' key to exit and Press 'Y' key to continue:");
ch=getchar();
i=i+1;
}
}
void insert (struct dllnode *node)
{
struct dllnode *curr;
```

```
curr=(struct dllnode *)malloc(sizeof(struct dllnode));
if(curr==NULL)
{
printf("\n Out of Memory");
exit(0);
}
curr->next=NULL;
printf("\n Enter the Value to be Insert:");
scanf("%d", &curr->info);
node->next=curr
curr->prev=node;
}
void display(struct dllnode*node)
{
struct dllnode *temp;
printf("\n Value of Nodes in the List is Forward Direction");
while(node!=NULL)
{
temp=node;
printf("%d", node->info);
node=node->next;
}
printf("\n Value of Nodes in the List is Reverse Direction");
node=temp;
while(node!=NULL)
{
printf("%d", node->info);
node=node->prev;
}
}
```

Output

```
Enter the value node: 10
Press 'E' key to exit and Press 'Y' key to continue: Y
Enter the value node: 20
Press 'E' key to exit and Press 'Y' key to continue: Y
```

Enter the value node: 30

Press 'E' key to exit and Press 'Y' key to continue: Y

Enter the value node: 40

Press 'E' key to exit and Press 'Y' key to continue: Y

Press 'E' key to exit and Press 'Y' key to continue: E

1. Insert at End
2. Display
3. Exit

Enter Your Choice: 2

10 20 30 40

Value of Nodes in the List is Forward Direction:

10 20 30 40

Value of Nodes in the List is Reverse Direction:

40 30 20 10

1. Insert at End
2. Display
3. Exit

Enter Your Choice:1

50

1. Insert at End
2. Display
3. Exit

Value of Nodes in the List is Forward Direction:

10 20 30 40 50

Value of Nodes in the List is Reverse Direction:

50 40 30 20 10

Enter Your Choice: 3

c. Insert at a particular location

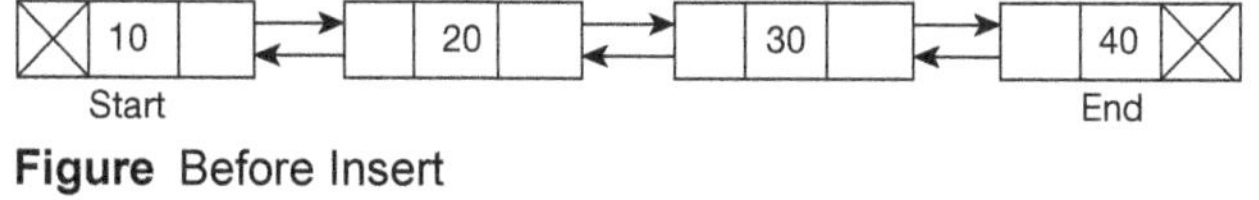

Figure Before Insert

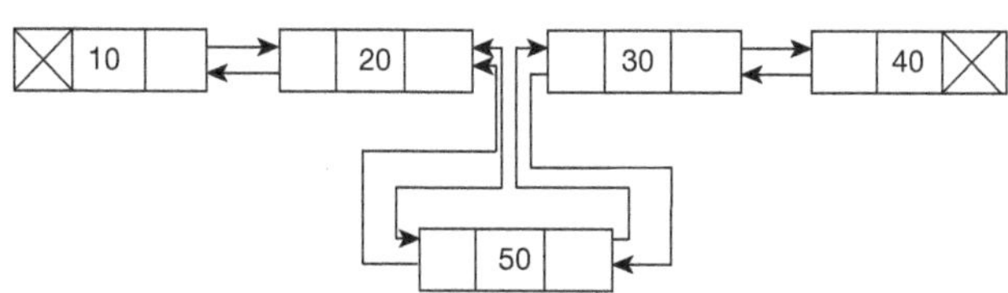

Figure After Insert (loc = 3, x = 50)

Algorithm

Steps

1. Start
2. Holds the address of the first node
3. Create a new node named as temp/node
4. If node = NULL then
5. Write "out of memory space" and
6. Exit
7. Set info [node] = x //copies new data into new node
8. Set next [node] = NULL
9. Set curr = start
10. Read loc
11. Set i = 1
4. Repeat steps 12 to 14 while curr ≠ NULL and i < loc
12. Set prev = curr
13. Set curr = next [curr]
14. Set i = i+1
15. End of step 17 loop
16. If curr = NULL then
17. Write "position not found" and
18. Exit
19. Set next [prev] = node
20. Set prev [node] = prev
21. Set next [node] = curr
22. Set prev [curr] = node
23. Stop

Program: Insert a Node at a Particular Location in a Double Linked List

```
#include<stdio.h>
#include<stdlib.h>
struct dllnode
{
int info;
struct dllnode *prev;
struct dll *next;
};
```

```
struct dllnode *start;
void create (struct dllnode *);
void insert(struct dllnode *);
int count(struct dllnode *);
void display(struct dllnode *);
void main()
{
struct dllnode *node;
char ch='1';
node=(struct dllnode *)malloc(sizeof(struct dllnode));
if(node==NULL)
{
printf("\n out of memory");
exit(0);
}
start=node;
create(node);
while(ch!='3')
{
printf("\n 1. Insert at Particular Location");
printf("\n 2. Display");
printf("\n 3. Exit");
printf("\n Enter your choice:");
ch=getchar();
switch(ch)
{
case '1':
insert(node);
node=start;
break;
case '2':
display(node);
break;
case '3':
break;
default:
```

```
printf("Wrong Choice");
}
}
}
void create (struct dllnode *node)
{
struct dllnode *curr;
char ch;
int i=1;
printf("\n Enter the value of %d node:", i);
scanf("%d", &node->info);
node->prev=NULL;
node->next=NULL;
i=i+1;
printf("\n Press 'E' key to exit and Press 'Y' key to continue:");
ch=getchar();
while(ch!='N')
{
curr=(struct dllnode *)malloc(sizeof(struct dllnode));
if(curr==NULL)
{
printf("\n Out of memory");
exit(0);
}
node->next=curr;
curr->prev=node;
node=node->next;
printf("\n Enter the value of %d node:", i);
scanf("%d", &node->info);
node->next=NULL;
printf("\n Press 'E' key to exit and Press 'Y' key to continue:");
ch=getchar();
i=i+1;
}
}
void insert (struct dllnode *node)
```

```
{
struct dllnode *curr;
int loc, c=0, i=1;
printf("\n Enter the location at which node will be inserted:");
scanf("%d", &loc);
c=count(node);
if(loc>c)
{
printf("\n Entered location Exceeds the Number of Nodes");
return;
}
curr=(struct dllnode *)malloc(sizeof(struct dllnode));
if(curr==NULL)
{
printf("\n Out of Memory");
exit(0);
}
while(i<loc)
{
node=node->next;
i=i+1;
}
printf("\n Input the Node value at %d location:", loc);
scanf("%d", &curr->info);
if(loc==1)
{
curr->next=node;
curr->prev=NULL;
node->prev=curr;
start=curr;
}
else
{
node->prev->next=curr;
curr->prev=node->prev;
curr->next=node;
```

```
node->prev=curr;
}
}
int count(struct dllnode *node)
{
int i=0;
while(node!=NULL)
{
i=i+1;
node=node->next;
}
return i;
}
void display(struct dllnode*node)
{
struct dllnode *temp;
printf("\n Value of Nodes in the List is Forward Direction");
while(node!=NULL)
{
temp=node;
printf("%d", node->info);
node=node->next;
}
printf("\n Value of Nodes in the List is Reverse Direction");
node=temp;
while(node!=NULL)
{
printf("%d", node->info);
node=node->prev;
}
}
```

Output

```
Enter the value node: 10
Press 'E' key to exit and Press 'Y' key to continue: Y
Enter the value node: 20
```

Press 'E' key to exit and Press 'Y' key to continue: Y

Enter the value node: 30

Press 'E' key to exit and Press 'Y' key to continue: Y

Enter the value node: 40

Press 'E' key to exit and Press 'Y' key to continue: Y

Press 'E' key to exit and Press 'Y' key to continue: E

1. Insert at Particular Location
2. Display
3. Exit

Enter Your Choice: 2

10 20 30 40

Value of Nodes in the List is Forward Direction:

10 20 30 40

Value of Nodes in the List is Reverse Direction:

40 30 20 10

1. Insert at Particular Location
2. Display
3. Exit

Enter Your Choice:1

Enter the location at which node will be inserted:3

Input the Node value at 3 location: 50

1. Insert at Particular Location
2. Display
3. Exit

Value of Nodes in the List is Forward Direction:

10 20 50 30 40

Value of Nodes in the List is Reverse Direction:

40 30 50 20 10

Enter Your Choice: 3

3. Deletion of a node

The deletion operation is used to delete an element from a double linked list. Before performing deletion one should remember the following points.

(*a*) If the list is empty, deletion is not possible

(*b*) If the list contains one node after deletion the list will be empty

(*c*) If the node to be deleted is not found, display a message "node not found"

(*d*) If the node is deleted, the memory space for the deleted node is de-allocated.

a. Delete at Beginning

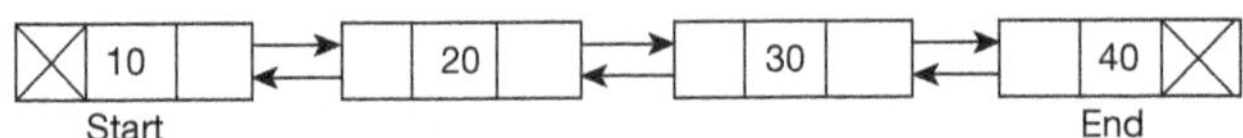

Figure Before Deletion

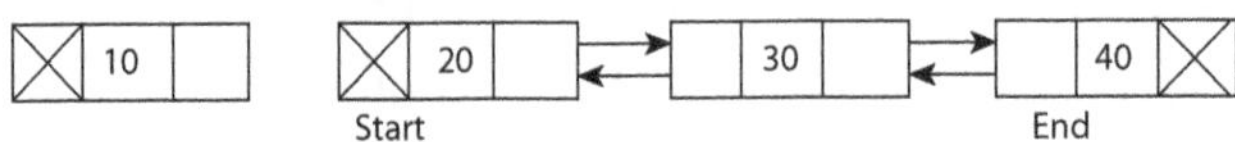

Figure After Delete the First Node

Algorithm

Steps

1. Start
2. Holds the address of the first node
3. Set temp = start
4. If start = NULL then
5. Write "UNDERFLOW" and
6. Exit
7. Set start = next [start]
8. Set prev [start] = NULL
9. Free the space associated with temp
10. Stop

Program: Delete a Node from the Beginning of a Double Linked List

```
#include<stdio.h>
#include<stdlib.h>
struct dllnode
{
int info;
struct dllnode *prev;
struct dll *next;
};
struct dllnode *start;
void create (struct dllnode *);
void delete(struct dllnode *);
void display(struct dllnode *);
void main()
{
```

```
struct dllnode *node;
char ch='1';
node=(struct dllnode *)malloc(sizeof(struct dllnode));
if(node==NULL)
{
printf("\n out of memory");
exit(0);
}
start=node;
create(node);
while(ch!='3')
{
printf("\n 1. Delete at Beg");
printf("\n 2. Display");
printf("\n 3. Exit");
printf("\n Enter your choice:");
ch=getchar();
switch(ch)
{
case '1':
delete(node);
node=start;
break;
case '2':
display(node);
break;
case '3':
break;
default:
printf("Wrong Choice");
}
}
}
void create (struct dllnode *node)
{
struct dllnode *curr;
```

```
char ch;
int i=1;
printf("\n Enter the value of %d node:", i);
scanf("%d", &node->info);
node->prev=NULL;
node->next=NULL;
i=i+1;
printf("\n Press 'E' key to exit and Press 'Y' key to continue:");
ch=getchar();
while(ch!='N')
{
curr=(struct dllnode *)malloc(sizeof(struct dllnode));
if(curr==NULL)
{
printf("\n Out of memory");
exit(0);
}
node->next=curr;
curr->prev=node;
node=node->next;
printf("\n Enter the value of %d node:", i);
scanf("%d", &node->info);
node->next=NULL;
printf("\n Press 'E' key to exit and Press 'Y' key to continue:");
ch=getchar();
i=i+1;
}
}
void delete (struct dllnode *node)
{
struct dllnode *temp;
if(node!=NULL)
{
temp=node;
node=node->next;
node->prev=NULL;
```

```
start=node;
free(temp);
}
}
void display(struct dllnode*node)
{
struct dllnode *temp;
if(node==NULL)
{
printf("\n Empty");
return;
}
printf("\n Value of Nodes in the List is Forward Direction");
while(node!=NULL)
{
temp=node;
printf("%d", node->info);
node=node->next;
}
printf("\n Value of Nodes in the List is Reverse Direction");
node=temp;
while(node!=NULL)
{
printf("%d", node->info);
node=node->prev;
}
}
```

Output

```
Enter the value node: 10
Press 'E' key to exit and Press 'Y' key to continue: Y
Enter the value node: 20
Press 'E' key to exit and Press 'Y' key to continue: Y
Enter the value node: 30
Press 'E' key to exit and Press 'Y' key to continue: Y
Enter the value node: 40
```

Press 'E' key to exit and Press 'Y' key to continue: Y

Press 'E' key to exit and Press 'Y' key to continue: E

1. Delete at Beg
2. Display
3. Exit

Enter Your Choice: 2

10 20 30 40

Value of Nodes in the List in Forward Direction:

10 20 30 40

Value of Nodes in the List is Reverse Direction:

40 30 20 10

1. Delete at Beg
2. Display
3. Exit

Enter Your Choice:1

10

1. Delete at Beg
2. Display
3. Exit

Enter Your Choice: 2

Value of Nodes in the List is Forward Direction:

20 30 40

Value of Nodes in the List is Reverse Direction:

40 30 20

Enter Your Choice: 3

b. Delete at End

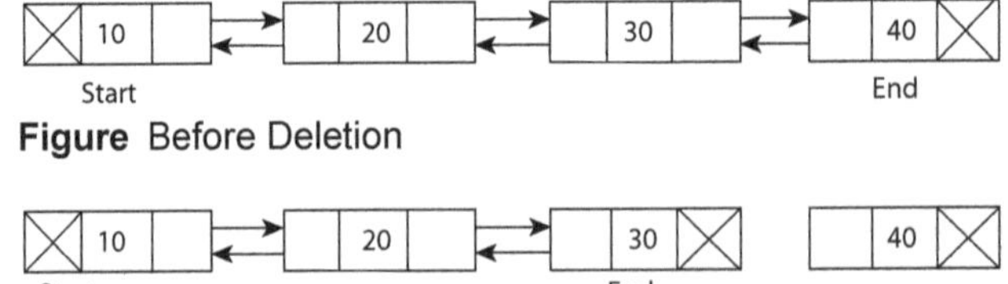

Figure Before Deletion

Figure After Delete the Last Node

Algorithm

Steps

1. Start

2. Holds the address of the first node
3. Set node = start
4. Set temp = start
5. If node = NULL then
6. Write "UNDERFLOW" and
7. Exit
8. Repeat steps 9 and 10 while next [node] ≠ NULL
9. Set temp = node
10. Set node = next [node]
11. End of step 8 loop
12. Set next [temp] = NULL
13. Free the space associated with node
14. Stop

Program: Delete a Node at the End of a Double Linked List

```
#include<stdio.h>
#include<stdlib.h>
struct dllnode
{
int info;
struct dllnode *prev;
struct dllnode *next;
};
struct dllnode *start;
void create (struct dllnode *);
void delete(struct dllnode *);
void display(struct dllnode *);
void main()
{
struct dllnode *node;
char ch='1';
node=(struct dllnode *)malloc(sizeof(struct dllnode));
if(node==NULL)
{
printf("\n out of memory");
exit(0);
```

```
}
start=node;
create(node);
while(ch!='3')
{
printf("\n 1. Delete at End");
printf("\n 2. Display");
printf("\n 3. Exit");
printf("\n Enter your choice:");
ch=getchar();
switch(ch)
{
case '1':
delete(node);
node=start;
break;
case '2':
display(node);
break;
case '3':
break;
default:
printf("Wrong Choice");
}
}
}
void create (struct dllnode *node)
{
struct dllnode *curr;
char ch;
int i=1;
printf("\n Enter the value of %d node:", i);
scanf("%d", &node->info);
node->prev=NULL;
node->next=NULL;
i=i+1;
```

```
printf("\n Press 'E' key to exit and Press 'Y' key to continue:");
ch=getchar();
while(ch!='N')
{
curr=(struct dllnode *)malloc(sizeof(struct dllnode));
if(curr==NULL)
{
printf("\n Out of memory");
exit(0);
}
node->next=curr;
curr->prev=node;
node=node->next;
printf("\n Enter the value of %d node:", i);
scanf("%d", &node->info);
node->next=NULL;
printf("\n Press 'E' key to exit and Press 'Y' key to continue:");
ch=getchar();
i=i+1;
}
}
void delete (struct dllnode *node)
{
struct dllnode *temp;
if(node->next==NULL)
{
temp=node;
node=node->next;
start=node;
free(temp);
return;
}
while(node->next!=NULL)
node=node->next;
temp=node;
node=node->prev;
```

```
node->next=NULL;
free(temp);
}
void display(struct dllnode*node)
{
struct dllnode *temp;
if(node==NULL)
{
printf("\n Empty");
return;
}
printf("\n Value of Nodes in the List is Forward Direction");
while(node!=NULL)
{
temp=node;
printf("%d", node->info);
node=node->next;
}
printf("\n Value of Nodes in the List is Reverse Direction");
node=temp;
while(node!=NULL)
{
printf("%d", node->info);
node=node->prev;
}
}
```

Output

```
Enter the value node: 10
Press 'E' key to exit and Press 'Y' key to continue: Y
Enter the value node: 20
Press 'E' key to exit and Press 'Y' key to continue: Y
Enter the value node: 30
Press 'E' key to exit and Press 'Y' key to continue: Y
Enter the value node: 40
Press 'E' key to exit and Press 'Y' key to continue: Y
```

Press 'E' key to exit and Press 'Y' key to continue: E

1. Delete at End
2. Display
3. Exit

Enter Your Choice: 2

Value of Nodes in the List in Forward Direction:

10 20 30 40

Value of Nodes in the List in Reverse Direction:

40 30 20 10

1. Delete at End
2. Display
3. Exit

Enter Your Choice: 1

Value of Nodes in the List is Forward Direction:

10 20 30

Value of Nodes in the List is Reverse Direction:

30 20 10

1. Delete at End
2. Display
3. End

Enter Your Choice: 3

c. Delete at a particular location

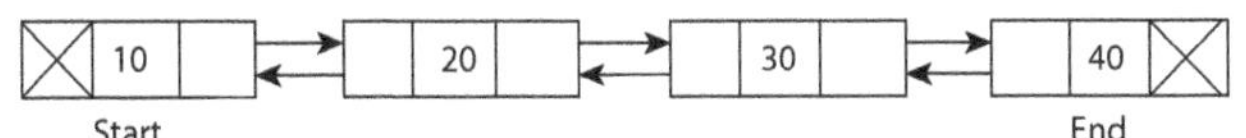

Figure Before Deletion

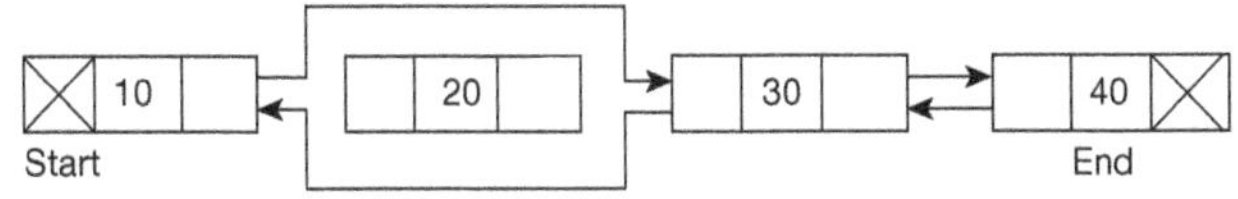

Figure After Deletion (loc = 2, x =20)

Algorithm

Steps

1. Start
2. Holds the address of the first node
3. Set node = start
4. If node = NULL then

5. Write "UNDERFLOW" and
6. Exit
7. Set i = 1
8. Read loc
9. If loc = 1 then node = NULL and
10. Exit
11. Repeat steps 12 and 13 while node ≠ NULL and i < loc
12. Set temp = node
13. Set node = next [node]
14. Set i = i+1
15. End of step 11 loop
16. If node = NULL then
17. Write "position not found" and
18. Exit
19. Set next [temp] = next [node]
20. Set prev [next[node]] = temp
21. Free the space associated with node
22. Stop

Program: Delete a Node at a Particular Location in a Double Linked List

```
#include<stdio.h>
#include<stdlib.h>
struct dllnode
{
int info;
struct dllnode *prev;
struct dllnode *next;
};
struct dllnode *start;
void create (struct dllnode *);
void delete(struct dllnode *);
int count(struct dllnode *);
void display(struct dllnode *);
void main()
{
struct dllnode *node;
char ch='1';
```

```
node=(struct dllnode *)malloc(sizeof(struct dllnode));
if(node==NULL)
{
printf("\n out of memory");
exit(0);
}
start=node;
create(node);
while(ch!='3')
{
printf("\n 1. Delete at a Particular Location");
printf("\n 2. Display");
printf("\n 3. Exit");
printf("\n Enter your choice:");
ch=getchar();
switch(ch)
{
case '1':
delete(node);
node=start;
break;
case '2':
display(node);
break;
case '3':
break;
default:
printf("Wrong Choice");
}
}
}
void create (struct dllnode *node)
{
struct dllnode *curr;
char ch;
int i=1;
```

```
printf("\n Enter the value of %d node:", i);
scanf("%d", &node->info);
node->prev=NULL;
node->next=NULL;
i=i+1;
printf("\n Press 'E' key to exit and Press 'Y' key to continue:");
ch=getchar();
while(ch!='N')
{
curr=(struct dllnode *)malloc(sizeof(struct dllnode));
if(curr==NULL)
{
printf("\n Out of memory");
exit(0);
}
node->next=curr;
curr->prev=node;
node=node->next;
printf("\n Enter the value of %d node:", i);
scanf("%d", &node->info);
node->next=NULL;
printf("\n Press 'E' key to exit and Press 'Y' key to continue:");
ch=getchar();
i=i+1;
}
}
void delete(struct dllnode *node)
{
struct dllnode *temp;
int loc, c=0, i=1;
printf("\n Enter the location at which node will be deleted:");
scanf("%d", &loc);
c=count(node);
if(loc>c)
{
printf("\n Enter location Exceeds the Number of Nodes");
```

```
return;
}
if(loc==1)
{
temp=node;
node=node->next;
if(node!=NULL)
node->prev=NULL;
free(temp);
start=node;
return;
}
while(i<loc)
{
node=node->next;
i=i+1;
}
temp=node;
node=node->prev;
node->next=temp->next;
temp->next->prev=node;
free(temp);
}
int count(struct dllnode *node)
{
int i=0;
while(node!=NULL)
{
i=i+1;
node=node->next;
}
return i;
}
void display(struct dllnode*node)
{
struct dllnode *temp;
```

```
if(node==NULL)
{
printf("\n Empty");
return;
}
printf("\n Value of Nodes in the List is Forward Direction");
while(node!=NULL)
{
temp=node;
printf("%d", node->info);
node=node->next;
}
printf("\n Value of Nodes in the List is Reverse Direction");
node=temp;
while(node!=NULL)
{
printf("%d", node->info);
node=node->prev;
}
}
```

Output

```
Enter the value node: 10
Press 'E' key to exit and Press 'Y' key to continue: Y
Enter the value node: 20
Press 'E' key to exit and Press 'Y' key to continue: Y
Enter the value node: 30
Press 'E' key to exit and Press 'Y' key to continue: Y
Enter the value node: 40
Press 'E' key to exit and Press 'Y' key to continue: Y
Press 'E' key to exit and Press 'Y' key to continue: E
   1. Delete at Particular Location
   2. Display
   3. Exit
Enter Your Choice: 2
Value of Nodes in the List is Forward Direction:
10 20 30 40
```

Value of Nodes in the List is Reverse Direction:

40 30 20 10

1. Delete at Particular Location
2. Display
3. Exit

Enter Your Choice: 1

Enter the location at which node will be deleted: 2

1. Delete at Particular Location
2. Display
3. Exit

Enter Your Choice: 2

Value of Nodes in the List is Forward Direction:

10 30 40

Value of Nodes in the List is Reverse Direction:

40 30 10

Enter Your Choice: 3

Program: Write a Program to Implement a Double Linked List

```
#include<stdio.h>
#include<stdlib.h>
struct node
{
        struct node *previous;
        int data;
        struct node *next;
}*head, *last;
void insert_begning(int value)
{
        struct node *var,*temp;
        var=(struct node *)malloc(sizeof(struct node));
        var->data=value;
        if(head==NULL)
        {
              head=var;
              head->previous=NULL;
              head->next=NULL;
              last=head;
```

```
        }
        else
        {
                temp=var;
                temp->previous=NULL;
                temp->next=head;
                head->previous=temp;
                head=temp;
        }
}
void insert_end(int value)
{
        struct node *var,*temp;
        var=(struct node *)malloc(sizeof(struct node));
                var->data=value;
        if(head==NULL)
        {
                head=var;
                head->previous=NULL;
                head->next=NULL;
                last=head;
        }
        else
        {
                last=head;
                while(last!=NULL)
                {
                        temp=last;
                        last=last->next;
                }
        last=var;
        temp->next=last;
        last->previous=temp;
        last->next=NULL;
        }
}
```

```
int insert_after(int value, int loc)
{
        struct node *temp,*var,*temp1;
        var=(struct node *)malloc(sizeof(struct node));
        var->data=value;
              if(head==NULL)
        {
              head=var;
              head->previous=NULL;
              head->next=NULL;
        }
        else
        {
              temp=head;
              while(temp!=NULL && temp->data!=loc)
              {
                       temp=temp->next;
              }
              if(temp==NULL)
              {
                       printf("\n%d is not present in list ",loc);
              }
              else
              {
              temp1=temp->next;
              temp->next=var;
              var->previous=temp;
              var->next=temp1;
              temp1->previous=var;
              }
        }
        last=head;
        while(last->next!=NULL)
        {
              last=last->next;
        }
```

```
}
int delete_from_end()
{
        struct node *temp;
        temp=last;
        if(temp->previous==NULL)
        {
            free(temp);
            head=NULL;
            last=NULL;
            return 0;
        }
        printf("\nData deleted from list is %d \n",last->data);
        last=temp->previous;
        last->next=NULL;
        free(temp);
        return 0;
}
void display()
{
        struct node *temp;
        temp=head;
        if(temp==NULL)
        {
            printf("List is Empty");
        }
        while(temp!=NULL)
        {
            printf("%d-> ",temp->data);
            temp=temp->next;
        }
}
int main()
{
        int value, i, loc;
        head=NULL;
```

```
printf("Select the choice of operation on link list");
printf("\n1.) insert at begning\n2.) insert at end\n3.) insert at middle");
printf("\n4.) delete from end\n5.) display list\n6.) exit");
while(1)
{
    printf("\n\nenter the choice of operation you want to do");
    scanf("%d",&i);
    switch(i)
    {
        case 1:
        {
        printf("enter the value you want to insert in node");
        scanf("%d",&value);
        insert_begning(value);
        display();
        break;
        }
        case 2:
        {
        printf("enter the value you want to insert in node at last");
        scanf("%d",&value);
        insert_end(value);
        display();
        break;
        }
        case 3:
        {
        printf("after which data you want to insert data");
        scanf("%d",&loc);
        printf("enter the data you want to insert in list");
        scanf("%d",&value);
        insert_after(value,loc);
        display();
        break;
        }
        case 4:
```

```
                    {
                    delete_from_end();
                    display();
                    break;
                    }
                    case 5:
                    {
                    display();
                    break;
                    }
                    case 6:
                    {
                    exit(0);
                    break;
                    }
            }
    }
    printf("\n\n%d",last->data);
    display();
}
```

Output

Select the choice of operation on link list

1. insert at begning
2. insert at end
3. insert at middle
4. delete from end
5. display list
6. exit

enter the choice of operation you want to do 1

enter the value you want to insert in node 2

2->

enter the choice of operation you want to do 2

enter the value you want to insert in node at last 3

2-> 3->

enter the choice of operation you want to do 1

enter the value you want to insert in node 4
4-> 2-> 3->
enter the choice of operation you want to do 3
after which data you want to insert data 12
enter the data you want to insert in list 2

12 is not present in list 4-> 2-> 3->

enter the choice of operation you want to do 3
after which data you want to insert data 2
enter the data you want to insert in list 12
4-> 2-> 12-> 3->

enter the choice of operation you want to do 4

Data deleted from list is 3
4-> 2-> 12->

enter the choice of operation you want to do 4

Data deleted from list is 12
4-> 2->

enter the choice of operation you want to do 5
4-> 2->

enter the choice of operation you want to do 6

3.9 CIRCULAR DOUBLE LINKED LIST

The main motive for consideration to implement a circular double linked is to simplify the insertion and deletion operations performed. In this list, the left link of the left most node contains the address of the right most node and the right link of the right most node contains the address of the left most node.

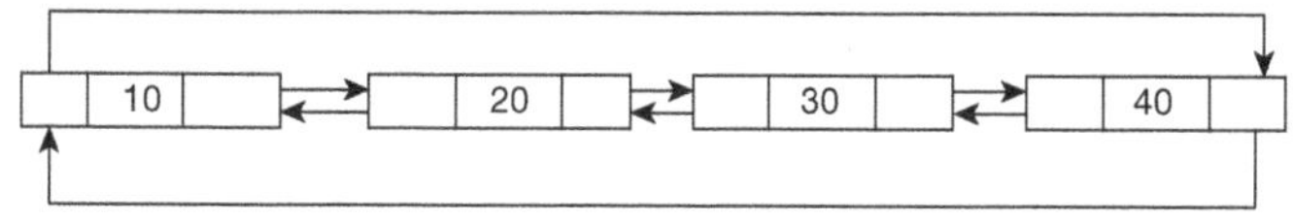

Figure Circular Double Linked List

3.10 OPERATIONS ON CIRCULAR DOUBLE LINKED LIST

1. Insertion Operation
   (*a*) Insert at Beg
   (*b*) Insert at End

2. Deletion Operation
   (*a*) Delete at Beg
   (*b*) Delete at End

1. Insertion Operation

a. Insertion at Beginning

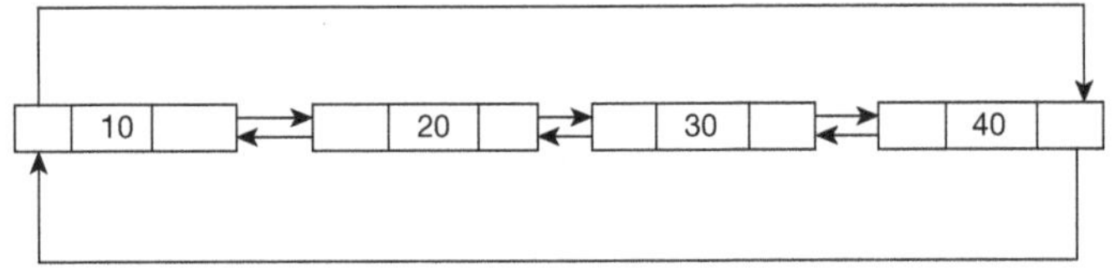

Figure Before Insertion at Beginning

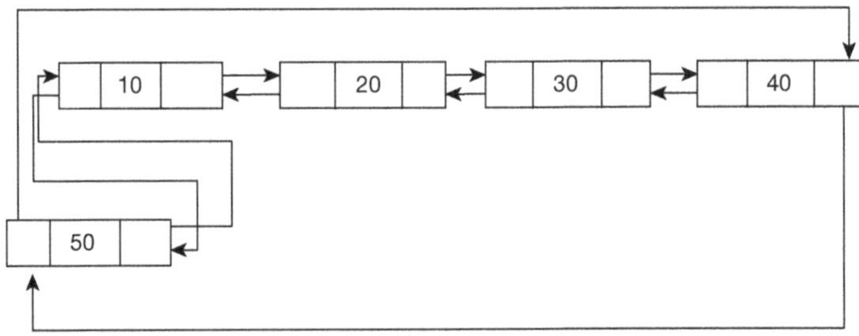

Figure After Insertion at Beginning (Say=50)

Algorithm

Steps

1. start
2. if avail=NULL then
3. print message "OVERFLOW" and then
4. stop
5. ptr←avail
6. avial←rightptr
7. avail←leftptr
8. read info
9. ptr←leftptr (first)
10. rightptr ←first
11. leftptr←ptr
12. leftptr←ptr
13. rightptr←ptr
14. first←ptr
15. stop

```
struct node *insertatbeg(struct node *start)
{
struct node *newnode, *ptr;
int num;
printf("\n Enter the Data");
scanf("%d", &num);
newnode=(struct node *)malloc(sizeof(struct node));
newnode->data=num;
ptr=start;
while(ptr->next!=start)
ptr=ptr->next;
newnode->prev=ptr;
ptr->next=newnode;
newnode->next=start;
start->prev=newnode;
start=newnode;
return start;
}
```

b. Insertion at End

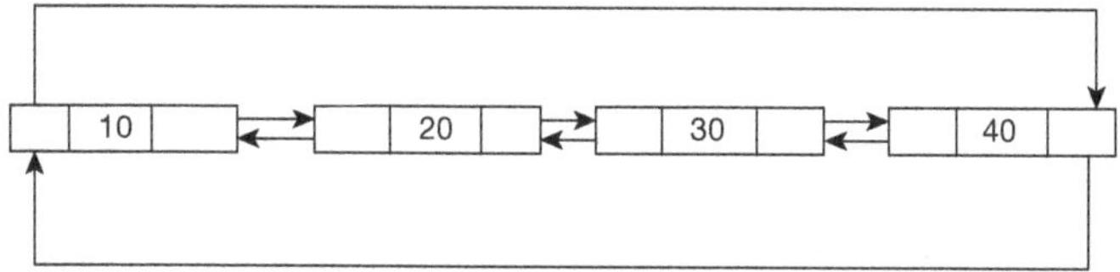

Figure Before Insertion at End

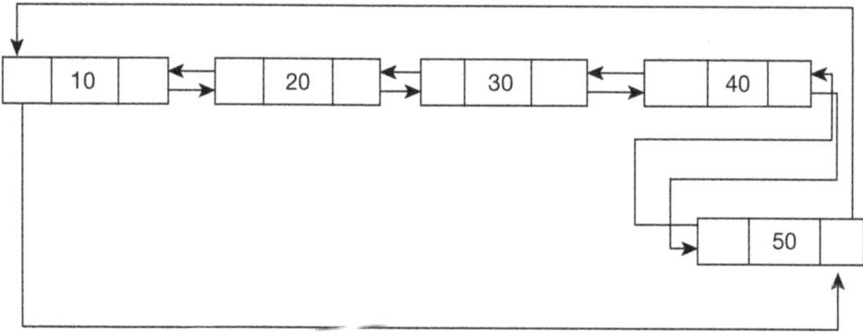

Figure After Insertion at End (Say=50)

Algorithm

Steps

1. start

2. if avail=NULL then
3. print message "OVERFLOW" and then
4. stop
5. ptr←avail
6. avail←leftptr
7. avail←rightptr
8. read info
9. ptr←leftptr (first)
10. rightptr←ptr
11. leftptr←ptr
12. rightptr←first
13. leftptr←ptr
14. stop

```
struct node *insertatend(struct node *start)
{
struct node *ptr, *newnode;
int num;
printf("\n Enter the Data");
scanf("%d", &num);
newnode=(struct node *)malloc(sizeof(struct node));
newnode->data=num;
ptr=start;
while(ptr->next!=start)
ptr=ptr->next;
ptr->next=newnode;
newnode->prev=ptr;
newnode->next=start;
start->prev=newnode;
return start;
}
```

2. Delete Operation

a. Deletion at Beg

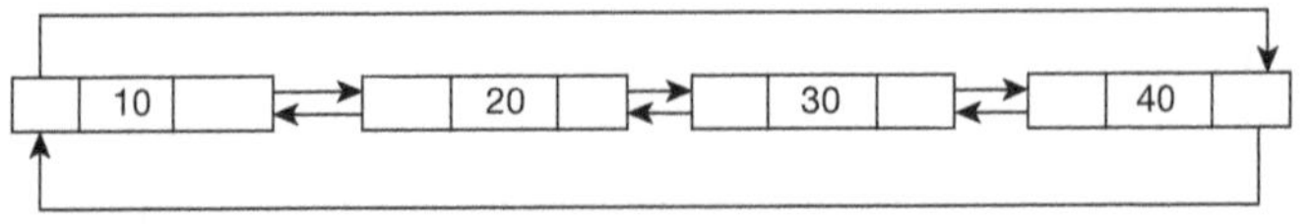

Figure Before Deletion at Beginning

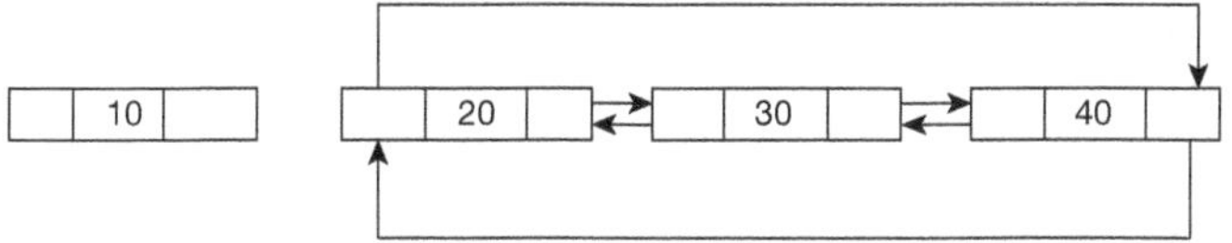

Figure After Deletion at Beginning (Say=10)

Algorithm

Steps

1. start
2. if first=NULL then
3. print message "UNDERFLOW" and then
4. stop
5. ptr←first
6. ptr←rightptr (first)
7. currptr←leftptr (first)
8. leftptr←currptr
9. rightptr←ptr
10. first←ptr
11. leftptr←avail
12. rightptr←avail
13. avail=ptr
14. stop

```
struct node *deleteatbeg(struct node *start)
{
struct node *ptr;
ptr=start;
while(ptr->next!=start)
ptr=ptr->next;
ptr->next=start->next;
tmp=start;
start=start->next;
start->prev=ptr;
free(tmp);
return start;
}
```

b. Deletion at End

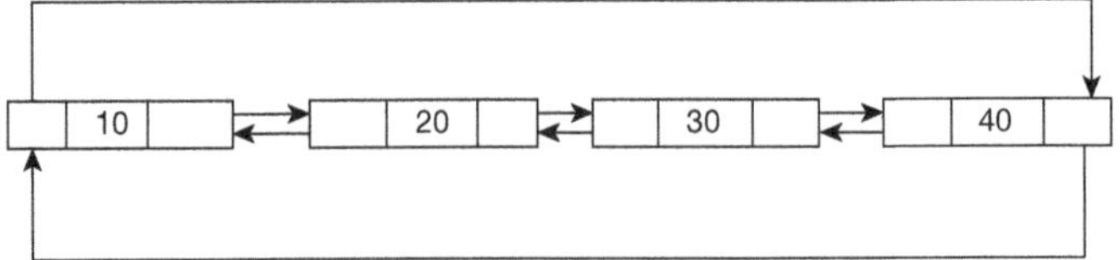

Figure Before Deletion at End

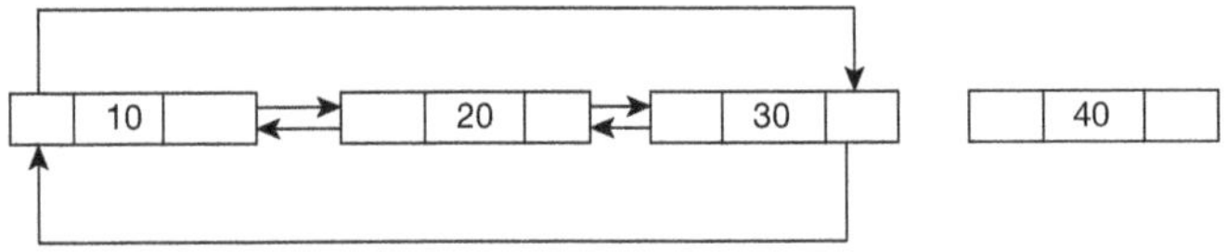

Figure After Deletion at End (Say=40)

Algorithm

Steps

1. Start
2. If first=NULLthen
3. Print message "UNDERFLOW" and then
4. Stop
5. ptr←leftptr (first)
6. currptr←leftptr
7. leftptr ←currptr
8. rightptr (currptr) ←first
9. leftptr←avail
10. rightptr←avail
11. avail←ptr
12. stop

```
struct node *deleteatend(struct node *start)
{
struct node *tmp;
tmp=start;
while(tmp->next!=start)
tmp=tmp->next;
tmp->prev->next=start;
start->prev=tmp->prev;
free(tmp);
return start;
}
```

Program: Write a Program to implement a Circular Double Linked List

```
#include<stdio.h>
#include<stdlib.h>
struct node
{
struct node *next;
int data;
struct node *prev;
};
struct node *start=NULL;
struct node *create(struct node *);
struct node *display(struct node *);
struct node *insertatbeg(struct node *);
struct node *insertatend(struct node *);
struct node *deleteatbeg(struct node *);
struct node *deleteatend(struct node *);
void main()
{
char ch='1';
while (ch!='7')
{
printf("\n 1. Create a Circular Double Linked List");
printf("\n 2. Display a Circular Double Linked List");
printf("\n 3. Insert at Beg");
printf("\n 4. Insert at End");
printf("\n 5. Delete at Beg");
printf("\n 6. Delete at End");
printf("\n 7. Exit");
printf("\n Enter Your Choice:");
ch=getchar();
switch(ch)
{
case '1':
start=create(start);
printf("\n Circular Double Linked List");
```

```
break;
case '2':
start=display(start);
break;
case '3':
start=insertatbeg(start);
break;
case '4':
start=insertatend(start);
break;
case '5':
start=deleteatbeg(start);
break;
case '6':
start=deleteatend(start);
break;
case '7':
break;
default:
printf("\n Wrong Choice");
}
}
}
struct node *create(struct node *start)
{
int num;
printf("\n Enter -1 to Last");
printf("\n Enter the Data");
scanf("%d", &num);
while(num!=-1)
{
if(start==NULL)
{
newnode=(struct node*)malloc(sizeof(struct node));
```

```
newnode->prev=NULL;
newnode->info=num;
newnode->next=start;
start=newnode;
}
else
{
newnode=(struct node*)malloc(sizeof(struct node));
newnode->data=num;
ptr=start;
while(ptr->next!=start)
ptr=ptr->next;
newnode->prev=ptr;
ptr->next=newnode;
newnode->next=start;
start->prev=newnode;
}
printf("\n Enter the Data:");
scanf("%d", &num);
}
return start;
}
struct node*display(struct node *start)
{
struct node *ptr;
ptr=start;
while(ptr->next!=start)
{
printf("%d", ptr->data);
ptr=ptr->next;
}
printf("%d",ptr->data);
return start;
}
struct node *insertatbeg(struct node *start)
```

```
{
struct node *newnode, *ptr;
int num;
printf("\n Enter the Data");
scanf("%d", &num);
newnode=(struct node *)malloc(sizeof(struct node));
newnode->data=num;
ptr=start;
while(ptr->next!=start)
ptr=ptr->next;
newnode->prev=ptr;
ptr->next=newnode;
newnode->next=start;
start->prev=newnode;
start=newnode;
return start;
}
struct node *insertatend(struct node *start)
{
struct node *ptr, *newnode;
int num;
printf("\n Enter the Data");
scanf("%d", &num);
newnode=(struct node *)malloc(sizeof(struct node));
newnode->data=num;
ptr=start;
while(ptr->next!=start)
ptr=ptr->next;
ptr->next=newnode;
newnode->prev=ptr;
newnode->next=start;
start->prev=newnode;
return start;
}
struct node *deleteatbeg(struct node *start)
```

```
{
struct node *ptr;
ptr=start;
while(ptr->next!=start)
ptr=ptr->next;
ptr->next=start->next;
tmp=start;
start=start->next;
start->prev=ptr;
free(tmp);
return start;
}

struct node *deleteatend(struct node *start)
{
struct node *tmp;
tmp=start;
while(tmp->next!=start)
tmp=tmp->next;
tmp->prev->next=start;
start->prev=tmp->prev;
free(tmp);
return start;
}
```

Header linked list

The header linked list is a special type of linked list where a special Header Node is inserted at the beginning of the list. The header node contains the address of first node in the linked list. The start pointer does not contain the address of actual first node of the list but it holds the address of header node. In this case, the header node is like a dummy node, it is also known as sentinel node.

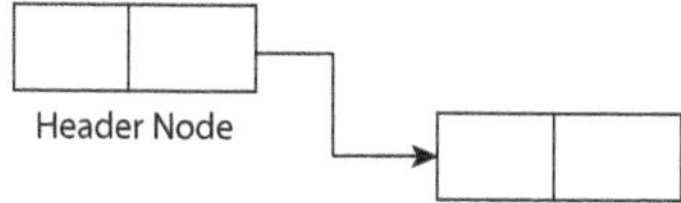

Here is the function in C to create a header node linked list.

```
#include<stdio.h>
struct node
```

```
{
int data;
struct node *next;
};
struct node *start=NULL;
struct node create(struct node *);
struct node *display(struct node *);
void main()
{
------------------
------------------
------------------
------------------
}
struct node *create(struct node *start)
{
struct node *tmp, &ptr;
int data;
printf("\n Enter -1 to end");
printf("Enter the Information");
scanf("%d", &data);
while (data!=-1)
{
tmp=(struct node*)malloc(sizeof(struct node));
tmp->info=data;
tmp->next=NULL;
if(start==NULL)
{
start=(struct node*)malloc(sizeof(struct node));
start->next=tmp;
}
else
{
ptr=start;
while(ptr->next!=NULL)
ptr=ptr->next;
```

```
ptr->next=tmp;
}
printf("\n Enter the information");
scanf("%d", &data);
}
return start;
}
struct node *display(struct node *start)
{
struct node *ptr;
ptr=start;
while(ptr!=NULL)
{
printf("%d", ptr->data);
ptr=ptr->next;
}
return start;
}
```

3.11 APPLICATIONS OF LINKED LIST

One useful application of linear linked list is in the representation of polynomial expression. We can use linked list to represent polynomial expression and for arithmetic operations also.

Applications of Doubly linked list can be

1. A great way to represent a deck of cards in a game.
2. The browser cache which allows you to hit the BACK button (a linked list of URLs)
3. Applications that have a Most Recently Used (MRU) list (a linked list of file names)
4. A stack, hash table, and binary tree can be implemented using a doubly linked list.
5. Undo functionality in Photoshop or Word (a linked list of state)

3.12 DIFFERENCE BETWEEN LINKED LISTS AND ARRAYS

Similar data element can be stored in memory with the use of array or a linked list. Arrays are easy to understand but they have the following limitations:

1. The size of arrays cannot be increased or decreased during execution.
2. The elements in an array are stored in contiguous memory locations.
3. The operations like insertion of a new element in an array or deletion of an existing element after the specified position.

Linked list can be used to overcome these limitations.

1. A linked list can grow or shrink during the execution of program.
2. There is no problem of shortage of memory as the nodes are stored in different memory locations.
3. In different operations like insertion and deletion no shifting of nodes is required.

POINTS TO REMEMBER

1. A linked list is a linear collection of data elements called as nodes in which linear representation is given by links from one node to another.
2. Linked list is a data structure which can be used to implement other data structures such as stacks, queues, and their variations.
3. Before we insert a new node in linked lists, we need to check for overflow condition, which occurs when no free memory cell is present in the system.
4. Before we delete a node from a linked list, we must first check for underflow condition which occurs when we try to delete a node from a linked list that is empty.
5. In a circular linked list, the last node contains a pointer to the first node of the list.
6. A doubly linked list is a linked list which contains a pointer to the next as well as the previous node in the sequence. Therefore, it consists of three parts: data, a pointer to the next node, and a pointer to the previous node.
7. The previous field of the first node and the next field of the last node contains NULL.
8. A header linked list is a special type of linked list which contains a header linked list Start will not point to the first node of the list but start will contains the address of the header node.

MULTIPLE CHOICE QUESTION

1. A linked list is a

   (*a*) Random access structure
   (*b*) Sequential access structure
   (*c*) Both a & b
   (*d*) None of these

2. An array is a
   (*a*) Random access structure (*b*) Sequential access structure
   (*c*) Both a & b (*d*) None of these
3. Linked list is used to implement data structures like
   (*a*) Stacks (*b*) Queues
   (*c*) Trees (*d*) All of these
4. Which type of linked list contains a pointer to the next as well as the previous node in the sequence?
   (*a*) Singly linked list (*b*) Circular linked list
   (*c*) Doubly linked list (*d*) All of these
5. Which type of linked list does not store NULL in next field?
   (*a*) Singly linked list (*b*) Circular linked list
   (*c*) Doubly linked list (*d*) All of these
6. Which type of linked list stores the address of the header node in the next field of the last node?
   (*a*) Singly linked list (*b*) Circular linked list
   (*c*) Doubly linked list (*d*) Circular header linked list
7. Which type of linked list can have four pointers per node?
   (*a*) Circular doubly linked list (*b*) Multi-linked list
   (*c*) Header linked list (*d*) Doubly linked list

TRUE OR FALSE

1. A linked list is a linear collection of data elements.
2. A linked list can grow and shrink during run time.
3. A node in a linked list can point to only one node at a time.
4. A node in a singly linked list can reference the previous node.
5. A linked list can store only integer values.
6. Linked list is a random access structure.
7. Deleting a node from a doubly linked list is easier than deleting it from a singly linked list.
8. Every node in a linked list contains an integer part and a pointer.
9. Start stores the address of the first node in the list.
10. Underflow is a condition that occurs when we try to delete a node from a linked list that is empty.

FILL IN THE BLANKS

1. __________ is used to store the address of the first free memory location.
2. The complexity to insert a node at the beginning of the linked list is ________.
3. The complexity to delete a node from the end of the linked list is__________.
4. Inserting a node at the beginning of the doubly linked list needs to modify _______ pointer.
5. Inserting a node in the middle of the singly linked list needs to modify _____ pointers.
6. Inserting a node at the end of the circular linked list needs to modify ________ pointers.
7. Inserting a node at the beginning of the circular doubly linked list needs to modify ________ pointers.
8. Deleting a node from the beginning of the singly linked list needs to modify ______ pointers.
9. Deleting a node from the middle of the doubly linked list needs to modify ________ pointers.
10. Deleting a node from the end of a circular linked list needs to modify ________ pointers.
11. Each element in a linked list is known as a ________.
12. First node in the linked list is called the _______.
13. Data elements in a linked list are known as __________.
14. Overflow occurs when ________.
15. In a circular linked list, the last node contains a pointer to the ________ node of the list.

EXERCISES

1. What is Linked List? How it is different from array? Write the different types of linked list?
2. Write a C function to reverse a Single Linked List?
3. Write a C function to reverse a Double Linked List?
4. Suppose DATA_1 is a list in memory. Write a algorithm which copies DATA_1 into a list DATA_2.
5. How a linked list can be used to represent a polynomial of type

   $6x^2y^2 - 4xy^2 + 8xy + 7y^2$
6. What is the advantage of a header node in a linked list?

7. Write a C function that removes all duplicate elements from a single linked list?
8. Write a C function to find the nth node in a single linked list?
9. Write a C function to count the total number of nodes in a single linked list?
10. Write a C function to merge two sorted single linked list?
11. Write a C function that removes the first element of a single linked list and adds it to the end of the list?
12. Write a C function to delete a node from a circular linked list?
13. Write a C function that concatenates two circular linked lists, producing a single circular linked list?
14. Write a C function to multiply two polynomial?
15. Write a C function to add two polynomial?

REFERENCES

1. Donal E. Knuth, The Art of Computer Programming, Addison-Wesley,Reading. Massachusetts, 1984.
2. Jean Paul Tremblay and G.Paul, Sorenson, An Introduction to Data Structures with Applications, McGraw-Hill, New York, 1987.
3. John Welsh, John Elder and David Bustard, Sequential Program Structures, Prentice-Hall, Englewood Cliff, New Jersey, 1981.
4. R. Hind, Efficient Dynamic Storage Management with buddy System, Proceeding of IEEE Symposium on Foundations of Computer Science, Vol. 19, 123-130, 1978.
5. Thomas L. Naps,Introduction to Data Structure with C, West Publishing Company, West Virginia, 1986.
6. Horowitz, Ellis, and Sartaj Sahni, Fundamentals of Data Structure, Computer Science Press, Rockville, Maryland, 1985.
7. Kruse, Robert L., Bruce P. Leung and L. Clovis Tondo, Data Structures and Program Design in C, Prentice Hall of India, New Delhi, 1995.

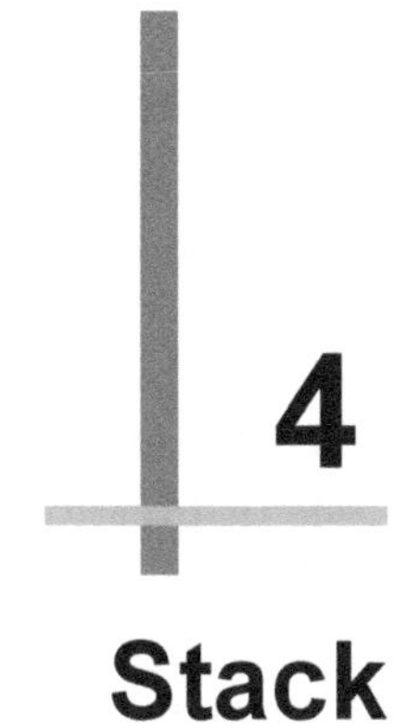

4 Stack

4.1 INTRODUCTION

Stack is a specialized data storage structure (Abstract data type). It has two main functions-push and pop. Insertion in a stack is done using push function and removal from a stack is done using pop function. Stack allows access to only the last element inserted hence, an item can be inserted or removed from the stack from one end called the top of the stack. It is therefore, also called Last-In-First-Out (LIFO) list. Stack has three properties:

(*a*) Capacity stands for the maximum number of elements stack can hold.

(*b*) Size stands for the current size of the stack.

(*c*) Elements are the array of elements.

The Linear data structure such as array and a linked list allows us to delete and insert an element at any place in the list, either at the beginning or at the end or even in the middle. However, sometimes it is required to permit the addition or deletion of elements only at one end. That is either at the beginning or at the end. Stack and queue are two types of data structures in which the addition or deletion of an element is done at end, rather than in the middle. A stack is a linear data structure in which all insertions and deletions are made at one end, called the top of the stack. It is very useful in many applications such as:

- We see stack (pile) of plates in restaurant, stack of books in bookshop.
- Even a packet of papers is also a stack of paper-sheet. A book is also a stack of written papers.
- When anybody takes a plate from a stack of plates, he takes it from the top.

Definition

A stack is an ordered collection of homogeneous data elements where the insertion and deletion operations occur at only one end. This end is often known as top of the stack. Here, the last element inserted will be top of the stack. Since deletion is done from the same end, last element inserted will be the first element to be removed out from the stack and so on. That is why the stack is also called Last-in-First-Out (LIFO).

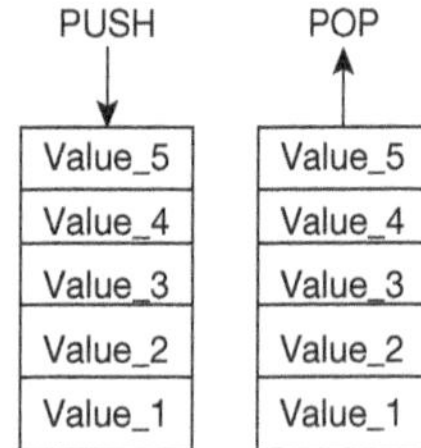

Initially, when stack is created using arrays the size is fixed, the stack base remains fixed while the stack top increase the position. So, most frequently accessible element in the stack is the top and the last accessible elements are the bottom of the stack.

4.2 OPERATIONS ON THE STACK

A stack is generally implemented with two basic operations such as PUSH and POP.

1. PUSH Operation
2. POP Operation

1. PUSH Operation

The process of adding a new element to the top of the stack is called push operation. Pushing an element in the stack invoke adding of element at the top. Suppose, after inserting an element max size is reached, i.e., stack is full. This situation is called the **stack overflow condition**. At this point the stack top is present at the highest location of the stack. Initially the stack is empty and it has one pointer *i.e.*, TOP.

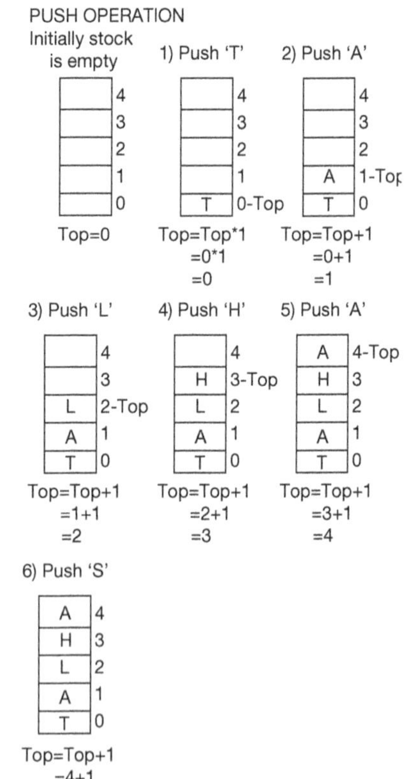

Figure shows the stack insertion (PUSH) operations.

Algorithm for PUSH Operation

Steps:

1. start
2. if top==maxsize−1 then
3. print message "stack is OVERFLOW and then
4. stop
5. read data
6. top=top+1

7. stack[top]=data
8. stop

2. POP Operation

The process of deleting an element from the top of the stack is called pop operation. After every pop operation the stack is decremented by 1. Finally, when all the elements are deleted, top points to bottom of the stack. When the stack is empty, it is not possible to delete any element and this situation is called the stack underflow. Thus, if there is no element on the stack and the Pop operation is performed then this will result into **UNDERFLOW** condition.

Algorithm for POP Operation

Steps:

1. start
2. if top==−1 then
3. print message "UNDERFLOW" and then
4. stop
5. stack [top]=data
6. top=top−1
7. stop

POP OPERATION 1) Pop 'A' 2) Push 'H'

A	4-Top		4		4
H	3	H	3-Top		3
L	2	L	2	L	2-Top
A	1	A	1	A	1
T	0	T	0	T	0

Top=Top-1 =4-1 =3 Top=Top-1 =3-1 =2

3) Push 'L' 4) Push 'A' 5) Push 'T'

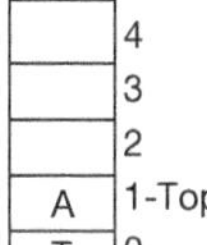

	4		4
	3		3
	2		2
	1		1
T	0-Top		0

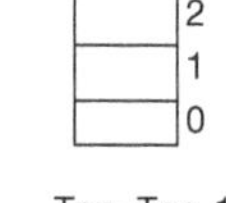

Top=Top-1 =2-1 =1 Top=Top-1 =1-1 =0 Top=Top-1 =0-1 =-1 (Underflow)

Figure below shows the stack deletion (POP) operations

4.3 IMPLEMENTATION OF STACK

A stack can be implemented in array or linked list

1. **Array Implementation of the Stacks**

A stack is an ordered collection of items and C language already contains a data type that is an ordered collection of items such as array. A stack and an array are two entirely different things. The number of elements in an array is fixed and is assigned by the declaration for the array. A stack on the other hand, is fundamentally a dynamic object whose size is constantly changing as items are popped and pushed. However, although an array cannot be a stack, it can be home of a stack.

Program: write a program to implement Stack Operation using array

```
#include<stdio.h>
#include<stdlib.h>
#define MAX_SIZE 5
int stack[MAX_SIZE];
void push();
```

```
int pop();
void traverse();
int is_empty();
int top_element();
int top = -1;
void main()
{
int element, choice;
while(1)
{
printf("Stack Operations.\n");
printf("1. Insert into stack (Push operation).\n");
printf("2. Delete from stack (Pop operation).\n");
printf("3. Print top element of stack.\n");
printf("4. Check if stack is empty.\n");
printf("5. Traverse stack.\n");
printf("6. Exit.\n");
printf("Enter your choice.\n");
scanf("%d",&choice);
switch ( choice )
{
case 1:
if ( top == MAX_SIZE - 1 )
printf("Error: Overflow\n\n");
else
{
printf("Enter the value to insert.\n");
scanf("%d",&element);
push(element);
}
break;
case 2:
if ( top == -1 )
printf("Underflow.\n\n");
else
{
```

```
element = pop();
printf("Element removed from stack is %d.\n", element);
}
break;
case 3:
if(!is_empty())
{
element = top_element();
printf("Element at the top of stack is %d\n\n", element);
}
else
printf("Stack is empty.\n\n");
break;
case 4:
if(is_empty())
printf("Stack is empty.\n\n");
else
printf("Stack is not empty.\n\n");
break;
case 5:
traverse();
break;
case 6:
exit(0);
}
}
}
void push(int value)
{
top++;
stack[top] = value;
}
int pop()
{
int element;
if ( top == -1 )
```

```
return top;
element = stack[top];
top--;
return element;
}
void traverse()
{
int d;
if ( top == - 1 )
{
printf("Stack is empty.\n\n");
return;
}
printf("There are %d elements in stack.\n", top+1);
for ( d = top ; d >= 0 ; d-- )
printf("%d\n", stack[d]);
printf("\n");
}
int is_empty()
{
if ( top == - 1 )
return 1;
else
return 0;
}
int top_element()
{
return stack[top];
}
```

Output

Stack Operations.

1. Insert into stack (Push operation).
2. Delete from stack (Pop operation).
3. Print top element of stack.
4. Check if stack is empty.

5. Traverse stack.
6. Exit.

Enter your choice.

1

Enter the value to insert.

2

Stack Operations.

1. Insert into stack (Push operation).
2. Delete from stack (Pop operation).
3. Print top element of stack.
4. Check if stack is empty.
5. Traverse stack.
6. Exit.

Enter your choice.

1

Enter the value to insert.

3

Stack Operations.

1. Insert into stack (Push operation).
2. Delete from stack (Pop operation).
3. Print top element of stack.
4. Check if stack is empty.
5. Traverse stack.
6. Exit.

Enter your choice.

1

Enter the value to insert.

4

Stack Operations.

1. Insert into stack (Push operation).
2. Delete from stack (Pop operation).
3. Print top element of stack.
4. Check if stack is empty.
5. Traverse stack.
6. Exit.

Enter your choice.

1

Enter the value to insert.

5

Stack Operations.

1. Insert into stack (Push operation).
2. Delete from stack (Pop operation).
3. Print top element of stack.
4. Check if stack is empty.
5. Traverse stack.
6. Exit.

Enter your choice.

5

There are 4 elements in stack.

5

4

3

2

Stack Operations.

1. Insert into stack (Push operation).
2. Delete from stack (Pop operation).
3. Print top element of stack.
4. Check if stack is empty.
5. Traverse stack.
6. Exit.

Enter your choice.

2

Element removed from stack is 5.

Stack Operations.

1. Insert into stack (Push operation).
2. Delete from stack (Pop operation).
3. Print top element of stack.
4. Check if stack is empty.
5. Traverse stack.
6. Exit.

Enter your choice.

5

There are 3 elements in stack.

4

3

2

Stack Operations.

1. Insert into stack (Push operation).
2. Delete from stack (Pop operation).
3. Print top element of stack.
4. Check if stack is empty.
5. Traverse stack.
6. Exit.

Enter your choice.

6

2. Linked List Implement of a Stack

The stack can be implemented as a linked list in which the top of the stack is represented by the first item in the list. The first element inserted into the stack is pointed out by the second element, the second element by the third and so on. In general the (n-1) th element is pointed out by the nth element.

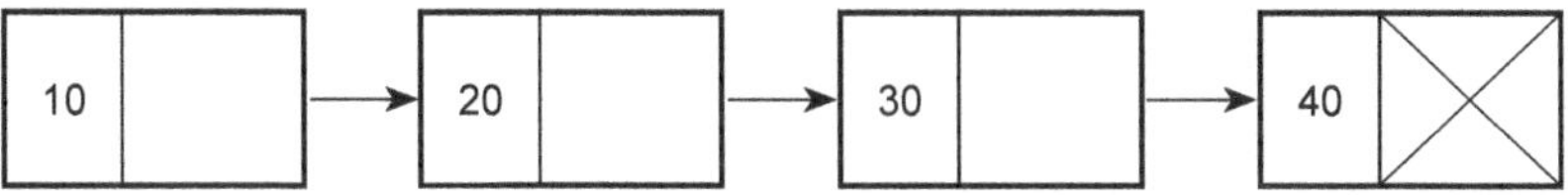

Top

In linked list implementation, the stack does not need to be of fixed size. There can be any number of elements or nodes in the stack. The second advantage of linked list method is that insertion and deletion operation do not involve more data movements. The other advantage of this method is that memory space is not wasted, because memory space is allocated only when the users wants to push an element into the stack. To implement a push, we create a new node in the list and attach it as the new first element. To implement a POP, we advance the Top of the stack to the second item in the first

Program: write a program to implement Stack Operation using Linked List

```
#include<stdio.h>
#include<stdlib.h>
void push();
void pop();
void display();
struct node
```

```
{
int info;
struct node *link;
}*top;
void main()
{
int i,ch,num;
top=NULL;
printf("Select the choice of operation on Stack");
printf("\n1.) Push\n2.) Pop");
printf("\n3.) display Stack\n4.) exit");
while(1)
{
        printf("\n\nenter the choice of operation you want to do");
        scanf("%d",&i);
        switch(i)
        {
              case 1:
              {
               printf("enter the value you want to insert in Stack");
               scanf("%d",&num);
               push(num);
               break;
               }
              case 2:
              {
               pop();
               break;
              }
              case 3:
              {
              display();
              break;
              }
              case 4:
              {
```

```
                exit(0);
                }
                default:printf("wrong choice");
          }
    }
    }
    void push(int a)
    {
    struct node *temp;
    temp=(struct node *)malloc(sizeof(struct node));
    temp->info=a;
    temp->link=top;
    top=temp;
    }
    void display()
    {
    struct node *temp;
    temp=top;
    if(temp==NULL)
    {
          printf("List is Empty");
    }
    while(temp!=NULL)
    {
          printf("%d-> ",temp->info);
          temp=temp->link;
    }
    printf("NULL");
    }
    void pop()
    {
    struct node *temp;
    if(top==NULL)
    printf("LIST IS EMPTY");
    else
    {
```

```
temp=top;
printf("%d->",temp->info);
top=top->link;
free(temp);
}
}
```

Output

Select the choice of operation on Stack

1. Push
2. Pop
3. Display Stack
4 Exit

enter the choice of operation you want to do 1
enter the value you want to insert in Stack 2
enter the choice of operation you want to do 1
enter the value you want to insert in Stack 3
enter the choice of operation you want to do 1
enter the value you want to insert in Stack 4
enter the choice of operation you want to do 1
enter the value you want to insert in Stack 5
enter the choice of operation you want to do 3
5-> 4-> 3-> 2-> NULL

4.4 APPLICATIONS OF STACK

Various applications of stack are known. A classical application in a compiler design is the evaluation of arithmetic expression; here the compiler uses a stack to translate an input arithmetic expression into its corresponding object code. Some machines are also known which use built-in stack hardware called stack machine. Another important application of a stack is during the execution of recursive programs; some programming languages use stacks to run recursive programs. One important feature of any programming language is the binding of memory variables. Such binding is determined by the scope rules.

1. Checking the validity of an Arithmetic Expression
2. Polish Notation
3. Recursion
4. Tower of Hanoi

1. Checking the Validity of an Arithmetic Expression

An arithmetic expression consists of operands and operators. Operands are variables or constants and operators are of various types. With the help of stack, we can check the validity of an arithmetic expression.

- Whenever an opening parenthesis is encountered, it is pushed on to the stack.
- Whenever a closing parenthesis is encountered, the stack is examined.
- If the stack is empty, the closing parenthesis does not have an opening parenthesis and the expression is therefore invalid.
- If the stack is not empty, we POP the stack and check whether the popped item corresponds to the closing parenthesis.
- If a match occurs, we continued. Otherwise the expression is invalid.
- When the end of the expression is reached, the stack must be empty; otherwise one or more opening parenthesis does not have corresponding closing parenthesis and the expression is invalid.

Example

[(P + Q) - {R + S}] - [T + U]

Symbol Scanned	Stack
[	[
(	[,(
P	[,(
+	[,(
Q	[,(
)	[
-	[
{	[,{
R	[,{
+	[,{
S	[,{
}	[
]	
-	
[	[
T	[

Symbol Scanned	Stack
+	[
U	[
]	

The stack is empty at the end, so the expression is valid.

2. Polish Notation

An arithmetic expression can be represented in various forms such as prefix, infix, postfix. The prefixes "pre", "in", and "post" refer to the relative position of the operator with respect to its operands.

Prefix: +PQ (operator before its operands)

Infix: P+Q (operator in the middle of its operands)

Postfix: PQ+ (operator after its operands)

The set of rules must be applied to expressions in order to determine the final value. These rules include precedence, BODMAS and associatively.

Table: Precedence and associatively of operator

Operator	Precedence	Associatively
-(unary), + (unary), NOT	6	--
^ (exponentiation)	6	Right to Left
* (multiplication), / (division)	5	Left to Right
+ (addition), -(subtraction)	4	Left to Right
<, <=, < >, >=	3	Left to Right
AND	2	Left to Right
OR, XOR	1	Left to Right

Convert Infix to postfix form

Infix to postfix conversion

Scan through an expression, getting one token at a time.

1. Fix a priority level for each operator.
2. If the token is an operand, do not stack it. Pass it to the output.
3. If token is an operator or parenthesis, do the following:
   a. Pop the stack until you find a symbol of lower priority number than the current one. An incoming left parenthesis will be considered to have higher priority than any other symbol. A left parenthesis on the stack will not be removed unless an incoming right parenthesis is found. The popped stack elements will be written to output.
   b. Stack the current symbol.

c. If a right parenthesis is the current symbol, pop the stack down to (and including) the first left parenthesis. Write all the symbols except the left parenthesis to the output (i.e. write the operators to the output).

d. After the last token is read, pop the remainder of the stack and write any symbol (except left parenthesis) to output.

Q1. P + Q - R

Solution: (PQ+) - R where X=PQ+

X - R

XR-

Put the value of X, we get

PQ + R-

Q2. P * Q + R / S

Solution: P*Q + RS/ where X=RS/

P*Q+X

PQ* +X where Y=PQ*

Y+X

YX+

Put the value of X and Y, we get

P Q * R S / +

Q3. (P + Q) * R / S + T ^ U / V

Solution: (PQ+) * R/S+T^U/V where A=PQ+

A * R / S + (T U ^) / V where B=TU^

A * R / S + B / V

A * (R S /) + B / V where C=RS/

A * C + (B V /) where D=BV/

A * C + D

(A C *) + D where E=AC*

E+ D

E D +

Put the values of A, B, C, D, E, we get

AC * D +

PQ + C * D +

PQ + RS / * BV / +

PQ+ RS / * TU^ V / +

Conversion of an infix expression to postfix expression

Suppose an arithmetic expression written in infix notation. Besides operands and operators, Arithmetic Expression may also contain left and right parenthesis. Suppose that Arithmetic Expression consists only of Exponentiations (^), multiplication (*), division (/), additions (+), subtractions (-). We also assumed that operators on the same level, including exponentiations are performed from left to right. This algorithm transforms the infix expression Arithmetic Expression into its equivalent postfix expression.

Algorithm

Steps:

1. start
2. infix_to_postfix(Arithmetic Expression)
3. push (‘(‘) //push left parenthesis ‘(‘ on to stack
4. repeat steps 5 to 27 while stack is not empty
5. set value = Arithmetic Expression.scan_ch() //scan the symbol from infix expression
6. if (value = operand)
7. write (“value”) //write symbol into the output expression
8. end of step 6 if structure
9. if (value = ‘(‘)
10. push (value) //push symbol ‘(‘ to the stack
11. end of step 9 if structure
12. if (value = operator)
13. x = pop()
14. if precedence (x) ≥ precedence (value)
15. repeat steps 16 and 17 while (precedence (x) ≥ precedence (value))
16. write x
17. x = pop()
18. end of step 15 loop
19. end of step 14 if structure
20. end of step 12 if structure
21. push (x)
22. push (value)
23. if (value = ‘)’)
24. x = pop()
25. repeat steps 26 and 27 while x ≠ ‘(‘
26. write (x)
27. x = pop()

28. end of step 25 loop
29. end of step 23 if structure
30. end of step 4 loop
31. stop

Example: Consider the following arithmetic infix expression Arithmetic Expression AE: P + (Q * R – (S / T ^ U) * V) * W)

Symbol Scanned	Stack	Expression (Postfix)
P	(	P
+	(+	P
(	(+ (	P
Q	(+ (	P Q
*	(+ (*	P Q
R	(+ (*	P Q R
-	(+ (-	P Q R *
(	(+ (- (	P Q R *
S	(+ (- (	P Q R * S
/	(+ (- (/	P Q R * S
T	(+ (- (/	P Q R * S T
^	(+ (- (/ ^	P Q R * S T
U	(+ (- (/ ^	P Q R * S T U
)	(+ (-	P Q R * S T U ^ /
*	(+ (- *	P Q R * S T U ^ /
V	(+ (- *	P Q R * S T U ^ / V
)	(+	P Q R * S T U ^ / V * -
*	(+ *	P Q R * S T U ^ / V * -
W	(+ *	P Q R * S T U ^ / V * - W
)		P Q R * S T U ^ / V * - W * +

Program: Write a program to convert infix expression to postfix expression

```
#include<stdio.h>
#include<ctype.h>
#include<string.h>
int top=-1,i=0,l;
```

```
char infix[50],stk[50],a;
void postfix(char);
int p(char);
void main()
{
        printf("Enter infix expression:-");
        gets(infix);
        l=strlen(infix);
        infix[l]='#';
        stk[++top]='#';
        printf("Postfix Expression:-");
        while(infix[i]!='#')
        {
        if(isalpha(infix[i]))
        printf("%c",infix[i]);
        else
        postfix(infix[i]);
        i++;
        }
        while((top!=-1)&&(stk[top]!='#'))
        printf("%c",stk[top--]);
}
void postfix(char a)
{
switch(a)
{
        case '(':stk[++top]=a;
        break;
        default:
        if(a==')')
        {
        while(stk[++top]!=')')
        printf("%c",stk[--top]);
        }
        else if(stk[++top]=='(')
        stk[++top]=a;
```

```
        else if(p(a)>p(stk[top]))
        stk[++top]=a;
        else
        {
        while(p(stk[top])>p(a))
        printf("%c ",stk[top--]);
        stk[++top]=a;
        }
}
}
int p(char a)
{
switch(a)
{
        case '^':
        return 3;
        break;
        case '/':
        case '*':
        return 2;
        break;
        case '+':
        case '-':
        return 1;
        break;
        default:
        return 0;
}
}
```

Output

Enter infix expression:- p+(q*r-(s/t^u)*v)*w

Postfix Expression:- pqr*stu^/v*-w*+

Enter infix expression:- a+b-c*d/f

Postfix Expression:- abcdf/*-+

a. **Convert infix expression into postfix expression in a tabular form**

The steps involved to convert the infix expression into postfix expression

1. Add the Unique symbol “#” into stack.
2. Scan the symbol of array infix one by one from left to right.
3. If symbol is left parenthesis “(“then add it to the stack.
4. If symbol is operand then add it to array postfix.
5. If symbol is operator then pop the operators which have same precedence or higher precedence than the operator which occurred.
6. Add the popped operator to array postfix.
7. Add the scanned symbol operator into stack.
8. If symbol is right parenthesis “)” then pop all the operators from stack until left parenthesis “(“ in stack.
9. Remove left parenthesis “(“from stack.
10. If symbol is “#” then pop all the symbols from stack and add them to array postfix except “#”.
11. Repeat the same steps until “#” comes in scanning array infix.

Evaluation of postfix expression

Assume: PN is an expression in postfix notation

Algorithm

Steps:

1. start
2. eval_postfix(PN)
3. append a right parenthesis ‘)’ at the end of the postfix expression
4. set value = PN.scan_ch() //scan the symbol from postfix expression
5. repeat steps 6 to 16 while value ≠ ‘)’
6. if value = operand
7. push (value) //operand is pushed in to the stack
8. end of step 6 if structure
9. if value = operator
10. set a = pop() // a is the second operands of the current operator
11. set b = pop() // b is the first operands of the current operator
12. set op = value
13. set result =b op a
14. push (result)
15. end of step 9 if structure
16. set value = PN.scan_ch()

17. end of step 5 loop
18. set result = pop
19. write "result"
20. stop

Example:

P * (Q + R ^ S) – T ^ U * (V / W)

Scanned Symbol	Operator in Stack	Postfix Expression
P	#	P
*	# *	P
(	# * (	P
Q	# * (	P Q
+	# * (+	P Q
R	# * (+	P Q R
^	# * (+ ^	P Q R
S	# * (+ ^	P Q R S
)	# *	P Q R S ^ +
-	# -	P Q R S ^ + *
T	# -	P Q R S ^ + * T
^	# - ^	P Q R S ^ + * T
U	# - ^	P Q R S ^ + * T U
*	# - *	P Q R S ^ + * T U ^
(	# - * (	P Q R S ^ + * T U ^
V	# - * (	P Q R S ^ + * T U ^ V
/	# - * (/	P Q R S ^ + * T U ^ V
W	# - * (/	P Q R S ^ + * T U ^ V W
)	# - *	P Q R S ^ + * T U ^ V W /
#		P Q R S ^ + * T U ^ V W / * -

Example: Evaluate postfix form: 5,9,8 + 4,6 * + 7 - *

Scanned Symbol	Stack
5	5
9	5,9
8	5,9,8
+	5,17
4	5 17,4

Scanned Symbol	Stack
6	5,17,4,6
*	5,17,24
+	5,41
7	5,41,7
-	5,34
*	170

b. **Convert Infix to Prefix Form**

Q1. P*Q+C

Solution: *PQ+C where X=*PQ

X+C

+XC

Put the values of X, we get

+*PQC

Q2. P/Q^R+S

Solution: P/^QR+SX=^QR (Exponentiation is having higher precedence than / that is the reason exponentiation operation is performed first.)

P/X+S

/PX+S where Y=/PX

Y+S

+YS

Put the values of X and Y, we get

+/PXS

+/P^QRS

Q3. (P-Q/R)*(S*T-U)

Solution: (P-/QR)*(S*T-U) where X=/QR

(P-X)*(S*T-U)

-PX*(*ST-U) where Y=*ST, Z=-PX

Z*(Y-U)

Z*-YU where W=-YU

Z*W

*ZW

Put the value of X, Y, Z and W, we get

*-PXW

*-P/QR-YU

*-P/QR-*STU

Algorithm

Arithmetic Expression in infix notation. Two stacks are used, push(stk1, x) means adding an item x to stack stk s1, pop(stk1) means removing the top most element from the stack stk1.

Steps:

1. start
2. infix_to_prefix(Arithmetic Expression)
3. initially add a left parenthesis '(' at the beginning of the infix expression Arithmetic Expression.
4. push (stk1, ')')
5. set item = Arithmetic Expression.reverseorder scan_ch() //scan the symbol from Arithmetic Expression in right to left
6. repeat steps 7 to 28 while stk1 is not empty
7. if item = operand
8. push (stk2, item)
9. end of step 7 if structure
10. if item = ')'
11. push (stk1,item)
12. end of step 10 if structure
13. if item = operator
14. set x = pop(stk1)
15. if precedence(x)>precedence(item)
16. repeat steps 17 and 18 while precedence (x)> precedence(item)
17. push (stk2, x)
18. set x = pop(stk1)
19. end of step 16 while loop
20. end of step 15 if structure
21. push(stk1, x)
22. push(stk1, item)
23. end of step 13 if structure
24. if item = '('
25. set x = pop(stk1)
26. repeat steps 27 and 28 while x ≠ ')'
27. push (stk2, x)
28. set x = pop(stk1)

29. end of step 26 while loop
30. end of step 24 if structure
31. end of step 6 loop
32. repeat step 33 and 34 while stack stk2 is not empty
33. set x = pop(stk2)
34. write "x"
35. end of step 32 loop
36. stop

Program: write a program to convert infix expression to prefix expression

```
#include<stdio.h>
#include<ctype.h>
#include<string.h>
int top=-1,t=-1;
char infix[20],sym[20],inf[20],pre[20];
void prefix(char);
int p(char);
void main()
{
        int l,i=0;
        printf("\n Convert Infix to Prefix Expression\n");
        printf("Enter infix expression:- ");
        gets(infix);
        l=strlen(infix);
        while(i<l)
        {
        inf[i+1]=infix[i];
        i++;
        }
        inf[0]='(';
        sym[++t]=')';
        i=strlen(inf)-1;
        while(i!=0)
        {
        if(isalpha(inf[i]))
        pre[++top]=inf[i];
        else
```

```
            prefix(inf[i]);
            i--;
            }
            while((t!=-1)&&(sym[t]!=')'))
            pre[++top]=sym[t--];
            printf("Prefix Expression:- ");
            while(top!=-1)
            printf("%c", pre[top--]);
    }
    void prefix(char a)
    {
            switch(a)
            {
            case ')':
            sym[++t]=a;
            break;
            default:
            if(a=='(')
            {
            while(sym[++t]!=')')
            pre[++top]=sym[t--];
            t--;
            }
            else if(a==')')
            sym[++t]=a;
            else if(p(a)>p(sym[t]))
            sym[++t]=a;
            else
            {
            while(p(a)<p(sym[t]))
            pre[++top]=sym[t--];
            sym[++t]=a;
            }
            }
    }
    int p(char a)
```

```
{
        switch(a)
        {
        case '^':
        return 3;
        break;
        case '/':
        case '*':
        return 2;
        break;
        case '+':
        case '-':
        return 1;
        break;
        default:
        return 0;
        }
}
```

Output

Convert Infix to Prefix Expression

Enter infix expression:- a+b-c*d/e

Prefix Expression:- -+ab/*cde

c. **Convert infix expression into prefix expression in a tabular form**

The steps involved to convert the infix expression into prefix expression

1. Reverse the input string.
2. Examine the next element in the input
3. If it is operand, add it to output string
4. If it is closing parenthesis, push it on stack
5. If it is operator, then
   (*a*) If stack is empty, push operator on stack
   (*b*) If the top of stack is closing parenthesis, push operator on stack
   (*c*) If it has same or higher priority than the top of stack, push operator on stack
   (*d*) Else pop the operator from the stack and add it to output string
6. If it is an opening parenthesis, pop operators from stack and add them to output string until a closing parenthesis is encountered. Pop and discard the closing parenthesis

7. If there is more input then go to step 2
8. If there is no more input, unstuck the remaining operators and add them to output string
9. Reverse the output string.

Evaluation of prefix Expression

PN is an expression in prefix notation

Algorithm

Steps:

1. start
2. eval_prefix(PN)
3. append a left parenthesis '(' at the beginning of the prefix expression
4. set item = PN.reverseorderscan_ch() //scan the symbol from PN in right to left
5. repeat steps 6 to 16 while item = '('
6. if item = operand
7. push(item)//operand is pushed into the stack
8. end of step 6 if structure
9. if item = operator
10. set a = pop() // a is the first operand of the current operator
11. set b = pop() // b is the second operand of the current operator
12. set op = item
13. set result = a op b
14. push (result)
15. end of step 9 if structure
16. set item = PN.reverseorderscan_ch()
17. end of step 5 loop
18. set result = pop()
19. write "result"
20. stop

Example:

Suppose we want to convert: P + Q * R * (S * T ^ U + V) – W + X into prefix form.

Reverse expression is: X + W -) V + U ^ T * S (* R * Q + P

Symbol Scanned	Stack stk1	Stack stk2
X	)	X
+	) +	X
W	) +	X W
-	) + -	X W
)	) + -)	X W
V	) + -)	X W V
+	) + -) +	X W V
U	) + -) +	X W V U
^	) + -) + ^	X W V U
T	) + -) + ^	X W V U T
*	) + -) + *	X W V U T ^
S	) + -) + *	X W V U T ^ S
(	) + -	X W V U T ^ S * +
*	) + - *	X W V U T ^ S * +
R	) + - *	X W V U T ^ S * + R
*	) + - * *	X W V U T ^ S * + R
Q	) + - * *	X W V U T ^ S * + R Q
+	) + - +	X W V U T ^ S * + R Q * *
P	) + - +	X W V U T ^ S * + R Q * * P
		X W V U T ^ S * + R Q * * P + - +
POP all the symbol of stack stk2 and print the result: + - + P * * Q R + * S ^ T U V W X		

Suppose we want to convert 3*4(3-2)+6*(5-2) into prefix form. Reverse expression is:

)2-5(*6+)2-3(4*3

Symbol Scanned	Stack Contents (Top on Right)	Prefix Expression (Right toLeft)
)	)	
2	)	2
-	)	2
5	)	2 5
(	Empty	2 5-
*	*	2 5 – 2 5 – 6

Symbol Scanned	Stack Contents (Top on Right)	Prefix Expression (Right toLeft)
6	*	2 5 – 6 *
+	+	2 5 – 6 *
)	+)	2 5 – 6 * 2
2	+)	2 5 – 6 * 2
-	+) -	2 5 – 6 * 2 3
3	+) -	2 5 – 6 * 2 3 -
(	+	2 5 – 6 * 2 3 -
/	+ /	2 5 – 6 * 2 3 – 4
4	+ /	2 5 – 6 * 2 3 – 4
*	+ / *	2 5 – 6 * 2 3 – 4 2
3	+ / *	2 5 – 6 * 2 3 – 4 2
	Empty	2 5 – 6 * 2 3 – 4 2 * / +
Reverse the output string is:		2 5 – 6 * 2 3 – 4 2 * / +

4.5 RECURSION

Recursion can be defined as a process in which a function calls itself with reduced input and has a base condition to stop the process, i.e., in order to solve a problem recursively, two conditions must be satisfied. First, the problem must be written in a recursive form, and second, the problem statement must include a stopping condition.

Definition: A function is said to be recursively defined, if a function containing either a Call statement to itself or a Call statement to a second function that may eventually result in a Call statement back to the original function.

A recursive function must have the following properties:

1. There must be certain criteria, called base criteria for which the function does not call itself.
2. Each time the function does call itself (directly or indirectly); the argument of the function must be close to a base value.

Principles of Recursion

Recursion is implemented through the use of functions. A function that contains a function call to itself or a function call to a second function which eventually calls the first function, is known as a **recursive function.**

Two important **conditions** must be satisfied by any recursive function

1. Each time a function calls itself it must be closer, in some sense to a solution.

2. There must be a decision criterion for stopping the process or computation.

For designing the good recursive program we must make certain assumptions such as:

(*a*) Base case: Base case is the terminating condition for the problem while designing any recursive function.

(*b*) If Conditions: If condition in the recursive algorithm defines the terminating condition.

(*c*) When a recursive program is subjected for execution function calls will not be executed immediately.

(*d*) The initial parameter input value pushed on to the stack.

(*e*) Each time a function is called a new set of local variable and formal parameters are again pushed on to the stack and execution starts from the beginning of the function using changed new value. This process is repeated till a base condition (stopping condition) is reached.

(*f*) Once a base condition or stopping condition is reached the recursive function calls popping elements from stack and returns a result to the previous values of the function.

(*g*) A sequence or returns ensures that the solution to the original problem is obtained.

Advantages and Disadvantages of Recursion

Advantages

1. We can create a simple and easy version of programs using recursion.
2. Always recursion will be written in the name of recursive definition. It can be translated into C code very easily.
3. We can avoid initialisation of variable inside the functions, but iterative solutions are required to be initialised.
4. Some specific applications are meant for recursion such as Binary tree traversal; tower of Hanoi etc. can be easily understood.

Disadvantages

1. It occupies lot of memory: When function is called outside or called within, the function stores formal parameters local variables and returns address to confirm function are working well. Apart from this, it stores function variables separately.
2. It consumes more time to get desired result: After matching the base condition, the function should restore the most recently saved parameters, local variables, and return address. This operation spends lot of time during pushing and popping the necessary items from the stack.

3. Function execution is slower than iterative method because of the overhead of calling functions repeatedly.

Comparison of Iteration and Recursion

Any iterative function consists of four parts.

1. **Initialisation**: The decision parameter is set to an initial value or more precisely, the loop variable is initialised, other pre-defined variables are also initialised.
2. **Decision**: The decision parameter is used to determine whether further looping is necessary. The loop variable is compared and based on the outcome, the loop is executed again.
3. **Computation**: Necessary computation is performed within the loop.
4. **Update**: The decision parameter is updated and transfer is made to the next iteration. The loop variable is incremented/decremented.

For a recursive function.

1. **Initialisation:** The variables in the form of arguments are passed on to the function.
2. **Decision:** The argument values are used to determine whether further recursive calls are required.
3. **Computation**: Necessary computation is performed using the local variables and the parameters at the current depth.
4. **Update**: The update is done so that the variables can be used for further recursive calls.

S.No	Iteration	Recursion
1	Iterative Instructions –are loop based repetitions of a process	Recursive function – is a function that is partially defined by itself
2	Iteration uses repetition structure	Recursion Uses selection structure
3	An infinite loop occurs with iteration if the loop-condition test never becomes false	Infinite recursion occurs if the recursion step does not reduce the problem in a manner that converges on some condition.
4	Iteration terminates when the loop-condition fails	Recursion terminates when a base case is recognized
5	Iteration does not use stack so it's faster than recursion	Recursion is usually slower then iteration due to overhead of maintaining stack
6	Iteration consume less memory	Recursion uses more memory than iteration
7	Infinite looping uses CPU cycles repeatedly	Infinite recursion can crash the system
8	Iteration makes code longer	Recursion makes code smaller

Recursion Through Stack

Some programming language like 'C' provides the facility of recursive function. So we can use it very easily. But in other language also we can provide recursion technique with stack implementation whenever the situation arises for recursion implementation. Even we can convert recursive function in 'C' into non - recursive function through stack implementation. We will see this approach in graph traversal where we use Depth first traversal using recursion as well as stack implementation. We have a need to do following things for using recursion through stack implementation.

1. One stack for each parameter of function.
2. Only one stacks for return address.
3. One stack for each local variable of function.

As a simple example, let us consider the case of calculation of the factorial value for an integer n.

n! = n * (n - 1) * (n - 2) * (n - 3) *........ * 3 * 2 * 1

The last expression is the recursive description of the factorial whereas the first is the iterative definition.

Algorithm

Steps:

1. start
2. if n = 0 then
3. fact = 1
4. else
5. fact = n * fact (n-1)
6. end if
7. return (fact)
8. stop

Program: Find the factorial of any given number with the help of recursion

```
#include <stdio.h>
void main()
        {
                int n, val;
                printf ("Enter the number");
        scanf("%d", &n);
        if (n < 0)
                printf ("Factorial not possible \n");
        else
```

```
            if (n == 0)
                        printf ("factorial of Zero is 1\n");
            else                {
                        val = fac (n, 1)
                        printf ("factorial of %d" = %d\n", n, val);        }
}

fac (int n, int fact)   {
            if (n = = 1)
            return fact;
else
        fac (n - 1, n * fact);  }
```

Output

Enter the number: 5

Factorial of 5 = 120

4.6 TOWER OF HANOI

Another complex recursive problem is that of towers of Hanoi. The problem has a historical basis in the ritual of the ancient Tower of Brahma. In this type of problems, recursion may be the only solution. In this problem, there are n disks of different sizes and there are three poles X, Y and T. Each disk has a hole in the centre. The problem of Tower of Hanoi is to move the disk from one pillar to another with the help of a temporary pillar. Suppose two pillars are X and Y. we want to move the disk from X to Y with the help of Temp pillar (T).

The rules for the movement of disks are as follows:

(*i*) Only one disk may be moved at a time.

(*ii*) A larger disk must never be stacked above a smaller one.

(*iii*) One and only one extra needle could be used for intermediate storage of disks.

For n = 1:

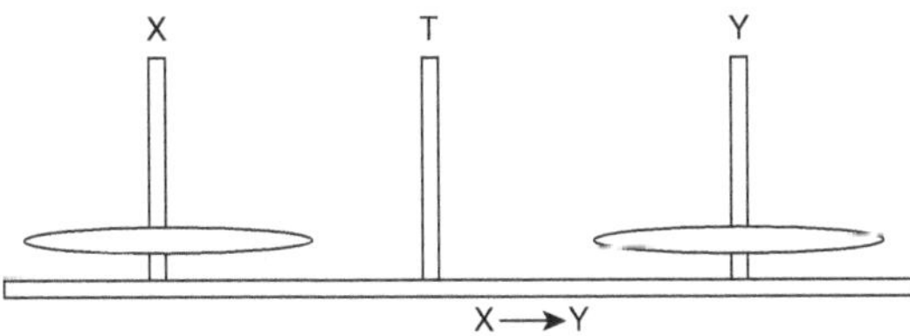

For n = 2:

1. X→T
2. X→Y
3. T→Y

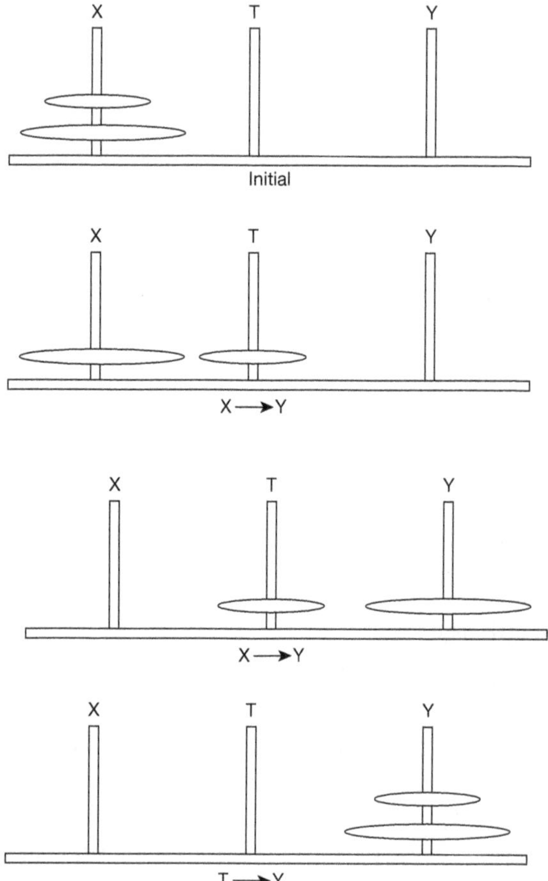

For n = 3:

1. X→Y
2. X→T
3. Y→T
4. X→Y
5. T→X
6. T→Y
7. X→Y

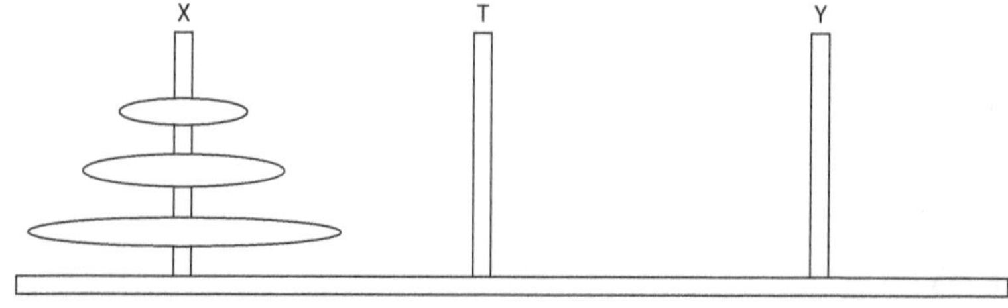

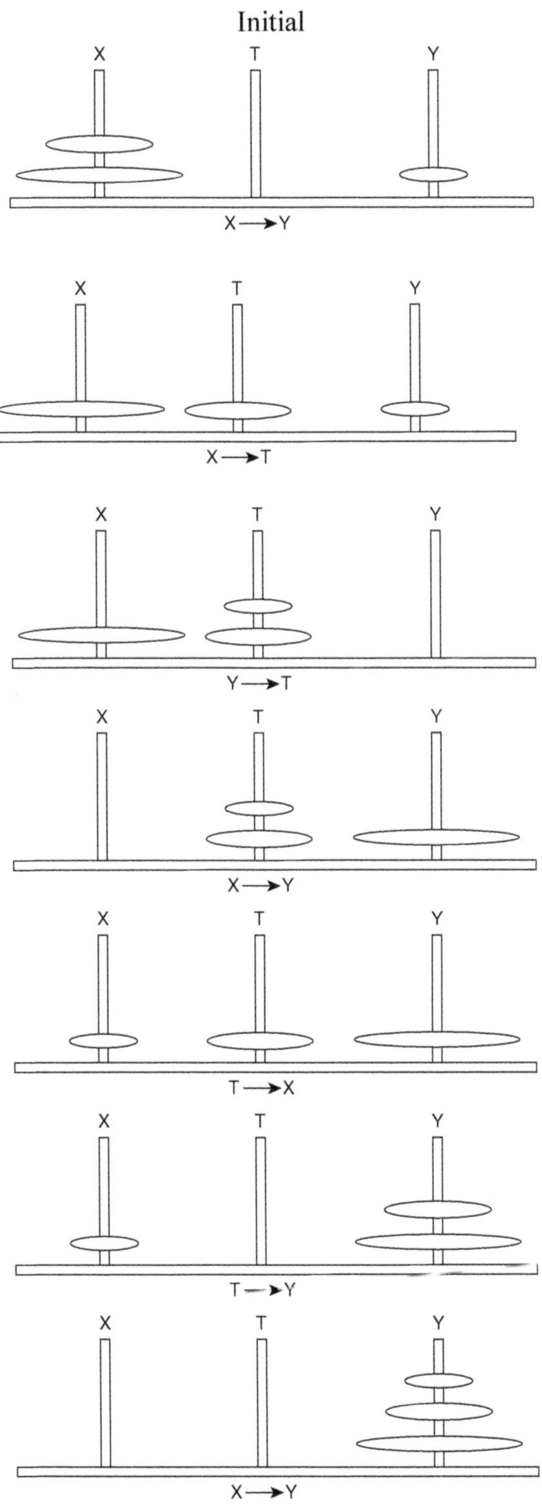
Initial
X
T
Y
X→Y
X
T
Y
X→T
X
T
Y
Y→T
X
T
Y
X→Y
X
T
Y
T→X
X
T
Y
T→Y
X
T
Y
X→Y

The formula for finding the number of steps it takes to transfer n disk from X to Y is 2^n-1

Number of disks (n)	Number of moves
1	2^1-1 = 2 - 1 =1
2	2^2-1 = 4 - 1 =3
3	2^3-1 = 8 – 1 =7
4	2^4-1 = 16 – 1 =15

POINTS TO REMEMBER

1. A stack is a linear data structure in which elements are added and remove only from one end, which is called the top. Hence, a stack is called a LIFO data structure as the element that is inserted last is the first one to be taken out.
2. In the computer's memory, stacks can be implemented using either linked lists or single arrays.
3. Infix, prefix, and postfix notations are three different but equivalent notations of writing algebraic expressions.
4. In postfix notation, operators are placed after the operands, whereas in prefix notation, operators are placed before the operands.
5. Postfix notations are expression that is scanned from left to right. If the character is an operands, it is pushed onto the stack. Else, if it is an operator, then the top two values are popped from the stack and the operator is applied on these values. The result is then pushed onto the stack.
6. Multiple stacks means to have more than one stack in the same array of sufficient size.

MULTIPLE CHOICE QUESTIONS

1. Stack is a
   (*a*) LIFO (*b*) FIFO
   (*c*) FILO (*d*) LILO
2. Which function places an element on the stack?
   (*a*) Pop() (*b*) Push()
   (*c*) Peek() (*d*) Isempty()

3. Disks piled up one above the other represent a
   (*a*) Stack (*b*) Queue
   (*c*) Linked list (*d*) array
4. Reverse polish notation is the other name of
   (*a*) Infix expression (b) Prefix expression
   (*c*) Postfix expression (*d*) Algebraic expression

TRUE OF FALSE

1. Pop () is used to add an element on the top of the stack.
2. Postfix operation does not allow the rules of operator precedence.
3. Recursive follows a divide-and-conquer technique to solve problems.
4. Using a recursive function takes more memory and time to execute.
5. Recursion is more of a bottom-up approach to problem solving.
6. An indirect recursive function if it contains a call to another function which ultimately calls it.
7. The peeks operation displays the topmost value and deletes it from the stack.
8. In a stack, the element that was inserted last is the first one to be taken out.
9. Underflow occurs when top=max-1.
10. Overflow can never occurs in case of multiple stacks.

FILL IN THE BLANKS

1. ________ is used to convert an infix expression into a postfix expression.
2. _________ is used in a non-recursive implementation of a recursive algorithm.
3. The storage requirement of a linked stack with n elements is _________.
4. Underflow takes when ____________.
5. The order of evaluation of a postfix expression is from ___________.
6. Whenever there is a pending operation to be performed, the function becomes ______ recursive.
7. A function is said to be ____________ recursive if it explicitly calls itself.

EXERCISES

1. What do you understand by stack overflow and underflow?
2. How does a stack implement using linked list?
3. How does a stack implement using array?

4. The following sequence of operation is done on an empty stack: PUSH 'S', PUSH 'S', PUSH 'T', PUSH 'U', POP, POP,PUSH 'A', PUSH 'L', PUSH 'G', POP, PUSH 'C', PUSH 'A', PUSH 'B', POP, POP. Show the stack configuration after each operation?
5. Convert the following infix expression to postfix expression:
   (*a*) A – B + C
   (*b*) A * B + C / D
   (*c*) (A - B) + C * D / E - C
   (*d*) (A * B) + (C / D) - (D + E)
   (*e*) ((A - B) + D / ((E + F) * G))
   (*f*) 14 / 7 * 3 – 4 + 9 / 2
6. Convert the following infix expression to prefix expression:
   (*a*) A – B + C
   (*b*) A * B + C / D
   (*c*) (A - B) + C * D / E - C
   (*d*) (A * B) + (C / D) - (D + E)
   (*e*) ((A - B) + D / ((E + F) * G))
   (*f*) 14 / 7 * 3 – 4 + 9 / 2
7. Differentiate between an iterative function and a recursive function?
8. Explain the Tower of Hanoi problem?

REFERENCES

1. Bruno, J.L and T. Lassagne, The generation of optimal code for a attack machine, journal of the ACM, July 1975.
2. Donald E. Knuth, The Art of Computer Programming, Vol. 2, Addison-Wesley, Reading, Massachusetts, 1984.
3. Forsythe, A.I., T.A. Keenan, et al., Computer Science: A First Course, John Wiley & Sons, New York, 1986.
4. Harrison, M.C., Data Structures and Programming, Glenview, Berkeley, California, 1985.
5. Seth, Rajeev and J. Ullman, The generation of optimal code for arithmetic expression, Journal of the ACM, Vol. 10, October 1970.

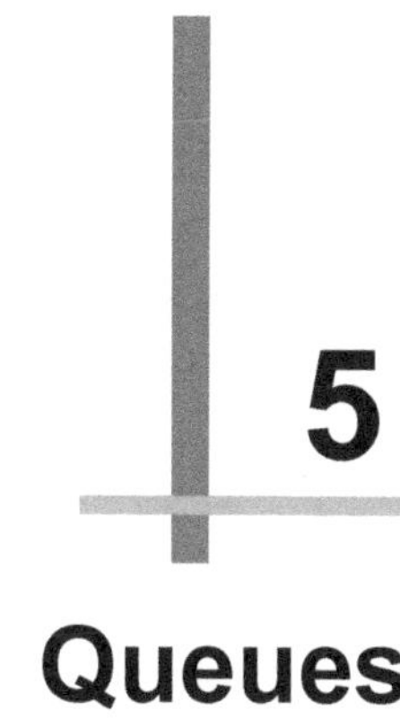

5 Queues

5.1 INTRODUCTION

Queues arise quite naturally in the computer for solution of many problems. Perhaps the most common occurrence of a queue in Computer Applications is for the scheduling of jobs. The name "queue" likely comes from the everyday use of the term. A real time example for a queue is people standing in a queue for billing in a shop, railway ticket counter, entry point in the shopping mall, etc. The first person in the queue will be the first person to get the service. Similarly the first element inserted in the queue will be the first one that will be retrieved and hence a queue is also called the First-in-First-out (**FIFO).**

Queue is a linear list which has two ends, one for insertion of elements and other for deletion of elements. The first end is called 'Rear' and the later is called 'Front'. Elements are inserted from Rear End and Deleted from Front End. Queues are called First-In-First-Out(FIFO) List, since the first element in a queue will be the first element out of the queue.

It is a homogeneous collection of elements in which new elements are added at one end called **rear,** and the existing elements are deleted from other end called **front.**

Push operation will insert (or add) an element to queue, at the rear end, by incrementing the array index. Pop operation will delete (or remove) from the front end by decrementing the array index and will assign the deleted value to a variable. Total number of elements present in the queue is front-rear+1, when implemented using arrays.

Example: Suppose we have an empty queue, with 8 memory cells:

0	1	2	3	4	5	6	7

Front=-1

Rear=-1

Insert S, T, A, L, H, A:

0	1	2	3	4	5	6	7
S	T	A	L	H	A		

Front=0 Rear=5

Delete S:

0	1	2	3	4	5	6	7
	T	A	L	H	A		

Front=1 Rear=5

5.2 REPRESENTATION OF QUEUES

Queues, being the linear data structure, can be represented by using both arrays and linked lists.

1. Queue Using Array

Array is data structure that stores a fixed number of elements. One of the major limitations of an array is that its size should be fixed prior to using it. But the size of the Queue keeps on changing as the elements are either removed from the front end or added at the rear end. Thus, if queue is implemented using arrays, we must be sure that the exact number of elements we want to store in the queue, because we have to declare the size of the array at design time or before the processing starts.

Operation on Queue using Array

(*a*) Insertion (Rear)

(*b*) Deletion (Front)

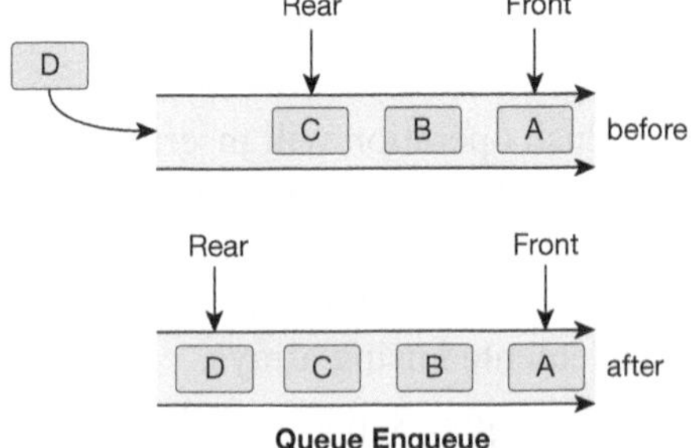

Queue Enqueue

Algorithm for queue insertion

Steps

1. start
2. check overflow condition
   if rear=max–1 then
   write "OVERFLOW" and then
   stop
3. read data

4. if front=0 then
5. queue[rear]=data
6. rear=rear+1
7. stop

Algorithm for queue deletion

Steps

1. start
2. check underflow condition
   if Front==–1 then
   write "UNDERFLOW" and then
   stop
3. if front=rear then
4. queue[front]=-1
5. front=0
6. front==front+1
7. stop

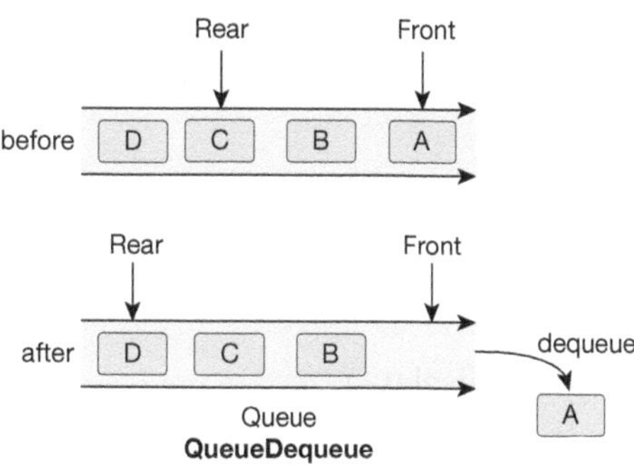

QueueDequeue

Program: write a program to implement a queue using array

```
#include<stdio.h>
#define MAX 7
void insert(int);
int del();
int queue[MAX], rear=0, front=0;
void display();
void main()
{
int choice, token;
printf("1.Insert");
printf("\n2.Delete");
printf("\n3.show or display");
while(1)
{
printf("\nEnter your choice for the operation: ");
scanf("%d",&choice);
switch(choice)
```

```
{
        case 1:insert(token);
display();
break;
case 2:token=del();
printf("\nThe token deleted is %d",token);
display();
break;
case 3:display();
break;
default:printf("Wrong choice");
break;
}
}
}
void display()
{
int i;
printf("\nThe queue elements are:");
for(i=rear;i<front;i++)
{
printf("%d ",queue[i]);
}
}
void insert(int token)
{
char a;
if(rear==MAX)
{
printf("\nQueue full");
return;
}
else
{
printf("\nEnter the token to be inserted:");
scanf("%d",&token);
        queue[front]=token;
```

```
front=front+1;
}
}
int del()
{
int t;
if(front==rear)
{
printf("\nQueue empty");
return 0;
}
rear=rear+1;
t=queue[rear-1];
return t;
}
```

Output

1. Insert
2. Delete
3. show or display

Enter your choice for the operation: 1

Enter the token to be inserted:2

The queue elements are:2

Enter your choice for the operation: 1

Enter the token to be inserted:3

The queue elements are:2 3

Enter your choice for the operation: 1

Enter the token to be inserted:4

The queue elements are:2 3 4

Enter your choice for the operation: 1

Enter the token to be inserted:5

The queue elements are:2 3 4 5

Enter your choice for the operation: 3

The queue elements are:2 3 4 5

Drawback of queues: One major drawback of representing a queue by using array is that a fixed amount of storage remains allocated even when the structure is actually using small amount or possibly no storage at all.

2. **Queue using linked list**

To represent queue using linked list each node is divided into two parts

(*i*) Info: which holds the data element

(*ii*) Next: which holds the address of the next node

Apart from that we need two more variables

(*i*) Front: which holds the address of the first node

(*ii*) Rear: which holds the address of the last node

Under the linked list representation of queue two pointers named as front and rear are used. However a special attention is required when the last element is removed from a queue, in that case rear must also set to NULL.

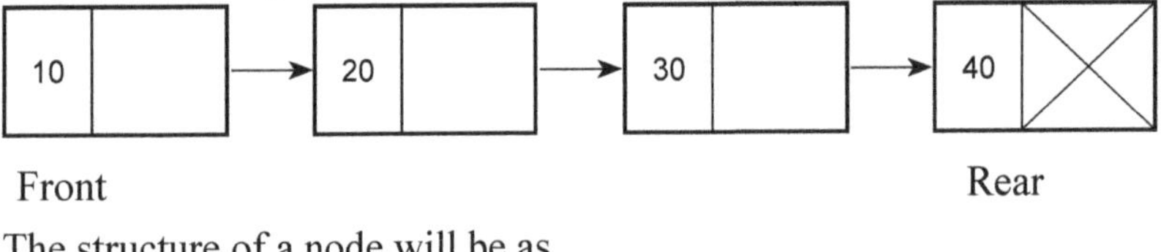

Front Rear

The structure of a node will be as

```
struct node
{
int info;
struct node *next;
}
struct node *front, *rear;
```

Program: write a program to implement a queue using linked list

```
#include<stdio.h>
#include<stdlib.h>
void insert();
void delete();
void display();
struct node
{
int info;
struct node *link;
}*rear=NULL,*front=NULL;
void main()
{
```

```
int i,ch,num;
printf("Select the choice of operation on Queue");
printf("\n1.) Insert\n2.) Delete");
printf("\n3.) display Queue\n4.) exit");
while(1)
{
        printf("\n\nenter the choice of operation you want to do ");
        scanf("%d",&i);
        switch(i)
        {
                case 1:
                insert();
                break;
                case 2:
                delete();
                break;
                case 3:
                display();
                break;
                case 4:
                exit(0);
                default:printf("wrong choice");
        }
}
}
void insert()
{
int num;
struct node *temp;
printf("enter the value you want to insert in Queue ");
scanf("%d",&num);
  temp=(struct node *)malloc(sizeof(struct node));
  temp->info=num ;
  temp->link=NULL;
  if(front==NULL)
  front=temp;
```

```
else
rear->link=temp;
rear=temp;
}
void display()
{
struct node *temp;
  temp=front;
  if(temp==NULL)
{
        printf("List is Empty");
}
while(temp!=NULL)
{
        printf("%d-> ",temp->info);
        temp=temp->link;
}
printf("NULL");
}
void delete()
{
struct node *temp;
if(front==NULL)
printf("LIST IS EMPTY");
else
{
temp=front;
printf("%d->",temp->info);
front=front->link;
free(temp);
}
}
```

Output

Select the choice of operation on Queue

1. Insert
2. Delete

3. display Queue
4. exit

enter the choice of operation you want to do 1
enter the value you want to insert in Queue 2
enter the choice of operation you want to do 1
enter the value you want to insert in Queue 3
enter the choice of operation you want to do 1
enter the value you want to insert in Queue 4
enter the choice of operation you want to do 3
2-> 3-> 4-> NULL
enter the choice of operation you want to do 2
2->
enter the choice of operation you want to do 3
3-> 4-> NULL

Types of Queue

1. Circular Queue
2. Double Ended Queue (DE-QUEUE)
3. Priority Queue

5.3 CIRCULAR QUEUE

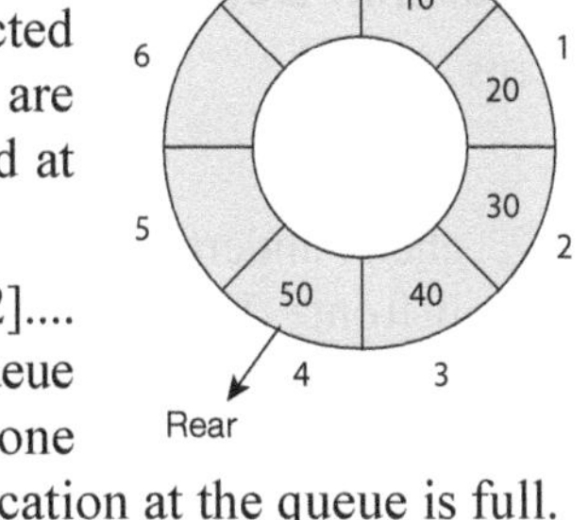

Circular queue is a linear data structure. It follows FIFO principle. In circular queue the last node is connected back to the first node to make a circle. Elements are added at the rear end and the elements are deleted at front end of the queue.

In circular queues the elements cq[0], cq[1], cq[2].... cq[n-1] is represented in a circular way. A circular queue is one in which the insertion of a new element is done at the very first location of the queue if the last location at the queue is full.

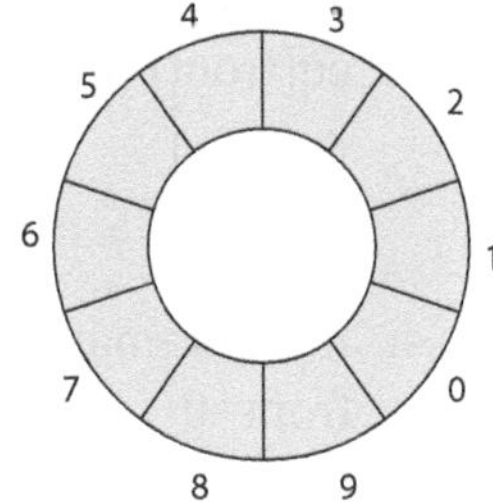

After inserting an element at last location cq[7], the next element will be inserted at the very first location (i.e., cq[0]). At any time the position of the element to be inserted will be calculated by the relation Rear = {(Rear+1) % SIZE}. After deleting an element from circular queue the position of the front end is calculated by the relation Front ={ (Front+1) % SIZE}. After locating the position of the new element to be inserted, rear, compare it with front. If (rear==front), the queue is full and cannot be inserted any more. when front==-1 and rear ==-1, circular queue is empty.

Algorithm Insert an element in circular queue

Steps

1. start
2. check overflow condition
   if(front==0 && rear==max-1) || (front==rear+1)) then
   write "OVERFLOW" and then
   stop
3. read data to insert
4. if(front==-1)
   front=0
   rear=0
5. if(rear=max-1) then
   rear=0
   else
   rear=rear+1
6. cq[rear]=data
7. stop

Algorithm Delete an element in circular queue

Steps

1. start
2. check underflow condition
   if(front=-1) then
   write "UNDERFLOW" and then
   stop
3. if(front==rear) then // circular queue has only one element
   cq[front]=0
   front=-1
   rear=-1
4. if(front=max-1)
   front=0
   else

front=front+1

5. stop

Program: Write a program to implement a circular queue

```
#include<stdio.h>
#define max 5
int front,rear,q[max];
void enqueue();
void dequeue();
void qdisplay();
void main()
{
    int c;
front=rear=-1;
do
{
    printf("\n 1: Insert\n 2: deletion\n 3: display\n 4: exit\n enter choice:");
    scanf("%d",&c);
    switch(c)
{
    case 1: enqueue();break;
    case 2: dequeue();break;
    case 3: qdisplay();break;
    case 4: printf("program Ends\n");break;
    default: printf("wrong choice\n");break;
     }
     }while(c!=4);
}
void enqueue()
{
    int x;
    if((front==0&&rear==max-1)||(front==rear+1))
    {
      printf("Queue is overflow\n");
      return;
}
```

```
if(front==-1)
{
      front=rear=0;
}
else
{
      if(rear==max-1)
{
      rear=0;
}
else
{
     rear++;
}
}
     printf("\nenter the no:\n");
     scanf("%d",&x);
     q[rear]=x;
     printf("%d successfully inserted\n",x);
     return;
}
     void dequeue()
{
     int y;
     if(front==-1)
{
     printf("q is underflow\n");return;
}
     y=q[front];
     if(front==rear)
{
     front=rear=-1;
}
else
{
     if(front==max-1)
```

```
{
front=0;
}
else
{
front++;
}
}
     printf("%d successfully deleted\n",y);
return;
}
    void qdisplay()
{
int i,j;
    if(front==rear==-1)
{
    printf("q is empty\n");return;
}
    printf("elements are :\n");
    for(i=front;i!=rear;i=(i+1)%max)
{
    printf("%d\n",q[i]);
}
    printf("%d\n",q[rear]);
return;
}
```

Output

```
1:insert
2:deletion
3:display
4:exit
enter choice:1
enter the no:
2
2 successfully inserted
1:insert
```

```
2:deletion
3:display
4:exit
enter choice:1
enter the no:
3
3 successfully inserted
1:insert
2:deletion
3:display
4:exit
enter choice:1
enter the no:
4
4 successfully inserted
1:insert
2:deletion
3:display
4:exit
enter choice:1
enter the no:
5
5 successfully inserted
1:insert
2:deletion
3:display
4:exit
enter choice:3
elements are :
2
3
4
5
1:insert
2:deletion
3:display
4:exit
```

```
enter choice:2
2 successfully deleted
1:insert
2:deletion
3:display
4:exit
enter choice:3
elements are :
3
4
5
1:insert
2:deletion
3:display
4:exit
enter choice:4
program ends
```

Example:

Consider the following queue characters, where queue is a circular array which is allocated 6 memory cells:

Front=2, Rear=4, Circular Queue: __, T, A, L, __, __

Do the following operation and show the front and rear position after each operation?

(*i*) H is added to the queue.
(*ii*) Two letters are deleting.
(*iii*) Three times A are added.
(*iv*) Two letters are deleting.
(*v*) T is added to the queue.
(*vi*) One letter is deleted.
(*vii*) S is added to the queue.
(*viii*) One letter is deleted.

Solution:

Initially

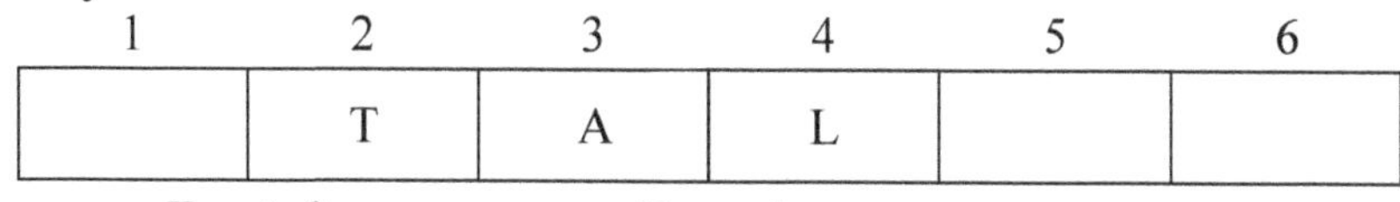

H is added

1	2	3	4	5	6
	T	A	L	H	
	Front=2			Rear=5	

Two Letters are deleting

1	2	3	4	5	6
			L	H	
			Front=4	Rear=5	

Three times A are added

1	2	3	4	5	6
A	A		L	H	A
	Rear=2		Front=4		

Two letters are deleted

1	2	3	4	5	6
A	A				A
	Rear=2				Front=6

T is added

1	2	3	4	5	6
A	A	T			A
		Rear=3			Front=6

One letter is deleted

1	2	3	4	5	6
A	A	T			
Front=1		Rear=3			

S is added

1	2	3	4	5	6
A	A	T	S		
Front=1			Rear=4		

One letter is deleted

1	2	3	4	5	6
	A	T	S		
	Front=2		Rear=4		

5.4 DOUBLE ENDED QUEUE (DE-QUEUE)

Another type of queue is called de-queue. In de-queue, both insertion and deletion operations are performed at either end of the queue. That is, we can insert an element from rear end or the front end. Also deletion is possible from either both ends.

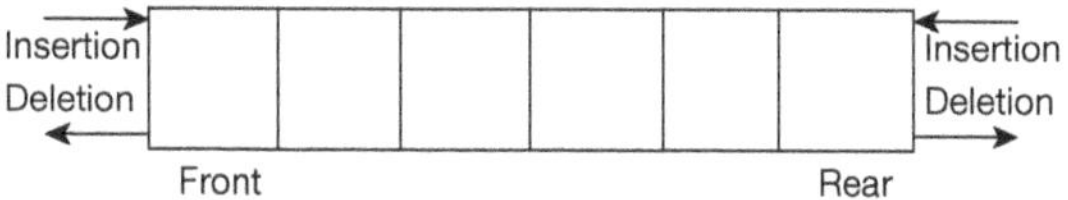

Figure Structure of a De-Queue

Types of De-queue

De-queue can be of two types

1. Input-restricted dequeue
2. Output-restricted dequeue

1. Input-restricted dequeue

In input-restricted dequeue, element can be added at only one end but we can delete the element from both ends.

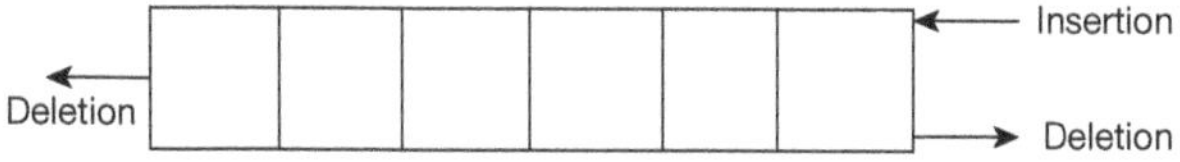

Figure Input Restricted DeQueue

2. An Output-restricted

An output-restricted dequeue is a dequeue where deletions take place at only one end but insertion at both ends.

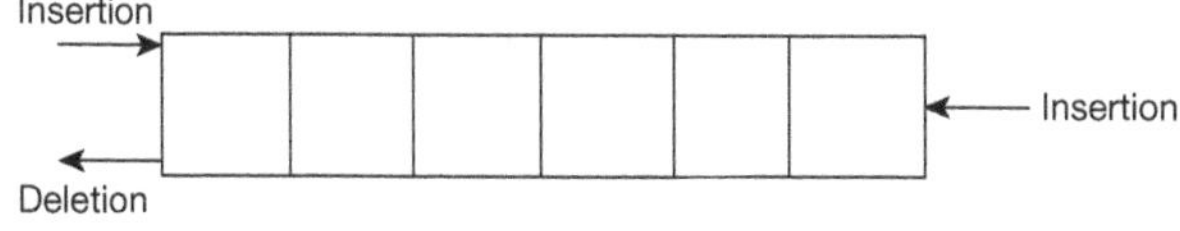

Figure Output Restricted Dequeue

The two possibilities that must be considered while inserting or deleting elements into the queue are:

(*a*) When an attempt is made to insert an element into a dequeue which is already full, an overflow occurs.

(*b*) When an attempt is made to delete an element from a dequeue which is empty, underflow occurs.

The four possible operation performed on dequeue is:

(*i*) Add an element at the rear side.
(*ii*) Add an element at the front side.
(*iii*) Delete an element from the front side.
(*iv*) Delete an element from the rear side.

Algorithm to implement a double ended queue

Steps

1. Start
2. Initialise and declare the variable
3. Enter your choice
4. If choice is ENQUEUE at FRONT then
   (*i*) Check if dequeue is full.
   (*ii*) Else check for FRONT at first position.
   (*iii*) Else decrement the FRONT position.
5. If choice is ENQUEUE at REAR then
   (*i*) Check if dequeue is full
   (*ii*) Else check for REAR at last position.
   (*iii*) Else increment the REAR position.
6. If choice is DEQUEUE at FRONT then
   (*i*) Check if dequeue is empty.
   (*ii*) Else check for dequeue contains only one element
   (*iii*) Else increment the FRONT position.
7. If choice is DEQUEUE at REAR then
   (*i*) Check if dequeue is empty
   (*ii*) Else check for dequeue contains only one element.
   (*iii*) Else decrement the REAR position.
8. Stop

Algorithm (Insertion)

1. **Insert an Element at the Right side of the Dequeue**
   Steps
   1. start
   2. input the data to be insert

3. if (left == 0 && right == max - 1) || (left == right + 1))
   message "OVERFLOW" and then
   stop
4. if (left == - 1)
   left = right = 0
   else
   if (right == max - 1)
   left = 0
   else
   right = right + 1
5. queue[right] = data
6. stop

2. **Insert an Element at the left side of the Dequeue**
   Steps

   1. start
   2. input the data to be insert
   3. if (left == 0 && right == max - 1) || (left == right + 1))
      message "OVERFLOW" and then
      stop
   4. if (left == - 1)
      left = right = 0
      else
      if (left == 0)
      left = max - 1
      else
      left = left - 1
   5. queue[left] = data
   6. stop

Algorithm (Deletion)

1. **Delete an Element at the Right side of the Dequeue**
   Steps

   1. start
   2. if (left == -1)
   3. message "UNDERFLOW" and then
   4. stop

5. data = q[right]
6. if(left == right)
7. left = right = - 1
   else
   if(right == 0)
   right = max - 1
   else
   right = right + 1
8. stop

2. **Delete an Element at the Right side of the Dequeue**
   Steps

   1. Start
   2. if (left == -1)
   3. message "UNDERFLOW" and then
   4. stop
   5. data = q[left]
   6. if(left == right)
   7. left = right = - 1
      else
      if(left == max - 1)
      left = 0
      else
      left = left + 1
   8. stop

5.5 PRIORITY QUEUE

A priority queue is another type of queue structure in which elements can be inserted or deleted based on the priority. A priority queue is a data structure in which each element has been assigned a value called the priority of the element and an element can be inserted or deleted not only at the end but at any position on the queue (included middle). A priority queue is a collection of elements such that each element has been assigned an explicit or implicit priority and such that the order in which elements are deleted and processed comes from the following rules:

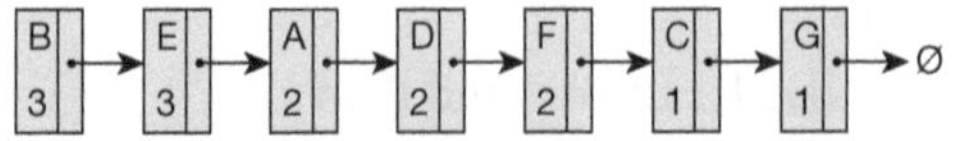

Figure General structure of priority queue

Rule 1:

An element of higher priority is processed before any element of lower priority.

Rule 2:

Two elements with the same priority are processed to the order in which they were inserted to the queue.

Types of Priority Queues

There are two types of priority queues:

1. Ascending Priority queue
2. Descending priority queue.
    1. **Ascending priority queue** elements can be inserted in an ascending order. But, while deleting elements from the queue a small element can only to be deleted first.
    2. **Descending priority queue** elements are inserted in descending order but while deleting elements from the queue a largest element should be deleted first.

Representation of the Priority Queue

There are various ways of maintaining a priority queue. These are:

- One way linked list.
- Multiple queues, one for each priority.
- Maximum or minimum heap.

One way List Representation

In this representation each node of the linked list will have three fields.

1. A Priority Number PN
2. An information field INFO
3. A link to next node LINK.

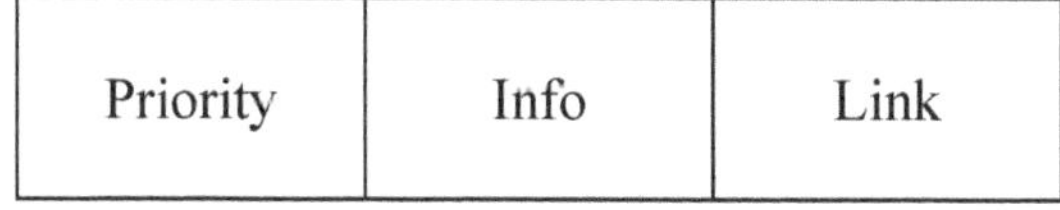

Figure Structure of a node in priority queue

Operation in priority queue

1. Add operation
2. Delete operation

Add operation in priority queue

Add operation in priority queue is same as the insert operation in sorted linked list. Here, we insert the new node element on the basis of priority. The new node element will be inserted before the element which has less priority than new node element.

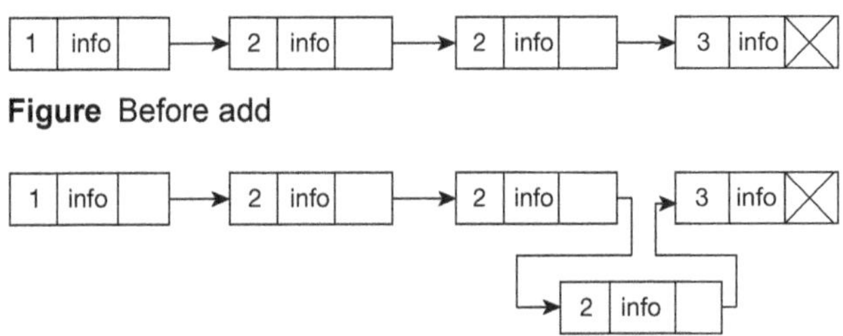

Figure Before add

Figure After add (whose priority is 2)

Delete operation in priority queue

A priority queue must at least support the following operations:

Pull Highest Priority Element: Remove the element from the queue that has the highest priority, and return it. This is also known as "pop element(Off)", "get_maximum_element" or "get_front(most)_element". Some conventions reverse the order of priorities, considering lower values to be higher priority, so this may also be known as "get_minimum_element", and is often referred to as "get-min" in the literature. This may instead be specified as separate "peek_at_highest_priority_element" and "delete_element" functions, which can be combined to produce "pull_highest_priority_element".

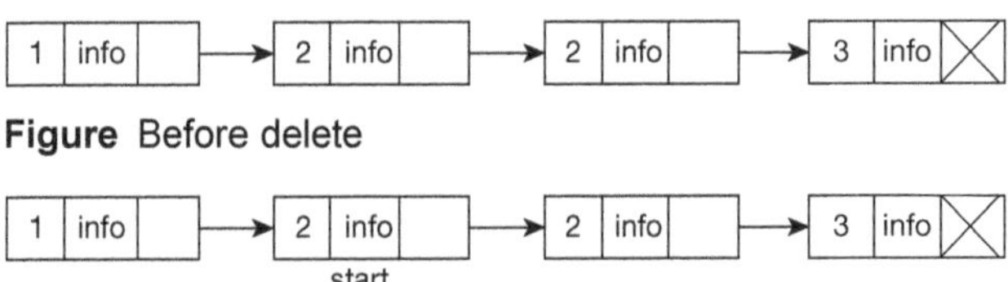

Figure Before delete

Figure After delete

Program: write a program to implement a priority queue

```
#include <stdio.h>
#include <stdlib.h>
#define MAX 5
void insert(int);
void delete(int);
void create();
void check(int);
```

```
void display_pqueue();
int pri_que[MAX];
int front,rear;
void main()
{
    int n, ch;
    printf("\n1 - Insert an element into queue");
    printf("\n2 - Delete an element from queue");
    printf("\n3 - Display queue elements");
    printf("\n4 - Exit");
    create();
    while (1)
{
    printf("\nEnter your choice : ");
    scanf("%d", &ch);
    switch (ch)
{
case 1:
    printf("\nEnter value to be inserted : ");
    scanf("%d",&n);
    insert(n);
    break;
case 2:
    printf("\nEnter value to delete : ");
    scanf("%d",&n);
    delete(n);
    break;
case 3:
    display_pqueue();
    break;
case 4:
    exit(0);
    default:
    printf("\nChoice is incorrect, Enter a correct choice");
}
}
```

```
}
void create()
{
front = rear = -1;
}
void insert(int data)
{
if (rear >= MAX - 1)
{
    printf("\nQueue overflow no more elements can be inserted");
    return;
}
if ((front == -1) && (rear == -1))
{
front++;
rear++;
    pri_que[rear] = data;
    return;
}
else
    check(data);
    rear++;
}
void check(int data)
{
int i,j;
    for (i = 0; i <= rear; i++)
{
    if (data >= pri_que[i])
{
    for (j = rear + 1; j > i; j--)
{
    pri_que[j] = pri_que[j - 1];
}
    pri_que[i] = data;
    return;
```

```
}
}
    pri_que[i] = data;
}
void delete(int data)
{
int i;
if ((front==-1) && (rear==-1))
{
    printf("\nQueue is empty no elements to delete");
return;
}
    for (i = 0; i <= rear; i++)
{
if (data == pri_que[i])
{
    for (; i < rear; i++)
{
    pri_que[i] = pri_que[i + 1];
}
    pri_que[i] = -99;
    rear--;
if (rear == -1)
front = -1;
return;
}
}
    printf("\n%d not found in queue to delete", data);
}
void display_pqueue()
{
if ((front == -1) && (rear == -1))
{
    printf("\nQueue is empty");
return;
}
```

```
for (; front <= rear; front++)
{
   printf(" %d ", pri_que[front]);
}
front = 0;
}
```

Output

```
1 - Insert an element into queue
2 - Delete an element from queue
3 - Display queue elements
4 - Exit
Enter your choice : 1
Enter value to be inserted : 2
Enter your choice : 1
Enter value to be inserted : 4
Enter your choice : 1
Enter value to be inserted : 6
Enter your choice : 1
Enter value to be inserted : 8
Enter your choice : 1
Enter value to be inserted : 10
Enter your choice : 3
10 8 6 4 2
Enter your choice : 2
Enter value to delete : 6
Enter your choice : 3
10 8 4 2
Enter your choice : 4
```

5.6 APPLICATIONS OF QUEUES

Some of the applications of queues are as follows:

1. There are several algorithms that use queues to solve problems easily. For example, BFS traversing of a binary tree etc.
2. Round-robin technique for processor scheduling is implemented using queues.
3. When the jobs are submitted to a network printer, they are arranged in order of arrival. *i.e.*, jobs sent to a printer are placed on a queue.

4. Every real-life line is queue. For example, lines at ticket counters at cinema halls, railway stations, bus stands etc., are queues because the service *i.e.*, ticket is provided on first come first served (FIFO) basis.

5.7 DIFFERENCE BETWEEN STACK AND QUEUE

S.No	Stack	Queue
1	Stack is an ordered list where all insertions and deletions are performed at one end called top	Queue is an ordered list where insertion are performed at rear side and deletion are performed at front side
2	Stack follow LIFO rule	Queue follow FIFO rule
3	Stack is full when top = MAXSIZE - 1	Queue is full when rear = MAXSIZE - 1
4	Stack is empty when top = - 1	Queue is empty when front ==-1
5	To insert an element into the stack; top is increment by 1. i.e. top = top + 1	To insert an element into the queue; rear is increment by 1. *i.e.* rear = rear + 1
6	To delete an element from the stack; top is decrement by 1. *i.e.* top = top - 1	To delete an element from the queue; front is decrement by 1. *i.e.* front = front + 1

POINTS TO REMEMBER

1. A queue is a FIFO data structure in which the element that is inserted first is the first one to be taken out.
2. The elements in a queue are added at one end called the rear and removed from the other end called the front.
3. In the computer memory, queues can be implemented using arrays and linked list.
4. In a circular queue, the first index comes after the last index.
5. A priority queue is a data structure in which each element is assigned a priority. The priority of the elements will be used to determine the order in which the elements will be processed.
6. A de-queue is a list in which elements can be inserted or deleted at either end. It is also known as a head-tail linked list because elements can be added to or removed from the front (head) or back (tail).

MULTIPLE CHOICE QUESTIONS

1. A line in a grocery store represents a

   (*a*) stack (*b*) queue

   (*c*) linked list (*d*) array

2. In a queue, insertion is done at

(*a*) rear (*b*) front
(*c*) back (*d*) top

3. The function that deletes values from a queue is called
   (*a*) enqueue (*b*) dequeue
   (*c*) pop (*d*) peek
4. Typical time requirement for operations on queues is
   (*a*) O (1) (*b*) O (n)
   (*c*) O (log n) (*d*) O (n^2)
5. The circular queue will be full only when
   (*a*) FRONT = MAX-1 and REAR = MAX-1
   (*b*) FRONT = 0 and REAR = MAX-1
   (*c*) FRONT = MAX-1 and REAR = 0
   (*d*) FRONT = 0 and REAR = 0

TRUE OR FALSE

1. A queue stores elements in a manner such that the first element is at the beginning of the list and the last element is at the end of the list.
2. Elements in a priority queue are processed sequentially.
3. In a linked queue, a maximum of 100 elements can be added.
4. Conceptually a linked queue is same as that of a linear queue.
5. The size of a linked queue cannot change during run time.
6. In a priority queue, two elements with the same priority are processed on FCFS basis.
7. Output-restricted dequeue allows deletions to be done only at one end of the dequeue, while insertion can be done at both the ends.

FILL IN THE BLANKS

1. New nodes are added at _______ of the queue.
2. __________ allows insertion of elements at either ends but not in the middle.
3. The typical time requirement for operations in a linked queue is __________.
4. In ____________, insertions can be done only at one end, while deletions can be done from both the ends.
5. Dequeue is implemented using ___________.
6. ________________ are appropriate data structures to process batch computer programs submitted to the computer centre.

7. ________ are appropriate data structures to process a list of employees having a contract for a seniority system for hiring and firing.

EXERCISES

1. Define priority queue and its applications?
2. Why do we use multiple queues?
3. Consider the queue : __, A,B,C,D,E,__,__,__,__

   Front=1 and Rear=5

   Do the following operation

   (*i*) Add F

   (*ii*) Delete two letters

   (*iii*) Add G, H

   (*iv*) Delete four letters

   (*v*) Add I
4. Consider the dequeue: __, A,B,C,D,E,__,__,__,__

   Left=1 and Right=5

   Do the following operation

   (*i*) Add F on the left

   (*ii*) Add G on the right

   (*iii*) Add H on the right

   (*iv*) Delete two letters from left

   (*v*) Add I on the right

   (*vi*) Add J on the left

   (*vii*) Delete two letters from right
5. Write a program to implement a priority queue using array?
6. Write a program to implement circular queue using array?
7. Define input restricted and output restricted queue with the help of suitable example?

REFERENCES

1. Ellis Horowitz and Sartaj Sahni, Fundamentals of Data Structures, Computer Science Press, Rockville, Maryland, New York, 1985.
2. Jean Paul Tremblay and Paul G. Sorenson, Introduction to Data Structures with Applications, McGraw-Hill, New York, 1987.
3. Robert L. Kruse, Bruse P. Leung and L. Clovis Tondo, Data Structures and Program Design in C, Prentice-Hall of India, New Delhi.
4. Thomas L. Naps, Introduction to Data Structures with C, West Publishing Company, West Virginia, 1986.

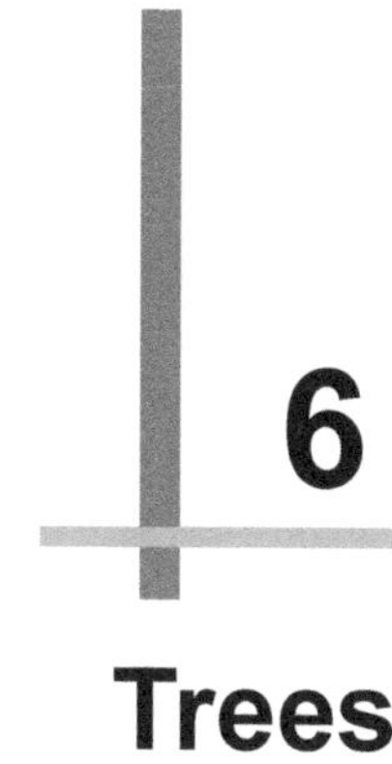

6 Trees

6.1 INTRODUCTION

So far we have studied about array, stack, queue and linked lists, which are known as linear data structures. These are termed as linear because the elements are arranged in a linear fashion. There are many applications in real life situations that make use of non-linear data structure such as trees and graphs. Tree is a data structure which allows you to associate a parent-child relationship between various pieces of data and thus allows us to arrange our records, data and files in a hierarchical fashion. Consider a tree representing your family structure.

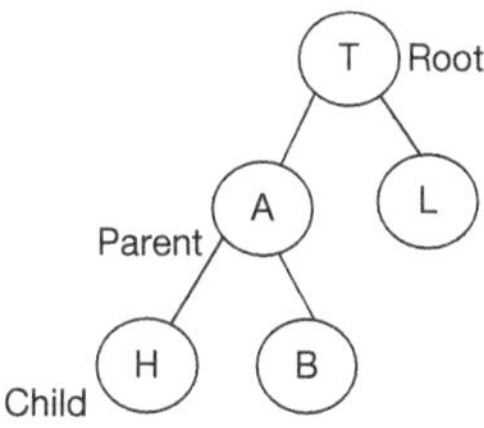

Figure: General Tree

6.2 BASIC TERMINOLOGY RELATED TO TREE

Node: Each element of a tree is called a node. This is the main component of any tree structure. It stores the actual data along with links to other nodes.

Root: A root is a specially designated node in a tree. Root is a node which has no parent. There can be only one root in a tree.

Parent: The parent of a node is the immediate predecessor of that node.

Child: The immediate successors of a node are called child nodes. A child which is placed at the left side is called the left child and a child which is placed at the right side is called the right child.

Degree of Node: The number of sub-trees of a node in a given tree is called degree of that node. Sub tree represents descendents of a node.

Terminal Node: A node with degree zero is called a terminal node or a leaf.

Non-Terminal Node: Any node except the root node whose degree is not zero is called non-terminal node.

Level: The entire tree structured is levelled in such a way that the root node is always at level 0. Then, its immediate children at level 1, and their immediate children at level 2 and so on. In general, if a node is at level n, then its children will be at level n+1.

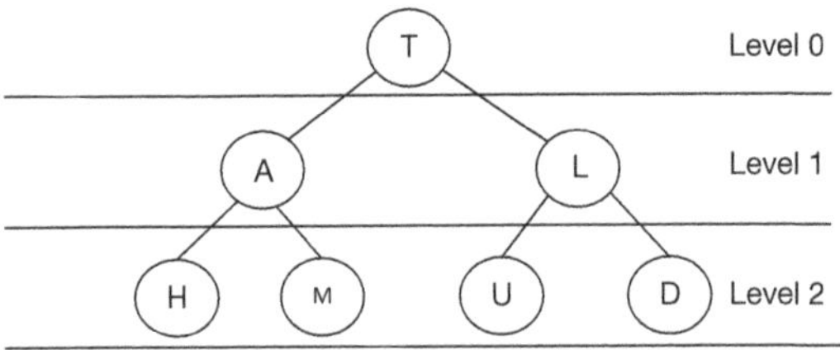

Edge: Edge represents a path between two nodes or a line between two nodes.

Path: Path is a sequence of consecutive edges from the source node to the destination node.

Depth: Depth is the length of the path from the root node to certain node.

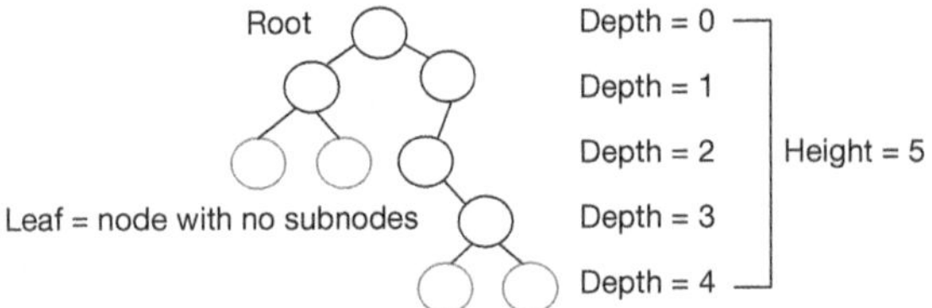

Height: Height of a tree is equal to the maximum level of any node in the tree. The height of the tree in above example is "5".

Ancestor and Descendant: An ancestor is any element which is connected further up in the hierarchy tree – no matter how many levels higher.

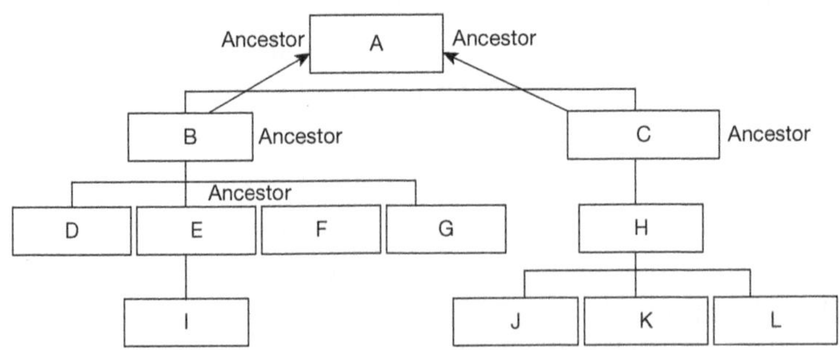

E, B and A are ancestors of I

C and A are ancestors of H

Descendant: A descendant refers to any element that is connected lower down the hierarchy tree – no matter how many levels lower.

E has one descendant – I

C has 4 descendants – H, J, K and L

G has no descendants

Forest: A forest is a disjoint union of trees. A set of disjoint (or forests) is obtained by deleting the root and the edges connecting the root node to nodes at level 1. We have already seen that every node of a tree is the tree of some sub-tree. Therefore, all the sub-trees immediately below a node form a forest. A forest can also be defined as an ordered set of zero or more general trees. While a general tree must have a root, a forest on the other hand may be empty because by definition it is a set, and sets can be empty.

6.3 BINARY TREES

A binary tree is made of nodes, where each node contains a "left" reference, a "right" reference, and a data element. The topmost node in the tree is called the root.

Every node (excluding a root) in a tree is connected by a directed edge from exactly one another node, this node is called a parent. On the other hand, each node can be connected to arbitrary number of nodes, called children. Nodes with no children are called leaves, or external nodes. Nodes which are not leaves are called internal nodes. Nodes with the same parent are called siblings.

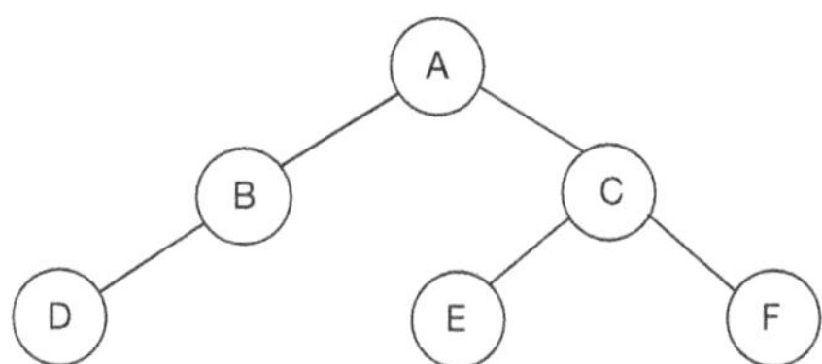

Fig: Binary Tree

6.4 TERMINOLOGY RELATED TO BINARY TREE

Parent: If N is any node in tree T that has left successor S_1 and right successor S_2, then N is called the parent of S_1, and S_2, Correspondingly S_1 and S_2 are called the left child and the right child of N. Every node other than the root node has a parent.

Level number: Every node in a binary tree is assigned a level number. The root node is defined to be at level 0.The left and the right child or the root node have a level number 1. Similarly, every node is at one level higher than its parents. So all child nodes are defined to have level number as parent's level number + 1.

Degree of a node: It is equal to the number of children that a node has. The degree of a leaf node is zero.

Sibling: All nodes that are at the same level and share the same parent are called siblings.

Leaf node: A node that has no children is called a leaf node or a terminal node.

Similar binary trees: Two binary trees T and $T^{/}$ are said to be similar if both these trees have the same structure.

Copies: Two binary trees T and T' are said to be copies if they have similar structure and if they have same content at the corresponding nodes.

Edge: It is the line connecting a node n to any of its successors. A binary tree of n nodes has exactly n-1 edges because every node except the root node is connected to its parent via an edge.

Path: A sequence of consecutive edges.

Depth: The depth of a node N is given as the length of the path from the root R to the node N.

Height of a tree: It is the total number of nodes on the path from the root node to the deepest node in the tree. A tree with only a root node has a height of 1.

6.5 PROPERTIES OF BINARY TREES

1. The number of external nodes in binary tree is equal to number of internal nodes+1.
2. The number of external nodes is at least h+1, where h is the height of the tree, and at most 2h.
3. The height h, of a binary tree with n nodes is at least logn+1 and at most n.
4. A binary tree with n nodes has exactly n-1 edges.

6.6 TYPES OF BINARY TREES

1. Strictly Binary Tree
2. Extended Binary Tree (2-Tree)
3. Complete Binary Tree
4. Almost Completed Binary Tree

1. Strictly Binary Tree

A binary tree is a finite set of elements that is either empty or is partitioned into three disjoint subsets. The first subset contains a single element called the root of the tree. The other two subsets are themselves binary trees, called the left and right subtrees of the original tree. Below given tree consists of 7 nodes and the root node is node A. Its left subtree is rooted at B and its right subtree is rooted at C. This is indicated by the two branches emanating from A to B on the left and A to C on the right.

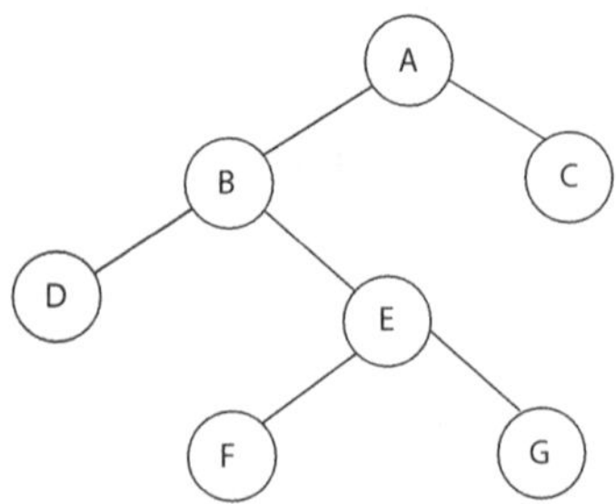

Fig: Strictly Binary Tree

The absence of a branch indicates an empty subtree. If every internal node (non terminal node) has its non empty left and right children then it is called strictly binary tree. In other words, if every non leaf node in a binary tree has non empty left and right sub-trees, the tree is termed as strictly binary tree.

Here, every internal node A, B, E has two non empty left and right children hence, it is strictly binary tree.

Properties

1. A strictly binary tree with n non leaf nodes has n+1 leaf node.
2. A strictly binary tree with n leaf nodes always has 2n-1 nodes.

2. Extended Binary Tree (2-Tree)

If in a binary tree, each empty sub-tree is replaced by a special node then the resulting tree is extended binary tree or 2-tree. So we can convert a binary tree to an extended binary tree by adding special nodes to leaf nodes and nodes that have only one child. The special nodes added to the tree are called external nodes and the original nodes of the tree are internal nodes. External nodes are shown by square and internal nodes by circles.

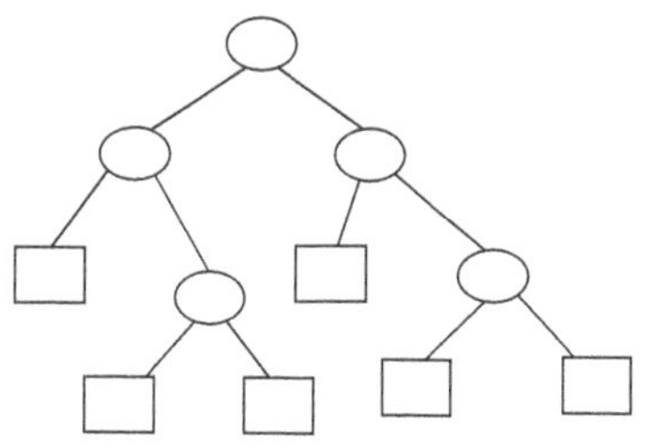

Fig: Extended Binary Tree

3. Complete Binary Tree

In computer science, a binary tree is a tree data structure in which each node has at most two children, which are referred to as the left child and the right child. A binary tree with n nodes and a depth d is a strictly binary tree all of whose terminal nodes are at level d. If a binary tree contains m nodes at level I, it contains at most 2m nodes at level I+1.

4. Almost Complete Binary Trees

A binary tree of depth d is an almost complete binary tree, if:

(*i*) Any node at level less than d-1 has two children.

(*ii*) For any node 'X' in the tree with a right descendant at level d, X must have a left child and every left descendant of X is either a leaf at level d or has two childrens.

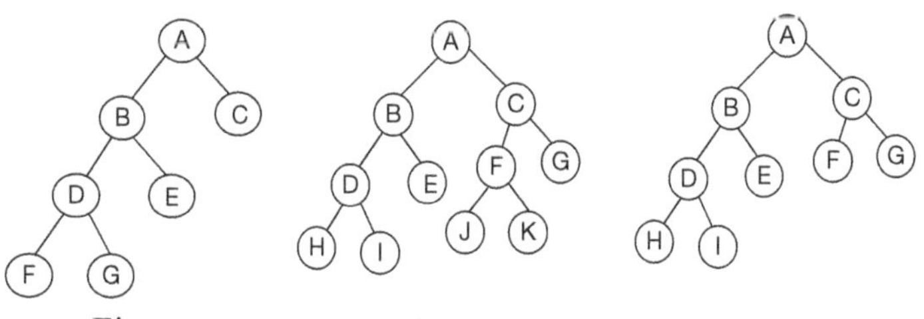

Figure: a Figure: b Figure: c

Figure (a), is not almost complete binary tree because it contains leaf nodes at level 1, 2 and 3. So, it is violating rule 1. Figure (b), satisfies rule 1, since every leaf is either at level 2 or at level 3. However, rule 2 is violating. Since A has a right descendant at level 3 (J) but also has a left descendant that is a leaf at level 2 (E). Figure (c), satisfies both rules 1 and 2 and is therefore an almost complete binary tree.

An almost complete strictly binary tree with n leaves has 2n-1 nodes and an almost complete binary tree with n leaves that is not strictly binary has 2n nodes. There are two distinct almost complete binary trees with n leaves one of which is strictly binary and one of which is not. An almost complete binary tree of depth d is intermediate between the complete binary tree of depth d-1 that contains 2^d-1 nodes and the complete binary tree of depth d, which contains 2^{d+1} -1 nodes.

6.7 REPRESENTATION OF A BINARY TREE

Binary trees can also be implemented in two ways one is array and the other is linked list.

1. Array Representation of Binary Tree

This is also called sequential representation or linear representation or contiguous representation based binary trees. We use one-dimensional array to maintain the nodes of the binary tree. We'll store the nodes in the array named tree from index 1 onwards. If a node is numbered k then the data of this node is stored in tree[k]. The root node is stored in tree [1] and it's left and right children in tree [2] and tree [3] and so on. We have left the index 0 empty for some other purpose.

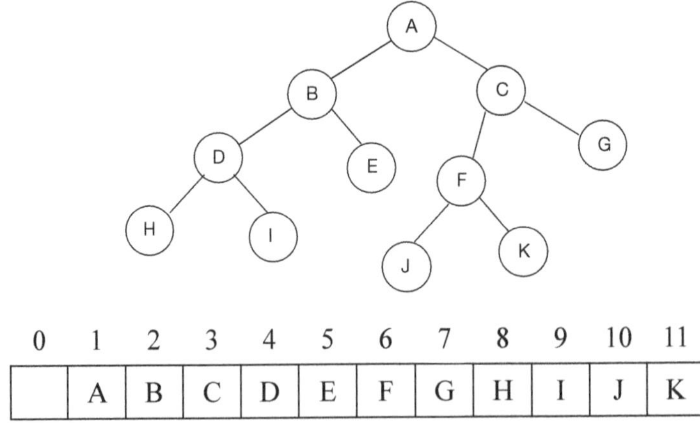

0	1	2	3	4	5	6	7	8	9	10	11
	A	B	C	D	E	F	G	H	I	J	K

2. Linked List Representation of Binary Tree

The binary tree can be represented using dynamic memory allocation of a node in a linked list form. In a linked list allocation technique a node in a tree contains three fields:

(*i*) Data: it contains the info value.

(*ii*) Left link: it contains address of the left sub-tree.

(*iii*) Right link: it contains address of the right sub-tree.

When a node has no children, the corresponding pointer fields are NULL. Here, first member data is for information field of node, second member is for left child of node which points to the structure itself, and it contains the address of left child. If node has no left child then it should be NULL. Third member is for right child of node which also points to the structure itself; it contains the address of right child. If node has no right child it should be NULL. This type of representation is dynamic block of memory. They are allocated only on demand.

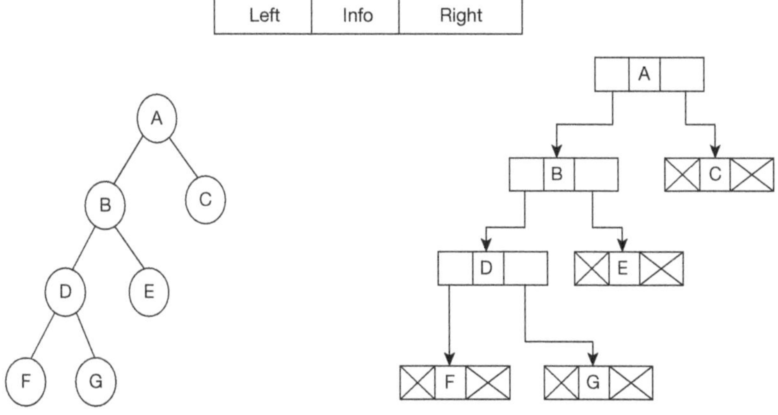

Fig: Linked List Representation of Binary Trees.

Declare structure of tree node

```
Struct node
{
Int info;
Struct node *left;
Struct node *righ;
};
```

6.8 TRAVERSING A BINARY TREE

Traversing a binary tree is the process of visiting each node in the tree exactly once in a systematic way. Unlike linear data structures in which the elements are traversed sequentially, tree is a non-linear data structure in which the elements can be traversed in many different ways. There are different algorithms for tree traversals. These algorithms differ in the order in which the nodes are visited.

1. **Pre-order Traversal (NLR)**
    1. Visiting the root node.
    2. Traversing the left sub-tree of root.
    3. Traversing the right sub-tree of root.
2. **In-order Traversal (LNR)**
    1. Traversing the left sub-tree of root.
    2. Visiting the root node
    3. Traversing the right sub-tree of root
3. **Post-order Traversal (LRN)**
    1. Traversing the left sub-tree of root
    2. Traversing the right sub-tree of root
    3. Visiting the root node.
4. **Level-order Traversal**

In level-order traversal, all the nodes at a level are accessed before going to the next level. This algorithm is also called as the traversal algorithm.

Example: let us take a binary tree and apply traversal.

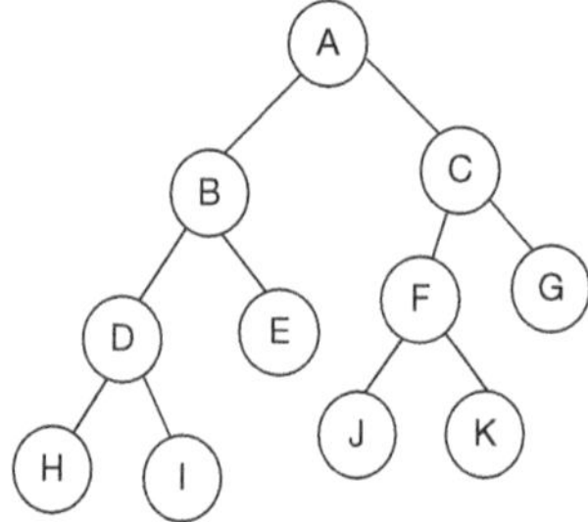

Preorder : A B D H I E C F J K G
Inorder : H D I B E A J F K C G
Postorder : H I D E B J K F G C A
Level Order : A B C D E F G H I J K

Example: let us take another example of a binary tree and apply each traversal.

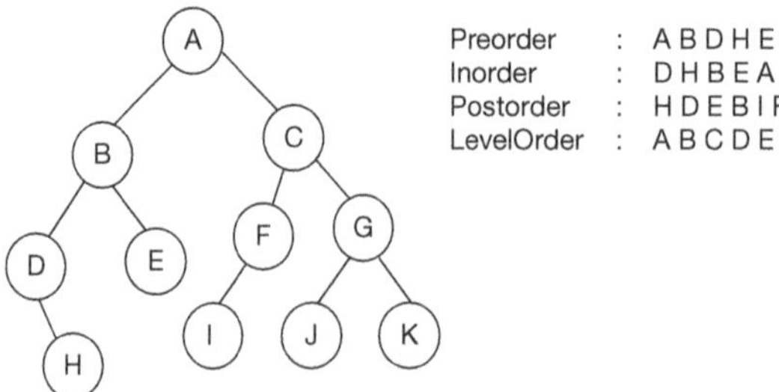

Preorder : A B D H E C F I G J K
Inorder : D H B E A I F C J G K
Postorder : H D E B I F J K G C A
LevelOrder : A B C D E F G H I J K

Algorithm for tree traversal

1. **Pre-order Traversal**

    Steps:

    A binary tree is in memory.

1. Node holds the address of the root node of the tree.
2. Preorder (node)
3. if node ≠ NULL
4. process (node)
5. preorder (left node)
6. preorder (right node)
7. stop

2. **In-order Traversal.**
   Steps:
   A binary tree is in memory.
   1. node hold the address of the root node of the tree.
   2. inorder (node)
   3. if node ≠ NULL
   4. inorder (left node)
   5. process (node)
   6. inorder (right node)
   7. stop
3. **Post-order Traversal.**
   Steps:
   A binary tree is in memory.
   1. node hold the address of the root node of the tree.
   2. postorder (node)
   3. if node ≠ NULL
   4. postorder (left node)
   5. postorder (right node)
   6. process (node)
   7. stop

Function for Pre-order traversal.

```
preorder(struct tree *ptr)
        {
        if (ptr!=NULL)
             {
              printf("%d",ptr->head);
              preorder(ptr->l);
              preorder(ptr->r);
        }
```

```
return(0);
        }
```

Function for Inorder traversal.

```
inorder(struct tree *ptr)
        {
            If (ptr!=NULL)
                  {
                  inorder(ptr->l);
                  printf("%d",ptr->head);
                  inorder(ptr->r);
                  }
                  return(0);
        }
```

Function for Postorder traversal.

```
postorder(struct tree *ptr)
        {
        if (ptr!=NULL)
        {
                  postorder(ptr->l);
                  postorder(ptr->r);
                  printf("%d",ptr->head);
        }
                  return(0);
        }
```

Program: write a program to Implement Binary Tree and apply Traversal like - Preorder, Inorder, Postorder.

```
#include<stdio.h>
#include<stdlib.h>
struct tree
{
int head;
struct tree *l, *r;
};
struct tree *r,*t;
int ch1,n,flag=0,in;
```

```
void main()
{
        char ch='y';
        r=NULL;
        while (ch=='y')
        {
           printf("\n 1.Create tree");
           printf("\n 2.Traverse In-Order");
           printf("\n 3.Traverse Pre-Order");
           printf("\n 4.Traverse Post-Order");
           printf("\n 5.Exit");
           printf("\n Enter chioce");
           scanf("%d",&ch1);
           switch (ch1)
        {
        case 1:
               if (insert(&r)==0)
               break;
        case 2:
               printf("\n\n Left,Root,Right");
               inorder(r);
               break;
        case 3:
               printf("\n \n Root,Left,Right");
               preorder(r);
               break;
        case 4:
               printf("\n\n Left,Right,Root");
               postorder(r);
               break;
        case 5:
               exit(0);
        default :
               printf(" Wrong Choice ");
        }// switch close
        }// while close
```

```
} //main close
insert(struct tree **ptr)
{
        if (*ptr==NULL)
            {
            *ptr=malloc (sizeof(struct tree));
            printf("\n Enter the element ");
            scanf("%d",&n);
            (*ptr)->head=n;
            (*ptr)->l=NULL;
            (*ptr)->r=NULL;
            return(0);
            }
//flag=1;}
        else
            printf("\n1. Left Element");
            printf("\n2. Right Element");
            printf("\n3. Exit");
            printf("\n Enter choice");
            scanf("%d",&in);
        switch(in)
        {
        case 1:
            insert(&(*ptr)->l);
            break;
        case 2:
            insert(&(*ptr)->r);
            break;
        case 3:
        break;
        default:
        printf("\n Choice is wrong");
        }// switch closed
        return(0);
} //fun closed
inorder(struct tree *ptr)
```

```
            {
            if(ptr!=NULL)
            {
            inorder(ptr->l);
            printf("%d",ptr->head);
            inorder(ptr->r);
            } // if close
            return(0);
            } //fun closed
   preorder(struct tree *ptr)
            {
             if (ptr!=NULL)
            {
            printf("%d",ptr->head);
            preorder(ptr->l);
            preorder(ptr->r);
            } // if close
            return(0);
            } //fun closed
   postorder(struct tree *ptr)
            {
            if (ptr!=NULL)
            {
            postorder(ptr->l);
            postorder(ptr->r);
            printf("%d",ptr->head);
            } // if close
            return(0);
            } //fun closed
```

Output

1. Crcate tree
2. Traverse In-Order
3. Traverse Pre-Order
4. Traverse Post-Order
5. Exit

Enter chioce 1

Enter the element 4

1. Create tree
2. Traverse In-Order
3. Traverse Pre-Order
4. Traverse Post-Order
5. Exit

Enter chioce 1

1. Left Element
2. Right Element
3. Exit

Enter choice1

Enter the element 2

1. Create tree
2. Traverse In-Order
3. Traverse Pre-Order
4. Traverse Post-Order
5. Exit

Enter chioce 1

1. Left Element
2. Right Ele ment
3. Exit

Enter choice 2

Enter the element 2

1. Create tree
2. Traverse In-Order
3. Traverse Pre-Order
4. Traverse Post-Order
5. Exit

Enter chioce 1

1. Left Element
2. Right Element
3. Exit

Enter choice 12

Choice is wrong

1. Create tree
2. Traverse In-Order

3. Traverse Pre-Order
4. Traverse Post-Order
5. Exit

Enter choice 1

1. Left Element
2. Right Element
3. Exit

Enter choice 2

1. Left Element
2. Right Element
3. Exit

Enter choice 2

Enter the element 4

1. Create tree
2. Traverse In-Order
3. Traverse Pre-Order
4. Traverse Post-Order
5. Exit

Enter choice 2

Left, Root, Right 2424

1. Create tree
2. Traverse In-Order
3. Traverse Pre-Order
4. Traverse Post-Order
5. Exit

Enter choice 3

Root, Left, Right 4224

1. Create tree
2. Traverse In-Order
3. Traverse Pre-Order
4. Traverse Post-Order
5. Exit

Enter choice 4

Left, Right, Root 2424

1. Create tree
2. Traverse In-Order

3. Traverse Pre-Order
4. Traverse Post-Order
5. Exit

Enter choice 5

Non-Recursive Function for Traversal

Non-recursive procedures for tree traversal will be implemented by using stack.

1. Pre order Traversal using stack

The procedure for traversing a tree in pre-order non-recursively is as:

Steps:

(*i*) Initially pointer (ptr) contains the address of root.
(*ii*) PUSH the address of root node on the stack.
(*iii*) POP an address from the stack.
(*iv*) If the POP address is not NULL
 (*a*) Traverse the node
(*v*) PUSH right child of node on stack
(*vi*) PUSH left child of node on stack
(*vii*) Repeat steps until the stack is empty.

Non-recursive function for preorder traversal is:

```
nonrec_preorder(struct node *ptr)
{
stack[++top]=ptr;
while(top!=-1)
        {
        ptr=stack[top--]
        if(ptr!=NULL)
            {
            printf("%d", ptr->info);
            stack[++top]=ptr->right;
            stack[++top]=ptr->left;
            }
        }
}
```

Example: Consider a binary tree.

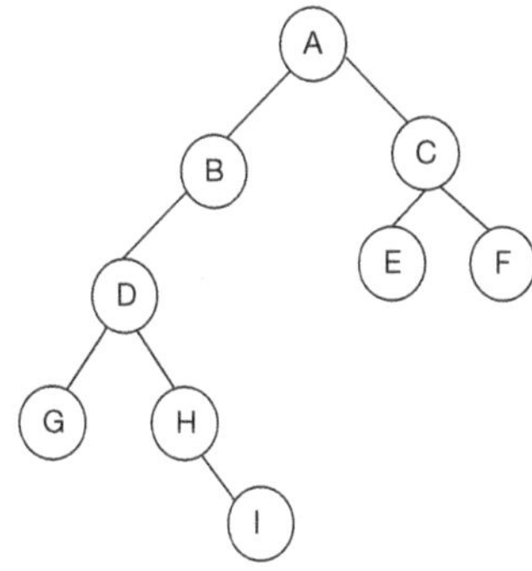

Initially set ptr = A, the root of tree. PUSH it and then POP it from the stack.

Since ptr ≠ NULL

Traverse the node A, and PUSH its right child C and left child B node on the stack. Now POP the top element B from the stack.

Stack:

B
C

POP the top element B from the stack. B ≠ NULL

Traverse the node B, and PUSH its right child (no right child) and left child D on the stack.

Stack:

D
C

POP the top element D from the stack. D ≠ NULL

Traverse the node D, and PUSH its right child H and left child G on the stack.

Stack:

G
H
C

POP the top element G from the stack. G ≠ NULL

Traverse the node G and PUSH its right child and left child (no right and left child)

Stack:

H
C

POP the top element H from the stack. H ≠ NULL

Traverse the node H and PUSH its right child I on the stack and its left child (no left child)

Stack:

I
C

POP the top element I from the stack. I ≠ NULL

Traverse the node I and PUSH its right child and left child (no right and left child)

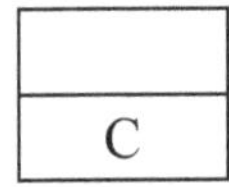

Stack:

POP the top element C from the stack. C ≠ NULL

Traverse the node C and PUSH its right child F and left child E on the stack.

Stack:

E
F

POP the top element E from the stack.

Stack:

F

Traverse the node E and PUSH its right and left child (no child)

POP the top element from the stack F

Traverse the node F and PUSH its right and left child (no child)

Now, no element in stack, stack is empty.

The Final Pre-order traversal is: A B D G H I C E F

2. Inorder Traversal using stack

The procedure for traversing a tree in in-order non-recursively is as follows:

Steps:

(*i*) repeat step while stack is not empty or pointer (ptr) ≠ NULL

(*ii*) if ptr ≠ NULL

(*a*) PUSH ptr on the stack

(*b*) ptr=left (ptr)

(*iii*) If ptr = NULL

(*a*) POP the element from the stack

(*b*) traverse the node

(*c*) ptr=right (ptr)

Non-recursive function for in-order traversal is:

```
nonrec_inorder(struct node *ptr)
{
while(top!=-1 || ptr!=NULL)
        {
        if(ptr!=NULL)
                {
                stack[++top]=ptr;
                ptr=ptr->left;
                }
else
                {
                ptr=stack[top--];
                printf("%d", ptr->info);
                ptr=ptr->right;
                }
        }
}
```

Example: Consider a Binary Tree.

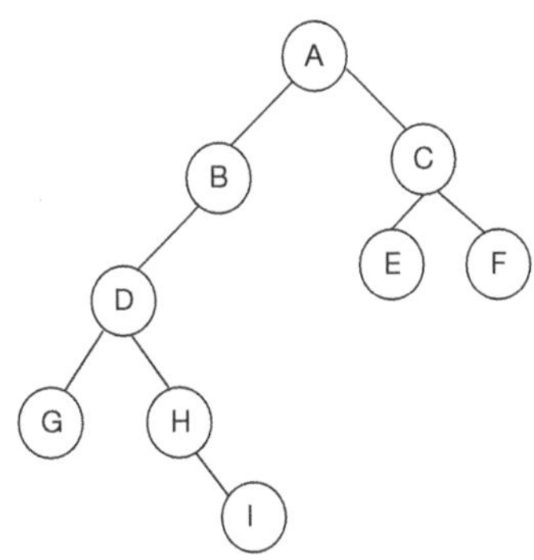

Initially ptr=root node

Now Ptr =A hence PUSH A on the stack.

Now Ptr=left of node (A) that means element B.

PUSH B on the stack and ptr moves to left (B) the element stored at left of B is D

PUSH D on the stack and ptr moves to left (D) the element stored at this location is G

PUSH G on the stack and ptr moves to left (G), G doesn't have any left element hence G is NULL.

After these operations of push; stack would be in the following form:

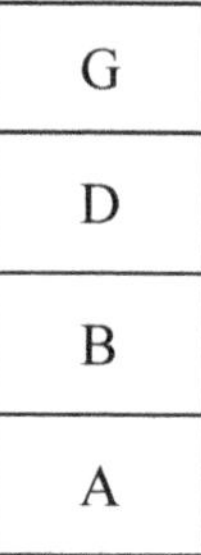

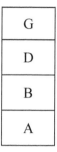

POP the top element from the stack *i.e.*; the element G.

Traverse the node G and ptr=right (G), i.e; ptr=NULL. Again POP the top element from the stack that is element D now pointer ptr points to ptr=right (D) i.e; ptr=H.

Traverse the node D

PUSH node H on the stack, and ptr=left(H)=ptr=NULL

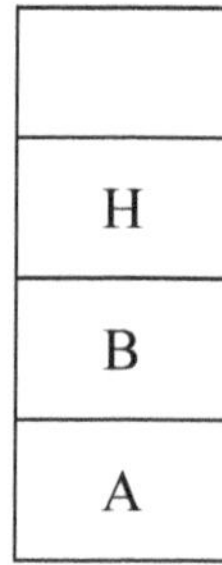

Stack:

POP the top element from the stack H

Traverse the node H and ptr= right (H) =ptr=I

PUSH the node I on the stack and ptr= left (I)= ptr=NULL

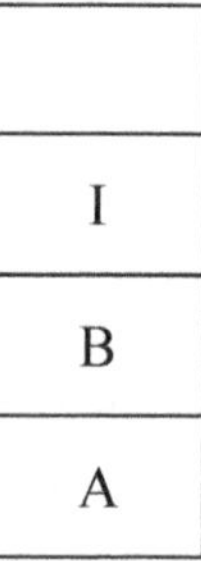

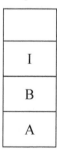

Stack

POP the top element from the stack I

Traverse the node I and ptr= right (I) = NULL

Again POP the element from the stack B

Traverse the node B and ptr= right (B)= ptr= NULL

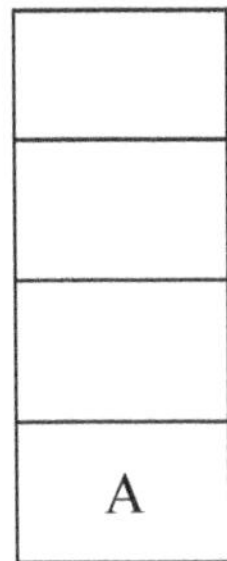

POP the top element from the stack A

Traverse the node A and ptr=right(A)=ptr=C

Ptr ≠ NULL, so PUSH the node C on the stack

Now ptr=left(C)=ptr=E

Ptr ≠ NULL, so PUSH the node E on the stack and ptr=left(E)=ptr=NULL

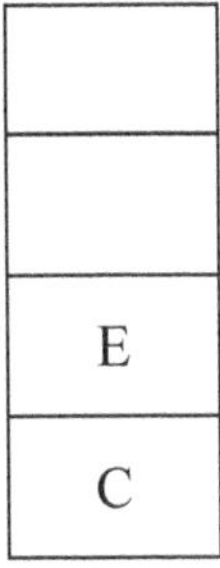

POP the top element from the stack

Traverse the node E, again POP the top element C from the stack

Traverse the node C and ptr= right(C) = ptr=F

PUSH the node F on the stack and ptr= left (F) = ptr=NULL

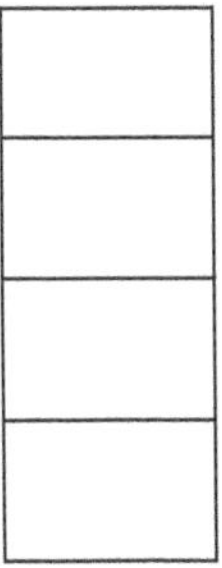

POP the top element from the stack

Traverse the node F, ptr= right (F)= ptr= NULL.

Stack is empty

Thus, the final in-order traversal is: G D H I B A E C F

3. **Postorder traversal using stack**

The procedure for traversing a tree in post-order non-recursively is as follows:

Steps:

(*i*) initially pointer ptr has the address of root
(*ii*) repeat step while ptr!=NULL
(*iii*) top=top+1
(*iv*) stack[top]=ptr
(*v*) if(right(ptr)!=NULL
(*vi*) {
(*vii*) top=top+1
(*viii*) stack[top]=right(ptr)
(*ix*) }
(*x*) ptr=left(ptr)
(*xi*) POP from the stack
(*xii*) while (ptr > 0)
(*xiii*) {
(*xiv*) traverse ptr
(*xv*) ptr=stack[top]
(*xvi*) top=top-1
(*xvii*) }
(*xviii*) if ptr < 0 then
(*xix*) {
(*xx*) ptr=right(ptr)
(*xxi*) }
(*xxii*) stop

Non-recursive function for post-order traversal is:

```
nonrec_postorder(struct node *ptr)
{
struct node *stack[30];
int top=-1;
int visited,i, visit[10];
do
{
while(ptr!=NULL)
{
```

```
printf("%d", ptr->info);
stack[++top]=ptr;
ptr=ptr->left;
}
if(top!=-1)
{
ptr=stack[top--];
visited=0;
for(i=0;i<top;i++)
if(visit[i]==ptr->right)
{
visited=1
break;
}
if(visited==1)
{
printf("%d", ptr->info);
ptr=NULL;
}
else
{
stack[++top]=ptr;
ptr=ptr->right;
visit[ptr]=1;
}
ptr=ptr->right;
}
}
while(top!=-1 || ptr!=NULL);
}
```

6.9 CREATION OF BINARY TREE WITH THE HELP OF TRAVERSAL

There are two different ways of creating binary tree:

1. pre-order and in-order traversal
2. post-order and in-order traversal

1. Creation of binary tree from pre-order and in-order traversal.

The general rule for creating a binary tree is as follows:

Rule 1: scan the pre-order traversal from left to right

Rule 2: for each node scanned, locate its position in in-order traversal. Assume the scanned node be X.

Rule 3: the node X preceding X in inorder from its left sub-tree and nodes succeeding it from right sub-tree.

Rule 4: repeat rule 1 for each symbol in the pre-order.

Example: Draw a binary tree of the following given orders

Pre-order: A B D H E C F G

In-order: D H B E A F C G

***Solution*:**

Pre-order: **A** B D H E C F G

In-order: D H B E **A** F C G

Step 1: In pre-order traversal root is the first node. So, A is the root node of the binary tree.

Root

A

Step 2: We can find the node of left sub-tree and right sub-tree with in-order sequence.

Nodes which are left sub-tree: D H B E

Nodes which are right sub-tree: F C G

Step 3: The left child of the root node will be the first node in the pre-order sequence after root node A. Hence, node B is the left child of A. Similarly, the right child of root A will be the first node after nodes of left sub-tree in pre-order sequence. Hence, node C is the right child of A.

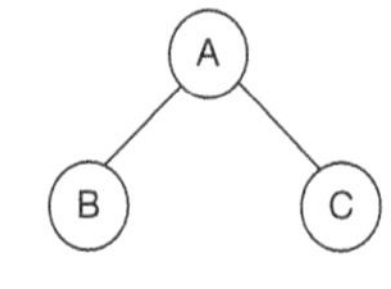

Nodes which are left sub-tree: D H E

Nodes which are right sub-tree: F G

Step 4: In in-order sequence, node D and node H are on the left side of B and E is on the right side of B. So node D and node H form left sub-tree and node E will be in the right sub-tree of node B.

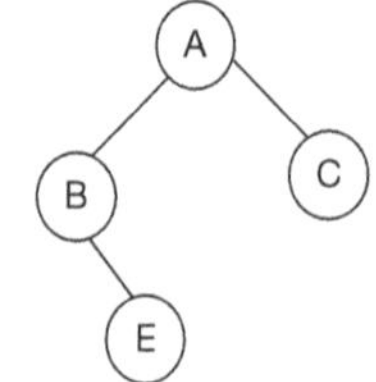

Nodes which are left sub-tree: D H

Nodes which are right sub-tree: F G

Step 5: In in-order sequence node F is on the left of node C and node G is on the right side of node C. So node F will be in left sub-tree of node C and node G in right sub-tree of node C.

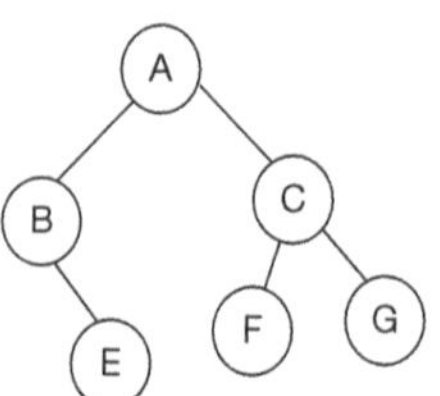

Nodes which are left sub-tree: D H

Step 6: again, in pre-order traversal node D is coming before node H. Hence node D is the root of left sub-tree of node B. To find out whether node H is in left or right sub-tree of node D. Now, we look at in-order sequence node H in right side of node D. So, node H will be in right sub-tree of node D. Thus, the final binary tree is.

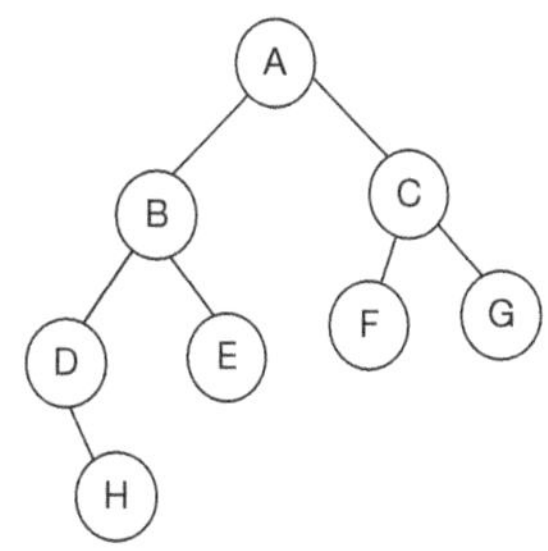

Example: Draw a binary tree

Pre-order: F A E K C D H G B

In-order: E A C K F H D B G

***Solution*:**

Root node is F

Nodes which are in left sub-tree: E A C K

Nodes which are in right sub-tree: H D B G

Now, apply the previous steps, we got the final tree.

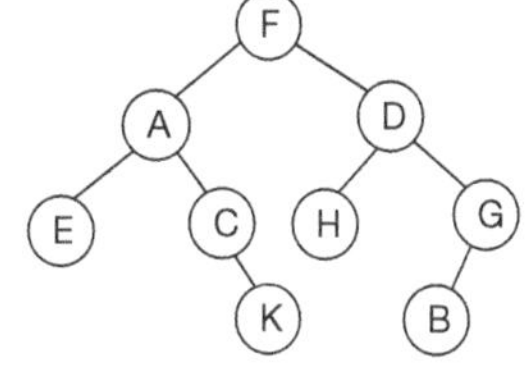

2. Creation of binary tree from post-order and in-order traversal. The general rule for creating a binary tree is as follows:

Rule 1: scan the post-order traversal from right to left.

Rule 2: for each node scanned locate its position in in-order traversal. Assume the scanned node be X.

Rule 3: the node preceding X in in-order from its left sub-tree and nodes succeeding it from right sub-tree.

Example: Draw a binary tree

Post-order: H D I E B J F K L G C A

In-order: H D B I E A F J C K G L

***Solution*:**

Post-order: H D I E B J F K L G C **A**

In-order: H D B I E **A** F J C K G L

Step 1: In post-order traversal root is the last node. Hence, node A is the root of the binary tree.

Nodes which are in left sub-tree: H D B I E

Nodes which are in right sub-tree: F J C K G L

Step 2: Now right child of node A will be the node which comes just before, node A *i.e.* node C and left child of node A will be the first node before nodes of right sub-tree in post-order traversal, node B.

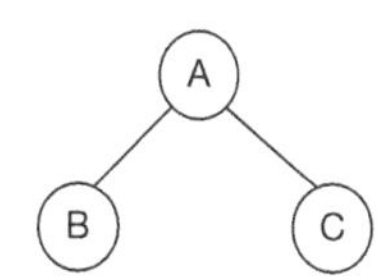

Nodes which are in left sub-tree: H D I E

Nodes which are in right sub-tree: F J K G L

Step 3: Now look at post-order traversal, node just before B is E, so node E is the right child of B and node just before C is G hence node G is right child of node C and node D is the first node before the nodes of right sub-tree of node B. Hence node D is the left child of node B and node F is the first node before nodes of right sub-tree of node C. Hence, node F is left child of node C.

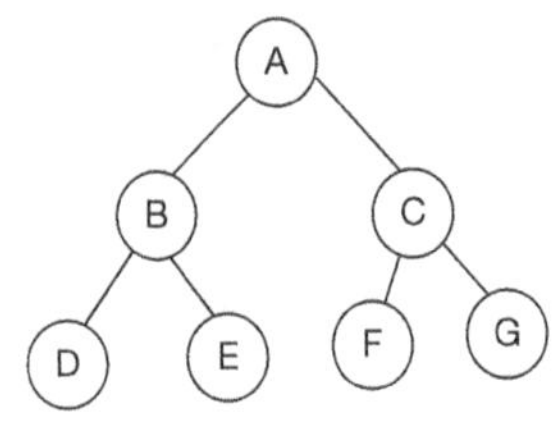

Now from in-order traversal node H is the left of node D hence it is left child of node D, node I is to the left of node E, hence it is left child of node E. Node J is to the right of node F, Hence it is right child of node F, node K is to the left of node G and node L to the right of node G, Hence node K is left child of node G and node L is right child of node G.

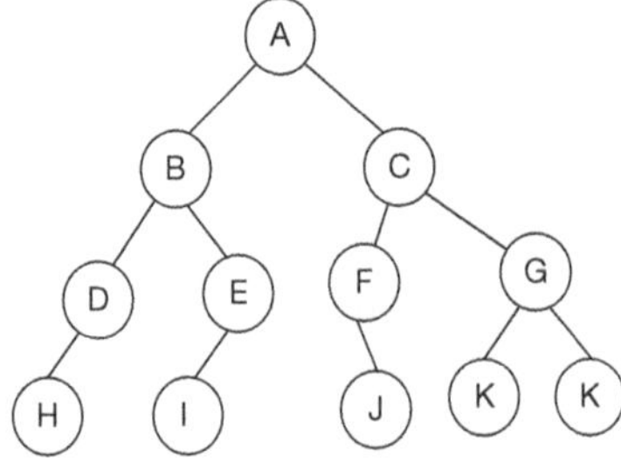

We got the final tree.

Converting algebraic expression into binary tree

The arithmetic expressions represented as binary trees are known as expression trees. In this, the root node is operator and the left and right child are operands. In case of unary operators the left child is not present and the right child is the operand.

Example: Draw the binary tree for the given expression: (A + B) * (C + D)

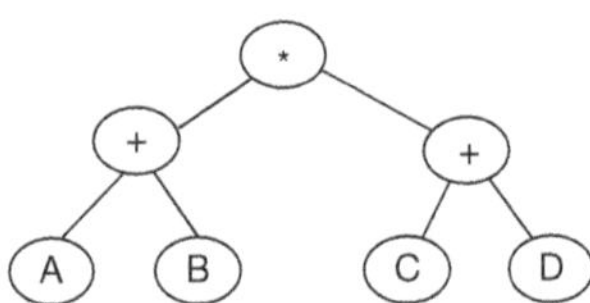

Example: Draw the binary tree for the given expression: (A - B) / ((C * D) + E)

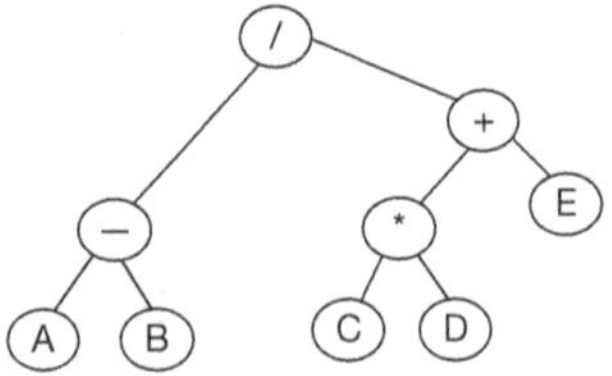

6.10 BINARY SEARCH TREE

A binary search tree is a binary tree. Such a tree can be represented by a linked data structure in which each node is an object. In addition to a key field, each node contains left, right and parent that points to the nodes corresponding to its left child, right child and its parent respectively.

Every element has a key.

1. The key in the left sub-tree are smaller than the root.
2. The key in the right sub-tree are greater than the root.
3. The left and right sub-trees are also binary search tree.

Example: create a binary search tree for the following numbers:

40 25 70 22 35 60 80 90 10 30

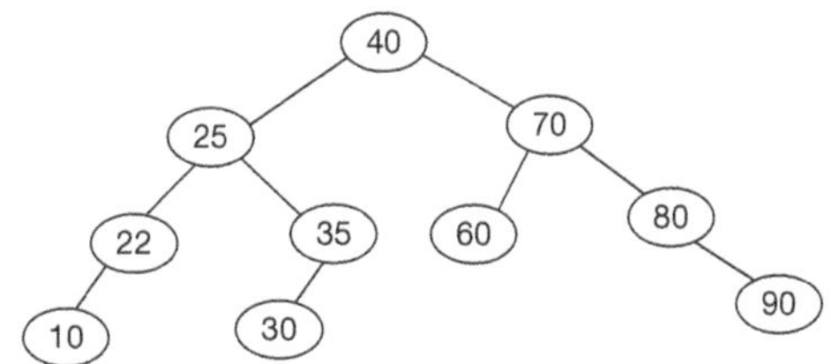

6.11 OPERATIONS IN BINARY SEARCH TREE

1. Traversal in Binary Search Tree
2. Searching in a Binary Search Tree
3. Finding nodes with Minimum and Maximum Values
4. Insertion in a Binary Search Tree
5. Deletion in a Binary Search Tree

1. Traversal in Binary Search Tree

Binary search tree is a binary tree so the traversal methods given for binary tree apply here.

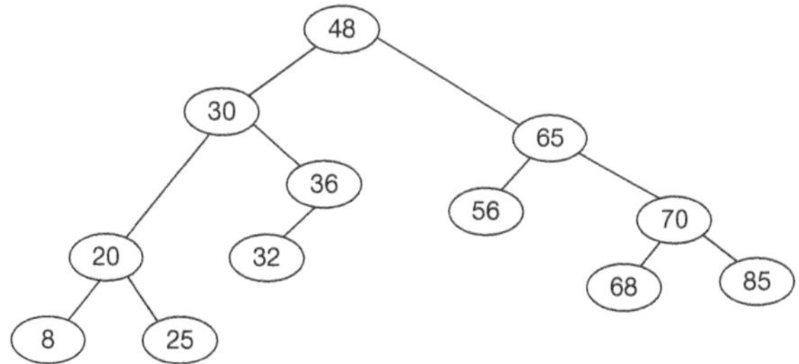

Pre-order : 48 30 20 8 25 36 32 65 56 70 68 85

In-order : 8 20 25 30 32 36 48 56 65 68 70 85

Post-order : 8 25 20 32 36 30 56 68 85 70 65 48

2. Searching in a Binary Tree

Start at the root node and move down the tree. To search a node in the tree, first the data element is compared with the value at the root node. If the data element is found there, then the search is successful. If the data element is less than the key in the root, then the search is performed in the left sub-tree. If the data element is greater than the key in the root, then the search is performed in the right sub-tree.

Search 25

(*i*) Compare 25 with 48
(*ii*) 25 < 48, move to left child
(*iii*) Now, compare 25 with 30
(*iv*) 25 < 30, move to left child
(*v*) Now, compare 25 with 20
(*vi*) 25 > 20, move to right child
(*vii*) 25 found

Search 50

(*i*) Compare 50 with 48
(*ii*) 50 > 48, move to right child
(*iii*) Now, compare 50 with 65
(*iv*) 50 < 65, move to left child
(*v*) Now, compare 50 with 56
(*vi*) 50 < 56, move to left child
(*vii*) NULL
(*viii*) 50 Not found

3. Finding nodes with Minimum and Maximum Values

To find minimum valued node in a binary search tree start at the root and move along the leftmost path until we get a node with no left child.

To find maximum valued node start at the root and move along the rightmost path until we get a node with no right child.

4. Insertion in a Binary Tree

To insert an element in a binary tree start at the root node and compare the value to be inserted with the value at root node and take following actions.

(*i*) If the value to be inserted is equal to the value at the root node then there is nothing to be done as duplicate values are not allowed.
(*ii*) If the value to be inserted is less than the value of the node then we move to left child.
(*iii*) If the value to be inserted is greater than the value of the node then we move to right child.

Insert 28

(*i*) Compare 28 with 48
(*ii*) 28 < 48, move to left child

(*iii*) Now, compare 28 with 30

(*iv*) 28 < 30, move to left child

(*v*) Now, compare 28 with 20

(*vi*) 28 > 20, move to right child

(*vii*) Now, compare 28 with 25

(*viii*) 28 > 25, move to the right child

(*ix*) NULL right child

(*x*) Insert at right child of 25

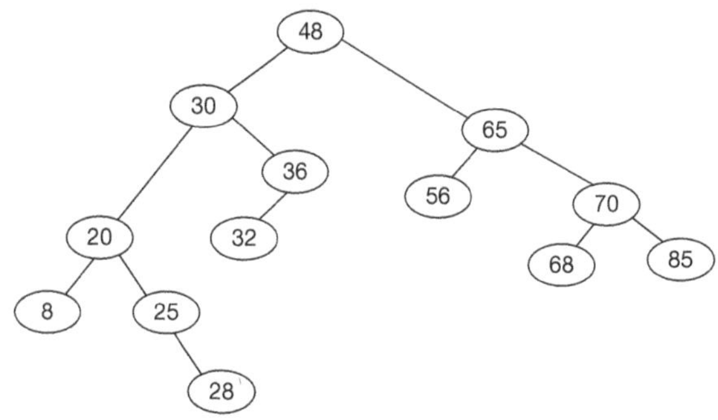

5. Deletion in a Binary Search Tree

Deletion of a node from a binary search tree depends on the number of its children. There are three cases that can occur.

Case 1: Node has no child, *i.e.* it is a leaf node.

Case 2: Node has exactly one child.

Case 3: Node has exactly two children.

Case 1: To delete a leaf node, the link to node is replaced by NULL. If the node is left child of its parent then the left link of its parent is set to NULL and if the node is right child of its parent then the right link of its parent is set to NULL. Then the node is de-allocated using free ().

To delete 20, the left link of node 30 is set to NULL.

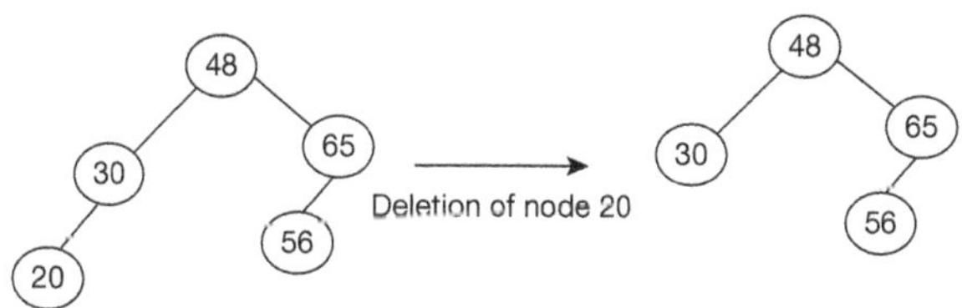

Case 2: In this case, the node to be deleted has only one child. After deletion this single child takes the place of the deleted node. For this we just change the appropriate pointer of the parent node so that after deletion it points to the child of deleted node. After this, the node is de-allocated using free ().

To delete node 65 from the below given tree. Node 65 is the right child of its parent node 48, so the single child 56 takes the place of 65 by becoming the right child of 65.

Case 3: This is the case when the node to be deleted has two children. Here we have to find the in-order successor of the node. The data of the in-order successor is copied to the node and then the in-order successor is deleted from the tree. In-order successor of a node is the node that comes just after that node in the in-order traversal of the tree.

Here node having the key 48 is to be deleted from the tree. In inorder successor node is having the key 56. So the data of node is copied to node and now node 48 has to be deleted from the tree.

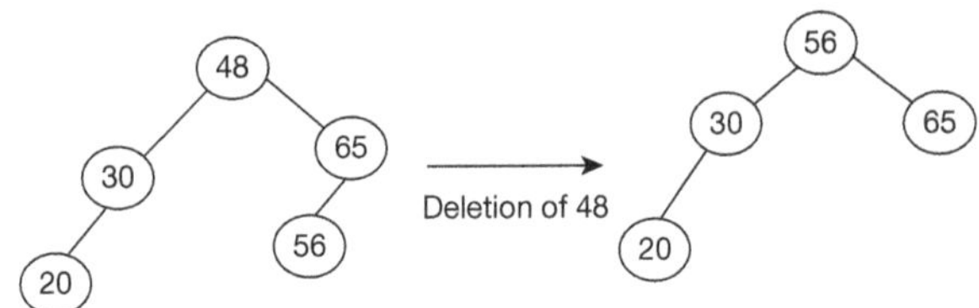

6.12 HUFFMAN'S TREE

Suppose, we are given n nodes and their weights the Huffman algorithm is used to find a tree with a minimum-weighted path length.The process essentially begins by merging (or adding up the values) of two smallest weights among given n valued nodes and hence leads to the creation of a new node, such that the new node's weight is equal to the sum of the merged childrens weight.This process is repeated until the tree has only one node. Such a tree with only one node is known as the Huffman tree.

The Huffman's algorithm can be implemented using a priority queue. Huffman tree is built from bottom up rather than top down i.e the creation of trees start from leaf nodes and proceeds upwards.

Huffman Algorithm

1. Suppose, there are n weights w_1, w_2, w_3... w_n.
2. Take two minimum weights among the n given weights. suppose w1 and w2 are two minimum weights then sub-tree will be:

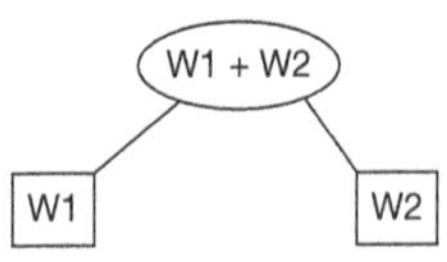

3. Now the remaining weights will be w_1+w_2, w_3, w_4,. ....,w_n
4. Create all sub-trees till the last weight.

Example: let us take 7 elements with weights and create an extended binary tree by using Huffman Algorithm.

Nodes	A	B	C	D	E	F	G
Weight	15	10	5	3	7	12	25

***Solution*:**

Step 1: take two nodes with minimum weights i.e, 5 and 3 and add up their weights to form new node

Now the remaining weighted elements in the list are:

15 10 8 7 12 25

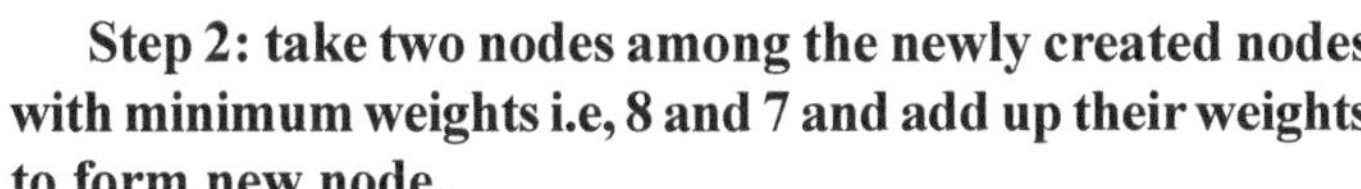

Step 2: take two nodes among the newly created nodes with minimum weights i.e, 8 and 7 and add up their weights to form new node.

Now the remaining elements in the list are:

15 10 15 12 25

Step 3: take two nodes with minimum weights i.e, 10 and 12 among this newly created list of nodes and add up their weights to form new node.

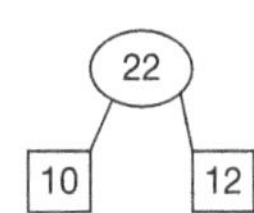

Now the remaining elements in the list are:

15 22 15 25

Step 4: take two nodes with minimum weights i.e, 15 and 15 among this newly created list of nodes and add up their weights to form new node.

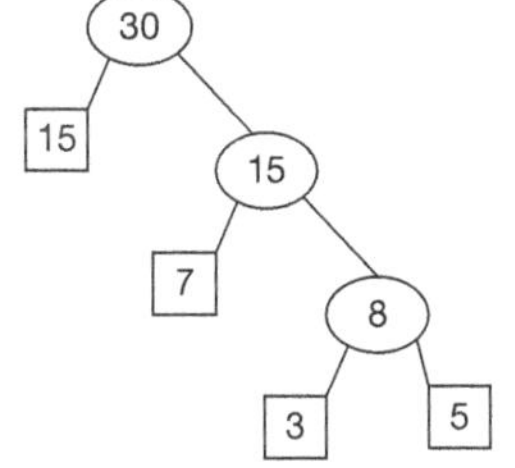

Now the remaining elements in the list are:

30 22 25

Step 5: take two nodes with minimum weights i.e, 22 and 25 among the newly created list of nodes and add them up for the creation of new node.

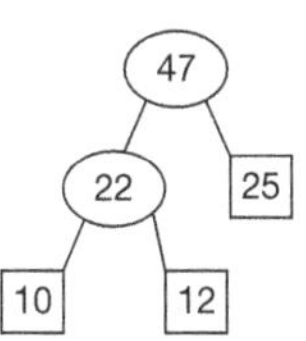

Now the remaining elements in the list are:

30 47

Step 6: take two nodes with minimum weights i.e, 30 and 47 and add them up, this leads to the creation of new node.

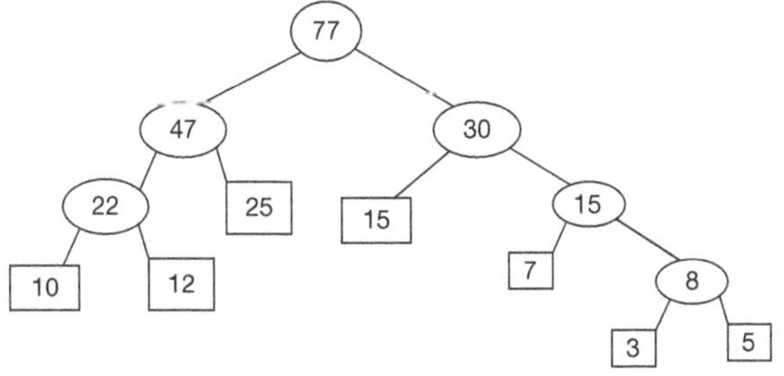

Figure: Huffman Tree

6.13 APPLICATIONS OF HUFFMAN'S TREE

The Huffman algorithm is used to perform the encoding and decoding of a long message consisting of a set of symbols. Suppose, we want to send a message that there are two options either it sends data as fixed size or to send it as variable length size. Assume a collection of data items A1, A2, A3.................An are to be coded by means of strings of bits. One way to do this is to code each item by an r-bit string where, $2^{n-1} < n \leq 2^r$ for example a 48 character set is frequently coded in memory by using 6-bit strings. One cannot use 5-bit strings since $2^5<48<2^6$. Now, we discuss a coding technique using variable-length string that is based on the Huffman tree for weighted data item.

Huffman coding

Huffman follows a bottom-up approach. Procedure is as follows:

1. Form the frequency list of all the symbols in the descending order.
2. Locate the two symbols in the list with the lowest frequencies. Frequencies referred as weights.
3. Create a parent node for these two nodes whose weight is equal to the sum of weights of two child nodes.
4. Remove the two children from the list and add newly created parent node of the list along with the weight.

Example:

Symbol	Weight
A	19
E	11
I	9
O	7
U	7

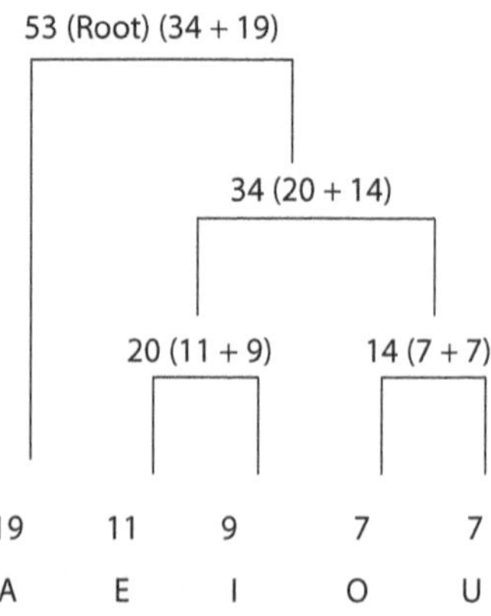

Thus, by using this method or technique the codes for all the symbols are given in the following table.

6.14 THREADED BINARY TREE

Consider the linked list representation of any binary tree, we notice that half of the entries in the pointer field left and right will contain NULL entries. This space may be more efficiently used by replacing the NULL entries by special pointers called Threads which point to the nodes higher in the tree. Such tree are called threaded binary tree.

In computer memory, an extra field called tag or flag is used to distinguish a thread from a normal pointer. Tree can be threaded using one-way threading or two-way threading. In a one-way threading a thread will appear in the right field of the node and will point to the successor node in the in-order traversal of tree. In two-way threading of tree a thread will appear in the left field of a node and will point to the preceding node in the in-order traversal of tree.

1. The Right NULL pointer of each node can be replaced by a thread to the successor of that node under in-order traversal called a right thread and the tree will be called as a right threaded tree.

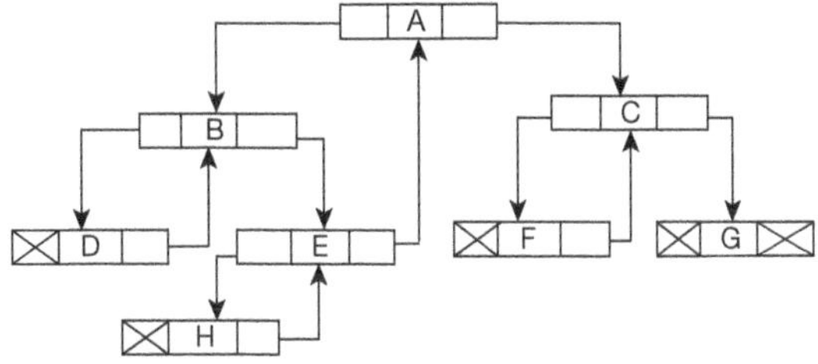

Figure: Right Threaded Binary Tree

2. The left NULL pointer of each node can be replaced by a thread to the predecessor of that node under in-order traversal called a left threaded and the tree will be called as a left threaded tree.

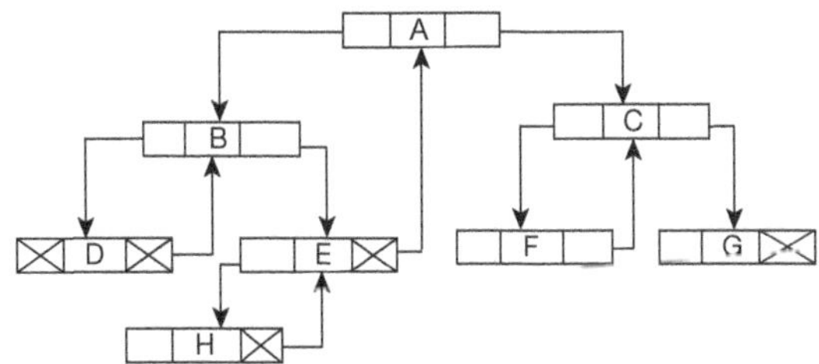

Figure: Left Threaded Binary Tree

3. Both left and right NULL pointers can be used to point to predecessor and successor of that node, respectively, under in-order traversal. Such a tree is called a fully threaded tree.

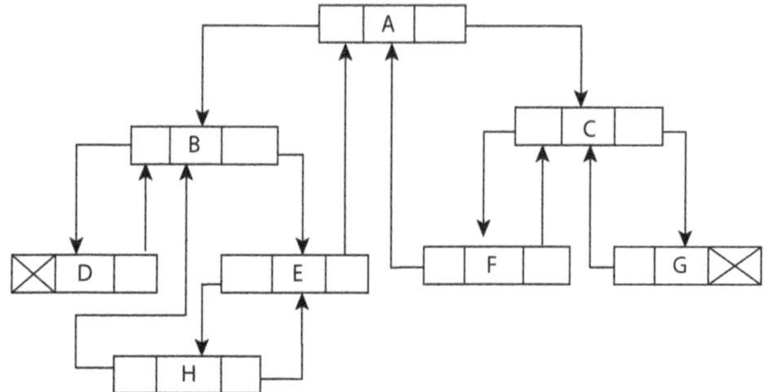

Figure: Fully Threaded Binary Tree

6.15 TRAVERSING IN A THREADED BINARY TREE

1. In-order traversal in Threaded Binary Tree
2. Pre-order traversal in Threaded Binary Tree

1. In-order traversal in Threaded Binary Tree:

If the tree is right threaded then we can traverse it in in-order without the use of stack or recursion. In in-order traversal the left most node of the tree is traversed first of all. So, first we traverse the leftmost node of the tree and then we find the in-order successor of each node and traverse it. As we know that the right most node of the tree is the last node in in-order traversal and its right pointer is a thread pointing to the header node, hence we will stop when we reach header node.

```
inorder()
{
struct node *ptr;
if(head->leftptr==head)
{
printf("tree is empty");
return;
}
ptr=head->leftptr;
while(ptr->left==link)
ptr=ptr->leftptr;
printf("%d", ptr->info);
while(1)
{
ptr=inordersuccessor(ptr);
if(ptr==head)
```

```
break;
printf("%d", ptr->info);
}
}
```

2. Pre-order traversal in Threaded Binary Tree:

In pre-order traversal we will start traversing from the left child of the header node. If the node has a left child then that left child will be traversed, otherwise if the node has a right child, then that right child will be traversed. If the node has neither left nor right child then with the help of right threads we will reach that in-order successor of the node which has a right sub-tree. Now, this sub-tree will be traversed as pre-order.

```
preorder()
{
struct node *ptr;
if(head->leftptr=head)
{
printf("tree is empty");
return;
}
ptr=head->leftptr;
while(ptr!=head)
{
printf("%d", ptr->info);
if(ptr->left==link)
ptr=ptr->leftptr;
else
if(ptr->rightptr==link)
ptr=ptr->rightptr;
else
{
while(ptr!=head && ptr->right==thread)
ptr=ptr->rightptr;
if(ptr!=head)
ptr=ptr->rightptr;
}
}
}
```

Insertion in a Threaded Binary Tree

The new node will be inserted as a leaf node so its left and right pointers both will be threads.

```
temp->leftptr=thread;
temp->rightptr=thread;
```

Case 1: When the tree is empty

When the tree is empty the left pointer of the head node is a thread pointing to it. We will insert the new node as the left child of header node. So now the left pointer of the head will be a link pointing to the new node. We know that the left pointer of first node in in-order traversal and the right pointer of last node in in-order traversal are threads pointing to the header node. Here, we have only one node which is the first and the last node so it's left right pointers will be threads pointing to the header node.

```
head->left=link;
head->leftptr=temp;
temp->leftptr=head;
temp->rightptr=head;
```

Case 2: When the new node inserted is the left child of its parent

The thread of new node will point to its in-order predecessor and successor. The node which was in-order predecessor of the parent is now the in-order predecessor of this node. The in-order successor of this node is its parent.

```
temp->leftchild=parent->leftchild;
temp->rightchild=parent;
```

The parent of new node has a thread in its left pointer pointing to its predecessor, but after insertion its left pointer will be a link pointing to the new node.

```
parent->left=link;
parent->rightchild=temp;
```

Case 3: When the new node inserted is the right child of its parent

The node which was in-order successor of the parent is now the in-order successor of this node. The in-order predecessor of this node is its parent. So, the left and right threads of the new node will be:

```
temp->leftptr=parent;
temp->rightptr=parent->child;
```

The parent of new node had a thread in its right pointer pointing to its successor, but after insertion its right pointer will be link pointing to the new node.

```
parent->right=link;
parent->rightchild=temp;
```

Deletion from a Threaded Binary Tree

There are three possibilities while performing deletion operation in threaded binary tree.

Case 1: Node to be deleted is root node

If the node to be deleted is the root node of the tree then the tree will become empty after its deletion so then left pointer of head will be a thread pointing to it.

```
head->left=thread;
head->leftptr=head;
```

If the node to be deleted is a left leaf node then the left pointer of parent will become a thread pointing to its in-order predecessor. Initially, its in-order predecessor was its left child but now its in-order predecessor will be that node which was predecessor of its left child.

```
parent->left=thread;
parent->leftptr=loc->leftptr;
```

If the node to be deleted is a right leaf node then the right pointer of parent will become a thread pointing to its in-order successor. Initially, its in-order successor was its right child but now its in-order successor will be that node which was successor of its right child.

```
paren->right=thread;
parent->rightptr=loc->rightptr;
```

Case 2: Node to be deleted has one child.

Delete the node as in binary search tree. Find the in-order successor and in-order predecessor of the node to be deleted.

```
successor=inordersucessor(loc);
predecessor=inorderpredecessor(loc);
```

If the node has right sub-tree then put the predecessor of the node in the left pointer of its successor.

```
if(loc->right==link)
successor->leftptr=predecessor;
```

If node has left sub-tree then put the successor of the node in the right pointer of its predecessor.

```
if(loc->left==link)
predecessor-rightptr=successor;
```

Case 3: Node to be deleted has two children

First, we will find the in-order successor of node and then copy the information of this in-order successor into node. After this in-order successor node is deleted using either case 1 or case 2.

6.16 AVL TREE

The first balanced binary search tree was the AVL tree. The AVL tree is a binary search tree that has an additional balance condition. This balance condition must be easy to maintain and ensures that the depth of the tree is O (log N). The simplest idea is to require that the left and right sub–trees have the same height. This balance condition ensures that the depth of the tree is logarithmic, but it is too restrictive because it is too difficult to insert new items while maintaining balance.

AVL is a height balance tree. A height balanced tree is one in which the difference in the height of the two sub-trees for any node is less than or equal to some specified amount. In AVL tree, the height difference may be no more than 1. In fact, for an AVL tree it will never be greater than 1.

Balance Factor

To implement an AVL tree each node must contain a balance factor, which indicates its states of balance relative to its sub-trees: Height of left sub-tree – Height of right sub-tree.

Then the balance factors in a balanced tree can have values of - 1, 0 or 1. For an AVL tree, the value of the balance factor of any node is -1, 0, or 1. If it is other than these three values then the tree is not balanced or it is not an AVL tree. If the value of the balance factor of any node is -1, then the height of the right sub-tree of that node is one more than the height of its left sub-tree. If the value of the balance factor of any node is 0 then the heights of its left and right sub-tree is exactly the same. If the value of the balance factor of any node is 1 then the height of the left sub tree of that node is one more than height of its right sub-tree.

6.17 ROTATIONS OF AVL TREE

(*i*) Left-to-Left rotation (LL Rotation)

(*ii*) Right-to-Right rotation (RR Rotation)

(*iii*) Left-to-Right rotation (LR Rotation)

(*iv*) Right-to-Left rotation (RL Rotation)

1. Left-to-Left rotation (LL Rotation)

The new node x is inserted in the left sub-tree of left sub-tree of A whose balance factor becomes + 2 after insertion. To rebalance the search tree, it is rotated to left.

Example:

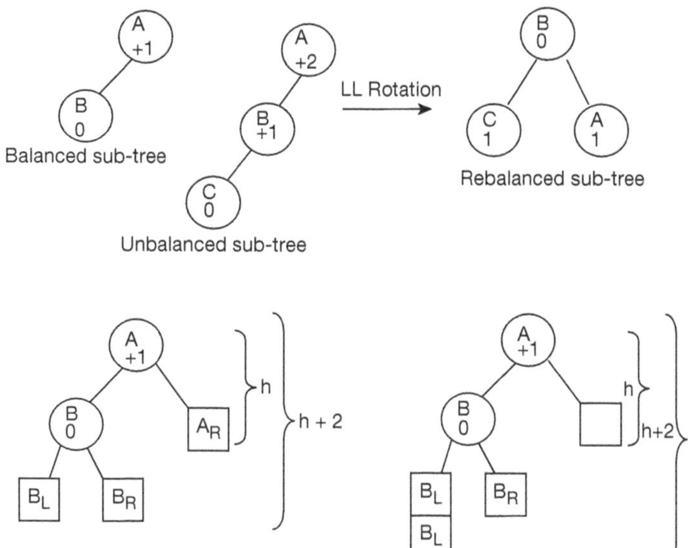

Figure: Balance sub-tree

Figure: Unbalanced sub-tree (height of B_L increased to height h+1)

Now Apply LL Rotation to the above given unbalanced sub-tree

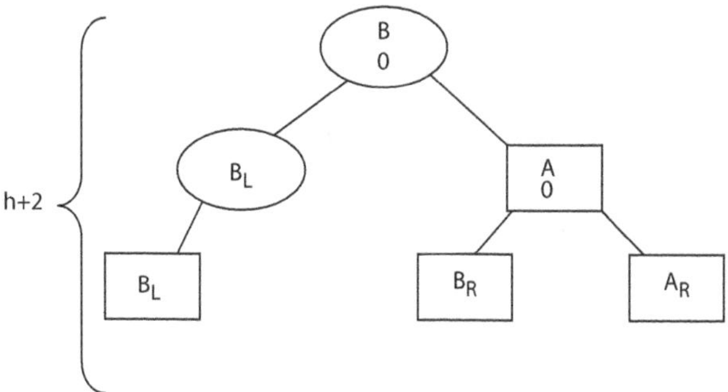

Figure: Rebalanced sub-tree (Height of sub-tree B remains h+1)

2. Right-to-Right rotation (RR Rotation)

The new node x is inserted in the right sub-tree of right sub-tree of A whose balance factor becomes + 2 after insertion. To rebalance the search tree, it is rotated.

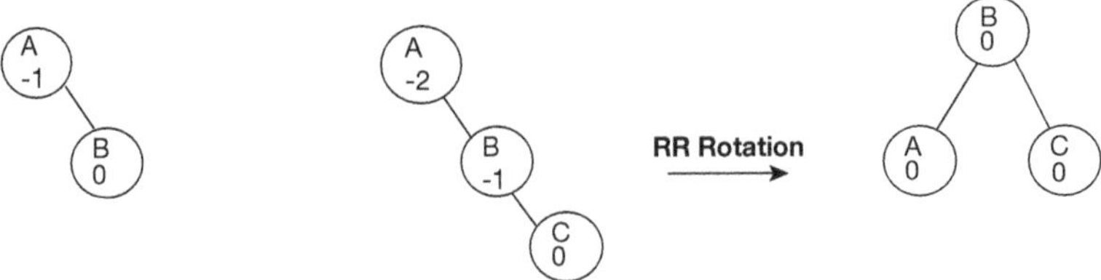

Figure: Balance sub-tree **Figure:** Rebalanced sub-tree **Figure:** Unbalanced sub-tree

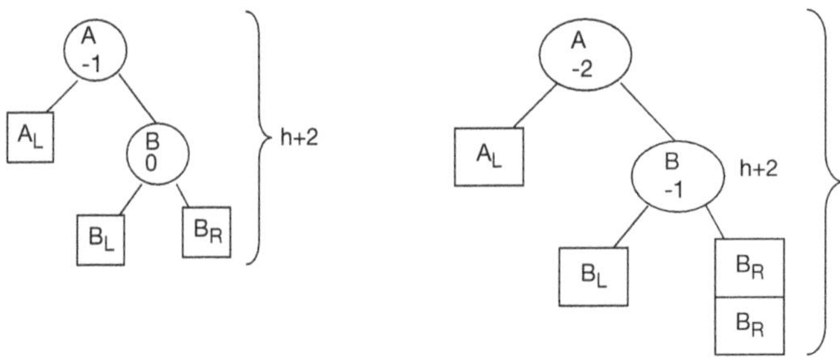

Figure: Balanced sub-tree **Figure:** Unbalanced sub-tree (height of B_R increased to height h+1)

Apply RR Rotation

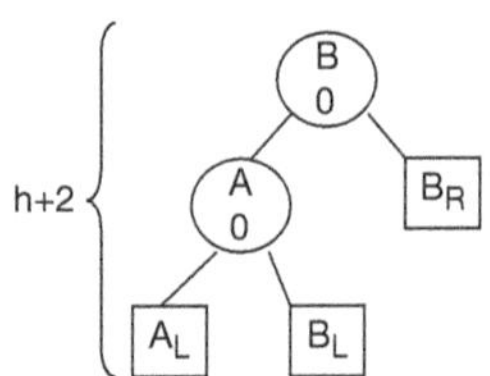

Figure: Rebalanced sub-tree (Height of sub-tree B remains h+1)

3. Left-to-Right rotation (LR Rotation)

In this, unbalance occurred due to the insertion in the right sub–tree of the left child of the root node. So, this is known as left to right insertion. LR rotation involves two rotations for the manipulation in pointers. In other words, it is used when the new node is inserted in the right sub-tree of left sub-tree of a node A.

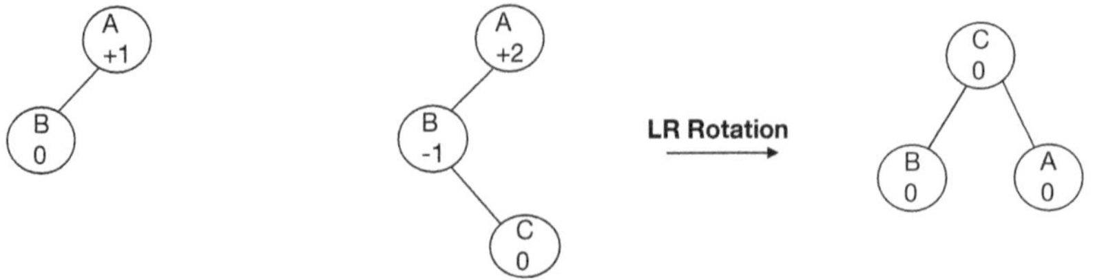

Figure: Balanced sub-tree **Figure:** Rebalanced sub-tree

Figure: Unbalanced sub-tree

Rotation 1 : The left sub-tree (C_L) of the right child (C) of the left child (B) of pivot node (A) becomes the right sub-tree of the left child (B). The left child (B) of the pivot node (A) becomes the left child of C.

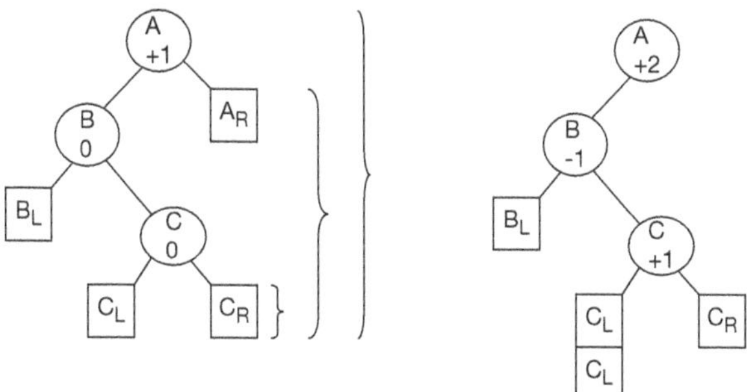

Figure: Balanced sub-tree

Figure: Unbalanced sub-tree (height of C_L increased to height h+1)

Apply R1 Rotation

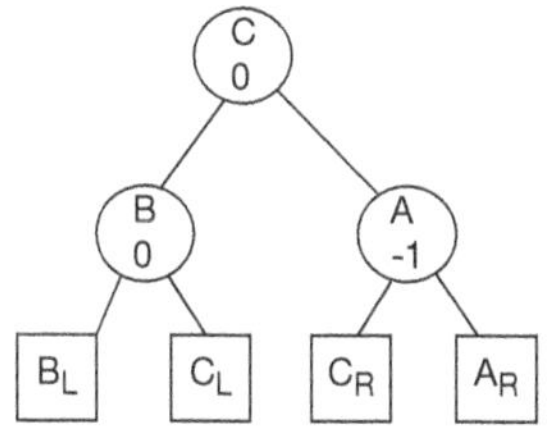

Figure: Rebalanced sub-tree

Rotation 2: The right sub-tree (C_R) of the left child (C) of the left child (B) of the pivot node becomes the left sub-tree of A and A becomes the right child of C.

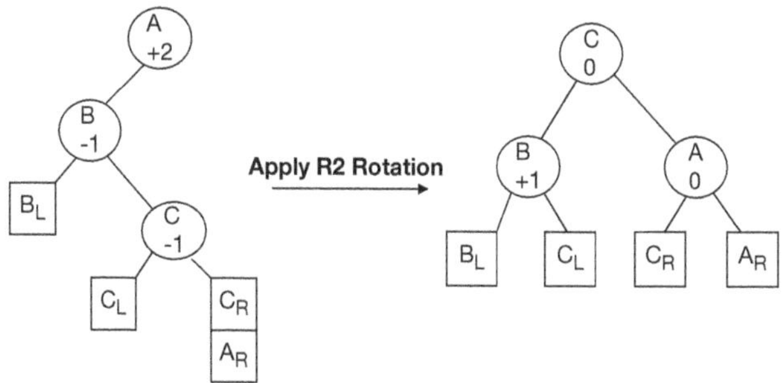

Figure: Unbalanced sub-tree (height of C_R Increased to height h+1)

Figure: Rebalanced sub-tree

4. Right-to-Left rotation (RL Rotation)

In this, unbalance occurred due to the insertion in the left sub-tree of the right child of the root node. This is known as right-to-left rotation. RL Rotation is the mirror image of LR–Rotation. Here there are two rotations for the manipulation of pointers. They are the following:

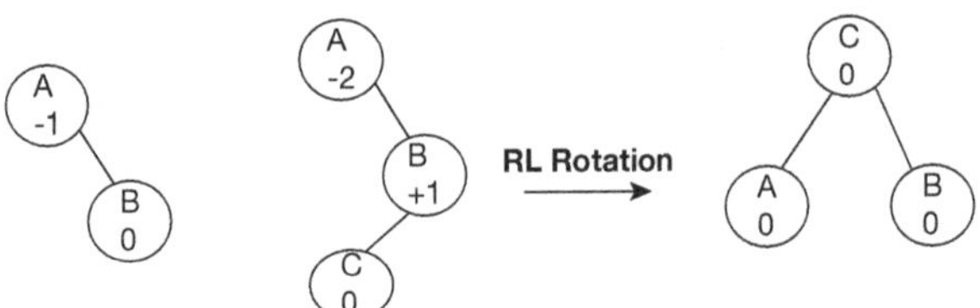

Figure: Balanced sub-tree **Figure:** Rebalanced sub-tree
Figure: Unbalanced sub-tree

Rotation 1 : The left sub-tree (CL) of the left child (C) of the right child (B) of the root node becomes the right sub-tree of A.

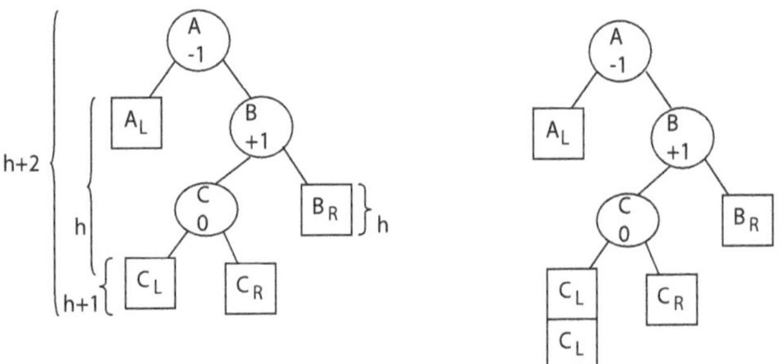

Figure: Balanced Tree **Figure:** Unbalanced sub-tree (height of C_L increased to height h+1)

Apply R1 Rotation

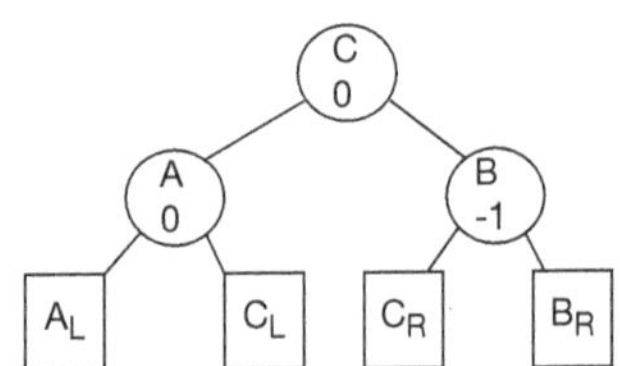

Figure: Rebalanced sub-tree

Rotation 2: The right sub-tree (C_R) of the left child (C) of the right child (B) of root node (A) becomes the left sub-tree of B and the right child (B) of the root node becomes the right child of C

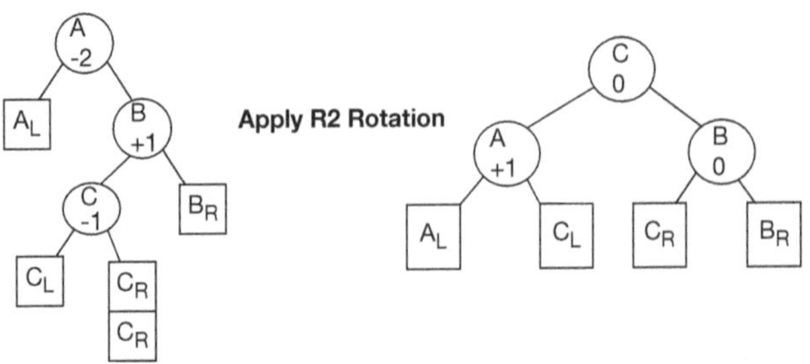

Figure: Unbalanced sub-tree (height of C_R increased to height h+1) **Figure:** Rebalanced sub-tree

6.18 INSERTION IN AN AVL TREE

We can insert a new node in an AVL tree by finding its appropriate position similar to that of the binary search tree. But insertion of a new node involves certain overheads since the tree may become unbalanced due to the increase in its height.

1. If the data item with key ‘k’ is inserted into empty AVL tree, then the node with key ‘k’ is set to be the root node. In this case, the tree node. In this case, the tree is height balanced.
2. If tree contains only single node, i.e., root node, then the insertion of the node with key ‘k’ depends upon its value. If the value of ‘k’ is less than the key value of the root then it is inserted to the left of the root otherwise right of the root. In this case the tree is height Balanced.
3. If on inserting the node with key ‘k’ the height of the right sub-tree of the root has increased.
4. If on inserting a node with key ‘k’ the height of the left sub-tree of the root is increased *i.e.*,
   (*a*) Height of the right sub-tree of the left sub-tree of the root node is increased.
   (*b*) Height of the left sub-tree of the root node is increased.

Example: insertion of the following keys in an AVL tree

55 66 77 15 11 33 22 35 25 44 88 99

Solution:

Insert 55: 55 0

Insert 66: 55 -1, 66 0

Insert 77:

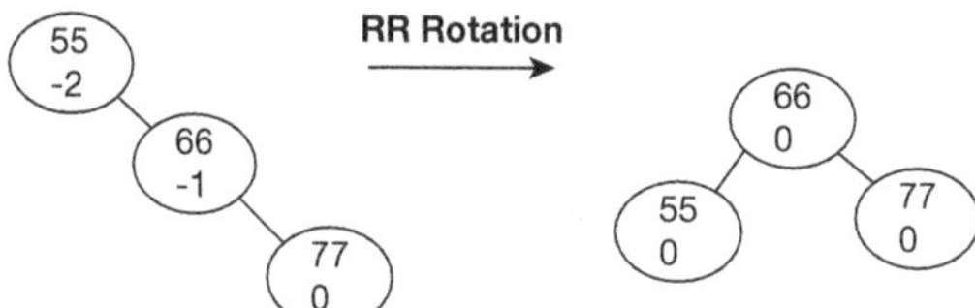

Insert 15:

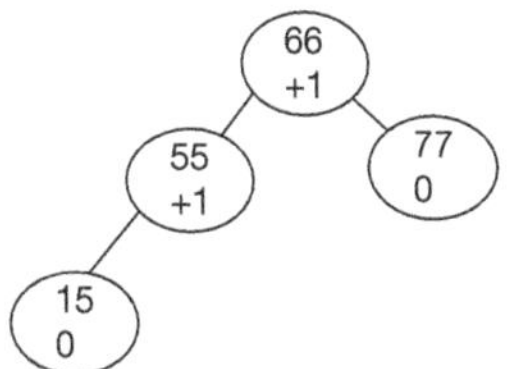

Insert 11:

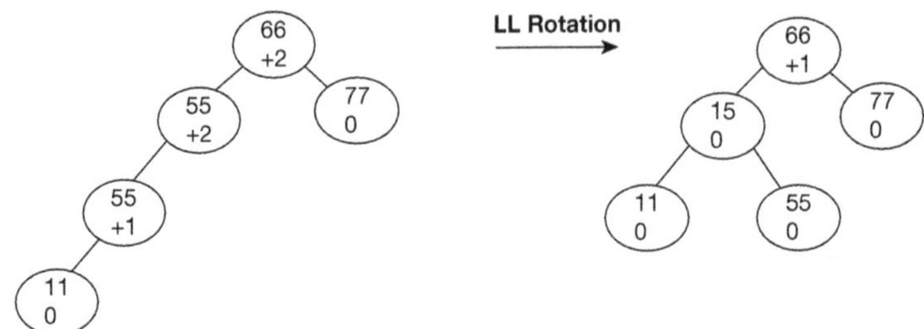

Insert 33:

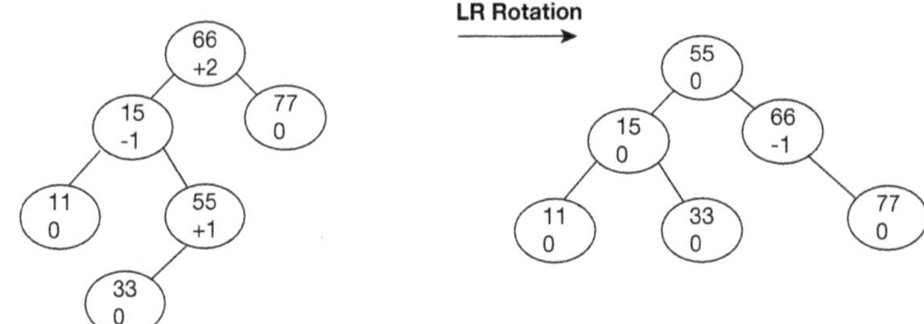

Insert 22:

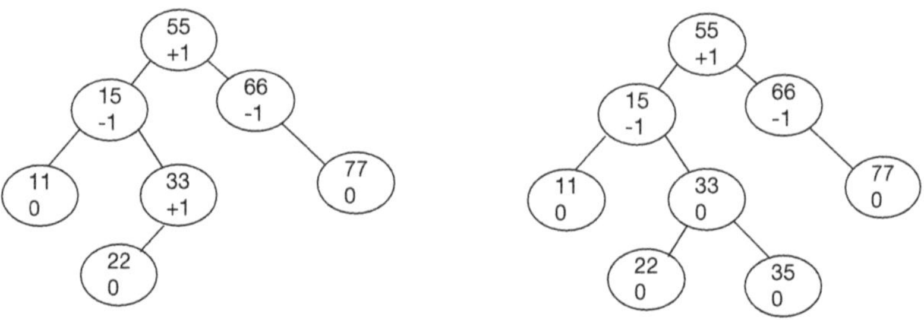

Insert 25: **RL Rotation**

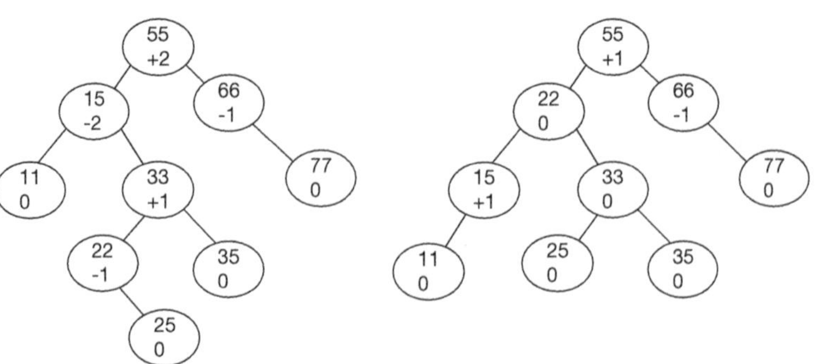

6.19 DELETION IN AN AVL TREE

The deletion of a node from an AVL tree is exactly the same as the deletion of a node from the BST. The sequence of steps to be followed in deleting a node from an AVL tree is as follows:

1. Initially, the AVL tree is searched to find the node to be deleted.
2. The procedure used to delete a node in an AVL tree is the same as deleting the node in the binary search tree.
3. After deletion of the node, check the balance factor of each node.
4. Rebalance the AVL tree if the tree is unbalanced. For this, AVL rotations are used.

Example: consider the AVL tree given in figure and deletes some nodes from it one by one:

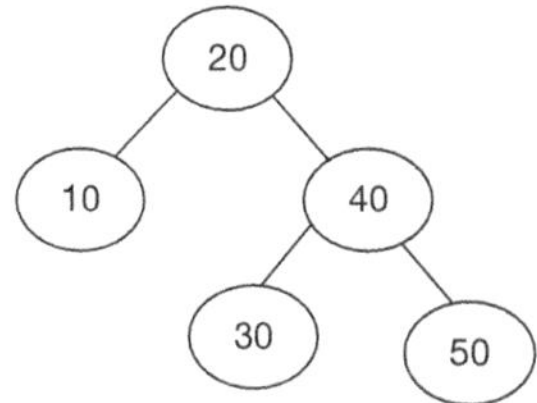

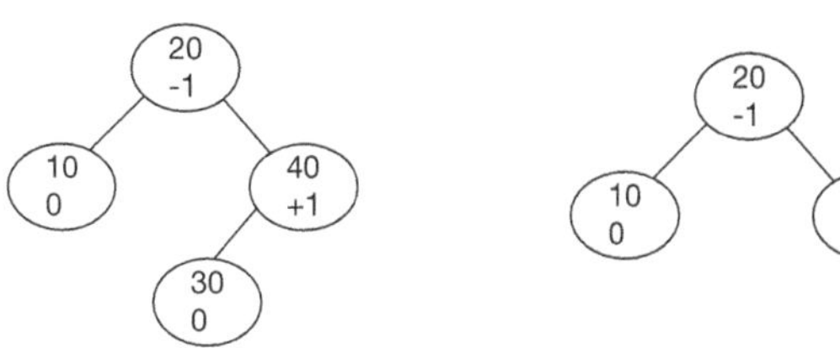

6.20 RED-BLACK TREE

A red-black tree is a binary search tree in which every node has a colour which is either red or black. Recall that an extended binary tree is a tree in which all NULL links are replaced by special nodes that are called external nodes. The properties of a red-black tree are as follows:

Property 1: The colour of a node is either red or black.

Property 2: The colour of the root node is always black.

Property 3: All leaf nodes are black.

Property 4: Every red node has both the children coloured in black.

Property 5: Every simple path from a given node to any of its leaf nodes has an equal number of black nodes.

All paths from a node n to any external node will have same number of black nodes. If a path from root to external node has all the black nodes, then it will be the longest possible path. Since, black height of root node is k, each path will have k black nodes. Therefore, the total nodes in shortest possible path will be k and total nodes in longest possible path will be 2k. Thus, we see that no path in a red-black tree can be more than twice another node is at most $2\log_2 (n+1)$.

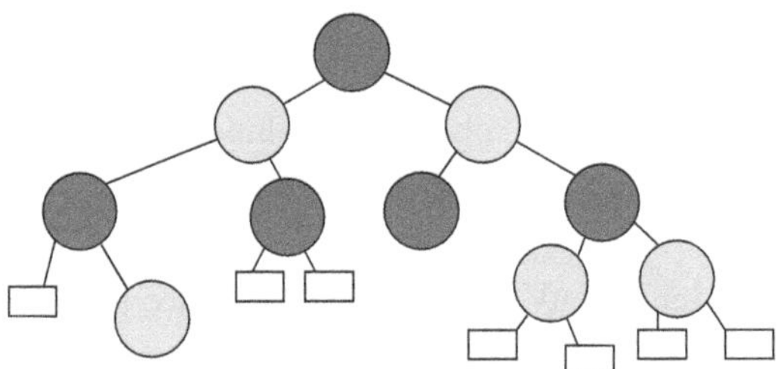

6.21 INSERTION A NODE IN A RED-BLACK TREE

The insertion operations start in the same way as we add a new node in the binary search tree. However, in a binary search tree, we always add the new node as a leaf, while in a red-black tree, leaf node contain no data. So instead of adding the new node as a leaf node, we add a red interior node that has two black leaf nodes. Remember that the colour of the new node is red and its leaf nodes are coloured in black. Once a new node is added, it may violate some property of the red-black tree. So in order to restore their property, we check for certain cases and restore depending on the case that turns up after insertion. Before learning these cases in detail, first let us discuss certain important terms that will be used.

(*i*) Grandparent node (G) of a node n refers to the parent of n's parent (P).

(*ii*) Uncle node (U) of a node n refers to the sibling of n's parents (P).

When we insert a new node in a red-black tree, note the following points:

1. All leaf nodes are always black. So property 3 always holds true.
2. Property 4 (both children of every red node are black) is threatened only by adding a red node, repainting a black node red, or a rotation.
3. Property 5 (all paths from any given node to its leaf nodes has equal number of black nodes) is threatened only by adding a black node, repainting a red node black, or a rotation.

Case 1: The new node n is added as the root of the tree

In this case, n is repainting black, as the root of the tree is always black. Since n adds one black node to every path at once.

Case 2: The new node's parent P is black

In this case, both children of every red node are black, so property 4 is not invalidated. Property 5 is also not threatened. This is because the new node n has two black leaf children, but because n is red, the paths through each of its children have same number of black nodes. In the following cases, it is assumed that n has a grandparent node G, because its parent P is red, and if it were the root, it would be black. Thus, n also has an uncle node U, irrespective of whether U is a leaf node or an internal node.

Case 3: If both the Parent (P) and the Uncle (U) are red

In this case, property 5 which says all paths from any given node to its leaf nodes have an equal number of black nodes is violated. In order to restore property 5, both node (P and U) are repainting black and the grandparent G is repainted red. Now, the new red node n has a black parent. Since, any path through the parent or uncle must pass through the grand parent, the number of black nodes on these paths has not changed. However, the grandparent G may now violate property 2 which says that the root node is always black or property 4 which states that both children of every red node are black. Property 4 will be violated when G has a red parent.

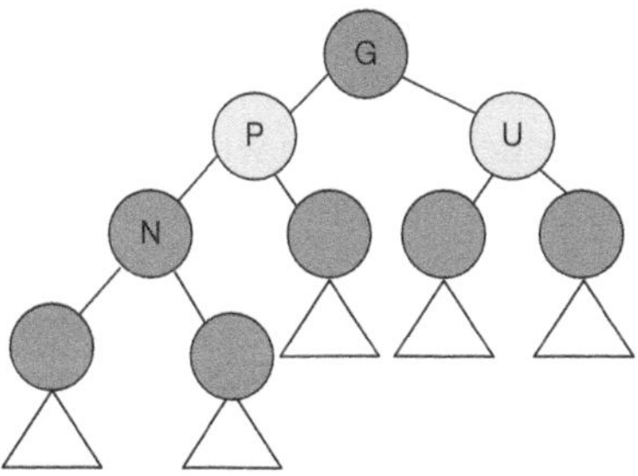

Case 4: the parent P is red but the uncle U is black and n is the right child of P and P is the left child of G

In this case, a left rotation is done to switch the roles of the new node n and its parent P. After the rotation, we have re-labelled n and P and then, case 5 is called to deal with the new node's parent. This is done because property 4 which says both children of every red node should be black is still violated.

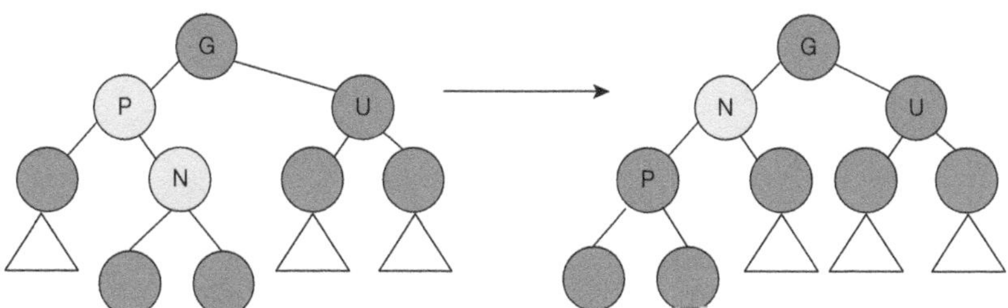

Case 5: The parent P is red but the uncle U is black and the new node n is the left child of P, and P is the left child of its parent G.

In this case, a right rotation on G the grandparent of n is performed. After this rotation, the former parent P is now the parent of both the new node n and the former grandparent G. We know that the colour of G is black because otherwise its former child P could not have been red, so now switch the colours of P and

G so that the resulting tree satisfies property 4 which states that both children of a red node are black. Note that in case n is the right child of P and P is the right child of G, we perform a left rotation.

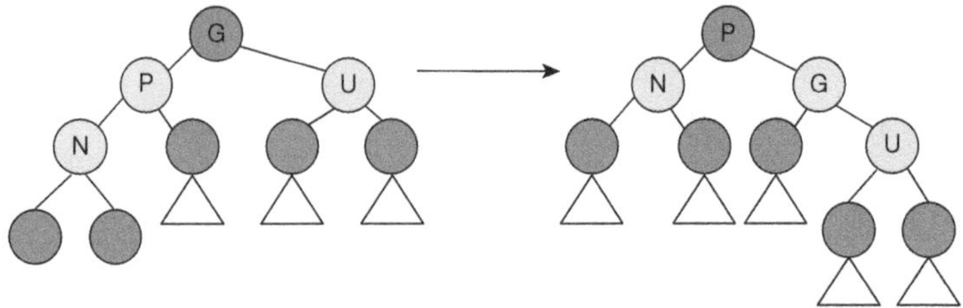

6.22 DELETING A NODE FROM RED-BLACK TREE

We start deleting a node from a red-black tree in the same way as we do in case of a binary search tree. In this section, we will assume that we are deleting a node with at most one non-leaf child, which we will call its child. In this case node has both leaf children, and then let one of them is its child. While deleting a node, if its colour is red, then we can simply replace it with its child, which must be black. All paths through the deleted node will simply pass through one less red node, and both the deleted node's parent and child must be black, so none of the properties will be violated. Another simple case is when we delete a black node that has a red child. In this case, property 4 and property 5 could be violated, so to restore them, just repaint the deleted node's child with black. However, a complex situation arises when both the node to be deleted as well as its child is black. In this case, we begin by replacing the node to be deleted with its child.

Case 1: n is the new root

In this case, we have removed one black node from every path, and the new root is black, so none of the properties are violated.

Case 2: Sibling S is red

In this case, interchange the colours of P and S, and then rotate left at P. In the resultant tree, S will become n's grandparent.

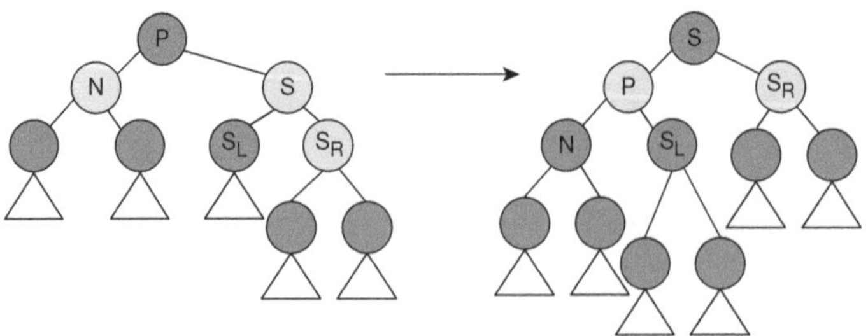

Case 3: P, S and S's Children are Black

In this case, simply repaint S with red. In the resultant tree, all the paths passing through S will have one less black node. Therefore, all the paths that pass through P now have one fewer black nodes than the paths that do not pass through P, so property 5 is still violated.

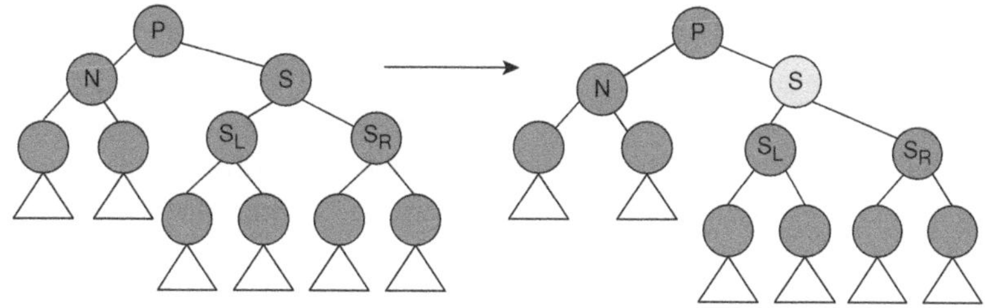

Case 4: S and S's Children are black, but P is red

In this case, we interchange the colours of S and P. Although this will not affect the number of black nodes on the paths going through S, it will add one black node to the paths going through n, making up for the deleted black node on those paths.

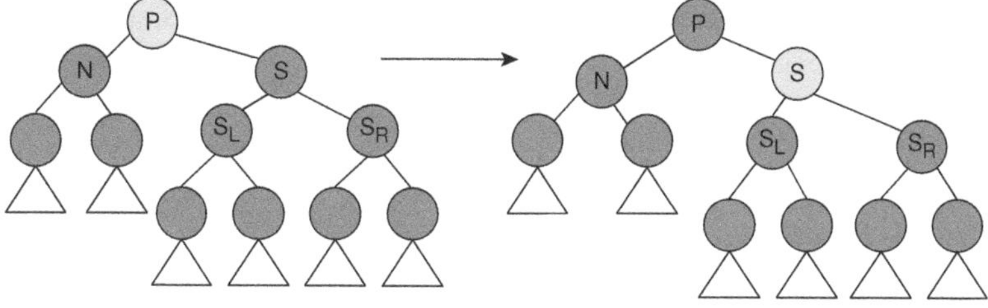

Case 5: n is the left child of P and S is black, S's left child is red and right child is black

In this case, perform a right rotation at S. After the rotation, S's left child become S's parent and n's new sibling. Also interchange the colours of S and its new parent.

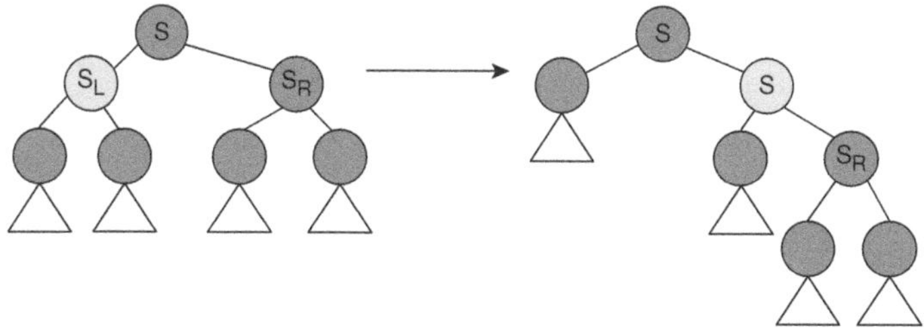

Case 6: S is black, S's right child is red, and n is the left child of its parent P

In this case, a left rotation is done at P to make S the parent of P and S's right child. After the rotation, the colours of P and S are interchanged and S's right child is coloured black.

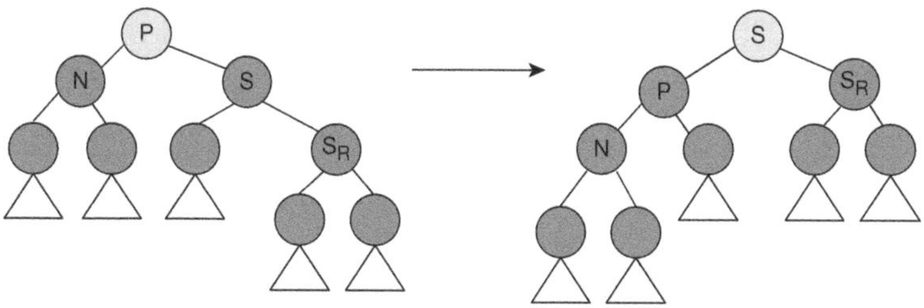

6.23 APPLICATIONS OF RED-BLACK TREE

Red-black trees are efficient binary search tree, as they offer worst case time guarantee for insertion, deletion and search operations. Red-black trees are not only valuable in time-sensitive applications such as real-time applications, but are also preferred to be used as a building block in other data structures which provides worst-case guarantee.

B-Tree and its Variants

All the data structures discussed so far favour data stored in the internal memory and hence support internal information retrieval. However, to favour retrieval and manipulation of data stored in external memory viz., storage devices such as disks etc. There is a need for some special data structures such as M-way search trees B-trees and B^+ trees.

Why do we need another tree structure?

1. In database programs, the data is too large to fit in memory; therefore, it is stored on secondary storage (disks or tapes).
2. Disk access is very expensive; the disk I/O operation takes milliseconds while CPU operation takes nanoseconds *i.e*; CPU is one million times faster.
3. When dealing with external storage the disk accesses dominate the running time.
4. Balance binary search trees (AVL & Red-Black) have good performance if the entire data can fit in the main memory.
5. These trees are not optimised for external storage and require many disk accesses, thus give poor performance for very large data.
6. Data is transfered to and from the disk in blocks.
7. To reduce disk accesses.

(*a*) Reduce tree height by increasing the number of children of a node.

(*b*) Store multiple records in a block on the disk.

8. To achieve above goals we use Multi way (M-way) search tree, which is a generalisation of BST, binary search tree.

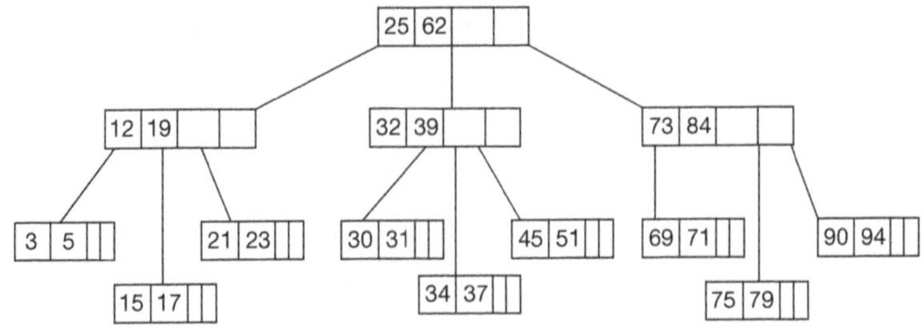

Figure: 4-way Search Tree

6.24 MULTI-WAY SEARCH TREES

M-way search trees are generalised versions of binary search trees. The goal of m-way search tree is to minimise the accesses while retrieving a key from a file. However, an M-way search tree of height h calls for O (h) number of accesses for an insert, delete, and retrieval operation. Hence, it pays to ensure that the height h is close to $\log_m (n+1)$, because the number of elements in an M-way search tree of height h ranges from a minimum of h to a maximum of M^h-1. This implies that an M-way search tree of n elements ranges from a minimum of height of $\log_m(n+1)$ to a maximum height of n. Therefore, there arises the need to maintain balanced M-way search trees.

Trees having (m-1) keys and m children are called M-way search trees. A binary tree is 2-way tree. It means that it has m-1=2-1=1 key (here m=2) in every node and it can have maximum of two children. A binary tree also called an M-way tree of order 3 is a tree in which key values could be either 1 or 2.

1. In an M-way tree all the nodes have degree < m.
2. The keys in each node are in ascending order $k_1 < k_2 < k_i$
3. The key K_i is larger than keys in sub-tree pointed by P_i and smaller than keys in sub tree pointed by P_{i+1}
4. The sub-trees are the M-way trees.

Searching a Multi-Way Tree

Searching for a key in an M-way search tree is similar to that of binary search trees. The procedure is as follows.

1. If the key is less than k_1 and k_2 then the search is continued in M-way search tree pointed to by pointer p_1
2. If the key lies between k_1 and k_2 than the search is continued in M-way search tree pointed to p_2
3. If the key lies between k_2 and k_3 then the search is continued in M-way search tree pointed to by pointer p_3
4. If the key is greater than k_{q-1} then search is continued in M-way search tree pointed by p_q

The steps are carried on recursively till either the key is found or the M-way search tree is empty.

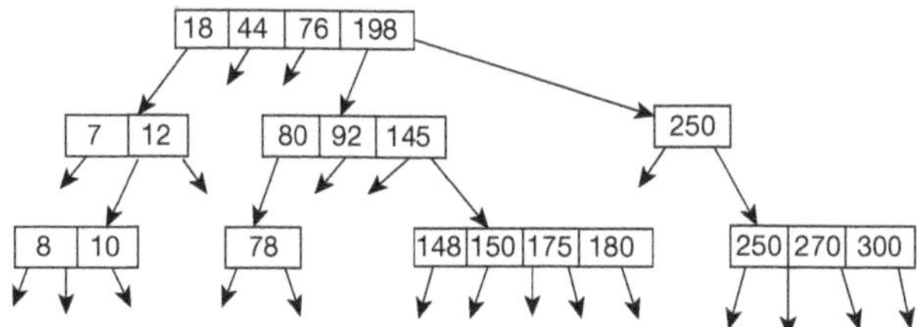

Insertion in an Multi-Way Search Tree

To insert a new element into an M-way search tree, we proceed in the same way as one would in order to search an element. To insert 9 into the 5-way search tree shown in figure, we proposed to search for 9 and find that we fall off the tree at the node [8, 10]. Since the node has only two keys and a 5-way search tree can accommodate upto 4 keys in a single node. 9 is inserted into the node.

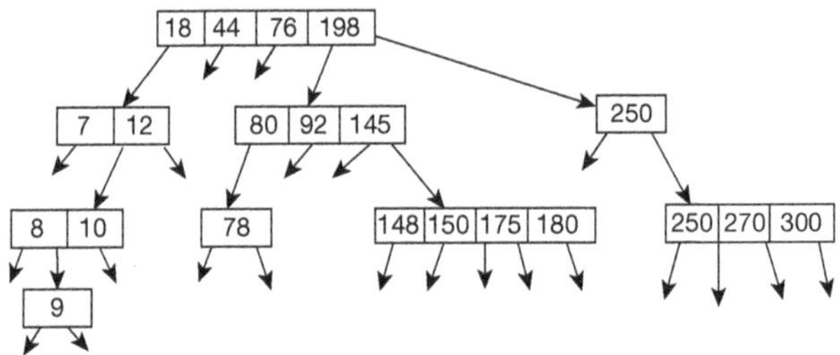

Deletion in Multi-Way Search Tree

Let K be a key to be deleted from the M-way search tree. To delete the key we proceed as one would to search for the key. Suppose the node accommodating the key is as follows.

1. If (A_i=A_j = NULL) then delete K.
2. If ($A_i \neq$ NULL, A_j = NULL) then choose the largest of the key elements K' in the child node pointed to by Ai delete the key K' and replace K by K'. Obviously deletion of K' may call for subsequent replacements and therefore deletions in similar manner, to enable the key K' moves up the tree.
3. If (A_i = NULL, $A_j \neq$ NULL) then choose the smallest of the key elements K" from the sub tree pointed to by A_j delete "K" and replace K by "K". Again deletion of "K" may trigger subsequent replacements and deletions to enable key "K" move up the tree.
4. If ($A_i \neq$ NULL, $A_j \neq$ NULL) then choose the largest of the key elements K' in the sub tree pointed to by Ai or the smallest of the key elements "K" from the sub tree pointed by A_j to replace K. As mentioned before to move K' or K" up the tree it may call for subsequent replacements and deletions.

To delete 175, we search for 175 and we get that in the leaf node [148, 150, 175, 180] where it is present. Hence, both Ai=NULL, Aj=NULL. So, We therefore, delete 175 and the node becomes [148, 150, 180].

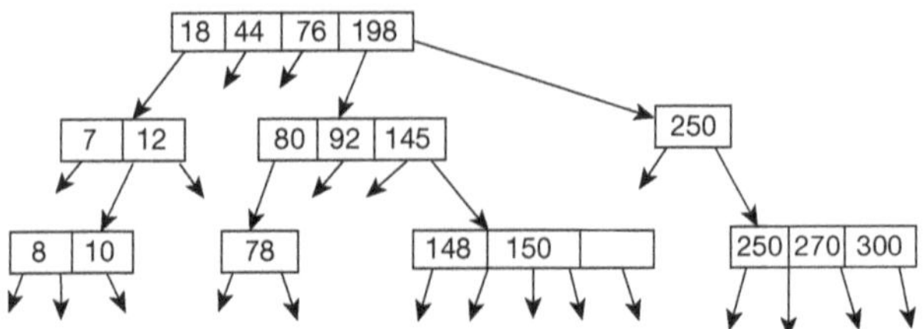

6.25 B TREE

In Multi-Way search tree, so many nodes have left sub tree but no right sub-tree. Similarly they have right sub-tree but no left sub tree. Insertion of key also increases the height of tree. As we know that the access time in tree is totally dependent on level of tree. So our aim is to minimise the access time which can be though balanced tree only. So we have a need to take all the leaf nodes at same level and non leaf nodes should not contain the empty sub-tree. So for an order where k<=n-1. For balancing the tree each node should contain n/2 keys. So the B- tree of order n can be defined as:

1. Each node has at least n/2 and maximum n non- empty children.
2. All leaf nodes will be at same level.
3. All leaf nodes can contain maximum n-1 keys.
4. All non-leaf nodes can contain m-1 keys where m is the number of children for that node.
5. Keys in non-leaf node will divide the left and right sub tree where value of left sub-tree keys will be less and value of right sub-tree keys will be more than that particular key.

A balanced order-n, multi-way search tree in which non root node contains at least [(n-1)/2] keys is called a B-tree of order n. A B-tree of order n is also called an n-(n-1) tree or an (n-1)-n tree. That is each node in the tree has a maximum of n-1 keys and n children thus, a 4-5 tree is a B-tree of order 5, as is a 5-4 tree. In particular, a 2-3 (or 3-2) tree is the most elementary nontrivial B- tree with one or two keys per node and two or three sons per node.

In discussing B-trees, the word ''order'' is used differently by different authors. It is common to find the order of a B-tree defined as the minimum number of keys in a non-root node. *i.e.*, (n-1)/2 and the degree of a B-tree to mean the maximum number of keys in a node *i.e.*, n-1. A B-tree is a rooted tree having the following properties:

1. Every node x has the following fields:
   (*a*) n [x] the number of keys currently stored in order x.
   (*b*) The n[x] keys themselves stored in non decreasing order, so, that $key_1 [x] \le key_2 [x] \le .... key_{n[x]}[x]$
   (*c*) Leaf [x], a Boolean value is TRUE if x is a leaf and FALSE if x is an internal node.
2. Each internal node x also contains n[x]+1 pointers $c_1[x]$, $C_2[x]....C_{n[x]+1} [x]$ to its children. Leaf nodes have no children, so their C_i fields are under fined.
3. The Keys key_i [x] separate the range of keys stored in each sub tree: if K_i is any key stored in the sub tree with root $C_i[x]$ then. $K_1 \le key_1[x] \le k_2 \le key_2 [x] \le .... \le key_{n[x]} [x] \le key_{n[x]} + 1$.

4. All leaves have the same depth, which is the tree's height h.
5. There are lower and upper bounds on the number of keys a node can contain. These bounds are expressed in terms of a fixed integer $i \geq 2$ called the minimum degree of the B-tree:
   (*a*) Every node other than the root must have at least t-1 key. Every internal node other than the root has at-least t children. If the tree is non empty, the root must have at-least one key.
   (*b*) Every node can contain at most 2t-1 key. Therefore, an internal node can have atmost 2t children. We say that a node is full if it contains exactly 2t-1 keys.

6.26 INSERTION IN B-TREE

The insertion of key in a B-tree requires first traversal in B-tree. Through traversal it will find that key to be inserted is already existing or not. Suppose key does not exist in tree then through traversal it will reach leaf node. Now we have two cases for inserting the key.

1. Node is not full
2. Node is already full

If the leaf node in which the key is to be inserted is not full, then the insertion is done in the node. A node is said to be full if it contains a maximum of (m-1) keys, given the order of the B-tree to be m. If the node were to be full, then insert the key in order into the existing set of keys in the node, split the node at its median into two nodes at the same level, pushing the median, and element up by one level. Note that the split nodes are only half full. Accommodate the median element in the parent node if it is not full. Otherwise repeat the same procedure and this may even call for rearrangement of the keys in the root node or the formation of a new root itself.

Example: Insert these numbers in a B-Tree of order 5.

20, 80, 55, 15, 116, 39, 76, 124, 103, 48, 200, 98, 175, 235, 28, 114, 132, 164

Solution:

Insert 20:

20

Insert 80:

20	80

Insert 55: after insertion of 55, the keys in node will be sorted.

20	55	80

Insert 15: after insertion of 15, the keys in node will be sorted.

15	20	55	80

Insert 116:

15	20	55	80	116

After insertion of 116, node is full, it splitted into two nodes, 55 is the median key so it will go in parent node but root node is splitted so it will become root.

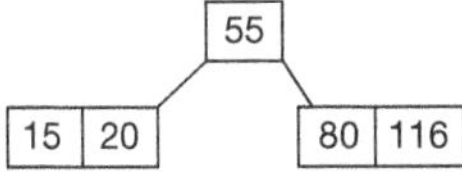

Insert 39:

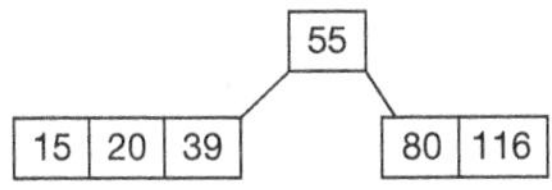

Insert 76:

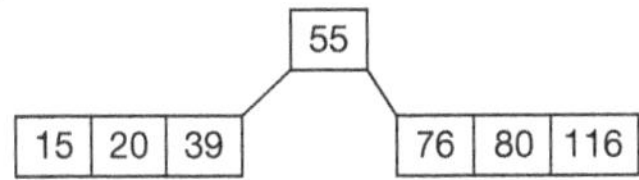

Insert 124:

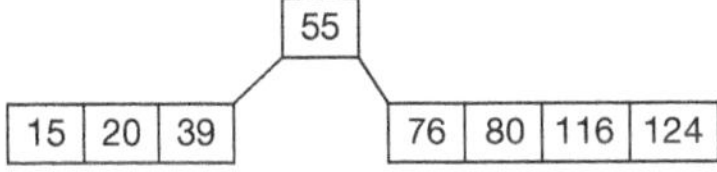

Insert103: After insertion of 103, node is full; it splitted into two nodes, 103 is the median key so it will go in parent node.

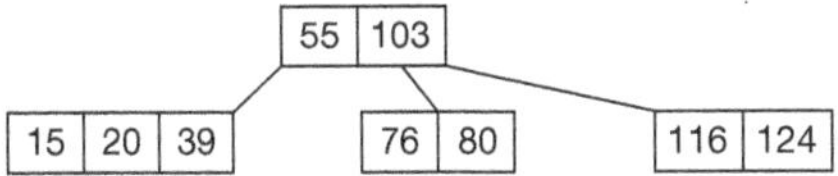

Insert 48:

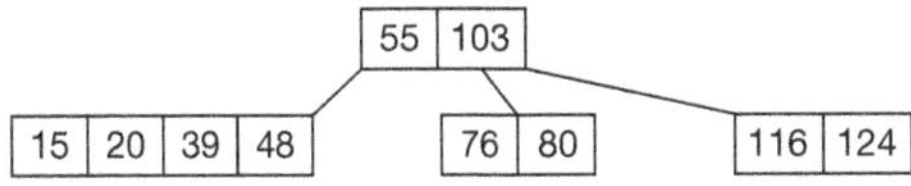

Insert 200:

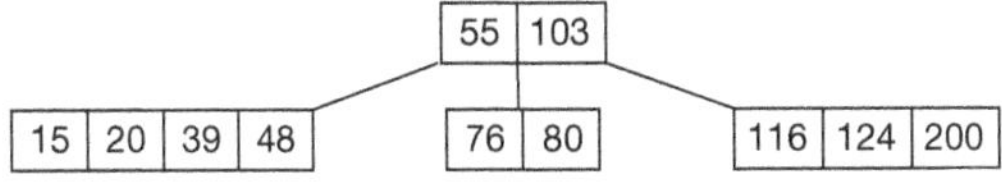

Insert 98:

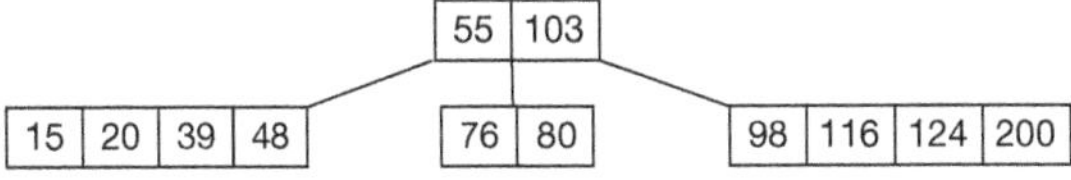

Insert 175: After insertion of 175, node is full; it splitted into two nodes, 124 is the median key so it will go in parent node

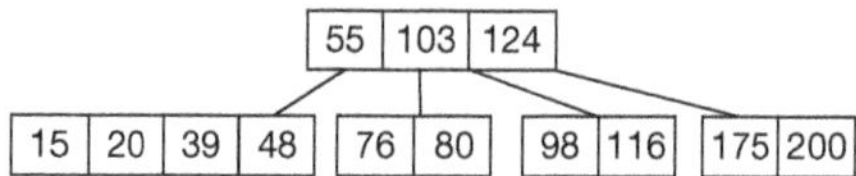

Insert 235:

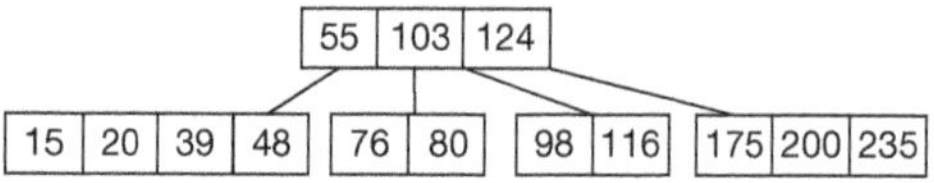

Insert 28: After insertion of 28, node is full; it splitted into two nodes, 28 is the median key so it will go in parent node.

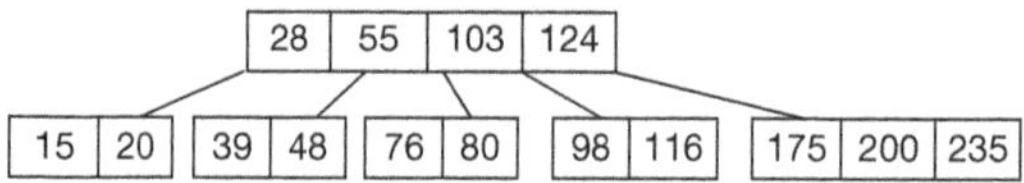

Insert 114:

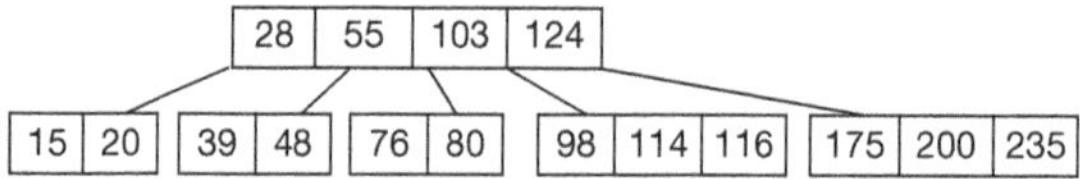

Insert 132:

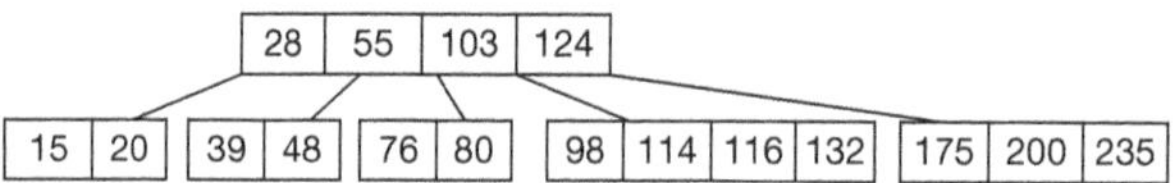

Insert 164: After insertion of 164, node is full; it splitted into two nodes, 116 is the median key so it will go in parent node. Here root is already full, so it splitted in two nodes, 103 is the median key so it will become the new root.

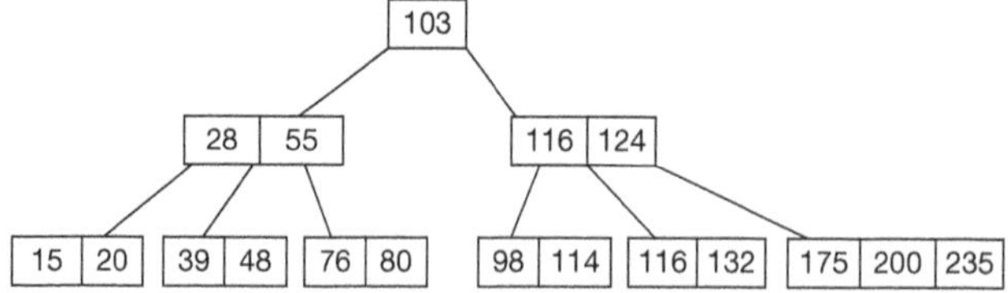

6.27 DELETION IN B-TREE

Deletion of key also requires first traversal in B-tree, after reaching on particular node, two cases may occur.

1. Node is leaf node
2. Node is non-leaf node

For the first case suppose node has more than minimum number of keys then it can be easily deleted. But suppose it has only minimum number of keys then first key of the adjacent node will go to the parent node and key in parent node which is partitioning will be combined together in one node. Suppose, now parent has also less than the minimum number of keys then the thing will be repeated until it will get the node which has more than the minimum number of keys. For the second case key will be deleted and its predecessor and successor key have minimum number of keys then the nodes of predecessor and successor keys will be combined. Thus, while removing a key from a leaf node, if the node contains more than the minimum number of elements, then key can be easily removed. However, if the leaf node contains just the minimum number of elements, then scout for an element from either the left sibling node or right sibling node to fill the vacancy. If the left sibling node has more than the minimum number of keys. Pull the largest key up into the parent node and move down the intervening entry from the parent node to the leaf node where the key is to be deleted. Otherwise, pull the smallest key of the right sibling node to the parent node and move down the intervening parent element to the leaf node.

If both the sibling nodes have only minimum number of entries, then create a new leaf node out of the two leaf nodes and the intervening element of the parent node, ensuring that the total number does not exceed the maximum limit for a node. If while borrowing the intervening element from the parent node, it leaves the number of keys in the parent node to be below the minimum number, then we propagate the process upwards ultimately resulting in a reduction of height of the B-tree.

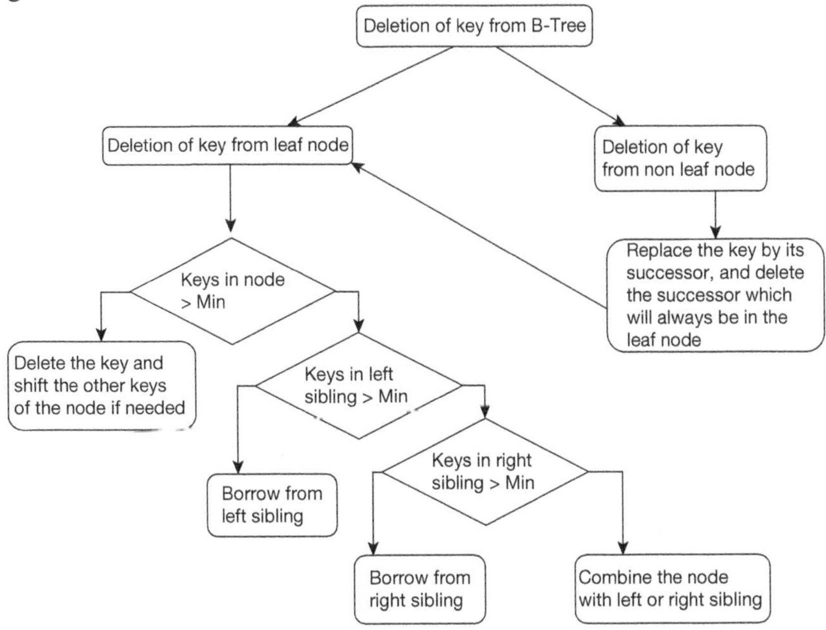

Example: Let us take a B-Tree of order 5

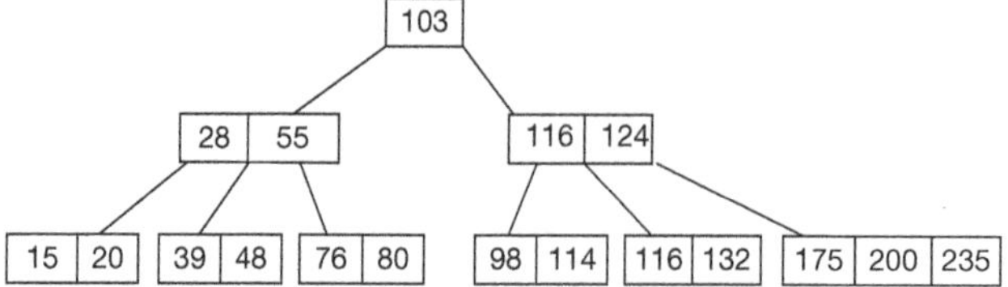

Delete 175: here 175 are in leaf node, so delete it from only leaf node.

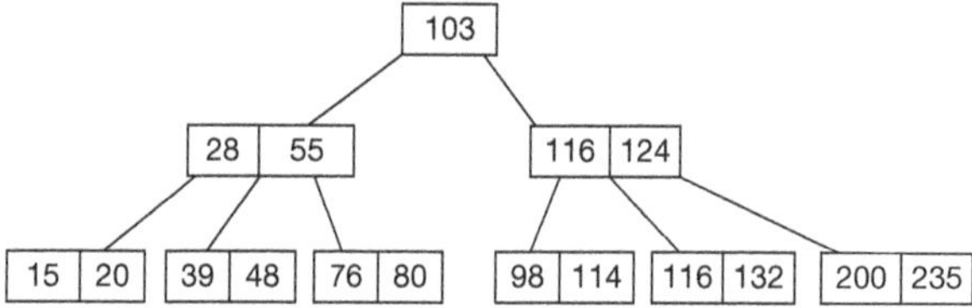

Delete 55: here 55 are in non leaf node. So first it will be deleted from the node and then the element of right side child will come in the node

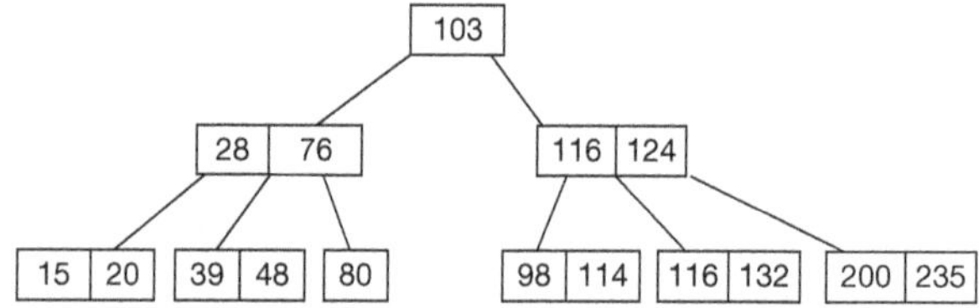

Delete 39: here first 39 will be deleted from leaf node then left side element in the parent node will come in leaf node and then last element of the left side node of the parent node will come in parent node.

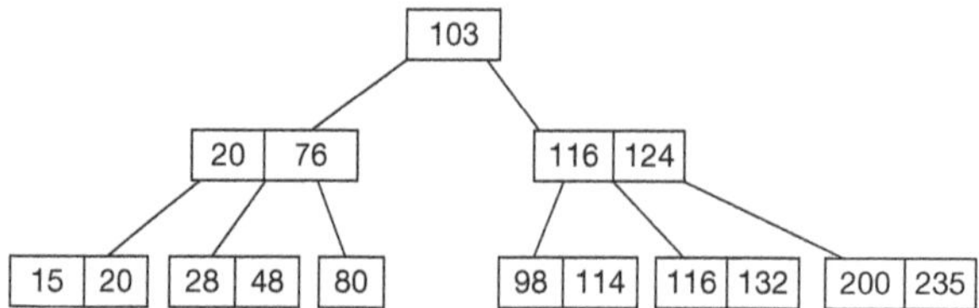

6.28 APPLICATION OF B-TREE

The main application of a B- tree is the organisation of a huge collection of records into a file structure. The organisation should be in such a way that any record in it can be searched very efficiently *i.e.*, insertion, deletion and modification operations can be carried out perfectly and efficiently.

6.29 B^+ TREES

The B-tree structure is the standard organisation for indexes in a database system. There are several variations of the B-tree, most well known being the B* tree and B^+ tree. The B-tree guarantees at least 50% storage utilisation that is at any given time, the tree has each of nodes at least 50% full. The B^+ tree is a slightly different data structure, which in addition to indexed access, also allows sequential data processing and stores all data in the lowest level of the tree.

One of the major drawbacks of the B-tree is the difficulty of traversing the keys sequentially. B^+ tree retains the rapid random access property of the B-tree, while also allowing rapid sequential access. In the B^+ tree, all keys are maintained in leaves and keys are replicated in non-leaf nodes to define the paths for locating individual records. The leaves are linked together to provide a sequential path for traversing the keys in the tree. The B^+ tree is called a balanced tree because every path from the root node to leaf node is the same length. A balance tree means that all searches for individual values require the same number of nodes to be read from the disk.

B^+ Tree

(*i*) is a structure of nodes linked by pointers

(*ii*) is anchored by a special node called the root and bounded by leaves

(*iii*) has a unique path to each leaf, and all paths are of equal length

(*iv*) store keys only at leaves, and stores reference values in other, internal node

(*v*) guides key search, via the reference values from the root to the leaves

B+ tree of order M (M>3) is a M-ary tree with the following properties:

(*i*) The data items are stored at leaves.

(*ii*) The root is either a leaf or has between two and M children.

(*iii*) Node

(*a*) The (internal node (non leaf) stores up to M-1 keys (redundant) to guide the searching; key i represents the smallest key in sub tree i+1.

(*b*) All nodes (except the root) have between [M/2] and M children.

(*iv*) Leaf:

(*a*) A leaf has between [L/2] and L data items, for some L (usually L << M, but we will assume M=L in most examples).

(*b*) All leaves are at the same depth.

(*v*) Less disk accesses due to fewer levels in the tree.

(*vi*) B^+ tree provides faster sequential access of data.

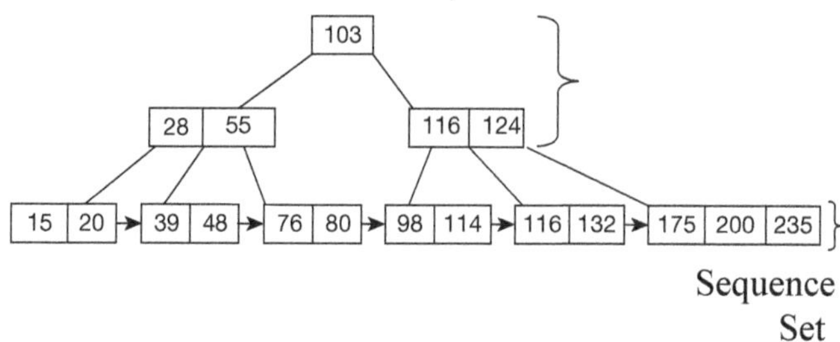

As we can see in the figure, the leaves have been connected to from a linked list of keys in sequential order. The B$^+$ Tree has two parts the first part is the index set that constitutes interior nodes and the second part is the sequential set that constitutes leaves.

B$^+$ Tree Structure

B$^+$ Tree consists of two parts:

Index Set

(*i*) Provide indexes for fast access of data.

(*ii*) Consist of internal nodes that store only key & sub tree pointers.

Sequence Set

(*i*) Consists of leaf nodes that contain data pointers.

(*ii*) Provides efficient sequential access of data (using doubly linked list).

Searching key in a B$^+$ Tree

(*i*) Start from the root

(*ii*) If an internal node is reached

(*iii*) Search KEY among the keys in that node

(*iv*) Linear search of binary search

(*v*) If KEY $\leq$ smallest key, follow the leftmost child pointer down

(*vi*) If KEY > largest key, follow the rightmost child pointer down

(*vii*) If $K_i \leq$ KEY K_j, follow the child pointer between K_i and K_j

(*viii*) If a leaf is reached

(*ix*) Search KEY among the keys stored in that leaf

(*x*) linear search or binary search

(*xi*) If found, return the corresponding record; otherwise report not found.

Insertion into a B^+ Tree

In order to insert a key into a B^+ Tree, first a B^+ Tree search is performed to find the correct location for the key. Actually, the procedure to insert a new key value into a B^+ Tree is almost as for B - Tree. The sequence to steps required to insert a node in a B^+ Tree are as follows:

1. The search operation is used to find the leaf node in which the value of node has to be inserted.
2. If the key value already exists in a leaf node, no more insertion is needed. Else if the said key value does not exist, insert the value in the leaf node in an ordered fashion.
3. When a node is split, the middle key is retained in the leaf half-node as well as being promoted to the father.

Deletion from a B^+ Tree

The sequence of steps required to delete a key value from the B+ Tree is as follows:

1. Search the B^+ Tree for the key value.
2. If the key value is in the B^+ Tree, remove it from the tree as that of B Tree.
3. When a key value is deleted from a leaf there is no need to delete that key from the index set of the key. That key value still can direct searches to proper leaves, since it is still a valid separator between the keys in the nodes below.

Difference between B-Tree and B^+ Tree

S.No	B-Tree	B^+ Tree
1	Data pointers are stored in all nodes.	Data printers are stored only in leaf nodes (sequential set).
2	Search can end at any node.	Search always ends at leaf node.
3	No redundant keys.	Redundant keys may exist.
4	Slow sequential access.	Efficient sequential access.
5	Higher trees.	Flatter trees. No data pointers in index set nodes.

6.30 APPLICATION OF TREES

1. Trees are used to store simple as well as complex data.
2. Integer value, character value and complex data means a structure or a record.

3. Trees are often used for implementing other types of data structures like hash tables, sets, and maps.
4. A self-balancing tree, Red-black tree is used to kernel scheduling, to pre-empt massively multi-processor computer operating system use.
5. Another variation of tree, B^+ trees is prominently used to store tree structures on disc. They are used to index a large number of records.
6. B-trees are also used for secondary indexes in databases, where the index facilitates a select operation to answer some range criteria.
7. Trees are an important data structure used for compiler construction.
8. Trees are also used in database design.
9. Trees are used in file system directories.
10. Trees are also widely used for information storage and retrieval in symbol tables.

POINTS TO REMEMBER

1. A tree is a data structure which is mainly used to store hierarchical data. A tree is recursively defined as collection of one or more nodes is designated as the root of the tree and the remaining nodes can be partitioned into non-empty sets each of which is a sub-tree of the root.
2. In a binary tree, every node has zero, one, or at the most two successors. A node that has no successors is called a leaf node or a terminal node. Every node other than the root node has a parent.
3. The degree of a node is equal to the number of children that a node has. The degree of a leaf node is zero. All nodes that are at the same level and share the same parent are called siblings.
4. Two binary trees having a similar structure are said to be copies if they have the same content at the corresponding nodes.
5. A binary tree of n nodes has exactly n-1 edges. The depth of a node N is given as the length of the path from the root R to the node N. the depth of the root node is zero
6. A binary tree of height h has at least h nodes and at most 2^{h-1} nodes.
7. In a complete binary tree, every level (except possibly the last) is completely filled and nodes appears as far left as possible.
8. The height of the binary tree with n nodes is at least $\log_2$ (n+1) and at most n. in-degree of a node is the number of edges arriving at that node. The root node is the only node that has an in-degree equal to zero.
9. A binary search tree, also known as an ordered binary tree, is a variant of binary tree in which all the nodes in the left sub-tree have a value less than that of the root node and all the nodes in the right sub-tree have a value either equal to or greater than the root node.

10. The average running time of a search operation is o ($\log_2$ n). However, in the worst case, a binary search tree will take o (n) time to search an element from the tree.
11. An AVL tree is a self-balanced tree which is also known as a height-balanced with it, which is calculated by subtracting the height of the right sub-tree from the height of the left sub-tree. In a height balanced tree, every node has a balanced factor of either 0, 1 or –1.
12. A red-black tree is a self-balancing binary search tree which is also called as a "symmetric binary B-Tree". Although a red-black tree is complex, it has good worst case running time for its operations and is efficient to use, as searching, insertion, and deletion can all be done in o (log n) time.
13. In a two-way threaded tree, also called a double threaded tree, threads will appear in both the left and the right field of the node.
14. An M-way search tree has M-1 values per node and M sub-trees. In such a tree, M is called the degree of the tree. M-way search tree consists of pointers to M sub-trees and contains M-1 keys, where M > 2.
15. A B-Tree of order M can have a maximum of M-1 keys and M pointers to its sub-trees. A B-Tree may contains a large number of key values and pointers to its sub-trees.
16. A B^+Tree is a variant of B-Tree which stores sorted data in a way that allows for efficient insertion, retrieval, and removal of records, each of which is identified by a key. B+Tree record data at the leaf level of the tree; only keys are stored in interior nodes.

MULTIPLE CHOICE QUESTIONS

1. Degree of a leaf node is

   (*a*) 0 (*b*) 1

   (*c*) 2 (*d*) 3

2. The depth of root node is

   (*a*) 0 (*b*) 1

   (*c*) 2 (*d*) 3

3. A binary tree of height h has at least h nodes and at most ________ nodes.

   (*a*) 2h (*b*) 2h

   (*c*) 2h+1 (*d*) 2h – 1

4. Pre-order traversal is also called

   (*a*) depth first (*b*) breath first

   (*c*) level order (*d*) in-order

5. The Huffman algorithm can be implemented using a
   (*a*) dequeue (*b*) queue
   (*c*) priority queue (*d*) none of these
6. Total number of nodes at the nth level of a binary tree can be given as
   (*a*) 2n (*b*) 2n
   (*c*) 2n+1 (*d*) 2n-1
7. In the worst case, a binary search tree will take how much time to search an element?
   (*a*) o (n) (*b*) o (log n)
   (*c*) o (n2) (*d*) o (n log n)
8. How much time does an AVL tree take to perform search, insert, and delete operations in the average case as well as the worst case?
   (*a*) o (n) (*b*) o (log n)
   (*c*) o (n2) (*d*) o (n log n)
9. When the left sub-tree of the tree is one level higher than that of the right sub-tree, then the balance factor is
   (*a*) 0 (*b*) 1
   (*c*) -1 (*d*) 2
10. Which rotation is done when the new node is inserted in the right sub-tree of the right sub-tree of the critical node?
    (*a*) LL (*b*) LR
    (*c*) RL (*d*) RR
11. When a node N is accessed it is splayed to make it the
    (*a*) Root node (*b*) Parent node
    (*c*) Child node (*d*) Sibling node
12. Every internal node of an M-way search tree consists of pointers to M sub-trees and contains how many keys?
    (*a*) M (*b*) M -1
    (*c*) 2 (*d*) M + 1
13. Every node in a B Tree has at most ______ children.
    (*a*) M (*b*) M -1
    (*c*) 2 (*d*) M + 1
14. Which data structure is commonly used to store a dictionary?
    (*a*) Binary Tree (*b*) Splay Tree
    (*c*) Trie (*d*) Red-Black Tree

15. In M-way search tree, M stands for
    (*a*) Internal nodes (*b*) External nodes
    (*c*) degree of node (*d*) leaf nodes
16. In best case, searching a value in a binary search tree may take.
    (*a*) O (n) (*b*) O (n log n)
    (*c*) O (log n) (*d*) O (n^2)

TRUE OR FALSE

1. Nodes that branch into child nodes are called parent nodes.
2. The size of a tree is equal to the total number of nodes.
3. A leaf node does not branch out further.
4. A node that has no successors is called the root node.
5. A binary tree of n nodes has exactly n -1 edges.
6. Every node has a parent.
7. The Huffman coding algorithm uses a variable length code table.
8. The internal path length of a binary tree is defined as the sum of all path lengths summed over each path from the root to an external node.
9. In a binary search tree, all the nodes in the left sub-tree have a value less than that of the root node.
10. If we take two empty binary search trees and insert the same elements but in a different order, then the resultant trees will be the same.
11. When we insert a new node in a binary search tree, it will be added as an internal node.
12. Mirror image of a binary search tree is obtained by interchanging the left sub-tree with the right sub-tree at every node of the tree.
13. If the thread appears in the right field, then it will point to the in-order successor of the node.
14. If the node to be deleted is present in the left sub-tree of A, then R rotation is applied.
15. Height of an AVL tree is limited to o (log n).
16. Critical node is the nearest ancestor node on the path from the root to the inserted node whose balance factor is -1, 0, or 1.
17. RL rotation is done when the new node is inserted in the right sub-tree of the right sub-tree of the critical node.
18. In a red-black tree, some leaf nodes can be red.
19. All leaf nodes in the B Tree are at the same level.
20. A B+ tree stores data only in the i-nodes.

21. B tree stores unsorted data.
22. Every node in the B-tree has at most (maximum) m-1 children.
23. The leaf nodes of a B tree are often linked to one another.
24. B+ tree stores redundant search key.
25. A trie is an ordered tree data structure.
26. A trie uses more space as compared to a binary search tree.
27. External nodes are called index nodes.

FILL IN THE BLANKS

1. Parent node is also known as the _________ node.
2. Size of a tree is basically the number of __________ in the tree.
3. The maximum number of nodes at the kth level of a binary tree is __________.
4. In a binary tree, every node can have a maximum of ________ successors.
5. Nodes at the same level that share the same parent are called ___________.
6. Two binary trees are said to be copies if they have similar ________ and ________.
7. The height of a binary tree with n nodes is at least _______ and at most ______.
8. A binary tree T is said to be an extended binary tree if ___________.
9. _________ traversal algorithm is used to extract a prefix notation from an expression tree.
10. In a Huffman tree, the code of a character depends on __________.
11. ________ is also called a fully threaded binary tree.
12. To find the node with the largest value, we will find the value of the right most node of the __________.
13. If the threaded appears in the right field, then it will point to the __________ of the node.
14. The balance factor of a node is calculated by __________.
15. Balance factor -1 means ___________.
16. Searching an AVL tree takes __________ time.
17. _________ rotation is done when the new node is inserted in the left sub-tree of the left sub-tree of the critical node.
18. In a red-black tree, the colour of the root node is ______ and the colour of leaf node is ___________.
19. The zig operation is done when___________.
20. In splay trees, rotation is analogous to _______ operation.

21. An M-way search tree consists of pointers to __________ sub-trees and contains ______ keys.
22. A B-Tree of order __________ can have a maximum of __________ keys and m pointers to its sub-trees.
23. Every node in the B-Tree except the root node and leaf nodes have at least _______ children.
24. In __________ data is stored in internal or leaf nodes.
25. A balanced tree that has height O (log N) always guarantees ________ time for all three methods.

EXERCISES

1. How many binary trees are possible with 4 nodes?
2. Prove that the root of a binary tree is an ancestor of every node in the tree except itself?
3. Prove that a strictly binary tree with n leaves contains 2n-1 nodes?
4. Write a C function to traverse a binary tree in pre-order and post-order?
5. Prove that the leftmost node at level n in an almost complete strictly binary tree is assigned the number 2^n?
6. Find the binary tree for the following expression:
   Expression: $(2x-3y)(4a+2b)^3$
7. Write a C function that finds height of a binary tree?
8. A binary tree has 9 nodes. The in-order and pre-order traversal of tree yields the following sequences of nodes:
   In-order: E A C K F H D B G
   Pre-order: F A E K C D H G B
9. Write a short node on threaded binary tree?
10. Explain the concept of a tree. Discuss its applications?
11. Explain the concept of a binary search tree. Discuss its various operations in binary search tree?
12. How many nodes will a complete binary tree with 32 nodes have in the last level? What will be the height of the tree?
13. How is an AVL tree better than a binary search tree?
14. How does a red-black tree perform better than a binary search tree?
15. Discuss the properties of a Red-Black tree. Explain the insertion and deletion cases?
16. Create a binary search tree with the data given below:
    98, 2, 48, 12, 56, 32, 4, 67, 23, 87, 23, 55, 46
    Insert 21, 39, 45, 54 and 63 into the tree

Delete values 23, 56, 2 and 45 from the tree

17. Create an AVL tree using the given data:
    50, 40, 35, 58, 48, 42, 60, 30, 33, 25

18. Suppose the following list of numbers is inserted into an empty binary search tree.
    20, 10, 18, 4, 8, 5, 13, 16, 17, 1, 27. Draw the final tree?

19. Difference between the B-Tree and B^+ Tree?

20. Create a B-Tree of order 5
    3, 14, 7, 1, 8, 5, 11, 17, 13, 6, 23, 12, 20, 26, 4, 16, 18, 24, 25, 19

21. Create a B-Tree of order 5
    10, 70, 60, 20, 110, 40, 80, 130, 100, 50, 190, 90, 180, 240, 30, 120, 140, 160

22. Create a Huffman tree with following numbers
    16, 11, 7, 20, 25, 5, 16

23. Consider the following algebraic expressions:
    (*i*) (A + B) * (C - D) / E
    (*ii*) A* (B + C) + D / (E - F)
    (*iii*) (A + B) / (C * D) – F / G
    Draw trees for these expressions and apply traversal.

24. Draw binary search tree from the in-order and pre-order traversal
    In-order: B E D A C H F G
    Pre-order: A B D E C F H G

25. Draw binary search tree from the in-order and post-order traversal
    In-order: J F C I H A B D G E
    Post-order: J F I H C G D E B A

REFERENCES

1. Adelson-Velskii, G.M. and E.M. Lendis, An algorithm for the organization of information soviet mathematic, English Translation.
2. Aho, A.V., J.E. Hopcroft, and J.D. Ullaman, Data Structures and Algorithms, Addison-Welsey.
3. Comer, D., The ubiquitous B Tree, Computing Surveys.
4. Donald E. Knuth, The art of Computer Programming: Fundamental Algorithms, vol 1, Addison-Wesley.
5. Edward Fredkin, Trie Memory, Communication of the ACM.
6. Eppinger, J.L., An empirical study of insertion and deletion in binary search trees, communication of the ACM.
7. Flajolet, P. And A.Odlyzko, The average height of binary trees and other simple trees, journal of computer and system sciences.

8. Gonnet, G.H., R. Baeza, and Yates, Handbook of algorithms and data structures, Addison-wesley.
9. Gudes, E. And S. Tsur, Experiments with B-Tree reorganization, proceeding of the ACM SIGMOD.
10. John L. Bentley, Programming pearls, Addison-Wesley.
11. Karlton, P.L., S.H. Fuller, et.al., performance of height balanced trees, communication of the ACM.
12. Melhorn. K., Data Structures and Algorithms: Searching and sorting, Springer-Verlag, New York.
13. Sheldon B. Akers, Binary Decision diagram, IEEE Transaction on Computing.
14. Sleator. D.D. and R.E. Tarjan, Self-adjusting binary search trees, Journal of the ACM.
15. Rudolf Bayer and E.M. McGreight, Organization and maintenance of large order indices, Acta Informatica.
16. Guibas and Sedgewick, symmetric binary tree, proceeding of the IEEE symposia on foundation of computer science.

7 Graphs

7.1 INTRODUCTION

A graph is another important non-linear data structure. Graphs are data structures which have wide range of applications in real life like airlines, analysis of electrical circuits, source, destination networks, finding shortest routes, flow chart of a program, statistical analysis etc.

Definition

Definitions: Graph, Vertices, Edges

Define a graph $G = (V, E)$ by defining a pair of sets:

1. V = a set of **vertices**
2. E = a set of **edges**

Edges:

- Each edge is defined by a pair of vertices
- An edge **connects** the vertices that defines it
- In some cases, the vertices can be the same

Vertices:

- Vertices are also called **nodes**
- Denote vertices with labels

Representation:

- Represent vertices with circles, perhaps containing a label
- Represent edges with lines between circles

Example:

- V = {A,B,C,D}
- E = {(A,B),(A,C),(A,D),(B,D),(C,D)}

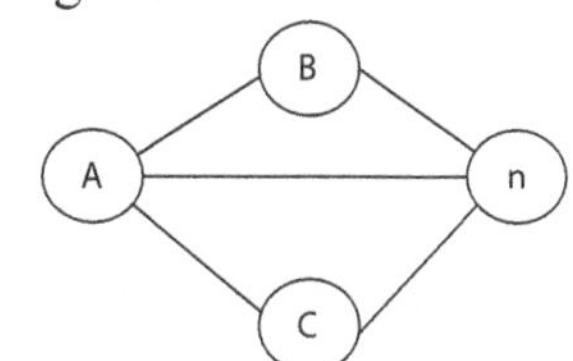

Motivation

Many algorithms use a graph representation to represent data or the problem to be solved

Examples:

- Cities with distances between
- Roads with distances between intersection points
- Course prerequisites
- Network
- Social networks
- Program call graph and variable dependency graph

7.2 BASIC TERM RELATED TO GRAPH

Graph Classifications

There are seveal common kinds of graphs

- Weighted or unweighted
- Directed or undirected
- Cyclic or acyclic

Choose the kind required for problem and determined by data. We examine each below

Kinds of Graphs: Weighted and Unweighted

- Graphs can be classified by whether or not their edges have **weights**
- **Weighted graph**: edges have a weight
  - Weight typically shows cost of traversing
  - Example: weights are distances between cities
- **Unweighted graph**: edges have no weight
  - Edges simply show connections
  - Example: course prerequisites

Kinds of Graphs: Directed and Undirected

- Graphs can be classified by whether or their edges have direction
  - **Undirected Graphs**: each edge can be traversed in **either direction**
  - **Directed Graphs**: each edge can be traversed **only in a specified direction**

Undirected Graphs

- **Undirected Graph**: no implied direction on edge between nodes

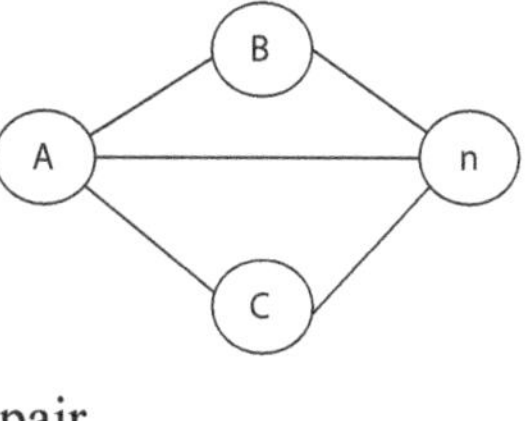

- The example from above is an undirected graph
- In diagrams, edges have no direction (*i.e.* they are not arrows)
- Can traverse edges in either directions

- In an undirected graph, an edge is an **unordered** pair
    - Actually, an edge is a set of 2 nodes, but for simplicity we write it with parents
        - For example, we write (A, B) instead of {A, B}
        - Thus, (A,B) = (B,A), etc
        - If (A,B) $\in$ E then (B,A) $\in$ E
    - Formally: $\forall$ u,v $\in$ E, (u,v)=(v,u) and u $\neq$ v
- A node normally does not have an edge to itself

Directed Graphs

- **Digraph**: A graph whose edges are directed (*i.e.* have a direction)
    - Edge drawn as arrow
    - Edge can only be traversed in direction of arrow
    - Example: E = {(A,B), (A,C), (A,D), (B,C), (D,C)}
    - Examples: courses and prerequisites, program call graph

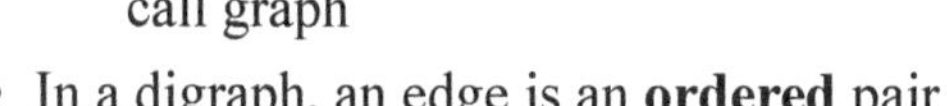

- In a digraph, an edge is an **ordered** pair
    - Thus: (u,v) and (v,u) are not the same edge
    - In the example, (D,C) $\in$ E, (C,D) $\notin$ E
    - What would edge (B,A) look like? Remember (A,B) $\neq$ (B,A)
- A node can have an edge to itself (eg (A,A) is valid)

Subgraph

- If graph G=(V, E)
    - Then Graph G'=(V',E') is a **subgraph** of G if V› $\subseteq$ V and E' $\subseteq$ E

Degree of a Node

- The **degree** of a node is the number of edges the node is used to define
- Can also define **in-degree** and **out-degree**
    - In-degree: Number of edges pointing **to** a node

   - Out-degree: Number of edges pointing **from** a node
   - Where are the in- and out-degree of the example?

Graphs: Terminology Involving Paths

- **Path**: sequence of vertices in which each pair of successive vertices is connected by an edge
- **Cycle**: a path that starts and ends on the same vertex
- **Simple path**: a path that does not cross itself
   - That is, no vertex is repeated (except first and last)
   - Simple paths cannot contain cycles
- **Length** of a path: Number of edges in the path
   - Sometimes the sum of the weights of the edges

Cyclic and Acyclic Graphs

- A **Cyclic** graph contains cycles
   - Example: roads (normally)
- An **acyclic** graph contains no cycles.
- Examples - Are these cyclic or acyclic?

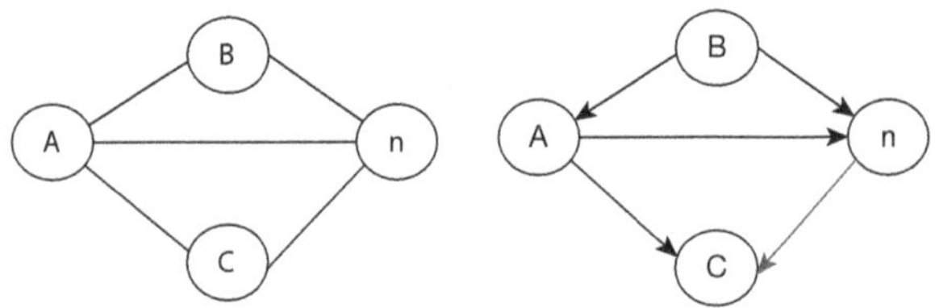

Connected and Unconnected Graphs and Connected Components

- An *undirected* graph is **connected** if every pair of vertices has a path between it
   - Otherwise it is unconnected
   - Give an example of a connected graph
- An unconnected graph can be broken into **connected components**
- A *directed* graph is **strongly connected** if every pair of vertices has a path between them, in **both directions**

Trees and Minimum Spanning Trees

- Tree: undirected, connected graph with no cycles
   - If G=(V, E) is a tree, how many edges in G?
- Spanning tree: a **spanning tree** of G is a connected subgraph of G that is a tree

- **Minimum spanning tree** (MST): a spanning tree with minimum weight
- Spanning trees and minimum spanning tree are not necessarily unique
- We will look at two famous MST algorithms: Prim's and Kruskal's

Data Structures for Representing Graphs

- Two common data structures for representing graphs:
  - Adjacency lists
  - Adjacency matrix

Adjacency List Representation

- Each node has a list of adjacent nodes
- Example (undirected graph):

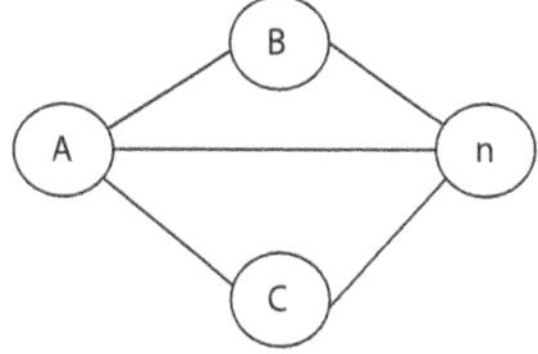

  - A: B, C, D
  - B: A, D
  - C: A, D
  - D: A, B, C
- Example (directed graph):

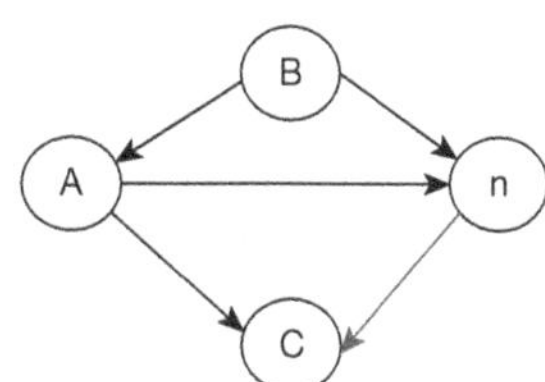

  - A: B, C, D
  - B: D
  - C: Nil
  - D: C
- Weighted graph can store weights in list
- Space: Θ(V + E) (ie |V| + |E|)
- Time:
  - To visit each node that is adjacent to node u: Θ(degree(u))
  - To determine if node u is adjacent to node v: Θ(degree(u))

Adjacency Matrix Representation

- **Adjacency Matrix**: 2D array containing weights on edges
  - Row for each vertex
  - Column for each vertex
  - Entries contain weight of edge from row vertex to column vertex
  - Entries contain ∞ (*i.e.* Integer'last) if no edge from row vertex to column vertex
  - Entries contain 0 on diagonal (if self edges not allowed)

- Example undirected graph (assume self-edges not allowed):

	A	B	C	D
A	0	1	1	1
B	1	0	∞	1
C	1	∞	0	1
D	1	1	1	0

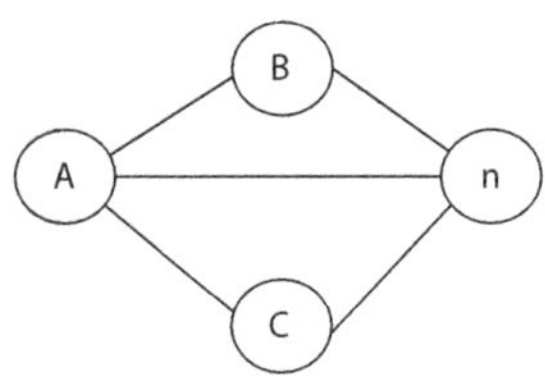

- Example directed graph (assume self-edges allowed):

	A	B	C	D
A	∞	1	1	1
B	∞	∞	∞	1
C	∞	∞	∞	∞
D	∞	∞	1	∞

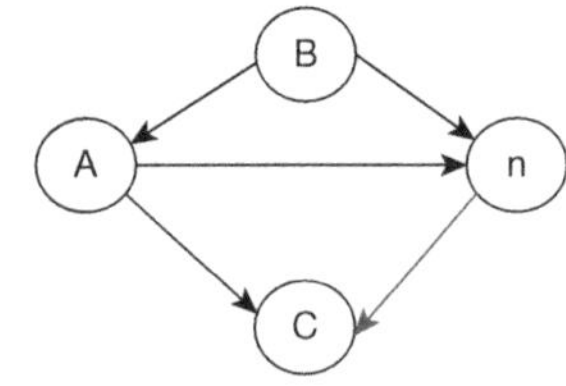

- Can store weights in cells
- Space: $\Theta(V^2)$
- Time:
    - To visit each node that is adjacent to node u: $\Theta(V)$
    - To determine if node u is adjacent to node v: $\Theta(1)$

7.3 REPRESENTATION OF GRAPH

There are two standard methods in common use, which differ fundamentally in the choice of abstract data types used, and there are several variations depending on the implementation of the abstract data type.

1. Sequential or Matrix Representation
2. Linked List Representation

7.4 MATRIX REPRESENTATION

The graphs can be represented as matrices. There are three most commonly used matrices.

(*i*) Adjacency Matrix
(*ii*) Incidence Matrix
(*iii*) Path Matrix

(i) Adjacency Matrix

The adjacency matrix is a matrix with one row and one column for each vertex. The values of matrix elements are either 0 or 1. The value of 1 for each row i and column j implies that edge (v_i, v_j) exists. A value of 0 indicates that there is no edge between vertices v_i and v_j. In other words, we can say that if graph G consists of v_1, v_2,. ...., v_n vertices then the adjacency matrix A = a[i][j] of the graph G is the n x n matrix and can be defined as:

a[i][j] = 1 if v_i is adjacent to v_j, that is, if there is an edge between v_i and v_j
0 if there is no edge between v_i and v_j

Example:

Let us take a directed graph

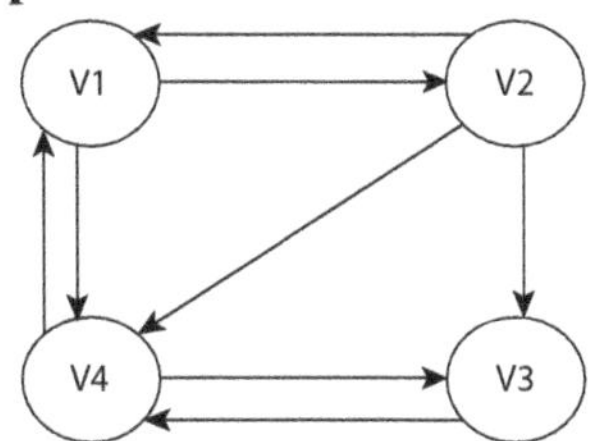

The corresponding adjacency matrix for this directed graph will be:

$$
\begin{array}{c} \\ v1 \\ v2 \\ v3 \\ v4 \end{array}
\begin{array}{c} \begin{array}{cccc} v1 & v2 & v3 & v4 \end{array} \\ \begin{pmatrix} 0 & 1 & 0 & 1 \\ 1 & 0 & 1 & 1 \\ 0 & 0 & 0 & 1 \\ 1 & 0 & 1 & 0 \end{pmatrix} \end{array}
$$

Let us take an undirected graph

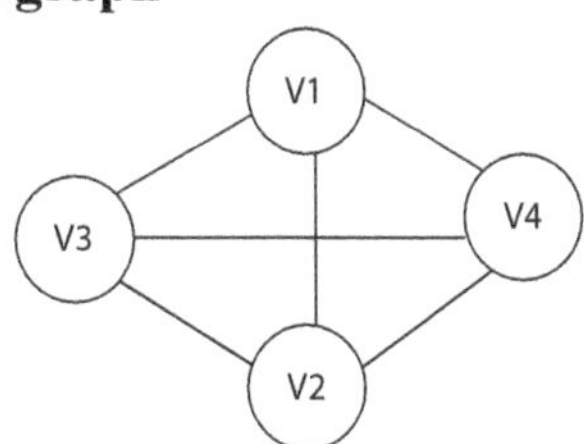

The corresponding adjacency matrix for this graph will be:

$$
\begin{array}{c} \\ v1 \\ v2 \\ v3 \\ v4 \end{array}
\begin{array}{c} \begin{array}{cccc} v1 & v2 & v3 & v4 \end{array} \\ \begin{pmatrix} 0 & 1 & 1 & 1 \\ 1 & 0 & 1 & 1 \\ 1 & 1 & 0 & 1 \\ 1 & 1 & 1 & 0 \end{pmatrix} \end{array}
$$

The matrix contains entries of only 0 and 1, so the matrix is called a bit matrix or Boolean matrix. When on constructing an adjacency matrix for a graph, one must follow the following points:

(*a*) Adjacency matrix A does not depend on the ordering of the vertex of a graph G, that is, different ordering of the vertices may result in a different adjacency matrix. One can obtain the same matrix by interchanging rows and columns.

(*b*) If graph G is undirected then the adjacency matrix of G will be symmetric. That is $[a_{ij}] = [a_{ji}]$ for every i and j

(ii) Incidence matrix

The incidence matrix consists of a row for every vertex and a column for every edge. The values of the matrix are -1, 0 or 1. The kth edge is (v_i, v_j), k^{th} column has a value 1 in the ith row, -1 in the jth row and 0 otherwise. For example, let us consider the following graph.

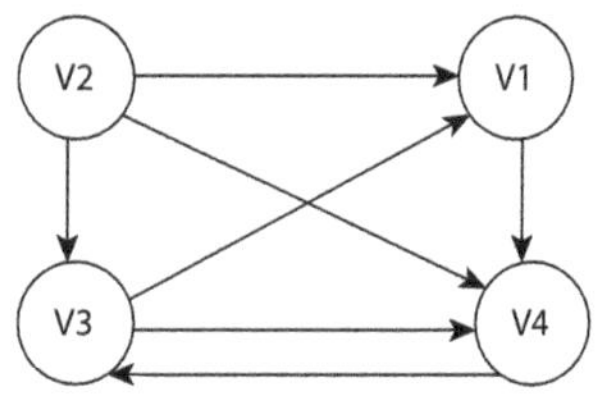

The adjacent matrix A of the above graph G is as follows:

A=

	v1	v2	v3	v4
v1	0	0	0	1
v2	1	0	1	1
v3	1	0	0	1
v4	0	0	1	0

Consider the powers A, A^2, A^3,. .... of the adjacency matrix A of a graph G.

Let a_k (i, j) = the ij entry in the matrix A^k. Observe that a_k (i, j) = a_{ij} gives the number of paths of length 1 from node v_i to v_j. Let A be the adjacency matrix of a graph G. Then a_k(i, j) the ij entry in the matrix a^k, gives the number of paths length k from v_i to v_j.

Consider the previous graph, whose adjacency matrix A is given above. The powers A, A^2, A^3, A^4,. .... of the matrix A are as follows:

A^2=

	v1	v2	v3	v4
v1	0	0	1	0
v2	1	0	1	2
v3	0	0	1	1
v4	1	0	0	1

A^3=

	v1	v2	v3	v4
v1	1	0	0	1
v2	1	0	2	2
v3	1	0	1	1
v4	0	0	1	1

A^4=

	v1	v2	v3	v4
v1	0	0	1	1
v2	2	0	2	3
v3	1	0	1	2
v4	1	0	1	1

Accordingly, in particular, there is a path of length 2 from v_4 to v_1, there are two paths of length 3 from v_2 to v_3 and there are three paths of length 4 from v_2 to v_4.

Suppose we now define the matrix B^r as follows

$B^r = A + A^2 + A^3 + A^4 + ... + A^r$

Then the ij entry of the matrix B^r, gives the number of paths of length r or less from node v_i to v_j.

(iii) Path Matrix

Let G be a simple directed graph with n vertices $v_1, v_2, ... V_n$. An n x n matrix P $[P_{ij}]$ is defined as follows:

$$Pij = \begin{cases} 1 \text{ if there is a path from } v_i \text{ to } v_j \\ 0 \text{ otherwise} \end{cases}$$

Suppose there is a path from v_i to v_j then there must be simple path from v_i to v_j when $v_i \neq v_j$ or there must be a cycle from v_i to v_j when $v_i = v_j$.

The path matrix P of a given graph G can be obtained from its adjacency matrix by following steps:

1. From the adjacency matrix of A, we can determine whether there exists an edge from one vertex to another.
2. Find A^n for some possible integer n.
3. Add the matrices $A, A^2, A^3, ... A^n$.
4. Now path matrix p can be obtained from B^n as follows:

   P_{ij}=1 if and only if there is a non-zero element in the I, j entry of the matrix B^n

Since G has only m nodes, such a simple path must have length m-1 or less, or such a cycle must have length m or less. This means that there is a non zero ij entry in the matrix B^m.

Let A be the adjacency matrix and $P = [P_{ij}]$ be the path matrix of a diagraph G. Then $p_{ij} = 1$ if and only if there is a non zero number in the ij entry of the matrix.

$B^m = A + A^2 + A^3 + ... + A^m$

Consider the following graph with m=4 nodes. Adding the matrix A, A^2, A^3, A^4, we obtain the following matrix B4 and replacing the non zero entries in B^4 by 1, we obtain the path matrix P of the graph G:

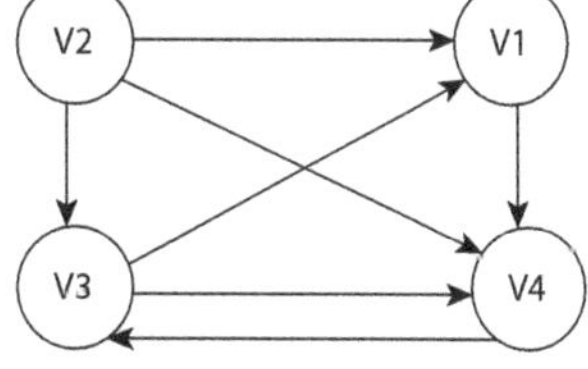

$$B^4 = \begin{array}{c} \\ v1 \\ v2 \\ v3 \\ v4 \end{array} \begin{array}{c} \begin{array}{cccc} v1 & v2 & v3 & v4 \end{array} \\ \begin{pmatrix} 1 & 0 & 2 & 3 \\ 5 & 0 & 6 & 5 \\ 3 & 0 & 3 & 5 \\ 2 & 0 & 3 & 3 \end{pmatrix} \end{array}$$

$$P = \begin{array}{c} \\ v1 \\ v2 \\ v3 \\ v4 \end{array} \begin{pmatrix} v1 & v2 & v3 & v4 \\ 1 & 0 & 1 & 1 \\ 1 & 0 & 1 & 1 \\ 1 & 0 & 1 & 1 \\ 1 & 0 & 1 & 1 \end{pmatrix}$$

Examine the matrix P; we see that the node v_2 is not reachable from any of the nodes. Recall that a directed graph G is said to be strongly connected if for any pair of nodes u and v in G, there are both a path from u and v and path from v to u. Accordingly G is strongly connected if and only if the path matrix P of G has no zero entries.

The adjacency matrix A and the path matrix P of a graph G may be viewed as logical Boolean matrices, where 0 represent false and 1 represents true. Thus, the logical operations of $\wedge$ (AND) and $\vee$ (OR) may be applied to the entries of A and P. The values of $\wedge$ and $\vee$ appears in the table:

$\wedge$	0	1
0	0	1
1	1	1

AND

$\vee$	0	1
0	0	0
1	0	1

Or

7.5 LINKED LIST REPRESENTATION

Let G be a directed graph with m nodes. The linked representation will contain two lists:

(*i*) A node list called "node"

(*ii*) An edge list called "edge"

Node List

Each element in the list node will correspond to a node in G and it will be a record of the form:

Node	Next	Adj	

Here node will be the name or key value of the node, next will be a pointer to the next node in the list node and adj will be a pointer to the first element in the adjacency list of the node, which maintained in the list edge. The blank area indicates that there may be other information in the record such as the in-degree of node, the out-degree of the node, the status of the node during the execution of an algorithm and so on. Node is an array of records containing fields such as name, indeg, outdeg, status, etc.

Edge List

Each element in the list edge will correspond to an edge of G and will be a record of the form;

destination	link	

The field destination will point to the location in the list Node of the destination or terminal nodes in the same adjacency list. The link field will link together the edges with the same initial node, the nodes in the same adjacency list. The blank area indicates that there may be other information in the record corresponding to the edge, such as a field edge containing the labelled data of the edge when G is a labelled graph, a field weight containing the weight of the edge when G is a weighted graph and so on.

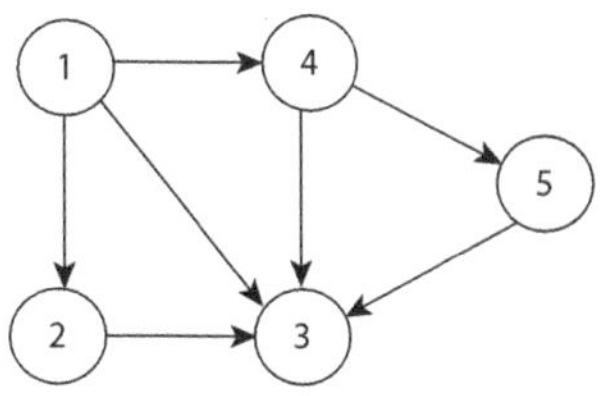

Graph "G"

Node	Adjacent List
1	2, 3, 4
2	3
3	
4	3, 5
5	3

Adjacent lists of G

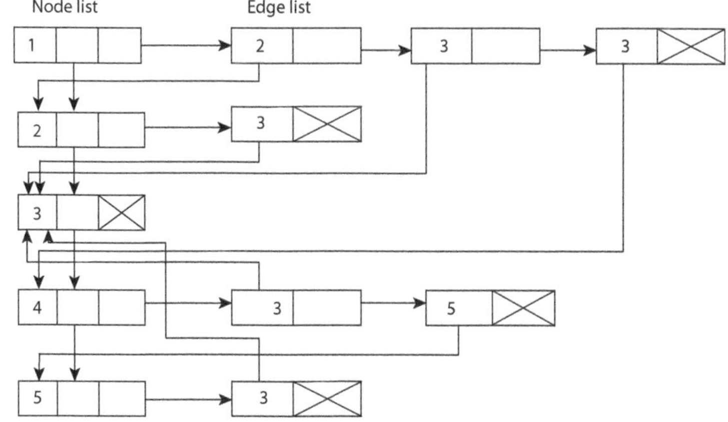

7.6 TRAVERSING A GRAPH

As we know that traversing is visiting each node in some systematic approach. Graph is represented by its nodes and edges. There are two graph traversal methods:

1. Breadth First Search (BFS) Using Queue
2. Depth First Search (DFS) Using Stack

In BFS, we use **queue** for keeping nodes, which will be used for next processing and in DFS, we use **stack**, which keeps the node for next processing.

1. Breadth first search using queue

This Graph traversal technique uses queue for traversing all the nodes of the graph. In this, first we take any node as a starting node then we take all the nodes adjacent to that starting node. We maintain the status of visited node in array so that no node can be traversed again.

Let us take a graph and apply BFS to it.

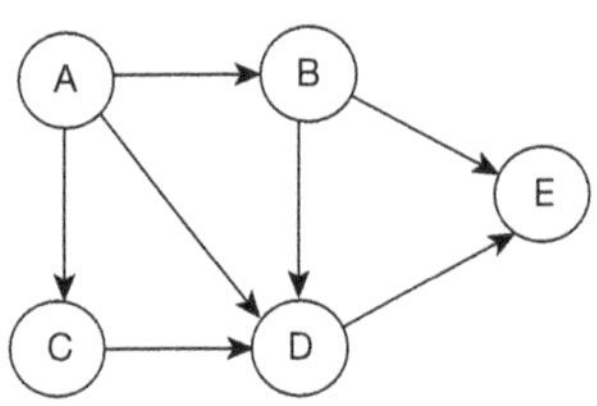

Vertex	Adjacency List
A	B, C, D
B	D, E
C	D
D	E
E	

Take the node A as the starting node and start the traversal of the given graph.

First we traverse node A, then we traverse all adjacent nodes to node A, *i.e.*, B,C, D. Now we traverse all nodes adjacent to B, then all the nodes adjacent to D, E

Now we traverse all nodes adjacent to C, then all the nodes adjacent to D. Now we traverse all nodes adjacent to D, then all the nodes adjacent to E now the traversal is: A, B, C, D, E

This was the traversal when we take node A as the starting node.

BFS through Queue

Take an array queue which will be used to keep the unvisited neighbours of the node. Take a Boolean array visited which will have value true if the node has been visited and will have value false if the node has not been visited.

Initially queue is empty and front = -1 and rear = -1

initially visited [i] = false where i =1 to n, n is total number of nodes.

Procedure

1. Insert starting node into the queue
2. Delete front element from the queue and insert all its unvisited neighbours into the queue at the end, and traverse them. Also make the value of visited array true for these nodes.
3. Repeat step 2 until the queue is empty.

Suppose the source vertex is A. Then following steps will illustrate the BFS:

Step 1: Initially push A to the queue.

0	1	2	3	4	
A					

Front = 0

Rear = 0

Step 2: Remove the front element A from the queue by incrementing front = front + 1 and display it. Then push all the neighbouring vertices of A to the queue by incrementing rear = rear + 1.

0	1	2	3	4	
	B	C	D		

Front = 1 Rear = 3

Traversed node = A

Step 3: Remove the front element B from the queue by incrementing front = front + 1 and display it. Then push all the neighbouring vertices of B to the queue by incrementing rear = rear + 1.

0	1	2	3	4	
		C	D	E	

Front = 2 Rear = 4

Traversed node = A, B

Step 4: Remove the front element C from the queue by incrementing front = front + 1 and display it. Then push all the neighbouring vertices of C to the queue by incrementing rear = rear + 1, if it is not in queue, D is already in queue, ignore it.

0	1	2	3	4	
			D	E	

Front = 3 Rear = 4

Traversed node = A, B, C

Step 5: Again the process is repeated remove the front element D of the queue and add the neighbouring vertex if it is not present in the queue.

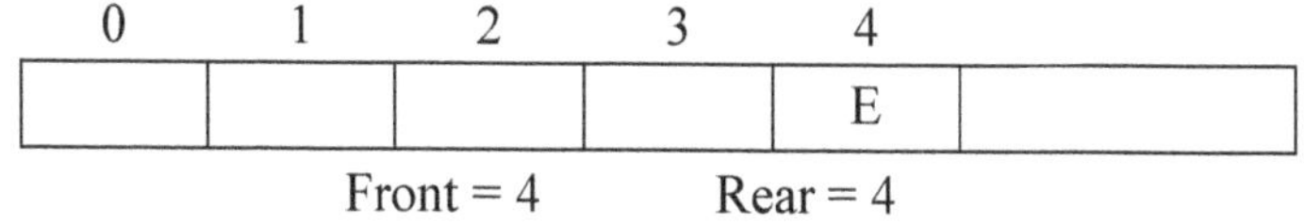

Traversed node = A, B, C, D

Step 6: Again the process is repeated until front > rear, i.e., remove the front element E of the queue and add the neighbouring vertex if it is present in the queue.

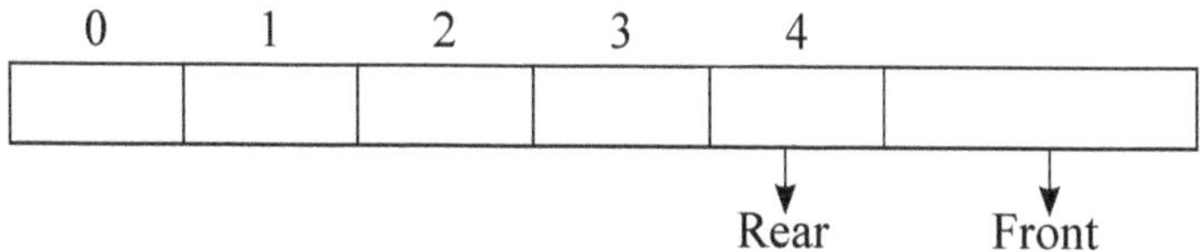

Traversed node = A, B, C, D, E

So, A, B, C, D, E is the BFS traversal of the graph.

Program: Write a Program to Implement Breadth First Search Traversal.

```
#include<stdio.h>
#include<stdlib.h>
#include<math.h>
#include<string.h>
void input();
void output();
int db(int);
void bfs();
int d,a[10],jj,ii,ti,b1,fi,ri;
char ch[10];
struct b
{
        char node[10];
        struct b *left,*right;
} *temp, *root=NULL,*t,*q[25];
void main()
{
input();
output();
}
void input()
{
        int n,m,r,i,f;
        printf("Enter the no of depth:-");
        scanf("%d",&d);
     n=pow(2,d+1)-1;
        for(i=1;i<=n;i++)
        {
                printf("Enter the %d node name:-",i);
                scanf("%s",ch);
                temp=(struct b *)malloc(sizeof(struct b));
                strcpy(temp->node,ch);
```

```
            temp->left=NULL;
            temp->right=NULL;
            if(root==NULL)
            {
            root=temp;
            }
            else
            {
            t=root;
            r=db(i);
            for(f=1;f<r;f++)
            {
            if(a[f]==0)
            {
            t=t->left;
            }
            else
            {
            t=t->right;
            }
            }
        if(a[r]==0)
        {
        t->left=temp;
        }
        else
        {
        t->right=temp;
        }
        }
        }
}
        void output()
        {
        t=root;
        printf("\n Enter the name Goal:-");
```

```
        scanf("%s",ch);
        bfs(t);
        }
        int db(int n)
        {
        int ji=0;
        while(n!=0)
        {
        a[ji++]=n%2;
        n=n/2;
        }
        for(ii=0,b1=ji-1;ii<b1;ii++,b1--)
        {
        ti=a[ii];
        a[ii]=a[b1];
        a[b1]=ti;
        }
        ji--;
        }
void bfs(struct b *t)
{
            int yes=0,index;
            fi=0;
            ri=1;
            q[fi]=t;
            printf("\n Breadth First search:-\n");
            while(fi<ri)
            {
            t=q[fi++];
            printf("%s",t->node);
            if(strcmp(t->node,ch)==0)
            {
            yes=1;
            index=fi;
            }
            if(t->left!=NULL)
```

```
            {
            q[ri++]=t->left;
            }
            if(t->right!=NULL)
            {
            q[ri++]=t->right;
            }
            }
            if(yes==1)
            printf("\n Goal State Are Present at Node %d",index);
            else
            printf("\n Goal State Are Not Present");
    }
```

Output

```
Enter the no of depth:-3
Enter the 1 node name:-A
Enter the 2 node name:-B
Enter the 3 node name:-C
Enter the 4 node name:-D
Enter the 5 node name:-E
Enter the 6 node name:-F
Enter the 7 node name:-G
Enter the 8 node name:-H
Enter the 9 node name:-I
Enter the 10 node name:-J
Enter the 11 node name:-K
Enter the 12 node name:-L
Enter the 13 node name:-M
Enter the 14 node name:-N
Entcr the 15 node name:-O
Enter the name Goal:-N
Breadth First search:-
ABCDEFGHIJKLMNO
Goal State Are Present at Node 14
```

2. Depth first search using stack

The Depth First Search (DFS) as its name suggest, is to search deeper in the graph. Given a input graph G= (V, E) and a source vertex S, from where the searching starts. First we visit the starting node, and then we travel through each node along a path, which begins at S. That is, we visit a neighbour vertex of S and again a neighbour of a neighbour of S and so on. DFS also works on both directed as well as on undirected graphs.

Depth first search using stack

Depth first Search technique uses stack. Take an array STACK, which will be used to keep the unvisited neighbours of the node. Take another Boolean array VISITED, which will have value TRUE if the node has been visited and will have FALSE if the node has not been visited.

Initially stack is empty and TOP = -1.

Initially VISITED [i] = FALSE where i = 1, n is total number of nodes

Procedure

1. Push starting node into the stack.
2. Pop an element from the stack, if it has not been traversed then traverse it, if it has already been traversed then just ignore it. After traversing make the value of visited array true for this node.
3. Now push all the unvisited adjacent nodes of the popped element on stack. Push the element even if it is already on the stack.
4. Repeat steps 3 and 4 until stack is empty.

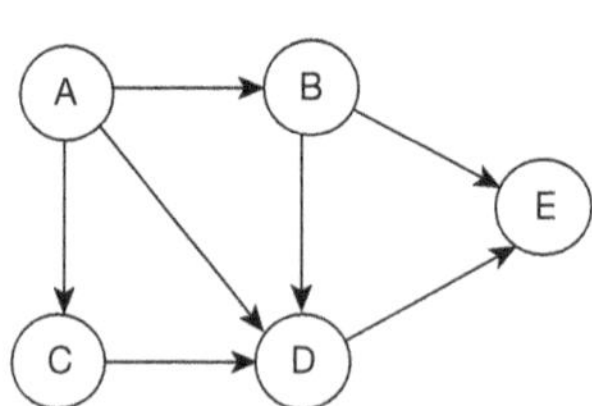

Vertex	Adjacency List
A	B, C, D
B	D, E
C	D
D	
E	D

Step 1: Push node A into stack

A

Now, Top = 0 and STACK = A.

Step 2: POP node A from stack and traverse it

So, Traversed node = A and VISITED [A] = TRUE

Now, push all the unvisited adjacent nodes B, C, D of the popped element on the stack.

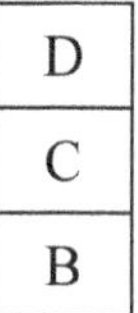

Now TOP = 2 and STACK = B, C, D

Traversal = A

Step 3: Pop the element node D from the stack, and push all its unvisited adjacent nodes. There is no adjacent node. So, Traversed node = D

VISITED [D] = TRUE

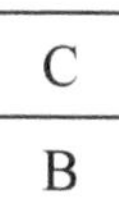

TOP = 1, STACK = B, C

Traversal = A, D

Step 4: POP the element C from the stack, traverse it and push all its unvisited adjacent nodes. Here node D is adjacent node of C but it is visited node. So, Traversed node = C

VISITED [C] = TRUE

B

TOP = 0, STACK = B

Traversal = A, D, C

Step 5: POP the element B from the stack, traverse it and push all its unvisited adjacent nodes *i.e.*, node E. Traversed node = B

VISITED [B] = TRUE

E

TOP = 0, STACK = E

Traversal = A, D, C, B

Step 6: POP the element E from the stack, traverse it and push all its unvisited adjacent nodes. No node is here.

Traversed node = E

VISITED [E] = TRUE

TOP = -1, STACK = EMPTY

Traversal = A, D, C, B, E

Since the stack is empty, so we will stop our process.

Program: Write a Program to Implement Depth First Search Traversal.

```
#include<conio.h>
#include<stdio.h>
#include<string.h>
#include<malloc.h>
#include<math.h>
void input();
void output();
int db(int);
void DFS(struct tree *);
struct tree
{
        char node[10];
        struct tree *left,*right;
} *temp, *root=NULL,*t,*s[25];
int d,a[10],jj,ii,ti,b,top;
char ch[10];
void main()
{
clrscr();
input();
output();
getch();
}
void input()
{
        int n,m,r,i,f;
        printf("Enter the no of depth:-");
        scanf("%d",&d);
        n=pow(2,d+1)-1;
        for(i=1;i<=n;i++)
        {
              printf("Enter the %d node name:-",i);
              scanf("%s",ch);
              temp=(struct tree *)malloc(sizeof(struct tree));
```

```
        strcpy(temp->node,ch);
        temp->left=NULL;
        temp->right=NULL;
        if(root==NULL)
        {
        root=temp;
        }
        else
        {
        t=root;
        r=db(i);
        for(f=1;f<r;f++)
        {
        if(a[f]==0)
        {
        t=t->left;
        }
        else
        {
        t=t->right;
        }
}
if(a[r]==0)
{
t->left=temp;
}
else
{
t->right=temp;
}
}
}
}
void output()
{
```

```
t=root;
printf("\n Enter the name Goal:-");
scanf("%s",ch);
DFS(t);
}
int db(int n)
{
int ji=0;
while(n!=0)
{
a[ji++]=n%2;
n=n/2;
}
for(ii=0,b=ji-1;ii<b;ii++,b--)
{
ti=a[ii];
a[ii]=a[b];
a[b]=ti;
}
ji--;
return ji;
}
void DFS(struct tree *t)
{
    int yes=0,top=1;
    s[top]=t;
    printf("\n Depth First search:-\n");
    while(top>0)
    {
    t=s[top];
    top--;
    printf("%s",t->node);
    if(strcmp(t->node,ch)==0)
    {
    yes=1;
    }
```

```
        if(t->left!=NULL)
        {
        s[++top]=t->left;
        }
        if(t->right!=NULL)
        {
        s[++top]=t->right;
        }
        }
        if(yes==1)
        printf("\n Goal State Are Present");
        else
        printf("\n Goal State Are Not Present");
    }
```

Output

```
Enter the no of depth:-2
Enter the 1 node name:-A
Enter the 2 node name:-B
Enter the 3 node name:-C
Enter the 4 node name:-D
Enter the 5 node name:-E
Enter the 6 node name:-F
Enter the 7 node name:-G

Enter the name Goal:-E

Depth First search:-
ACGFBED
Goal State Are Present
```

7.7 SPANNING TREE

A spanning tree is a subset of Graph G, which has all the vertices covered with minimum possible number of edges. Hence, a spanning tree does not have cycles and it cannot be disconnected.

By this definition we can draw a conclusion that every connected & undirected Graph G has at least one spanning tree. A disconnected graph does not have any spanning tree, as it cannot span to all its vertices.

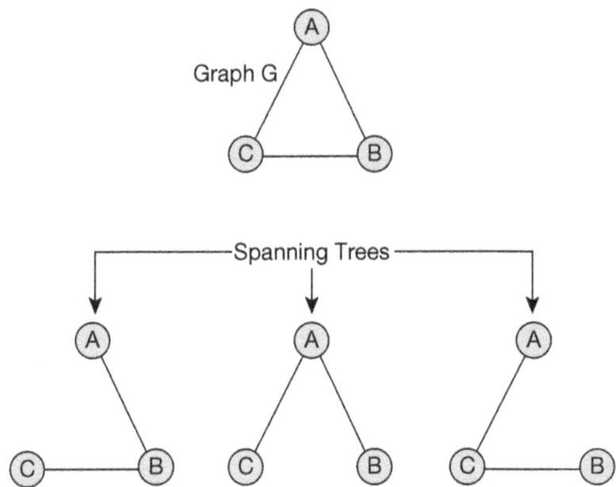

We found three spanning trees off one complete graph. A complete undirected graph can have maximum $\mathbf{n^{n-2}}$ number of spanning trees, where n is the number of nodes. In addressed example, n is 3, hence $\mathbf{3^{3-2} = 3}$ spanning trees are possible.

General properties of spanning tree

We now understand that one graph can have more than one spanning trees. Below are few properties is spanning tree of given connected graph G –

- A connected graph G can have more than one spanning tree.
- All possible spanning trees of graph G, have same number of edges and vertices.
- Spanning tree does not have any cycle (loops)
- Removing one edge from spanning tree will make the graph disconnected *i.e.* spanning tree is **minimally connected**.
- Adding one edge to a spanning tree will create a circuit or loop *i.e.* spanning tree is **maximally acyclic**.

Mathematical properties of spanning tree

- Spanning tree has n-1 edges, where n is number of nodes (vertices)
- From a complete graph, by removing maximum **e-n+1** edges, we can construct a spanning tree.
- A complete graph can have maximum $\mathbf{n^{n-2}}$ number of spanning trees.

So, we can conclude here that spanning trees are subset of a connected Graph G and disconnected Graphs do not have spanning tree.

Application of Spanning Tree

Spanning tree is basically used to find minimum paths to connect all nodes in a graph. Common application of spanning trees is –

- **Civil Network Planning**

- **Computer Network Routing Protocol**
- **Cluster Analysis**

Let's understand this by a small example. Consider city network as a huge graph and now plan to deploy telephone lines such a way that in minimum lines we can connect to all city nodes. This is where spanning tree comes in the picture.

7.8 MINIMUM SPANNING TREE (MST)

In a weighted graph, a minimum spanning tree is a spanning tree that has minimum weight that all other spanning trees of the same graph. In real world situations, this weight can be measured as distance, congestion, traffic load or any arbitrary value denoted to the edges.

Minimum Spanning-Tree Algorithm

We shall learn about two most important spanning tree algorithms here –

- Krukshal's Algorithm
- Prim's Algorithm

Both are greedy algorithms.

7.9 KRUKSHAL'S ALGORITHM

This algorithm creates a forest of trees. Initially the forest consists of n single node trees and no edges. That is, in the method initially we take n district trees for all nodes of the graph. At each step, we add one edge, so that it joins two trees together.

1. Initially construct a separate tree for each node in a graph.
2. Edges are placed in a priority queue, we take edges in ascending order. We can use a heap for the priority queue.
3. Until we have added n-1 edges.
   - (*a*) Extract the cheapest edge from the queue.
   - (*b*) If it forms a cycle, reject it

     else

     add it to the forest.
4. Whenever we insert an edge, two trecs will be joined, every step will have joined two trees in the forest together so that at the end, there will be only one tree.

In this method, first we examine all the edges one-by-one starting from the smallest edge. To decide whether the selected edge should be included in the spanning tree or not, we will examine the two nodes connecting the edge. If the two nodes belong to the same tree then we will not include the edge in the spanning tree, since the two nodes are in the same tree, they are already connected and adding these edges would result in a cycle. So we will insert an edge in the spanning tree only if its nodes are in different trees.

Now, we will see how to decide whether two nodes are in the same tree or not. For this, we need a UNION - FIND structure.

To understand the UNION - FIND structure, we need to look at a partition of a set.

(*a*) Every element of the set belongs to one of the sets in the partition.

(*b*) No element of the set belongs to more than one of the sub-sets.

(*c*) Every element of a set belongs to one and only one of the sets of a partition.

A partition of a set may be thought of as a set of equivalence classes. Each sub-set of the partition contains a set of equivalent elements. For each subset, we denote one element as the representative of that sub-set. Each element in the sub-set is, somehow, equivalent and represented by the representative. When we add elements to the sub-set, we arrange that all the elements point to their representative. Initially, each node is its own representative. As the initial pairs of nodes are joined to form a tree, the representative pointer of one of the nodes is made to point to the other, which becomes the representative of the tree. As trees, are joined the representative pointer of the representative of one of them is set to point to any element of the other. Let x denote an object, we wish to support the following operations.

1. MAKE - SET (x) creates a new set whose only member is pointed to by x.
2. FIND - SET (x) returns a pointer to the representative of the set containing x.
3. UNION (x, y) unites the dynamic sets that contain x and y, say S_x and S_y into a new set that is the union of these two sets. The representative of the resulting set is some member of $S_x \cup S_y$. Since we require the sets in the collection to be disjoint, we "destroy" sets S_x and S_y removing them from the collection.

MST - KRUSKAL (G, W)

1. A = ø
2. for each vertex v V[G]
   do MAKE-SET (v)
3. sort the edges of E into increasing order by weight w.
4. for each edge (u,v) E taken in increasing order.
   do if FIND-SET (u) ≠ FIND-SET (v)
   then A = A U {u, v}
   UNION (u, v)
5. return A.

Consider a graph

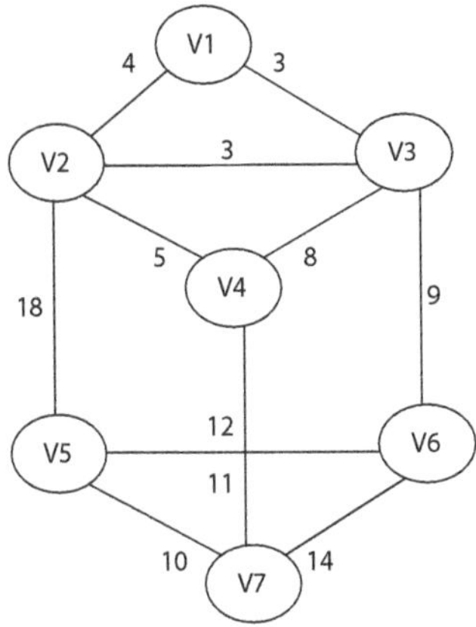

Edge	Weight
V1, V3	3
V3, V2	3
V2,V1	4
V2, V4	5
V4, V3	8
V3, V6	9
V5,V7	10
V5, V6	11
V4,V7	12
V7, V6	14
V2, V5	18

Solution:

Step 1: Initial Step

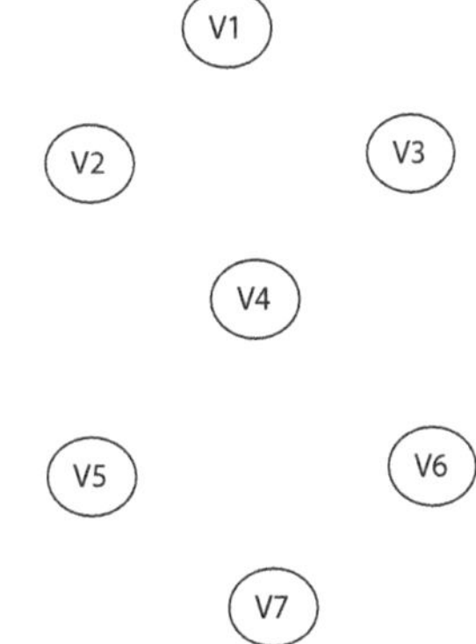

Step 2: take V1, V3 edge, minimum weight 3

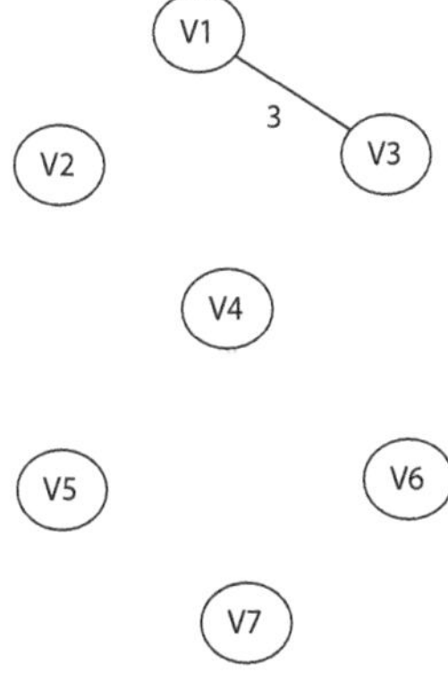

Step 2: take V3, V2 edge, minimum weight 3

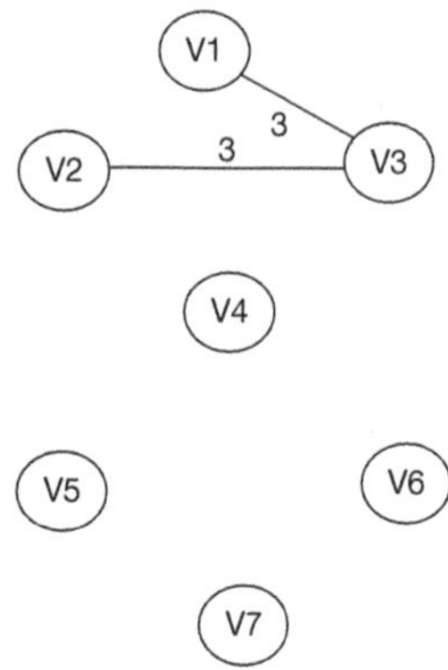

Step 3: take V2, V1 edge, this cannot be added, because it forms a cycle, reject it.

Step 4: take V2, V4 edge, minimum weight 5

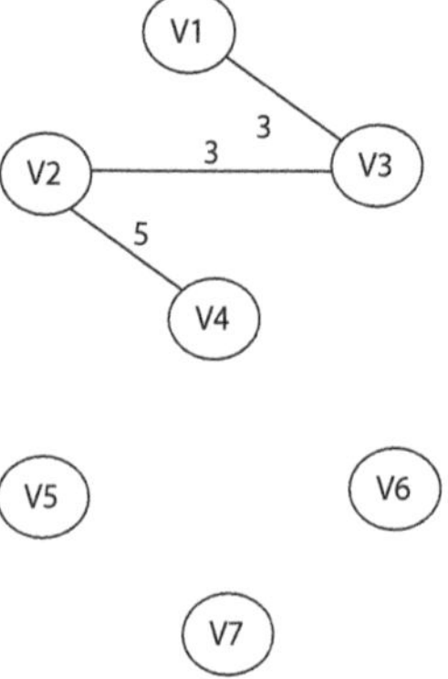

Step 5: take V4, V3 edge, this cannot be added, because it forms a cycle, reject it.

Step 6: take V3, V6 edge, minimum weight 9

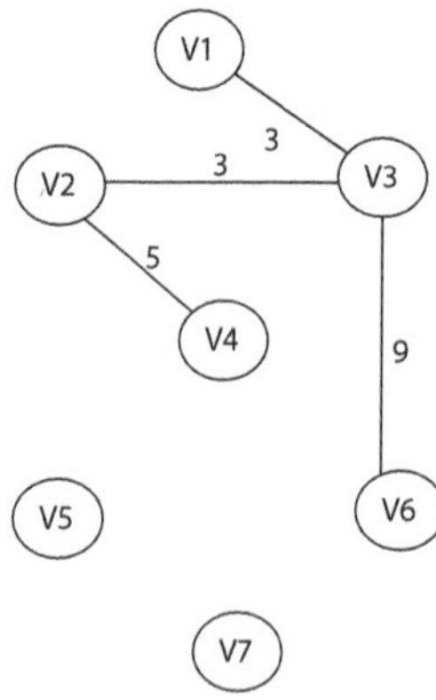

Step 7: take V5, V7 edge, minimum weight 10

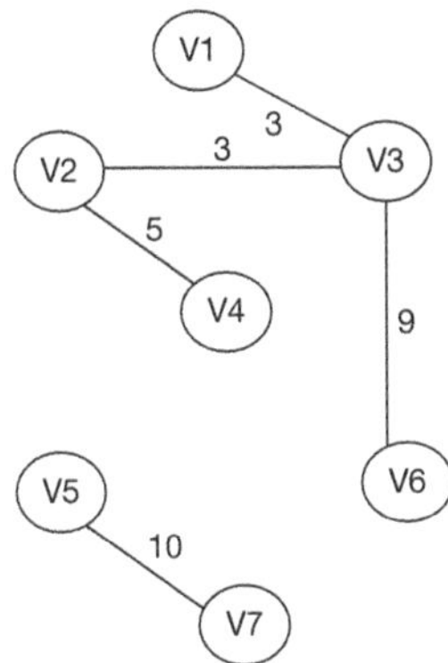

Step 8: take V5, V6 edge, minimum weight 11

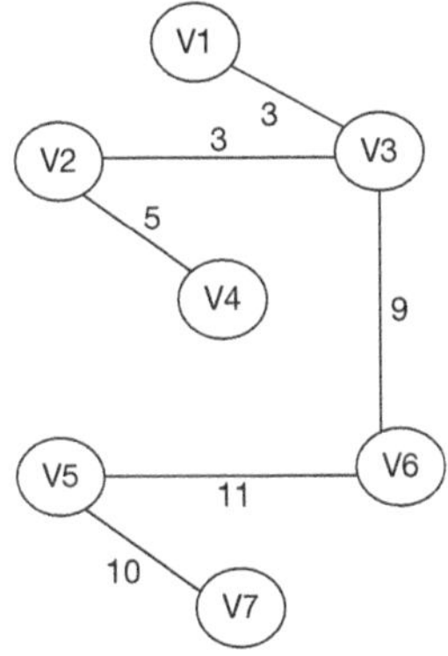

Step 9: take V4, V7 edge, this cannot be added, because it forms a cycle, reject it

Step 10: take V7, V6 edge, this cannot be added, because it forms a cycle, reject it

Step 11: take V2, V5 edge, this cannot be added, because it forms a cycle, reject it

The edge that belong to minimum spanning tree

{(V1,V3), (V3,V2), (V2,V4), (V3,V6), (V5,V7), (V5,V6)}

Weight of the minimum spanning tree: 3+3+5+9+10+11

The total cost of a minimum spanning tree is 41

Program: Write a Program to implement a minimum spanning tree from Kruskal's Algorithm

```
#include<stdio.h>
#define MAX 20
struct edge
{
```

```
int u, v, weight;
struct edge *link;
}* front = NULL
int father [MAX]                 //Holds father of each node
struct edge tree[MAX]            //will contain the edge of spanning tree
int n;                     //denote total number of nodes in the graph
int weight_tree = 0        //weight of the spanning tree
int count = 0              //denote number of edge include in the tree
void make_tree();
void insert_tree(int i, int j, int weight);
void insert_priority_queue(int i, int j, int weight);
struct edge *del_priority_queue();
main()
{
int i;
create_graph();
make_tree();
printf("Edges to be included in spanning tree are:");
for(i=0;i<=count;i++)
{
printf("%d->", tree[i].u);
printf("%d->", tree[i].v);
}
printf("Weight of this minimum spanning tree is", weight_tree);
}
create_graph()
{
int i, weight, maxedge, origin, destination;
printf("Enter number of nodes:");
scanf("%d", &n);
maxedge = n*(n-1)/2;
for(i=1;i<=maxedge;i++)
{
printf("Enter edge %d(0 0 to quit):", i);
scanf("%d %d", &origin, &destination);
```

```
if((origin == 0) && (destination ==0))
break;
printf("Enter weight for this edge:");
scanf("%d", &weight);
if(origin > n || destination > n || origin <=0 || destination <=0)
{
printf("Invalid Edge");
i--;
}
else
insert_priority_queue(origin, destination, weight);
}
if(i < n-1)
{
printf("Spanning tree is not possible");
exit (1);
}
}
void make_tree()
{
struct edge *temp;
int node1, node2, root_n1, root_n2;
while(count < n-1)    //loop till n-1 edges included in the tree
{
temp = del_priority_queue();
node1 = temp->u;
node2 = temp->v;
printf("n1 = %d", node1);
printf(n2 = %d", node2);
while(node1 > 0)
{
root_n1 = node1;
node1 = father[node];
}
while(node2 > 0)
{
```

```
root_n2 = node2;
node2 = father[node];
}
printf("rootn1 = %d", root_n1);
printf(rootn2 = %d", root_n2);
if(root_n1!=root_n2)
{
insert_tree(temp->u, temp->v, temp->weight);
weight_tree = weight_tree + temp->weight;
father[root_n2] = root_n1;
}
}
}
void insert_tree(int i, int j, int weight)
{
printf("This edge inserted in the spanning tree");
count++;
tree[count].u=i;
tree[count].v=j;
tree[count].weight=weight;
}
void insert_priority_queue(int i, int j, int weight)
{
struct edge *temp, *q;
temp = (struct edge*) malloc(sizeof(struct edge));
temp->u=i;
temp->v=j;
temp->weight=weight;
if(front ==NULL || temp->weight < front->weight)
{
temp->link = front;
front = temp;
}
else
{
q=front;
```

```
while(q->link!=NULL && q->link->weight <=temp->weight)
q=q->link;
temp->link = q->link;
q->link = temp;
if(q->link == NULL)          //edge to be added at the end
temp->link = NULL;
}
}
struct edge *del_priority_queue()
{
struct edge *temp;
temp = front;
printf("Edge processed is %d->%d %d\n", temp->u, temp->v, temp->weight);
front = front->link;
return temp;
}
```

7.10 PRIM'S ALGORITHM

In this, we start with any node and add the other node in spanning tree on the basis of weight of edge connecting to that node. Suppose, we start the node 'N' then we have a need to all the connecting edges and which edge has minimum weight. Then, we will add that edge and node to the spanning tree. Suppose, if two nodes N1 and N2 are in spanning tree and both have edge connecting to an edge. Which has minimum weight will be added in spanning tree.

The main idea of Prim's algorithm is similar to that of Dijkstra's algorithm for finding shortest path in a given graph. Prim's algorithm has the property that the edges in the set A from a single tree. We begin with some vertex u in a given graph G = (V, E), defining the initial set of vertices A. Then, in each iteration, we choose a minimum weight edge (u, v) connecting a vertex v in the set A to the vertex u outside set A. Then vertex u is brought into A. This process is repeated until a spanning tree is formed. Like Krushal's algorithm, here too, the important fact about MSTs is we always choose the smallest - weight edge joining a vertex inside set A to the one outside the set A.

MST-Prim (G, w, r)

1. for each u v[G]
2. do key[u] = ∞
3. π[u] = NIL
4. key [r] = 0

```
Q = V[G]
while Q ≠ 0
do u = EXTRACT-MIN (Q)
for each v Adj[u]
do if v Q and w (u, v) < key [v]
then π [u] = u
key[v] = w(u, v)
```

Solution

Step 1:

Suppose the starting vertex is V1

Edges, which have exactly one end belonging to the partial minimal spanning tree

{(V1, V2),(V1, V3)}

The edge chosen based on the minimal spanning tree (V1,V3)

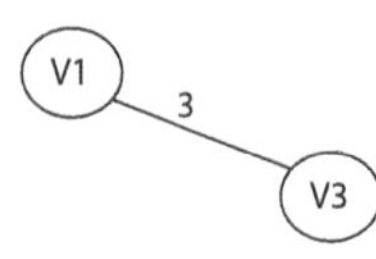

Step 2: set of vertices in the minimal spanning tree (V1, V3)

Edges, which have exactly one end belonging to the partial minimal spanning tree

{(V1, V2), (V2, V3),(V3, V4),(V3, V6)}

The edge chosen based on the minimal spanning tree (V2, V3)

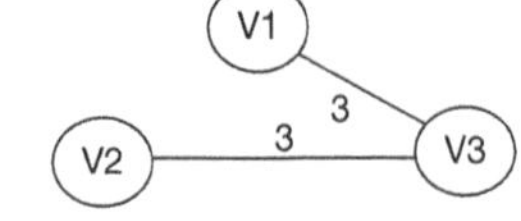

Step 3: set of vertices in the minimal spanning tree (V1, V2, V3)

Edges, which have exactly one end belonging to the partial minimal spanning tree

{(V3, V4), (V3, V6),(V2, V4),(V2, V5)}

The edge chosen based on the minimal spanning tree (V2, V4)

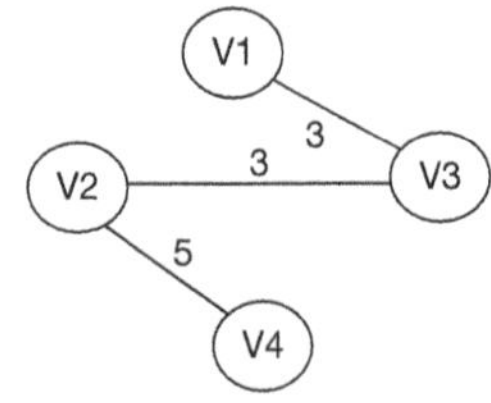

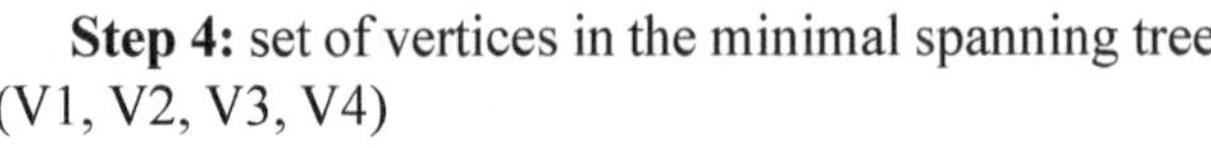

Step 4: set of vertices in the minimal spanning tree (V1, V2, V3, V4)

Edges, which have exactly one end belonging to the partial minimal spanning tree

{(V3, V6), (V2, V5),(V4, V7)}

The edge chosen based on the minimal spanning tree (V3, V6)

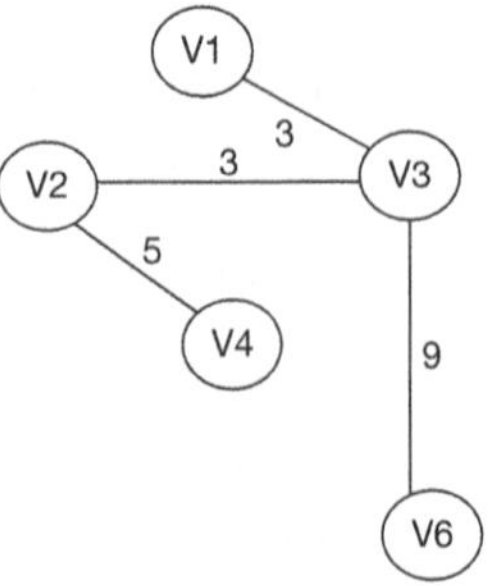

Step 5: set of vertices in the minimal spanning tree (V1, V2, V3, V4, V6)

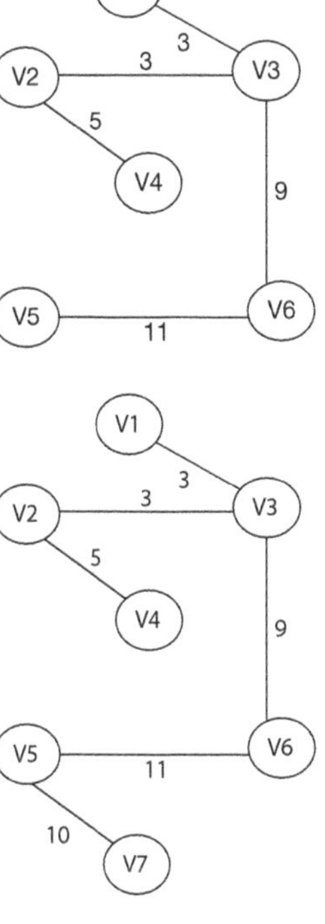

Edges, which have exactly one end belonging to the partial minimal spanning tree

{(V2, V5), (V4, V7), (V5, V6), (V6, V7)}

The edge chosen based on the minimal spanning tree (V5, V6)

Step 6: set of vertices in the minimal spanning tree (V1, V2, V3, V4, V5, V6)

Edges, which have exactly one end belonging to the partial minimal spanning tree

{(V4, V7), (V6, V7), (V5, V7)}

The edge chosen based on the minimal spanning tree (V5, V7)

The edge that belong to minimum spanning tree

{(V1, V3), (V2, V3), (V2, V4), (V3, V6), (V5, V6), (V5, V7)}

Weight of the minimum spanning tree 3+3+5+9+11+10

The total cost of a minimum spanning tree is 41

Program: Write a Program to Implement Minimum Spanning Tree for Prim's Algorithm.

```
#include<stdio.h>
int a,b,u,v,n,i,j,ne=1;
int visited[10]={0},min,mincost=0,cost[10][10];
void main()
{
printf("\n Enter the number of nodes:");
scanf("%d",&n);
printf("\n Enter the adjacency matrix:\n");
for(i=1;i<=n;i++)
for(j=1;j<=n;j++)
{
scanf("%d",&cost[i][j]);
if(cost[i][j]==0)
cost[i][j]=99;
}
visited[1]=1;
printf("\n");
```

```
while(ne<n)
{
   for(i=1,min=99;i<=n;i++)
    for(j=1;j<=n;j++)
    if(cost[i][j]<min)
    if(visited[i]!=0)
    {
     min=cost[i][j];
     a=u=i;
     b=v=j;
     }
if(visited[u]==0 || visited[v]==0)
{
printf("\n Edge %d:(%d %d) cost:%d",ne++,a,b,min);
mincost+=min;
visited[b]=1;
}
cost[a][b]=cost[b][a]=99;
}
printf("\n Minimun cost=%d",mincost);
}
```

Output

```
Enter the number of nodes:3
Enter the adjacency matrix:
1
2
1
2
3
2
1
2
1
Edge 1:(1 3) cost:1
Edge 2:(1 2) cost:2
Minimun cost=3
```

7.11 SHORTEST PATHS (DIJKSTRA'S ALGORITHM)

A path from source vertex s to t is shortest path from s to t if there is path from s to t with lower weights. In a shortest paths problem, we are given a weighted directed graph G = (V, E) with weight function w: E→R mapping edges to real - valued weights. The weight of path p = < V_0, V_1. ..... V_m > is the sum of the weights of its constituent edges.

$$w(p) = \sum_{i=1}^{k} w(V_{i-1}, V_i)$$

We define the shortest path weight from u to v by

δ(u,v) = min (w(p): u→v)

Dijkstra's algorithm

Dijkstra's algorithm, named after its discover, Dutch computer scientist Edsger Dijkstra, is a greedy algorithm that solve the single-source shortest path problem for a directed graph G = (V,E) with non-negative edge weights, *i.e.*, we assume that w(u,v) > each edge (u,v) E.

Dijkstra's algorithm maintains a set S of vertices whose final shortest - path weights from the source s have already been determined. That is, for all vertices v E S, we have d[v] = (s,v). The algorithm repeatedly selects the vertex u E V- S with the minimum shortest - path estimate, insert u into S, and relaxes all edges leaving u. We maintain a priority queue Q that contains all the vertices in v -s, keyed by their d values. Graph G is represented by adjacency lists.

1. INITIALIZE - SINGLE - SOURCE (G, s)
2. S - 0
3. Q - V[G]
4. While Q = 0
5. do u - EXTRACT - MIN (Q)
6. S - S U {u}
7. for each vertex vE Adj [u]
8. do RELAX (u, v, w)

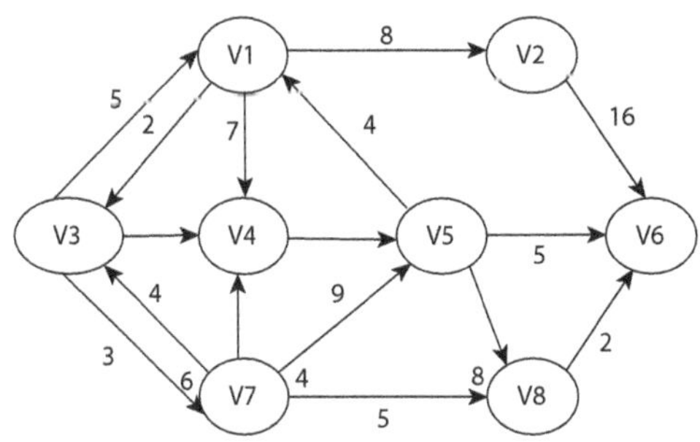

The procedure is as:

1. Initially make source node permanent and make it the current working node. All other nodes are made temporary.
2. Examine all the temporary neighbours of the current working node and after checking the condition for minimum weight, relabel the required nodes.
3. From all the temporary nodes, find out the node which has minimum value of distance, make this node permanent and now this is our current working node.
4. Repeat steps 2 and 3 until destination node is made permanent.

Suppose the source node is V1

V1 is the current working node.

Node	Destination	Precedence	Status
V1	0	0	Permanent
V2	∞	0	Temporary
V3	∞	0	Temporary
V4	∞	0	Temporary
V5	∞	0	Temporary
V6	∞	0	Temporary
V7	∞	0	Temporary
V8	∞	0	Temporary

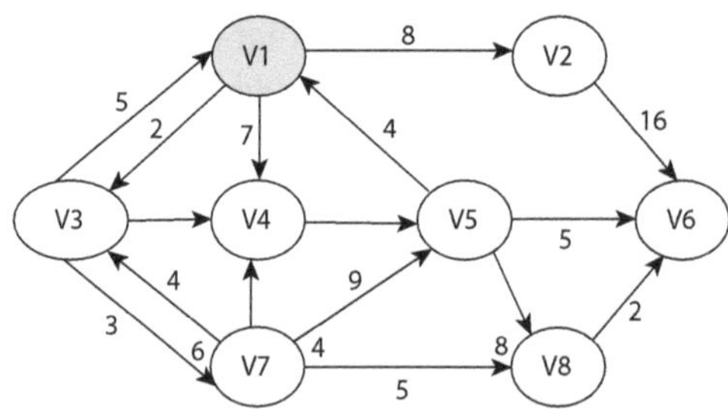

Now we will check the adjacent nodes of V1, which are temporary also. Here, V2,V3,V4 are adjacent to V1 and are temporary.

V2.distance > V1.distance + distance (V1,V2) ∞ > 0 + 8 relabel V2

V3.distance > V1.distance + distance (V1,V3) ∞ > 0 + 2 relabel V3

V4.distance > V1.distance + distance (V1,V4) ∞ > 0 + 7 relabel V4

Now we will change the precedence and distance of V2, V3, V4

Node	Destination	Precedence	Status
V1	0	0	Permanent
V2	8	V1	Temporary
V3	2	V1	Temporary
V4	7	V1	Temporary

Node	Destination	Precedence	Status
V5	∞	0	Temporary
V6	∞	0	Temporary
V7	∞	0	Temporary
V8	∞	0	Temporary

Now from all the temporary nodes find out the node that has the smallest distance from source *i.e.* smallest value of distance. V3 has the smallest value of distance in all temporary nodes so make it permanent and now V3 is our current working node.

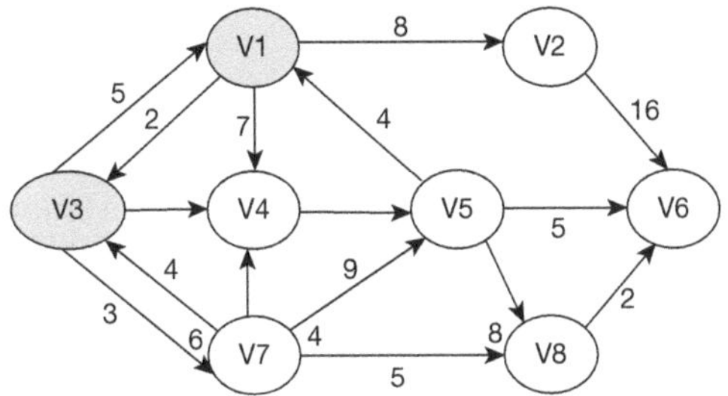

Adjacent nodes of V3 are V4, V7 both are temporary.

V4.distance > V3.distance + distance (V3,V4) 7 > 2 + 7 relabel V4

V7.distance > V3.distance + distance (V3,V7) ∞ > 2 + 3 relabel V3

Now we will change the precedence and distance of V4 and V7.

Node	Destination	Precedence	Status
V1	0	0	Permanent
V2	8	V1	Temporary
V3	2	V1	Permanent
V4	6	V3	Temporary
V5	∞	0	Temporary
V6	∞	0	Temporary
V7	5	V3	Temporary
V8	∞	0	Temporary

Now from all the temporary nodes V7 has smallest value of distance so make it permanent and now V7 is our current working node.

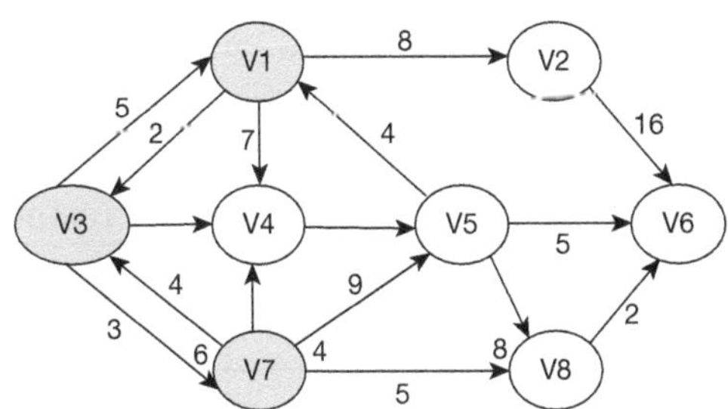

Adjacent nodes of V7 are V3,V4,V5, since V3 is permanent we will not relabel it.

V4.distance < V7.distance + distance (V7,V4) 6 < 5 + 3 don't relabel V4

V5.distance > V7.distance + distance (V7,V5) ∞ > 5 + 4 relabel V5

Now precedence and distance of V5 will be changed.

Node	Destination	Precedence	Status
V1	0	0	Permanent
V2	8	V1	Temporary
V3	2	V1	Permanent
V4	6	V3	Temporary
V5	9	V7	Temporary
V6	∞	0	Temporary
V7	5	V3	Permanent
V8	∞	0	Temporary

Now from all temporary nodes V4 has smallest value of distance so make it permanent. Now V4 is the current working node.

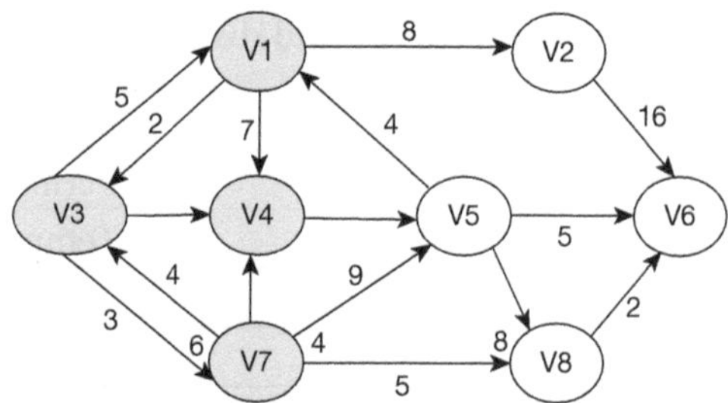

Adjacent nodes of V4 are V5, V1. Node V1 is already permanent, so we will check for V5 only.

V5.distance < V4.distance + distance (V4,V5) 9 < 6 + 9 don't relabel V5

Node	Destination	Precedence	Status
V1	0	0	Permanent
V2	8	V1	Temporary
V3	2	V1	Permanent
V4	6	V3	Permanent
V5	9	V7	Temporary
V6	∞	0	Temporary
V7	5	V3	Permanent
V8	∞	0	Temporary

Now from all temporary nodes V2 has smallest value of distance so make it permanent. Now V2 is our current working node.

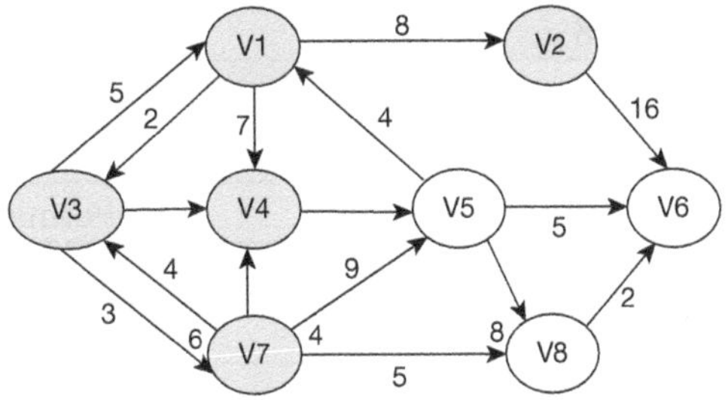

An adjacent node of V2 is V6.

V6.distance < V2.distance + distance (V2, V6) ∞ > 8 + 16 relabel V6

Now precedence and distance of V6 will be changed.

Node	Destination	Precedence	Status
V1	0	0	Permanent
V2	8	V1	Permanent
V3	2	V1	Permanent
V4	6	V3	Permanent
V5	9	V7	Temporary
V6	24	V2	Temporary
V7	5	V3	Permanent
V8	∞	0	Temporary

Now from all temporary nodes V5 has smallest value of distance, so make it permanent, now V5 is our current working node.

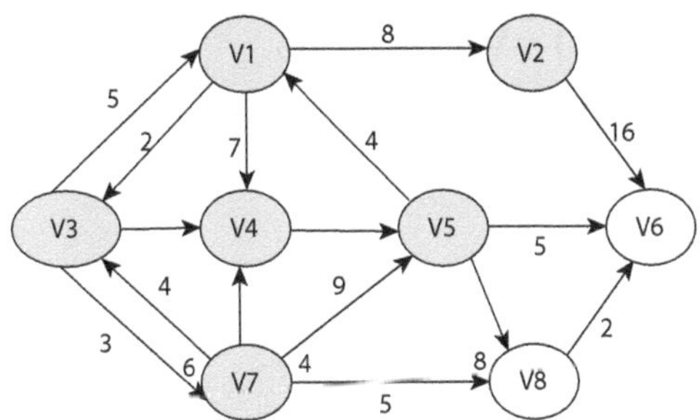

Adjacent nodes of V5 are V6, V8.

V6.distance < V5.distance + distance (V5, V6) 24 > 9 + 5 relabel V6

V8.distance < V5.distance + distance (V5, V8) ∞ > 9 + 8 relabel V8

Now precedence and distance of V6 and V8 will be changed.

Node	Destination	Precedence	Status
V1	0	0	Permanent
V2	8	V1	Permanent
V3	2	V1	Permanent
V4	6	V3	Permanent
V5	9	V7	Permanent
V6	14	V5	Temporary
V7	5	V3	Permanent
V8	17	V5	Temporary

Now from all temporary nodes V6 has smallest value of distance so make it permanent. Since V6 is our destination node and it has been made permanent, so we will stop our process.

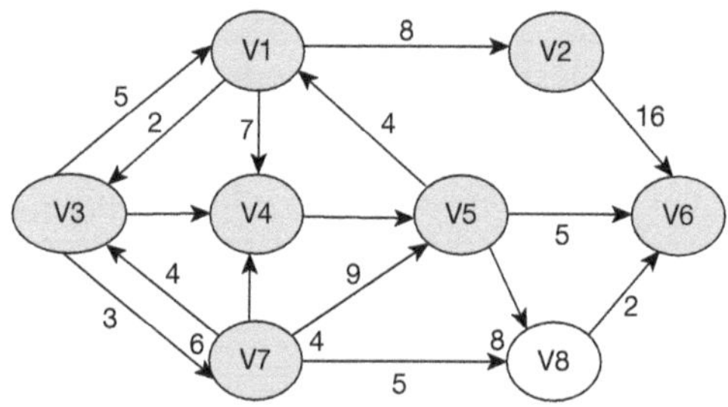

We can find out the shortest path from the last table. Start from the destination node and keep on seeing the predecessors until we get source node as a predecessor.

Predecessor of V6 is V5

Predecessor of V5 is V7

Predecessor of V7 is V3

Predecessor of V3 is V1

So the path is V1—V3—V7—V5—V6

Program: Write a program to find the shortest path between two node in graph using Dijkshtra Algorithm.

```
#include<stdio.h>
#define MAX 10
#define TEMP 0
#define PERM 1
#define infinity 9999
struct node
{
int predecessor
```

```
int dist;
int status;
};
int adj[MAX][MAX];
int n;
void main()
{
int i, j;
int source, dest;
int path[MAX];
int shortest_distance, count;
create graph();
printf("The adjacency matrix is:");
display();
while (1)
{
printf("Enter source node (0 to quit):");
scanf("%d", &source);
printf("Enter destination node(0 to quit):");
scanf("%d", &dest);
if(source==0 || dest==0)
exit (1);
count = findpath(source, dest, path, & shortest_distance);
if(shortest_distance!=0)
{
printf("Shortest distance is :", shortest_distance);
printf("Shortest path is:");
for(i=count; i>1;i--)
printf("%d->", path[i]);
printf("%d", path[i]);
printf("\n");
}
else
printf("There is no path from source to destination node:");
}
```

```
}
create graph()
{
int i, max_edge, origion, dest, weight;
printf("Enter number of vertices:");
scanf("%d", &n);
max_edge=n*(n-1);
for(i=1;i<=max_edge;i++)
{
printf("Enter edge %d(0 0 to quit):",i);
scanf("%d %d", &origion, &dest);
if((origion==0 && (dest==0))
break;
printf("Enter weight for this edge:");
scanf("%d", &weight);
if(origion > n || dest > n || origion <=0 || dest <=0)
{
printf("invalid edge");
i--;
}
else
adj[origion][dest]=weight;
}
}
display()
{
int i, j;
for(i=1;i<=n;i++)
{
for(j=1;j<=n;j++)
printf("%3d", adj[i][j]);
printf("\n");
}
}
int findpath(int s, int d, int path[MAX], int *sdist)
```

```
{
struct node state[MAX];
int i, min, count=0, current, newdist, u, v;
*sdist=0;
for(i=1;i<=n;i++)
{
state[i].predecessor=0;
state[i].dist=infinity;
state[i].status=TEMP;
}
state[s].predecessor=0;
state[s].dist=0;
state[s].status=PERM;
current=s;
while(current!=d)
{
for(i=1;i<=n;i++)
{
if(adj[current][i]>0 && state[i].status==TEMP)
{
newdist=state[current].dist +adj[current][i];
if(newdist <state[i].dist)
{
state[i].predecessor=current;
state[i].dist=newdist;
}
}
}
min=infinity;
current=0;
for(i=1;i<=n;i++)
{
if(state[i].status==TEMP & state[i].dist<min)
{
min=state[i].dist;
```

```
current=i;
}
}
if(current==0)
return 0;
state[current].status=PERM;
}
while(current!=0)
{
count++;
path[count]=current;
current=state[current].predecessor;
}
for(i=count;i>1;i--)
{
u=path[i];
v=path[i-1];
*sdist+=adj[u][v];
}
return (count);
}
```

7.12 WARSHALL'S ALGORITHM

Let G be a directed graph with n nodes, V_1, V_2,. .... V_n. Suppose we want to find the path matrix P of the graph G. Warshall gave an algorithm for this purpose that is much more efficient than calculating the powers of the adjacency matrix A.

First we define n square Boolean matrices P_0, P_1,. .... P_n as follows. Let P_k[i][j] denote the ij entry of the matrix P_k. Then we define:

P_k[i][j] = { 1 if there is a simple path from V_i to V_j which does not use any other nodes except possibly V_1, V_2,. ....V_k.
0.otherwise

In other words:

P_0 [i][j] = 1 if there is an edge from V_i to V_j

P_1 [i][j] = 1 if there is a simple path from V_i to V_j which does not use any other nodes except possible V_1.

P_2 [i][j] = 1 if there is a simple path from V_i to V_j which does not use any other nodes except possible V_1 and V_2.

....

....

First observe that the matrix $P_0 = A$, the adjacency matrix of G. Furthermore, since G has only n nodes, the last matrix $P_n = P$, the path matrix of G.

Warshall observed that $P_k[i][j] = 1$ can occur only if one of the following two cases occurs:

1. There is a simple path from V_i to V_j which does not use any other nodes except possibly V_1, V_2,. .... V_{k-1}; hence $P_{k-1}[i][j] = 1$

$$V_i \rightarrow \ldots\ldots\ldots \rightarrow V_j$$

2. There is a simple path from V_i to V_k and a simple path from V_k to V_j where each path does not use other nodes except possibly V_1, V_2,. ......V_{k-1}; hence $P_{k-1}[i][j] = 1$ and $P_{k-1}[k][j] = 1$

$$V_i \rightarrow \ldots\ldots\ldots \rightarrow V_k \rightarrow \ldots\ldots\ldots\ldots \rightarrow V_j$$

Accordingly, the elements of the matrix P_k can be obtained by

$P_k[i][j] = P_{k-1}[i][j] \wedge (P_{k-1}[i][j] \wedge P_{k-1}[k][j])$

Where we use the logical operations $\wedge$ (AND) and $\vee$ (OR). In other words, we can obtain each entry in the matrix P_k by looking at only three entries in the matrix P_{k-1}. Warshall's algorithm is as follows:

Algorithm

A directed graph G with n nodes is maintained in memory by its adjacency matrix A. This algorithm finds the Boolean path matrix P of the graph G.

1. Repeat steps 2 and 3 for i, j = 0, 1,. ..... n-1 //initializes P
2. If A[i][j] = 0 then set P[i][j] = 0
3. Else set P[i][j]
4. End of step1 loop
5. Repeat steps 6 to 8 for k = 0, 1,. ..... n-1 //updates P
6. Repeat steps 7 to 8 for i = 0, 1,. n-1
7. Repeat step 8 for j = 0, 1,. n-1
8. Set P[i][j] = P[i][j] $\vee$ (P[i][k] $\wedge$ P[k][j])
9. End of step 5 loop
10. End of step 3 loop
11. End of step 2 loop
12. Stop

Example: let us take a graph and find out the values of P_0, P_1, P_2, P_3, P_4

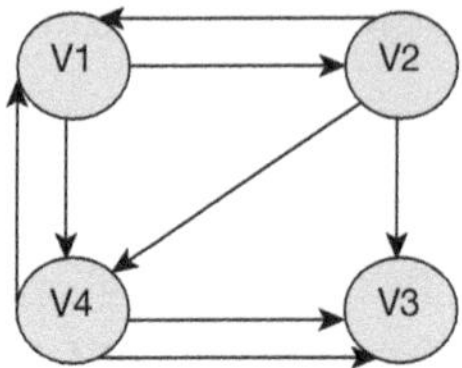

Solution

The first matrix P_0 is the adjacency matrix

$P_0 =$

	v1	v2	v3	v4
v1	0	1	0	1
v2	1	0	1	1
v3	0	0	0	1
v4	1	0	1	0

Now we have to find P_1

Now wherever $P_0[i][j] = 1$ $\quad P_1[i][j] = 1$

If $P_0[i][j] = 0$ then see $P_0[i][1]$ and $P_0[1][j]$, if both are 1 then $P_1[i][j] = 1$

$P_1 =$

	v1	v2	v3	v4
v1	0	1	0	1
v2	1	1	1	1
v3	0	0	0	1
v4	1	1	1	1

Similarly P_2

$P_2 =$

	v1	v2	v3	v4
v1	1	1	1	1
v2	1	1	1	1
v3	0	0	0	1
v4	1	1	1	1

Similarly P_3

$P_3 =$

	v1	v2	v3	v4
v1	1	1	1	1
v2	1	1	1	1
v3	0	0	0	1
v4	1	1	1	1

Similarly P_4

$$P_4 = \begin{array}{c} \\ v1 \\ v2 \\ v3 \\ v4 \end{array} \begin{array}{c} \begin{array}{cccc} v1 & v2 & v3 & v4 \end{array} \\ \begin{pmatrix} 1 & 1 & 1 & 1 \\ 1 & 1 & 1 & 1 \\ 1 & 1 & 1 & 1 \\ 1 & 1 & 1 & 1 \end{pmatrix} \end{array}$$

Here P_0 is the adjacency matrix and P_4 is the path matrix of the graph.

Program: Write a program to find path matrix by Warshall's Algorithm

```
#include<stdio.h>
#define MAX 20
main()
{
int i,j,k,n;
int weighted_adj[MAX][MAX], adj[MAX][MAX], path[MAX][MAX];
printf("enter the number of vertices");
scanf("%d", &n);
printf("Enter weighted adjacency matrix:");
for(i=0;i<n;i++)
for(j=0;j<n;j++)
scanf("%d", &weighted_adj[i][j]);
printf("The weighted adjacency matrix is:");
display(weighted_adj,n);
//change weighted adjacency matrix into Boolean adjacency matrix
for(i=0;i<n;i++)
for(j=0;j<n;j++)
if(weighted_adj[i][j] ==0)
adj[i][j] = 0;
else
adj[i][j] = 1;
printf("The adjacency matrix is:");
display(adj,n);
for(i=0;i<n;i++)
for(j=0;j<n;j++)
path[i][j]=adj[i][j];
```

```
for(k=0;k<n;k++)
{
printf("P %d is:", k);
display(path,n);
for(i=0;i<n;i++)
for(j=0;j<n;j++)
path[i][j]=(path[i][j] || (path[i][k] && path[k][j]));
}
printf("Path matrix P %d of the given graph is:", k);
display(path,n);
}
display(int matrix[MAX][MAX],int n)
{
int i,j;
for(i=0;i<n;i++)
{
for(j=0;j<n;j++)
printf("%3d", matrix[i][j]);
printf("\n");
}
}
```

7.13 MODIFIED WARSHALL'S ALGORITHM (SHORTEST PATH)

Let G be a directed graph with n nodes $V_0, V_1, \ldots\ldots V_{n-1}$, suppose G is weighted; that is, suppose each edge e in G is assigned a non-negative number w(e) called the weighted or length of the edge e. Then may be maintained in memory by its weight matrix W= $[W_{ij}]$, defined as follows:

$$W_{ij} = \begin{cases} w(e) & \text{if there is an edge from } V_i \text{ to } V_j \\ 0 & \text{if there is no edge from } V_i \text{ to } V_j \end{cases}$$

The path matrix P tells us whether or not there are path between the nodes. Now we want to find a matrix Q which will tell us the lengths of the shortest paths between the nodes or, more exactly, a matrix $Q = [q_{ij}]$ where q_{ij} = length of a shortest path from V_i to V_j

Next we describe a modification of Warshall's algorithm which finds us the matrix Q. Here we define a sequence of matrices $Q_0, Q_1, \ldots\ldots Q_n$ (the previous described matrices $P_0, P_1, \ldots\ldots P_n$) whose entries are defined as follows:

$Q_k[i][j]$ = the smaller of the length of the preceding path from V_i to V_j or the sum of the lengths of the preceding paths from V_i to V_k and from V_k to V_j.

More exactly,

$Q_k[i][j] = \min(Q_{k-1}[i][j], Q_{k-1}[i][k] + Q_{k-1}[k][j])$

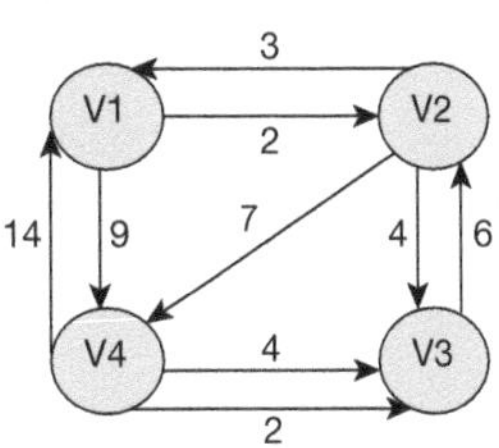

The initial matrix Q_0 is the same as the weight matrix W except that each 0 in W is replaced by ∞ or a very, very large number. The final matrix Q_n will be the desired matrix Q.

Example: let us take a graph and find out the values of Q_0, Q_1, Q_2, Q_3, Q_4

Solution

Weighted adjacency matrix for this graph is

W =

	V1	V2	V3	V4
V1	0	2	0	9
V2	3	0	4	7
V3	0	6	0	2
V4	14	0	4	0

Q_0 =

	V1	V2	V3	V4
V1	∞	2	0	9
V2	3	∞	4	7
V3	∞	6	∞	2
V4	14	∞	4	∞

	V1	V2	V3	V4
V1	--	V1V2	--	V1V4
V2	V2V1	--	V2V3	V2V4
V3	--	V3V2	--	V3V4
V4	V4V1	--	V4V3	--

After including node V1 (k=1)

Q_1 =

	V1	V2	V3	V4
V1	∞	2	0	9
V2	3	**<u>5</u>**	4	7
V3	∞	6	∞	2
V4	14	**<u>16</u>**	4	**<u>23</u>**

	V1	V2	V3	V4
V1	--	V1V2	--	V1V4
V2	V2V1	**V2V1V2**	V2V3	V2V4
V3	--	CB	--	V3V4
V4	V4V1	**V4V1V2**	V4V3	**V4V1V4**

After including node V2 (k=2)

$Q_2 =$

	V1	V2	V3	V4
V1	**5**	2	**6**	9
V2	3	5	4	7
V3	**9**	6	**10**	2
V4	14	16	4	23

	V1	V2	V3	V4
V1	**V1V2V1**	V1V2	**V1V2V3**	V1V4
V2	V2V1	V2V1V2	V2V3	V2V4
V3	**V3V2V1**	V3V2	**V3V2V3**	V3V4
V4	V4V1	V4V1V2	V4V3	V4V1V4

After including node V3 (k=3)

$Q_3 =$

	V1	V2	V3	V4
V1	5	2	6	**8**
V2	3	5	4	**6**
V3	9	6	10	2
V4	**13**	**10**	4	**6**

	V1	V2	V3	V4
V1	V1V2V1	V1V2	V1V2V3	**V1V2V3V4**
V2	V2V1	V2V1V2	V2V3	**V2V3V4**
V3	V3V2V1	V3V2	V3V2V3	V3V4
V4	**V4V3V2V1**	**V4V3V2**	V4V3	**V4V3V4**

After including node V4 (k=4)

$Q_4 =$

	V1	V2	V3	V4
V1	5	2	6	8
V2	3	5	4	6
V3	9	6	**6**	2
V4	13	10	4	6

$$\begin{array}{c} \\ V1 \\ V2 \\ V3 \\ V4 \end{array} \begin{array}{cccc} V1 & V2 & V3 & V4 \\ \left[\begin{array}{cccc} V1V2V1 & V1V2 & V1V2V3 & V1V2V3V4 \\ V2V1 & V2V1V2 & V2V3 & V2V3V4 \\ V3V2V1 & V3V2 & \underline{\mathbf{V3V4V3}} & V3V4 \\ V4V3V2V1 & V4V3V2 & V4V3 & V4V3V4 \end{array}\right] \end{array}$$

$Q_1(1, 3) = \text{Minimum } [Q_0(1, 3), Q_0(1, 1) + Q_0(1, 3)]$
$= \text{Minimum } (\infty, \infty)$
$= \infty$

$Q_1(2, 2) = \text{Minimum } [Q_0(2, 2), Q_0(2, 1) + Q_0(1, 2)]$
$= \text{Minimum } (\infty, 3+2)$
$= 5$

$Q_2(3, 1) = \text{Minimum } [Q_1(3, 1), Q_1(3, 2) + Q_1(2, 1)]$
$= \text{Minimum } (\infty, 6+3)$
$= 9$

$Q_3(1, 4) = \text{Minimum } [Q_2(1, 4), Q_2(1, 3) + Q_2(3, 4)]$
$= \text{Minimum } (9, 6+2)$
$= \text{Minimum } (9, 8)$
$= 8$

$Q_4(3, 3) = \text{Minimum } [Q_3(3, 3), Q_2(3, 4) + Q_2(4, 3)]$
$= \text{Minimum } (10, 2+4)$
$= \text{Minimum } (10, 6)$
$= 6$

Program: Write a program to modified Warshall's Algorithm to find shortest path matrix

```
#include<stdio.h>
#define infinity 9999
#define MAX 20

main()
{
int i,j,k,n;
int adj[MAX][MAX], path[MAX][MAX];
printf("enter the number of vertices");
scanf("%d", &n);
printf("Enter weighted matrix:");
for(i=0;i<n;i++)
```

```
for(j=0;j<n;j++)
scanf("%d", &adj[i][j]);
printf("The weighted matrix is:");
display(adj, n);
//replace all zero entries of adjacency matrix with infinity
for(i=0;i<n;i++)
for(j=0;j<n;j++)
if(adj[i][j] ==0)
path[i][j] = infinity;
else
path[i][j]=adj[i][j];
for(k=0;k<n;k++)
{
printf("Q %d is:", k);
display(path,n);
for(i=0;i<n;i++)
for(j=0;j<n;j++)
path[i][j]=minimum(path[i][j], path[i][k] + path[k][j]);
}
printf("Shortest Path matrix Q %d is:", k);
display(path,n);
}
minimum (int a,int b)
{
if(a<=b)
return a;
else
return b;
}
display(int matrix[MAX][MAX],int n)
{
int i,j;
for(i=0;i<n;i++)
{
for(j=0;j<n;j++)
```

```
printf("%7d", matrix[i][j]);
printf("\n");
}
}
```

7.14 APPLICATIONS OF GRAPH

Graphs are constructed for various types of application such as:

1. In circuit networks where points of connection are drawn as vertices and component wires become the edges of the graph.
2. In transport networks where stations are drawn as vertices and routes become the edges of the graph.
3. In maps that draw cities/state/regions as vertices and adjacency relations as edge.
4. In program flow analysis where procedures or modules are treated as vertices and calls to these procedures are drawn as edges of the graph.
5. Once we have a graph of a particular concept, they can be easily used for finding shortest paths, project planning, etc.
6. In flow charts or control-flow graphs, the statements and conditions in a program are represented as nodes and the flow of control is represented by the edges.
7. In state transition diagram, the nodes are used to represent states and the edges represent legal moves from one state to the other.
8. Graphs are also used to draw activity network diagrams. These diagrams are extensively used as a project management tool to represent the interdependent relationships between groups, steps, and tasks that have a significant impact on the project.
9. An activity network diagram also known as an arrow diagram or a PERT is used to identify time sequences of events which are pivotal to objectives. It is also helpful when a project has multiple activities which need simultaneous management. Activity network diagrams help the project development team to create a realistic project schedule by drawing graphs that exhibit.

POINTS TO REMEMBER

1. A graph is basically a collection of vertices also called nodes and edges that connect these vertices.
2. A graph in which there exists a path between any two of its nodes is called a connected graph. An edge that has identical end-points is called a loop. The size of a graph is the total number of edges in it.

3. The out-degree of a node is the number of edges that originate at u.
4. The in-degree of a node is the number of edges that terminates at u. A node u is known as a sink if it has a positive in-degree but a zero out-degree.
5. A transitive closure of a graph is constructed to answer reachability questions.
6. A vertex v of G is called an articulation points if removing v along with the edges incidents to v result in a graph that has at least two connected components.
7. Breadth first search is a graph search algorithm that begins at the root node and explores all the neighbouring nodes. Then for each of those nearest nodes, the algorithm explores their unexplored neighbour nodes, and so on, until it finds the goal.
8. The depth first search algorithm progresses by expanding the starting node of G and thus going deeper and deeper until a goal node is found, or until a node that has no children is encountered.
9. A spanning tree of a connected, undirected graph G is a sub-graph of G which is a tree that connects all the vertices together.
10. Kruskal's algorithm is an example of a greedy algorithm, as it makes the locally optimal choice at each stage with the hope of finding the global optimum.
11. Dijkstra's algorithm is used to find the length of an optimal path between two nodes in a graph.

MULTIPLE CHOICE QUESTIONS

1. An edge that has identical end-points is called a

   (*a*) Multi-path (*b*) Loop
   (*c*) Cycle (*d*) Multi-edge

2. The total number of edges containing the node u is called

   (*a*) in-degree (*b*) out-degree
   (*c*) degree (*d*) none of these

3. A graph in which there exists a path between any two of its nodes is called

   (*a*) complete graph (*b*) connected graph
   (*c*) diagraph (*d*) in-degree graph

4. The number of edges that originates at u are called

   (*a*) in-degree (*b*) out-degree
   (*c*) degree (*d*) source

5. The memory use of an adjacency matrix is

   (*a*) o (n) (*b*) o (n^2)
   (*c*) o (n^3) (*d*) o (log n)

6. The term optimal can means
   (*a*) shortest (*b*) cheapest
   (*c*) fastest (*d*) all of these
7. How many articulation vertices does a biconnected graph contains?
   (*a*) 0 (*b*) 1
   (*c*) 2 (*d*) 3

TRUE OR FALSE

1. Graph is a linear data structure.
2. In-degree of a node is the number of edges leaving that node.
3. The size of a graph is the total number of vertices in it.
4. A sink has a zero in-degree but a positive out-degree.
5. The space complexity of depth first search is lower than that of breadth first search.
6. A node is known as a sink if it has a positive out-degree but the in-degree = 0.
7. A directed graph that has no cycles is called a directed acyclic graph.
8. A graph G can have many different spanning trees.
9. Kruskal's algorithm is an example of a greedy algorithm.

FILL IN THE BLANKS

1. _________ has a zero degree.
2. In-degree of a node is the number of edges that _________ at u.
3. Adjacency matrix is also known as a __________.
4. A path p is known as a __________ path if the edge has the same end-points.
5. A graph with multiple edges and/ or a loop is called a __________.
6. Vertices that are a part of the minimum spanning tree T are called.
7. A __________ of a graph is constructed to answer reachability questions.
8. An ________ is a vertex v of G if removing v along with the edges incident to v results in a graph that has at least two connected components.
9. A________ graph is a connected graph that is not broken into disconnected pieces by deleting any single vertex.
10. An edge is called a __________ if removing that edge results in a disconnected graph.

EXERCISES

1. Explain the relationship between a linked list structure and a diagraph?
2. Define graph? Explain its key term?
3. How are graphs represented inside a computer's memory? Which method do you prefer and why?
4. Explain the graph traversal algorithms in detail with the help of suitable example?
5. Differentiate between BFS and DFS?
6. Define spanning tree? When is a spanning tree called a minimum spanning tree? Take a weighted graph of your choice and find out its minimum spanning tree?
7. Write short notes on Prim's, Kruskal and Dijkstra Algorithm?
8. Briefly discuss Warshall's Algorithm. Also, discuss its modify version?
9. Write a program to create and print a graph?

REFERENCES

1. Berge, C., The Theory of graphs and its applications, John Wiley & Sons, New York, 1983.
2. Deo, N., Graph theory with applications to engineering and computer science, Prentice-Hall of India, New Delhi.
3. Dijkstra, E. W., A note on two problems in connection with graphs, Numerishche Mathematik, Vol. 1, 1959.
4. Euler, L., Leonerd Euler, The Konigsberg's Bridges, Scientific American, 189, 1953.
5. Gabow, N.H., Z. Galil, et al., Efficient algorithms for finding minimum spanning trees on directed and undirected graphs, Combinatorica, 6, 1986.
6. Harary, F., Graph Theory, Addison-Wesley, Reading Massachusetts, 1979.
7. Hopcroft, J.E. and R.E. Tarjan, Efficient Algorithms for Graph Manipulation, 1984.
8. Randal E. Bryant, Graph based algorithms for Boolean function manipulation, IEEE Transactions on Computers, C-35, 8, August 1986.
9. Sahner, R.A., K.S. Trivedi, and A. Puliafito, Performance of reliability Analysis of Computer System, Kluwer Academic Publishers, Boston, 1996.
10. Sheldon B. Akers, Binary Decision Diagram, IEEE Transactions on Computer, C-27, 6, June 1978.
11. Shimon Even, Graph Algorithms, Computer Science Press, 1984.
12. Tarjan, R.E., Depth First Search and Linear Graph Algorithm, SIAM Journal of Computing, 1, 1972.
13. Writh, N., Algorithm + Data Structure = Programs, Prentice Hall, Englewood Cliffs, New Jersey, 1997.
14. Faster Algorithm for the shortest path, Journal of the ACM, 37, 1990.

8

Searching and Sorting

8.1 INTRODUCTION

The process of finding the location of a specific data item or record with a given key value or finding the locations of all records, which satisfy one or more conditions in a list, is called "Searching". If the item exists in the given list then search is said to be successful otherwise if the element if not found in the given list then search is said to be unsuccessful.

1. External searching
2. Internal searching

External searching means searching the records using keys where there are many records which reside in files stored on disks. Internal searching means searching the records using keys where there are less number of records residing entirely within the computer's main memory.

There are many different searching algorithms. The algorithm that one chooses generally depends on the way information in DATA is arranged. Following are the three important searching techniques:

- Linear or Sequential Searching
- Binary Searching
- Interpolation Search

The time required for a search operation depends on the complexity of the searching algorithm. Basically, we have to consider three cases when we search for a particular element in the list.

1. Best Case: The best case is that in which the element is found during the first comparison.
2. Worst Case: The worst case is that in which the element is found only at the end *i.e.*, in the last comparison.

3. Average Case: The average case is that in which the element is found in comparisons more than best case but less than worst case.

8.2 LINEAR OR SEQUENTIAL SEARCHING

Suppose DATA is a linear array with n elements. Given no other information about DATA. The most intuitive way to search for a given ITEM in DATA is to compare ITEM with each element of DATA one-by-one. That is, first we test whether DATA (1) = ITEM, and then we test whether DATA (2) = ITEM, and so on. This method which traverses DATA sequentially to locate ITEM, is called linear search or sequence search. Each element of an array is read one-by-one sequentially and it is compared with the desired element. A search will be unsuccessful if all the elements are read and the desired element is not found. Linear search is the least efficient search technique among the quantity dependent search techniques. This technique should be chosen for searching the records when the records are stored without considering the order or when the storage medium lacks the direct access facility. Some important points are:

- It is the simplest way for finding an element in a list.
- It searches the element sequentially in a list, no matter whether list is sorted or unsorted.
- In case of sorted list the search is started from 1st element and continue until the desired element is found or the element whose value is smaller than the value being searched.
- If the list is unsorted searching started from 1st location and continued until the element is found or the end of the list is reached.

Algorithm

Let A be an array of n elements, A(1), A(2), A(3),...... A(n) and let "data" is the element to be searched. Then this algorithm will find the location "loc" of data in array A. Set loc = -1, if the search is unsuccessful.

1. Input an array A of n element and "data" to be searched and initialise loc = -1.
2. Initialise i =0: and repeat through step 3 if (i<n) by incrementing i by one.
3. If (data = A [i])
   (*a*) Loc = i
   (*b*) GOTO step 4
4. If (loc >0)

   Print "data is found and searching is successful"

   Else

   Print "data is found and searching is unsuccessful"
5. Exit

Drawbacks

- It is a very slow process.
- It is used only for small amount of data.
- It is a very time consuming method

Program: Write a Program to implement Linear Search using array.

```
#include<stdio.h>
void main()
{
int a[5],i,flag=0,m;
printf("Enter the number of Array elements \n");
for(i=0;i<5;i++)
{
scanf("%d",&a[i]);
}
printf("The Array Elements are:-\n");
for(i=0;i<5;i++)
{
printf("%d\t",a[i]);
}
printf("\n Enter the number to be searched: ");
scanf("%d",&m);
for(i=0;i<5;i++)
{
if(a[i]==m)
{
flag=1;
break;
}
}
if(flag==1)
printf("Element Found at position %d ",i);
else
printf("Element Not Found");
}
```

Output

Enter the number of Array Elements

12

34

4

67

23

The Array Elements are:-

12 34 4 67 23

Enter the number to be searched: 34

Element Found at position 1

8.3 BINARY SEARCH

If we place our items in an array and sort those in either ascending or descending order. Then we can obtain much better performance with an algorithm called **binary Search.**

General Idea about Binary Search Algorithm

1. Find the middle element of the array.
2. Compare the middle element with the data to be searched, and then there are following three cases.
   (*a*) If it is a desired element, then search is successful.
   (*b*) If it is less than desired data, then search only the first half of the array, *i.e.*, the elements which come to the left side of the middle element.
   (*c*) If it is greater than the desired data, then search only the second half of the array, *i.e.*, the elements which come to the right side of the middle element.

Algorithm

1. Input an array A of elements and "data" to be searched.
2. LB = 0, UB=n; mid = int (LB + UB)/2
3. Repeat steps 4 and 5 while (LB< = UB) and (A [mid]! = data)
4. If (data < A [mid])

        UB = mid-1

    Else

        LB = mid+1

5. Mid = int (LB + UB)/2
6. If (A[mid] == data)

   Print "the data is found"

   Else

   Print "the data is not found"
7. Exit

Example: Suppose an array A [7] whose elements are

5	8	15	25	30	40	55
0	**1**	**2**	**3**	**4**	**5**	**6**

Suppose data = 30

Solution: Following steps are used if we use binary search to search a data = 30 in the above array.

Here n = 6

So, LB = 0, UB = 6

$$\text{mid} = \frac{(0+6)}{2} = 3 \text{ i.e., } A[\text{mid}] = A[3] = 25$$

Since, A[3] < data i.e., 25 < 30.

So, reinitialise the variable LB as LB = mid +1

i.e., LB = 3+1 =4

Now, $\text{mid} = \frac{4+6}{2} = 5$

i.e., A[mid] = A [5] = 40

Now, data < A [mid] i.e., 30 < 40

So reinitialise the variable UB = mid -1 = 5-1 =4

Now, LB =4 and UB =5

So, $\text{mid} = \frac{4+5}{2} = \frac{9}{2} = 4$ i.e., A[4] = 30

Since (A[mid] = data) i.e., 30 = 30

Thus searching is successful and 30 is found in the given array

Program: Write a program to implement Binary Search using array.

```
#include<stdio.h>
void main()
{
int a[10],i,n,m,c=0,l,u,mid;
```

```
printf("Enter the size of an array: ");
scanf("%d",&n);
printf("Enter the elements in ascending order: ");
for (i=0;i<n;i++)
{
scanf("%d",&a[i]);
}
printf("Enter the number to be searched: ");
scanf("%d",&m);
l=0,u=n-1;
while(l<=u)  {
                    mid=(l+u)/2;
                    if(m==a[mid])
                         {
                          c==1;
                          break;
                          }
else if(m<a[mid]) {
             u=mid-1;   }
else
             l=mid+1;
             }
if(c==1)
printf("Element found.");
else
printf("Element not found.");
}
```

Output

```
Enter the size of an array: 6
Enter the elements in ascending order:
2
4
6
8
10
12
```

Enter the number to be search: 10

Element found.

8.4 INTERPOLATION SEARCH

Another technique for searching an ordered array is called interpolation search. This method is even more efficient than binary search, if the elements are uniformly distributed (or sorted) in an array A.

In a binary search, the search space is always divided in two parts to guarantee logrithmic time; however, when we search for "Arham" in the phone book, we do not start in the middle - we start towards the front and work from there. That is the idea of an interpolation search. Instead of cutting the search space by a fixed half, we cut it by an amount that seems most likely to succeed. This amount is determined by interpolation.

Consider an array A of elements and the elements are uniformly distributed. Initially, as in binary search, low is set to 0 and high is set to n-1.

Now we are searching an element key in an array between A[low] and A[high]. The key would be expected to be at mid.

Mid = low + (high - low) * ((key - A[low]/A[high] - A[low]))

If key is lower than A [mid], reset high to mid -1; else reset low to mid +1. Repeat the process until the key is found or low > high.

Algorithm

Suppose A be array of sorted elements and key is the elements to be searched and low represents the lower bound of the array and high represents higher bound of the array.

1. Input a sorted array of n elements and the key to be searched.
2. Initialise low = 0 and high = n-1
3. Repeat the steps 4 through 7 until if (low < high)
4. Mid = low + (high - low) * ((key - A[low])/A[high] - A[low])
5. If (key == A(mid)

       print "key is found"
6. If (key < A[mid])

       high − mid + 1

   else if (key > A[mid])

       low = mid +1

   else

       print " The key is not in the array and Exit"
7. STOP

Example 14.2: Let us consider 7 numbers as 4, 15, 20, 35, 45, 55, 65

Solution: Suppose we are searching 45 from the given array

Here n=7, key= 45, low = 0, high = n -1 = 6

mid = 0 +(6 - 0) X {(45 - 4)/(65 - 4)}

= 0 + 6 X (41/61) = 4.032

Consider only the integer part of the mid *i.e.*, mid = 4.

Now the statement if (key = = A[mid]) gives the following output

Key = = A[mid]. i.e; key== A [4]

i.e; A [4] = 45.

Hence 45 = 45

Thus, key is found.

8.5 SORTING TECHNIQUES

Sorting is nothing but storage of data in some order; it can be in ascending or descending order. The term Sorting comes into picture with the term Searching. There are so many things in our real life that we need to search, like a particular record in database, roll numbers in merit list, a particular telephone number, any particular page in a book etc.

Sorting arranges data in a sequence which makes searching easier. Every record which is going to be sorted will contain one key. Based on the key the record will be sorted. For example, suppose we have a record of students, every such record will have the following data:

- Roll No.
- Name
- Age
- Class

Here Student roll no. can be taken as key for sorting the records in ascending or descending order. Now suppose we have to search a Student with roll no. 15, we don't need to search the complete record we will simply search between the Students with roll no. 10 to 20.

Sorting Efficiency

There are many techniques for sorting. Implementation of particular sorting technique depends upon situation. Sorting techniques mainly depends on two parameters. First parameter is the execution time of program, which means time taken for execution of program. Second is the space, which means space, taken by the program.

The efficiency of data handling can often be substantially increased if the data are sorted

Types of Sorting

1. Bubble sort
2. Insertion Sort
3. Selection sort
4. Merger Sort
5. Heap Sort
6. Quick sort
7. Radix Sort

The sorting problem is to arrange a sequence of records so that values of their key fields form a non-decreasing sequence. That is, given records r_1, r_2,..... r_n, with key values k_1, k_2,....k_n, respectively, we must produce the same records in an order r_{i1}, r_{i2}, r_{in}, such that $k_{i1} \leq k_{i2} \leq . .. \leq k_{in}$

8.6 BUBBLE SORT

Also called as sinking sort

Bubble sort, is a simple sorting algorithm. Comparing two items at a time and swapping them if they are in the wrong order. Pass through the list is repeated until no swaps are needed, which means the list is sorted. The idea applied for the bubble sort is as follows:

(*a*) Suppose if the array contains n elements, then (n-1) iterations are required to sort this array.

(*b*) First compare the 1st and 2nd element of array, if 1st element < 2nd element then compare the 2nd element with 3rd element.

(*c*) If 2nd element > 3rd element, then interchange the value of 2nd and 3rd elements.

(*d*) Now compare the value of 3rd element with 4th element, if 3rd element > 4th element then interchange the value of 3rd and 4th elements.

(*e*) Similarly n-1th element is compared with nth element.

(*f*) Now the highest value element is reached at the nth position.

The bubble sort is generally considered to be the most inefficient sorting algorithm in common usage.

Algorithm

Bubble sort (A)

1. start
2. for i= 1 to length [A]
3. for j= length [A] to i+1
4. if A[j] < A[j-1]
5. exchange (A[j], A[j-1])

Example: let us take the element and apply bubble sort technique.

5	1	6	2	4	3

Solution:

Pass 1:

(*a*) Compare 1st element and 2nd element, 5>1, interchange

5	1	6	2	4	3

Now the elements are as follows:

1	5	6	2	4	3

(*b*) Compare 2nd element and 3rd element, 5 < 6, no interchange.

(*c*) Compare 3rd and 4th element, 6>2 interchange

1	5	6	2	4	3

Now the elements are as follows:

1	5	2	6	4	3

(*d*) Compare 4th and 5th element, 6> 4, interchange

1	5	2	6	4	3

Now the element areas follows:

1	5	2	4	6	3

(*e*) Compare 5th and 6th element, 6>3, interchange.

1	5	2	4	6	3

Now the element are as follows:

1	5	2	4	3	6

After the Pass 1, the elements are as follows:

1	5	2	4	3	6

Pass 2:

(*a*) Compare 1st and 2nd element, 1<5, no interchange.

(*b*) Compare 2nd and 3rd element, 5>2, interchange.

1	5	2	4	3	6

Now the elements are as follows:

1	2	5	4	3	6

(*c*) Compare 3rd and 4th element, 5>4, interchange.

1	2	4	5	3	6

Now the elements are as follows:

1	2	4	5	3	6

(*d*) Compare 4th and 5th element, 5>3, interchange.

Now the elements are as follows:

1	2	4	3	5	6

After the Pass 2, the element are as follows:

1	2	4	3	5	6

Pass3:

(*a*) Compare 1st and 2nd element,1<2, no interchange.
(*b*) Compare 2nd and 3rd element,2<4 no interchange.
(*c*) Compare 3rd and 4th element, 4>3, interchange.

1	2	4	3	5	6

Now the elements are as follows:

1	2	3	4	5	6

So, final sorted elements are

1	2	3	4	5	6

Program: Write a program to implement a bubble sort using array

```
#include <stdio.h>
int main()
{
int array[100], n, c, d, swap;
printf("Enter number of elements\n");
scanf("%d", &n);
printf("Enter %d integers\n", n);
for (c = 0; c < n; c++)
scanf("%d", &array[c]);
for (c = 0 ; c < ( n - 1 ); c++)
{
   for (d = 0 ; d < n - c - 1; d++)
```

```
{
  if (array[d] > array[d+1])
  {
    swap = array[d];
    array[d] = array[d+1];
    array[d+1] = swap;
  }
 }
}
printf("Sorted list in ascending order:\n");
for ( c = 0 ; c < n ; c++ )
printf("%d\t", array[c]);
return 0;
}
```

Output

```
Enter number of elements
8
Enter 8 integers
44
55
33
88
77
22
11
66
Sorted list in ascending order:
11 22 33 44 55 66 77 88
```

8.7 INSERTION SORT

It is a simple Sorting algorithm which sorts the array by shifting elements one by one. Following are some of the important characteristics of Insertion Sort.

1. It has one of the simplest implementation
2. It is efficient for smaller data sets, but very inefficient for larger lists.
3. Insertion Sort is adaptive, that means it reduces its total number of steps if given a partially sorted list, hence it increases its efficiency.

4. It is better than Selection Sort and Bubble Sort algorithms.
5. Its space complexity is less but like Bubble Sort, insertion sort also requires a single additional memory space.
6. It is **Stable**, as it does not change the relative order of elements with equal keys

Algorithm

Insertion sort (A)

1. start
2. for j=2 to length [A]
3. do key = A[j]
4. i = j-1
5. while i > 0 and A[i] > key
6. do A[i+1]=A[i]
7. i = i - 1
8. A[i+1] = key

Step 1: array [0] is already sorted because of only one element.

Step 2: array [1] is inserted before or after array [0]

So array [0], array [1] are sorted

Step 3: array [2] is inserted before array [0], in between array [0] and array [1] or after array [1]

So array [0], array [1], array [2] are sorted

Step 4: array [3] is inserted in its proper place in array

So array [0], array [1], array [2], array [3] are sorted

And so on............................

Finally, array [n-1] is inserted into its proper place in array

So array [0], array [1], array[2],. ...., array [n-1] are sorted.

Example: let us take the element and apply insertion sort technique.

30	20	35	14	90	25	32

Solution:

Step1: 20<30, interchange the elements, we get

20	30	35	14	90	25	32

Step 2: 30<35, no need to interchange the elements

20	30	35	14	90	25	32

Step 3: 14 is less than 35, 30, 20 so insert 14 before 20, we get

14	20	30	35	90	25	32

Step 4: 90>35, no need to interchage the elements

14	20	30	35	90	25	32

Step 5: 25 is less than 90, 35, 30, so insert 25 before 30

14	20	25	30	35	90	32

Step 6: 32 is less than 90, 35, therefore insert 32 before 35, we get

14	20	25	30	32	35	90

Hence the array is sorted

Program: Write a program to implement an insertion sort using array

```
#include <stdio.h>
int main()
{
 int n, array[10], c, d, t;
 printf("Enter number of elements\n");
 scanf("%d", &n);
 printf("Enter %d integers\t", n);
 for (c = 0; c < n; c++)
{
 scanf("%d", &array[c]);
}
 for (c = 1 ; c <= n - 1; c++)
{
 d = c;
 while ( d > 0 && array[d] < array[d-1])
 {
    t=array[d];
    array[d]=array[d-1];
    array[d-1]=t;
    d--;
 }
}
printf("Sorted list in ascending order:\n");
for (c = 0; c <= n - 1; c++)
{
```

```
    printf("%d\t", array[c]);
  }
  return 0;
  }
```

Output

```
Enter number of elements
7
Enter 7 integers
30  20  35  14  90  25  32
Sorted list in ascending order:
14  20  25  30  32  35  90
```

8.8 SELECTION SORT

The idea of selection sort is rather simple: we repeatedly find the next largest (or smallest) element in the array and move it to its final position in the sorted array. Assume that we wish to sort the array in increasing order, *i.e.*, the smallest element at the beginning of the array and the largest element at the end. We begin by selecting the largest element and moving it to the highest index position; we can do this by swapping the element at the highest index and the largest element. We then reduce the effective size of the array by one element and repeat the process on the smaller sub-array.

Let us take an array of elements. First you will search the position of smallest element from array [0]. .... array[n-1]. Then you will interchange that smallest element with array [0]. Now you will search the position of the second smallest element from array [1]. .... array [n-1], then interchange that smallest element with array [1], and so on.....

Algorithm

Selection sort (A)

1. start
2. n=length[A]
3. for j=1 to n-1
4. smallest=j
5. for i=j+1 to n
6. if A[i] < A[smallest]
7. then smallest=i
8. exchange (A[j], A[smallest])

Steps

1. Search the smallest element from array [0]........ array[n-1]
2. Interchange array [0] with smallest element.
3. Result: array [0] is sorted.
4. Again search the second smallest element from array[1]..... array[n-1]
5. Interchange array [1] with second smallest element.
6. Result: array [0], array [1] is sorted.
7. Repeat these steps until we get the array in sorted order.

How Selection Sorting Works

Original Array	After 1st pass	After 2nd pass	After 3rd pass	After 4th pass	After 5th pass
3	1	1	1	1	1
6	6	3	3	3	3
(1)	(3)	6	4	4	4
8	8	8	8	5	5
4	4	(4)	6	(6)	6
5	5	5	(5)	8	8

In the first pass, the smallest element found is 1, so it is placed at the first position, then leaving first element, smallest element is searched from the rest of the elements, 3 is the smallest, so it is then placed at the second position. Then we leave 1 and 3, from the rest of the elements, we search for the smallest and put it at third position and keep doing this, until array is sorted.

Program: Write a program to implement a selection sort using array

```
#include <stdio.h>
int main()
{
  int array[100], n, c, d, position, swap;
  printf("Enter number of elements\n");
  scanf("%d", &n);
  printf("Enter %d integers\n", n);
  for ( c = 0 ; c < n ; c++ )
  scanf("%d", &array[c]);
  for ( c = 0 ; c < ( n - 1 ) ; c++ )
  {
    position = c;
```

```
        for ( d = c + 1 ; d < n ; d++ )
        {
          if ( array[position] > array[d] )
            position = d;
        }
        if ( position != c )
        {
          swap = array[c];
          array[c] = array[position];
          array[position] = swap;
        }
      }
      printf("Sorted list in ascending order:\n");
      for ( c = 0 ; c < n ; c++ )
      printf("%d\t", array[c]);
      return 0;
    }
```

Output

```
Enter number of elements
6
Enter 5 integers
3 6 1 8 4 5
Sorted list in ascending order:
1 3 4 5 6 8
```

8.9 MERGE SORT

Merge sort is a sorting algorithm that uses the idea of divide and conquers approach. The procedure MERGE SORT (A, p, r) sorts the elements in the sub array A [p....r]. If $p \leq r$ the sub array has at most one element and is therefore already sorted. Otherwise, the divide step simply computes an index q that partitions A [p.....r] into two sub arrays: A [p.....q], containing [n/2] elements, and A [q+1....r] containing [n/2] elements. To sort the entire sequence A=(A[1],A[2],....A[n]) we call MERGE - SORT (A,1, length[A]) where once again length [A]=n. If we look at the operation of the procedure bottom-up when n is a power of two, the algorithm consists of merging pairs of 1 item sequence to form sorted sequences of length 2, merging pairs of sequences of length 2 to form sorted sequences of length 4, and so on, until two sequences of length n/2 are merged to form the final sorted sequence of length n.

Algorithm

MERGE-SORT (A, p, r)

1. start
2. if p < r
3. then q = (p + r) / 2
4. MERGE-SORT(A, p, q)
5. MERGE-SORT(A, q+1, r)
6. MERGE(A, p, q, r)

MERGE (A, p, q, r)

1. $N_1 = q - p + 1$
2. $N_2 = r - q$
3. create arrays L[1......n_1+1] and R[1......n_2+1]
4. for i=1 to n_1
5. do L[i] = A[p + i - 1]
6. for j = 1 to n_2
7. do R[j] = A[q + j]
8. $L[n_1 + 1] = \infty$
9. $R[n_2 + 1] = \infty$
10. i = 1
11. j = 1
12. for k = p to r
13. do if L[i] ≤ R[j]
14. then A[K] = L[i]
15. i = i + 1
16. else A[k] = R[j]
17. j = j + 1

Example: let us take a list of element and apply merge sort technique

194 34 12 756 54 1 88 55 897 23 96 33

Solution:

Step 1: merge the two unsorted pairs in a single sorted pair. Initially we have pair size 1. Merge these pair of size 1 into pairs of size 2.

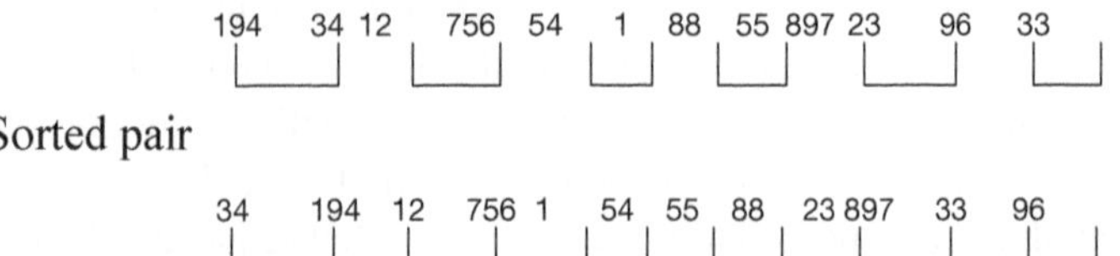

Sorted pair

Step 2: similarly merge the pairs of size 2 into pair of size 4

34 194 12 756 | 1 54 55 88 | 23 897 33 96

Sorted pair

12 34 194 756 | 1 54 55 88 | 23 33 96 897

Step 3: merge the pairs of size 4 into a pair of 8 in sorted fashion

1 12 34 54 55 88 194 756 23 | 897 33 96

Step 4: merge two pairs into a single pair

1 12 23 33 34 54 55 88 96 194 756 897

Now the sorted list is:

1 12 23 33 34 54 55 88 96 194 756 897

Program: Write a program to implement a merge sort using array

```
#include<stdio.h>
#define MAX 50
void mergeSort(int arr[],int low,int mid,int high);
void partition(int arr[],int low,int high);
void main()
{
  int merge[MAX],i,n;
  printf("Enter the total number of elements: \n");
  scanf("%d",&n);
  printf("Enter the elements which to be sort: \n");
  for(i=0;i<n;i++)
  {
    scanf("%d",&merge[i]);
  }
  partition(merge,0,n-1);
  printf("After merge sorting elements are: \n");
  for(i=0;i<n;i++)
  {
    printf("%d ",merge[i]);
  }
}
```

```
void partition(int arr[],int low,int high)
{
   int mid;
   if(low<high)
   {
      mid=(low+high)/2;
      partition(arr,low,mid);
      partition(arr,mid+1,high);
      mergeSort(arr,low,mid,high);
   }
}
void mergeSort(int arr[],int low,int mid,int high)
{
   int i,m,k,l,temp[MAX];
   l=low;
   i=low;
   m=mid+1;
   while((l<=mid)&&(m<=high))
   {
      if(arr[l]<=arr[m])
      {
         temp[i]=arr[l];
         l++;
      }
      else
      {
         temp[i]=arr[m];
         m++;
      }
      i++;
   }
   if(l>mid)
   {
      for(k=m;k<=high;k++)
      {
```

```
            temp[i]=arr[k];
            i++;
        }
    }
    else
    {
        for(k=l;k<=mid;k++)
        {
            temp[i]=arr[k];
            i++;
        }
    }
    for(k=low;k<=high;k++)
    {
        arr[k]=temp[k];
    }
}
```

Output

```
Enter the total number of elements:
12
Enter the elements which to be sort:
194  34  12  756  54  1  88  55  897  23  96  33
After merge sorting elements are:
1  12  23  33  34  54  55  88  96  194  756  897
```

8.10 HEAP SORT

Heap sort was invented by **John Williams** and uses the approach just opposite to selection sort. The selection sorts find the smallest element among n elements, then the smallest element among n-1 elements and so on, until the end of the array where as heap sort finds the largest element and puts it at the end of the array, then the second largest item is found and this process is repeated for all other elements. Before discussing heap sort, we will begin by defining a new structure, the heap. We can define minimum heap and maximum heap. A **max (or min) heap** is a complete binary tree with the property that the value at each node is at least as large as (or as small as) the values of its children (if they exist). This is called **Heap property.** A heap is complete balanced binary tree in which each node satisfies the heap property and every leaf is of depth d or d-1. The definition of a **max heap** implies that one of the largest elements is at the root of the heap. If the elements are distinct, then the root contains the largest element.

We do following steps for heap sorting

1. Replace the root with last node of heap tree
2. Keep the last node (now root) at the proper position, it means do the delete operation in heap tree but here deleted node is root.

Example: Let us take a heap tree and apply heap tree sorting algorithm

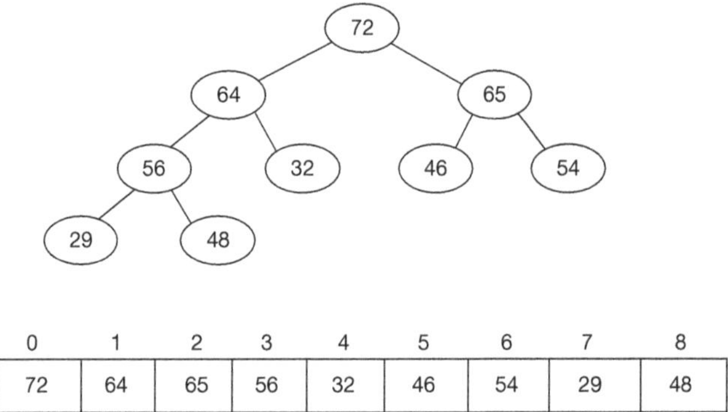

0	1	2	3	4	5	6	7	8
72	64	65	56	32	46	54	29	48

Solution:

Step 1:

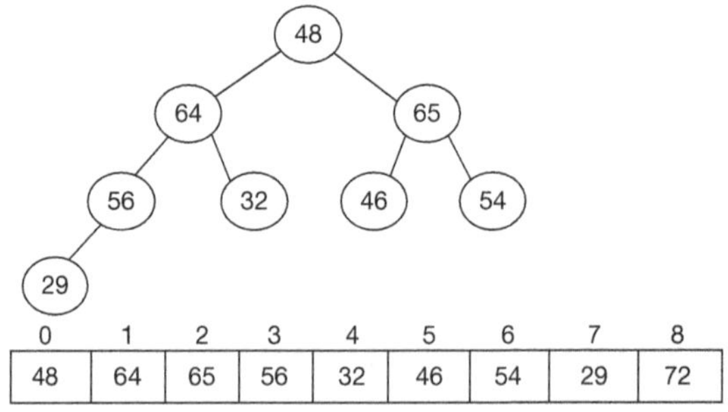

0	1	2	3	4	5	6	7	8
48	64	65	56	32	46	54	29	72

Now the root is at the position of last node and last node at the position of root. Here left and right child of 48 is 64 and 65.

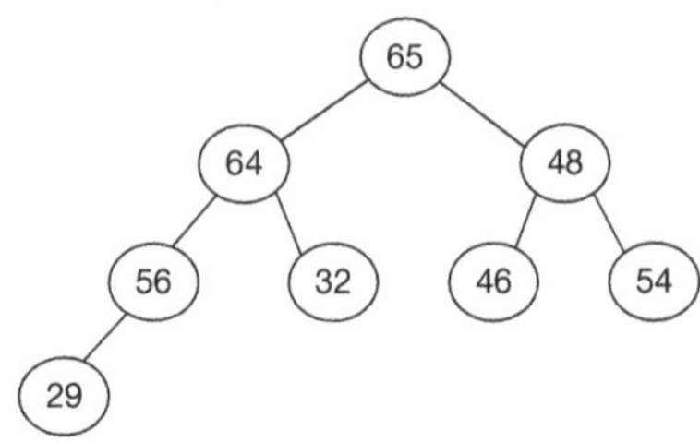

Here right child of 48 is 54, which is greater than 48, hence replace it with 54.

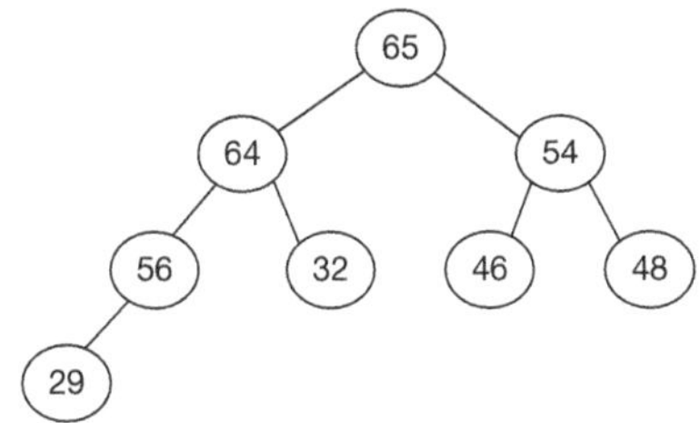

Now the elements of heap tree in array are as:

0	1	3	4	5	6	7	8	
65	64	54	56	32	46	48	29	**72**

Now 29 is the last node. So replace it with root 65 and do the same operation.

Step 2:

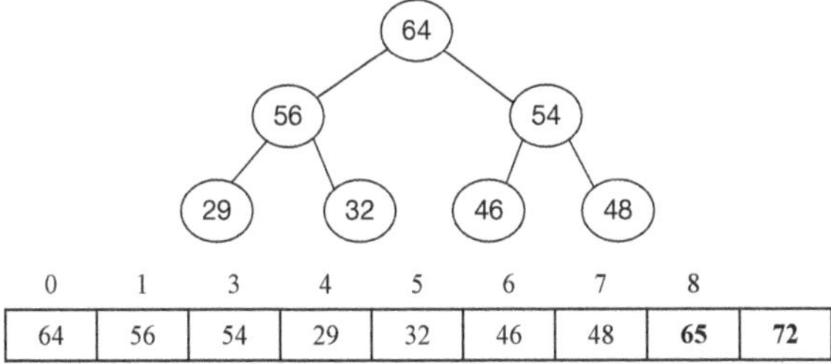

0	1	3	4	5	6	7	8	
64	56	54	29	32	46	48	**65**	**72**

Step 3: same as step 1 and step 2

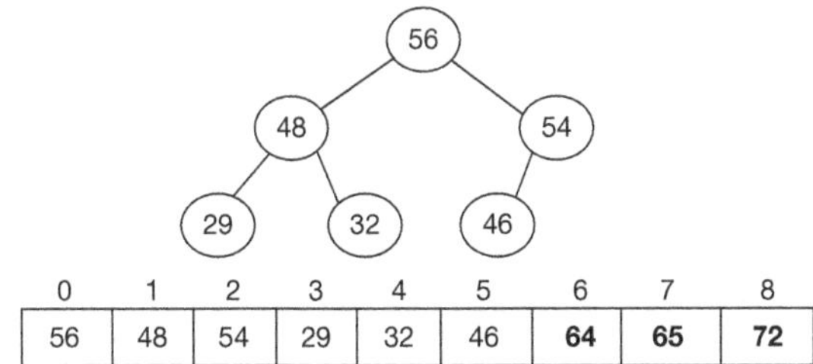

0	1	2	3	4	5	6	7	8
56	48	54	29	32	46	**64**	**65**	**72**

Step 4:

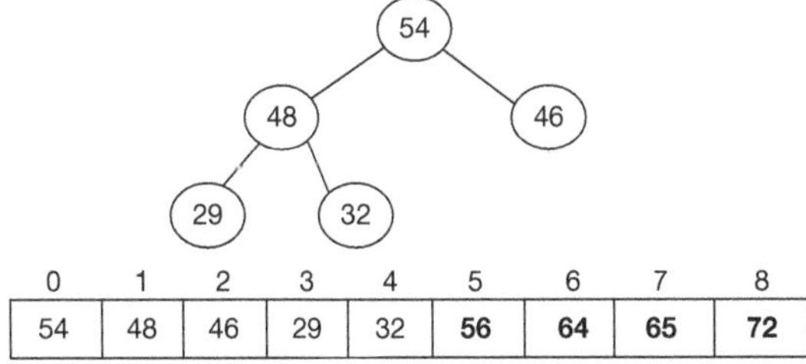

0	1	2	3	4	5	6	7	8
54	48	46	29	32	**56**	**64**	**65**	**72**

Step 5:

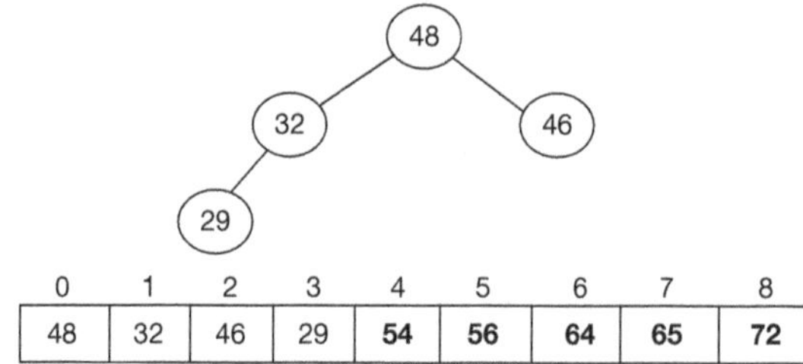

Step 6:

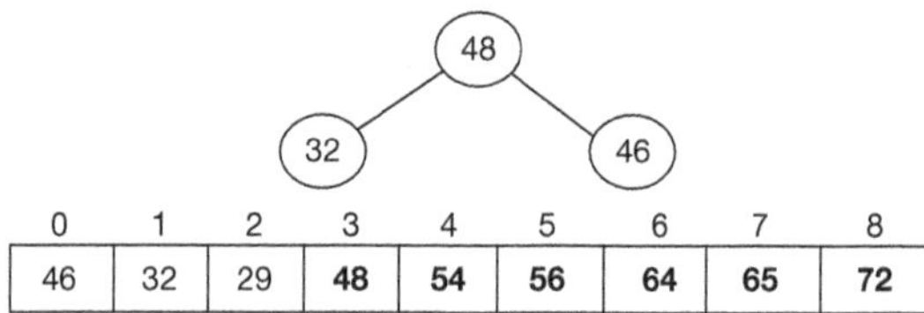

Step 7:

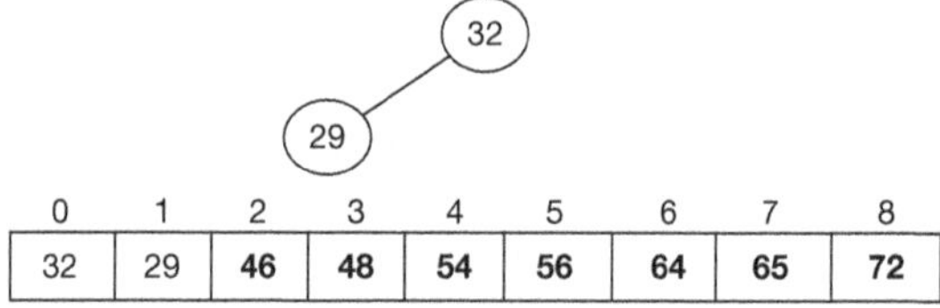

Step 8:

29

0	1	2	3	4	5	6	7	8
29	32	46	48	54	56	64	65	72

Now all the numbers are in sorted order

Program: Write a program Implement heap sort

```
#include<stdio.h>
void main()
{
int a[20],i,j,temp,n,root,c;
printf("Enter size of array : ");
scanf("%d",&n);
printf("Enter element in array : ");
for(i=0;i<n;i++)
scanf("%d",&a[i]);
for(i=1;i<n;i++)
```

```
{
c=i;
        do
        {
        root=(c-1)/2;
        if(a[root]<a[c])
        {
        temp=a[root];
        a[root]=a[c];
        a[c]=temp;
        }
        c=root;
        }while(c!=0);
}
printf("Heap array : ");
for(i=0;i<n;i++)
printf(" %d",a[i]);
for(j=n-1;j>=0;j--)
{
temp=a[0];
a[0]=a[j];
a[j]=temp;
root=0;
        do
        {
        c=2*root+1;
        if(a[c]<a[c+1] && c<j-1)
        c++;
        if(a[root]<a[c] && c<j)
        {
        temp=a[root];
        a[root]=a[c];
        a[c]=temp;
        }
        root=c;
        }while(c<j);
```

```
}
printf("\n\n\a\a\a\aSorted array : ");
for(i=0;i<n;i++)
printf(" %d",a[i]);
}
```

Output

```
Enter size of array : 8
Enter element in array : 72
64
65
56
32
46
54
29
48
Heap array : 72 64 65 56 32 46 54 29 48
Sorted array : 29 32 46 48 54 56 64 65 72
```

8.11 QUICK SORT

C.A.R. Hoare implements quick sort by divide and conquer method. That means divide the big problem into two small problems and then those two small problems into small ones and so on. To Quick sort, we divide the original list into two sub lists. We choose the item from list called key or pivot from which all the left side of elements are smaller and all the right side of elements are greater than that element. So we can create two lists, one list on the left side of pivot element and the second list is on light side of the pivot. Thus, quick sort works by partitioning a given array A[p.......r] into two non-empty sub-arrays A[p.....q] and A[q+1......r] such that every key in A[p......q] is less than or equal to every key in A[q+1......r]. Then the two sub-arrays are stored by recursive calls to quick sort. The exact position of the partition depends on the given array and index q is computed as a part of the partitioning procedure.

Algorithm

Quick SORT (A, p, r)

1. if p < r then
2. q = PARTITION (A, p, r)

3. QUICK-SORT (A, p, q-1)
4. QUICK-SORT (A, q+1, r)

Note that to sort entire array, the initial call is quick sort (A, 1, length [A]) as a first step, quick sort choose as pivot one of the items in the array to be sorted. Then array is partitioned on either side of the pivot. Elements that are less than or equal to pivot will move towards the left and elements that are greater than or equal to pivot will move towards the right.

Partitioning the Array

Algorithm

PARTITION (A, p, r)

1. x = A[r]
2. i = p - 1
3. for j = p to r - 1
4. do if A[j] ≤ x
5. then i = i + 1
6. exchange A[i] = A[j]
7. exchange A[i + 1] = A [r]
8. return i + 1

1. All the elements on the left side of pivot should be smaller or equal to the pivot.
2. All the elements on the right side of pivot should be greater than or equal to pivot.

The process for sorting the elements through quick sort is as:

1. Take the first element of list as pivot.
2. Place pivot at the proper place in list.
3. For placing the pivot at proper place we have a need to do the following process:
   (*a*) Compare the pivot element one by one right to left for getting the element which has value less than pivot element.
   (*b*) Interchange the element with pivot element.
   (*c*) Now the comparison will start from the interchanged element position from left to right for getting the element which has higher value than pivot.
   (*d*) Repeat the same process until pivot is at its proper position.

Example: Let us take list of element and process through quick sort

46 27 6 57 70 86 40 63 93 17 80 66

Solution:

Taking 46 as pivot, we have to start comparison from right to left.

Pivot value: 46

Smallest value less than pivot: 17

Interchange it with pivot

17 27 6 57 70 86 40 63 93 46 80 66

Now the comparison will start from 17, left to right

Value greater than pivot: 57

Interchange it with pivot

17 27 6 46 70 86 40 63 93 57 80 66

Now the comparison will start from 57, right to left

Smallest value less than pivot: 40

Interchange it with pivot

17 27 6 40 70 86 46 63 93 57 80 66

Now the comparison will start from 40, left to right

Value greater than pivot: 70

Interchange it with pivot

17 27 6 40 46 86 70 63 93 57 80 66

Sub-array1: 17 27 6 40

Pivot value: 46

Sub-array2: 86 70 63 93 57 80 66

Now we have a need to do the same process for sub-arrays and at the end all the elements of list will be at its proper position.

Now all the element in sorted order:

6 17 27 40 46 57 63 66 70 80 86 93

Program: Write a program to Implement a quick sort

```
#include<stdio.h>
void quicksort(int [10],int,int);
int main()
{
int x[20],size,i;
printf("Enter size of the array: ");
scanf("%d",&size);
printf("Enter %d elements: ",size);
```

```
for(i=0;i<size;i++)
scanf("%d",&x[i]);
quicksort(x,0,size-1);
printf("Sorted elements: \n");
for(i=0;i<size;i++)
printf(" %d",x[i]);
return 0;
}
void quicksort(int x[10],int first,int last)
{
int pivot,j,temp,i;
        if(first<last)
        {
pivot=first;
i=first;
j=last;
while(i<j)
        {
while(x[i]<=x[pivot]&&i<last)
i++;
while(x[j]>x[pivot])
j--;
if(i<j)
        {
temp=x[i];
x[i]=x[j];
x[j]=temp;
}
}
temp=x[pivot];
x[pivot]=x[j];
x[j]=temp;
quicksort(x,first,j-1);
quicksort(x,j+1,last);
        }
}
```

Output

Enter size of the array: 12
Enter 12 elements:
46
27
6
57
70
86
40
63
93
17
80
66
Sorted elements:
6 17 27 40 46 57 63 66 70 80 86 93

8.12 RADIX SORT

This sort is based on the values of the actual digits in the positional representations of the numbers being sorted. For example, the number 475 in decimal notation is written with a 4 in the hundred position, a 7 in the tens position, and a 5 in the unit position. The larger of the two such integer of equal length can be determined as follows: start at the most significant digit and advance through the least significant digits as long as the corresponding digits in the two numbers match. The number with the larger digit in the first position in which the digits of the two numbers do not match is the larger of the two numbers. Of course, if all the digits of both numbers match, the numbers are equal. To sort decimal numbers, we need ten buckets, since the base or radix is ten. These buckets are numbered 0,1,2,3,4,5,6,7,8,9.

Example: let us take number in unsorted order and sort them by applying radix sort.

235 126 211 347 499 569 330 165

Solution:

Step 1: Take these numbers on the basis of unit digit

Numbers	0	1	2	3	4	5	6	7	8	9
235						235				
126							126			
211		211								
347								347		
499										499
569										569
330	330									
165						165				

After step 1, numbers are: 330 211 235 165 126 347 499 569

Step 2: Take these numbers on the basis of tens digit

Numbers	0	1	2	3	4	5	6	7	8	9
330				330						
211		211								
235				235						
165							165			
126			126							
347					347					
499										499
569							569			

After step 2, numbers are: 211 126 330 235 347 165 569 499

Step 3: Take these numbers on the basis of hundred

Numbers	0	1	2	3	4	5	6	7	8	9
211			211							
126		126								
330				330						
235			235							
347				347						
165		165								
569						569				
499					499					

After step 3, numbers are: 126 165 211 235 330 347 499 569

Now the sorted numbers are: 126 165 211 235 330 347 499 569

Algorithm

RADIX SORT

1. start
2. radix (a, n)
3. set large = largest element in the array
4. set num = total number of digits in the array
5. set digit = num
6. set pass = 1
7. repeat steps 8 to 15 while ≤ num
8. initialize buckets
9. set i = 0
10. repeat steps 11 to 13 while i ≤ n-1
11. set l = pass-1 position of number a[i]
    // 0th position of number 123
12. put the number a[i] into bucket l
13. set i = i+1
14. end of step 10 loop
15. set pass = pass+1
16. end of step 7 loop
17. write all the numbers from the bucket in order
18. stop

Program: Write a program to implement a radix sort

```
#include<stdio.h>
#include<conio.h>
int largest (int arr[], int n);
void radixsort(int arr[], int n)
void main()
{
int arr[20], i, n;
printf("enter the number of element in the array:");
scanf("%d", &n);
printf("enter the elements of the array");
```

```
for(i=0;i<n;i++)
{
scanf("%d", &arr[i]);
}
radixsort(arr,n);
printf("sorted array is:");
for(i=0;i<n;i++)
printf("%d \t", arr[i]);
getch();
}
int largest(int arr[], int n)
{
int large = arr[0], i;
for (i=1;i<n;i++)
{
if(arr[i]>large)
large=arr[i];
}
return large;
}
void radixsort(int arr[], int n)
{
int bucket[10][10], bucketcount[10];
int i,j,k,remainder,number_of_position=0,division=1,large,pass;
large=largest(arr,n);
while(large>0)
{
number_of_position++;
large/=10;
}
for(pass=0;pass<number_of_position;pass++)
{
for(i=0;i<20;i++)
bucketcount[i]=0;
for(i=0;i<n;i++)
{
```

```
//sort the number according to the digit
remainder=(arr[i]/divisor)%10;
bucket[remainder][bucketcount[remainder]]=arr[i];
bucketcount[remainder]+=1
}
//collect the numbers after pass
i=0;
for(k=0;k<20;k++)
{
for(j=0;j<bucketcount[k];j++)
{
arr[i]=bucket[k][j];
i++;
}
}
divisor*=10;
}
}
```

Output

```
enter the number of element in the array:8
enter the elements of the array:
235
126
211
347
499
569
330
165
sorted array is:
126
165
211
235
330
```

347

499

569

Table: Best, Average, Worst case Complexity

Algorithm	Time Complexity			Space Complexity
	Best Case	Average Case	Worst Case	
Bubble Sort	Ω(n)	Θ(n^2)	O(n^2)	O(1)
Insertion Sort	Ω(n)	Θ(n^2)	O(n^2)	O(1)
Selection Sort	Ω(n^2)	Θ(n^2)	O(n^2)	O(1)
Merge Sort	Ω(n log(n))	Θ(n log(n))	O(n log(n))	O(n)
Heap Sort	Ω(n log(n))	Θ(n log(n))	O(n log(n))	O(1)
Quick Sort	Ω(n log(n))	Θ(n log(n))	O(n^2)	O(log(n))
Radix Sort	Ω(nk)	Θ(nk)	O(nk)	O(n+k)

POINTS TO REMEMBER

1. Searching refers to finding the position of a value in a collection of values.
2. In bubble sorting, consecutive adjacent pairs of elements in the array are compared with each other.
3. Selection sort works by finding the smallest value and placing it in the first position.
4. Insertion sort works by moving the current data element past the already sorted values and repeatedly interchanging it with the proceeding value until it is in the correct place.
5. Merge sort is a sorting algorithm that uses the divide, conquer and combine algorithm paradigm.
6. Heap sort an array in two phases. In the first phase, it built a heap of the given array. In the second phase, the root element is deleted repeatedly and inserted into an array.
7. Quick sort works by using divide-and-conquer strategy.
8. Radix sort is a linear sorting algorithm that uses the concept of sorting names in alphabetical order.
9. Linear search works by comparing the value to be searched with every element of the array one by one is a sequence until a match is found.
10. Binary search works efficiently with a sorted list. In this algorithm, the value to be searched is compared with the middle element of the array segment.

11. Internal sorting deals with sorting the data stored in the memory, whereas external sorting deals with sorting the data stored in files.

MULTIPLE CHOICE QUESTIONS

1. The worst case complexity is ______ when compared with the average case complexity of a binary search algorithm.
   (*a*) Equal (*b*) Greater
   (*c*) Less (*d*) None of these
2. The complexity of binary search algorithm is
   (*a*) O (n) (*b*) O (n^2)
   (*c*) O (n log n) (*d*) O (log n)
3. Which of the following cases occurs when searching an array using linear search the value to be searched is equal to the first element of the array?
   (*a*) Worst case (*b*) Average case
   (*c*) Best case (*d*) Amortized case
4. A card game player arranges his cards and picks them one by one. With which sorting technique can you compare this example?
   (*a*) Bubble sort (*b*) Selection sort
   (*c*) Merge sort (*d*) Insertion sort
5. Which of the following techniques deals with sorting the data stored in the computer's memory?
   (*a*) Insertion sort (*b*) Internal sort
   (*c*) External sort (*d*) Radix sort
6. In which sorting, consecutive adjacent pairs of elements in the array are compared with each other?
   (*a*) Bubble sort (*b*) Selection sort
   (*c*) Merge sort (*d*) Radix sort
7. Which term means sorting the two sub-arrays recursively using merge sort?
   (*a*) Divide (*b*) Conquer
   (*c*) Combine (*d*) All of these
8. Which sorting algorithm sorts by moving the current data element past the already sorted values and repeatedly interchanging it with the preceding value until it is in its correct place?
   (*a*) Insertion sort (*b*) Internal sort
   (*c*) External sort (*d*) Radix sort

9. Which algorithm uses the divide, conquer, and combine algorithmic paradigm?
   (*a*) Selection sort (*b*) Insertion sort
   (*c*) Merge sort (*d*) Radix sort
10. Quick sort is faster than
   (*a*) Selection sort (*b*) Insertion sort
   (*c*) Bubble sort (*d*) All of these
11. Which sorting algorithm is also known as tournament sort?
   (*a*) Selection sort (*b*) Insertion sort
   (*c*) Bubble sort (*d*) Heap sort

TRUE OR FALSE

1. Binary search is also called sequential search.
2. Linear search is performed on a sorted array.
3. For insertion sort, the best case occurs when the array is already sorted.
4. Selection sort has a linear running time complexity.
5. The running time of merge sort in the average case and the worst case is o (n log n).
6. The worst case running time complexity of quick sort is o (n log n).
7. Heap sort is an efficient and a stable sorting algorithm.
8. External sorting deals with sorting the data stored in the computer's memory.
9. Insertion sort is less efficient than quick sort, heap sort, and merge sort.
10. The average case of insertion sort has a quadratic running time.
11. The partitioning of the array in quick sort is done in o (n) time.

FILL IN THE BLANKS

1. Performance of the linear search algorithm can be improved by using a ________.
2. The complexity of linear search algorithm is___________.
3. Sorting means___________.
4. _____________ sort shows the best average-case behaviour.
5. ___________ deals with sorting the data stored in files.
6. O (n^2) is the running time complexity of __________ algorithm.
7. In the worst case, insertion sort has a __________ running time.
8. __________ sort uses the divide, conquer, and combine algorithm paradigm.
9. In the average case, quick sort has a running time complexity of__________.

10. The execution time of bucket sort in an average case is __________.
11. The running time of merge sort in the average and the worst case is__________.
12. The efficiency of quick sort depends on __________.

EXERCISES

1. Show all the passes using bubble sort with following list:

   234 54 12 76 11 87 32 12 45 67 76
2. Show all the passes using insertion sort with following list:

   13 33 27 77 12 43 10 432 112 90
3. Show all the passes using selection sort with following list:

   10 22 65 223 87 343 98 244 543 22 4
4. Show all the passes using quick sort with following list:

   19 123 43 78 242 98 34 75 135 87 24
5. Show all the passes using radix sort with following list:

   123 76 456 244 654 865 124 987 222 890
6. Show all the passes using merge sort with following list

   194 34 12 756 54 1 88 54 897 23 96 34
7. Which techniques of searching an element in an array would you prefer to use in which condition?
8. Define sorting? What is importance of sorting?
9. What are the different types of sorting techniques?
10. Write a program to implement a bubble sort?
11. Write a program to implement a insertion sort?
12. Write a program to implement a selection sort?
13. Write a program to implement a merge sort?
14. Write a program to implement a heap sort?
15. Write a program to implement a quick sort?
16. Write a program to implement a radix sort?
17. Write a program to implement a merging of two sorted array?

REFERENCES

1. A simple merge algorithm that merges two contiguous lists in time proportional to n while using a small fixed amount of additional storage space appears in Bing-Chao Huang, Michael A. Langston, Practical in place Merging, Communication of the ACM,31 pp. 348-352.

2. Ashenhurst, R.L., External Sorting based on the radix sorting principle, Theory of switching, Harvard University Press.
3. Bentley, J.L., and M.D. McIcroy, Better way of partitioning, software practice and experience, 23, pp. 1249-1265.
4. Betz, B.K., Memorandum, Minneapolis-Honeywell Regulator Co., 1956.
5. Bing-Chao Huang, Michael A. Langston, Practical in place Merging, Communication of the ACM, 31 pp. 348-352.
6. Demuth, H.B., Ph.D. Thesis, Stanford University, A Sorting method using Bubble sort principle with two tapes, 1956.
7. Frager W.D., and A.C. McKeller, Multipartition quick sort, Journal of the ACM, 17, pp. 496-497.
8. Friend, E.H., Quadric sorting, 44, pp. 246-253.
9. Gilstad, R.L., Poly phase merge sort, proceeding of Eastern joint computer conference, 18, pp. 143-148.
10. Hadian and M. Sobel, A Survey on external sorting techniques, technical report, University of Minnesota, No. 121, 1969.
11. Hildebrandt, P., H. Isbitz, H. Rising and J.Schwartz, in the word of sorting, journal of ACM, 6, pp. 156-163.
12. Hoare, C.A., Quick sort, computer journal 5 (1), pp. 10-15.
13. Hwang, F.K., and Lin, S., Binary Merging SICOMP (Journal of Computing (SICOMP), Society for Industrial and Applied Mathematics (SIAM), 1, pp. 31-39.
14. Incerpi, Janet, and Sedgewick, Robert, How to sort better a large collection? Journal of computer system and science, 31, pp. 210-224.
15. Isaac, E.J., and R.C.Singleton, Efficient partitioning method for quick sorting, journal of ACM,3, pp. 169-174.
16. Knuth, D.E., The art of computer programming, 2nd Ed., 3, Addison-Wesley, New York, USA.
17. Knuth Donald E., The art of computer programming, 2nd Ed., 3. Sorting and searching, Stanford University, Addison-Wesley, CA, USA.
18. Lomuto, N., Programming pearls, Addison-Wesley, Reading MA, New York.
19. Sedgewick, Robert, let's make quick sort more quick, communication of ACM, 21, pp. 847-857.
20. Sedgewick, Robert, sorting algorithm for linear data, journal of algorithm, 7, pp. 159-173.
21. Shell, Donald, L., Better than N^2 sorting with sequential data storage, communication of the ACM, 2, 7, pp.30-32.
22. Sobel, Sheldo, Oscillatory Sorting: An external sorting approach, journal of ACM, 9, pp. 327-375.
23. Tanner, R. Michael, Minimean merging and sorting: an algorithm, SIAM, journal of computing, 7, pp. 18-38.
24. Weiss, M.A., Improving the $O(N^2)$ sorting for large sequential storage data, computer journal, 34, pp. 88-91.
25. Williams, J.W.J., Non-linear sorting with heap data structure, communication of the ACM, 6, pp. 347-358.
26. Yoash, N.B., A technique of the partition exchange or quick sort on data stored on two tapes, ACM, 8, pp. 649-657.

9

Hashing Techniques

9.1 INTRODUCTION

We have seen different searching techniques where search time basically dependent on the number of elements. Sequential search, binary search and all the search trees totally depend on number of elements and key comparisons involved. Suppose, all the elements are in an array having size n. Let us say all the keys are unique and in the range 0 to n-1. Now we are storing the records in array based on the key where array index and keys are same. Now we can access the record in constant time and comparisons.

9.2 HASH TABLES

Hash tables support one of the most efficient types of searching: hashing. Fundamentally, a hash table consists of an array in which data is accessed via a special index called a key. The primary idea behind a hash table is to establish a mapping between the set of all possible keys and positions in the array using a hash function. A hash function accepts a key and returns its hash value. Keys vary in type, but coding are always integers. Since both computing a hash value and indexing into an array can be performed in constant time, the beauty of hashing is that we can use it to perform constant time searches. When a hash function can guarantee that no two keys will generate the same hash coding, the resulting hash table is said to be directly addressed. This is ideal, but direct addressing is rarely possible in practice. Typically, the number of entries in a hash table is small relative to the universe of possible keys. Consequently, most hash functions map some keys to the same position in the table. When two keys map to the same position, they collide. A good hash function minimises collisions, but we must still be prepared to deal with them.

9.3 APPLICATIONS OF HASH TABLES

Some applications of hash tables are:

1. Database Systems

Generally, database systems try to optimise between two types of access method: sequential and random. Hash tables are an important part of efficient random access because they provide a way to locate data in a constant amount of time.

2. Symbol Tables

The tables used by compilers to maintain information about symbols from a program. Compilers access information about symbols frequently. Therefore, it is important that symbol tables be implemented very efficiently.

3. Tagged Buffers

A mechanism for storing and retrieving data in a machine - independent manner. Each data member resides at fixed offset in the buffer. A hash table is stored in the buffer so that the location of each tagged member can be ascertained quickly. One use of a tagged buffer is sending structured data across a network to a machine whose byte ordering and structure alignment may not be same as the original host's. The buffer handles these concerns as the data is stored and extracted member by member.

4. Data Dictionaries

Data Structures that support adding, deleting, and searching for data. Although the operations of a hash table and a data dictionary are similar, other data structures may be used to implement data dictionaries. Using a hash table is particularly efficient.

9.4 HASHING

Hashing is a technique to convert a range of key values into a range of indexes of an array. We're going to use modulo operator to get a range of key values. Consider an example of hash table of size 20 with following items stored in it. Item are in (key, value) format.

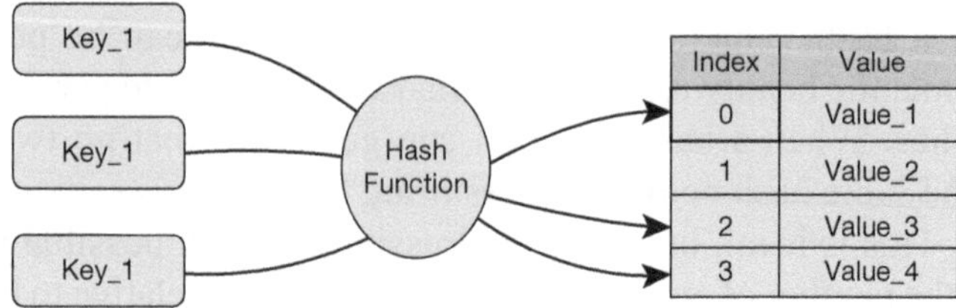

- (1,20)
- (2,70)
- (42,80)

- (4,25)
- (12,44)
- (14,32)
- (17,11)
- (13,78)
- (37,98)

S.n.	Key	Hash	Array Index
1	1	1 % 20 = 1	1
2	2	2 % 20 = 2	2
3	42	42 % 20 = 2	2
4	4	4 % 20 = 4	4
5	12	12 % 20 = 12	12
6	14	14 % 20 = 14	14
7	17	17 % 20 = 17	17
8	13	13 % 20 = 13	13
9	37	37 % 20 = 17	17

9.5 HASH FUNCTIONS

A hash function is any function that can be used to map data of arbitrary size to data of fixed size. The values returned by a hash function are called hash values, hash codes, hash sums, or simply hashes. The intent is that elements will be relatively randomly and uniformly distributed. Perfect Hash function is a function which, when applied to all the members of the set of items to be stored in a hash table, produces a unique set of integers within some suitable range. Such function produces no collisions. Good Hash Function minimises collisions by spreading the elements uniformly throughout the array. There is no magic formula for the creation of the hash function. It can be any mathematical transformation that produces a relatively random and unique distribution of values within the address space of the storage.

Characteristics of a Good Hash Function

There are four main characteristics of a good hash function:

1. The hash value is fully determined by the data being hashed.
2. The hash function uses all the input data.
3. The hash function “uniformly” distributes the data across the entries set of possible hash values.
4. The hash function generates very different hash values for similar strings.

Rule 1

If something else besides the input data is used to determine the hash, then the hash value is not as dependent upon the input data, thus allowing for a worse distribution of the hash values.

Rule 2

If the hash function does not use all the input data, then slight variations to the input data would cause an inappropriate number of similar hash values resulting in too many collisions.

Rule 3

If the hash function does not uniformly distribute the data across the set of possible hash values, a large number of collisions will result, cutting down on the efficiency of the hash table.

Rule 4

In real world applications, many data sets contain very similar data elements. We would like these data elements to still be distributable over a hash table.

9.6 TYPES OF HASH FUNCTIONS

1. Division Method

Perhaps the simplest of all the methods of hashing is *division method hashing* which states that an integer x is to divide x by M and then to use the remainder modulo M. In this case, the hash function is

$$h(x) = x \bmod M$$

Generally, this approach is quite good for just about any value of M. However, in certain situations some extra care is needed in the selection of a suitable value for M. For example, it is often convenient to make M an even number. But this means that $h(x)$ is even if x is even; and $h(x)$ is odd if x is odd. If all possible keys are equiprobable, then this is not a problem. However, if we say, even keys are more likely than odd keys, the function $h(x) = x \bmod M$ will not spread the hashed values of those keys evenly.

Similarly, it is often tempting to let M be a power of two. *e.g.*, $M = 2^k$ for some integer $k>1$. In this case, the hash function $h(x) = x \bmod 2^k$ simply extracts the bottom k bits of the binary representation of x. While this hash function is quite easy to compute, it is not a desirable function because it does not depend on all the bits in the binary representation of x.

For these reasons M is often chosen to be a prime number. For example, suppose there is a bias in the way the keys are created that makes it more likely for a key to be a multiple of some small constant, say two or three. Then making M a prime increases the likelihood that those keys are spread out evenly. Also, if M is a prime number, the division of x by that prime number depends on all the bits of x, not just the bottom k bits, for some small constant k.

A potential disadvantage of the division method is due to the property that consecutive keys map to consecutive hash values:

$$h\,(i) = i$$

$$h\,(i{+}1) = i{+}1 \pmod{M}$$

$$h\,(i{+}2) = i{+}2 \pmod{M}$$

While this ensures that consecutive keys do not collide, it does mean that consecutive array locations will be occupied. We will see that in certain implementations this can lead to degradation in performance. In the following sections we consider hashing methods that tend to scatter consecutive keys. In the division method for creating hash functions, we map a key k into one of m slots by taking the remainder of k divided by m. That is, the hash function is:

h (k) = k mod m or h(k) = k mod m +1

For example, if the hash table has size m =11 and the key is k = 90, then h(k) = 2, since it requires only a single division operation, hashing by division is quite fast.

2. Multiplication Method

A very simple variation on the middle-square method that alleviates its deficiencies is the so-called, *multiplication hashing method.* Instead of multiplying the key x by itself, we multiply the key by a carefully chosen constant a, and then extract the middle k bits from the result. In this case, the hashing function is

$$h(x) = \left\lfloor \frac{M}{W}(ax \bmod W) \right\rfloor.$$

What is a suitable choice for the constant a? If we want to avoid the problems that the middle-square method encounters with keys having a large number of leading or trailing zeroes, then we should choose a that has neither leading nor trailing 0's.

Furthermore, if we choose an a that is *relatively prime* to W, then there exists another number a' such that $aa' = 1 \pmod{W}$. In other words, a' is the *inverse* of a modulo W, since the product of a and its inverse is one. Such a number has the nice property that if we take a key x, and multiply it by a to get ax, we can recover the original key by multiplying the product again by a', since $axa' = aa'x = 1x$.

There are many possible constants with the desired properties. One possibility which is suited for 32-bit arithmetic (*i.e.*, $W = 2^{32}$) is $a = 2654435769$. The binary representation of a is

$$10011110001101101111001101111001$$

This number has neither many leading nor trailing zeroes. Also, this value of a and $W = 2^{32}$ are relatively prime and the inverse of a modulo W is $a' = 340573321$.

The multiplication method for creating hash functions operates in two steps: First, we multiply the key k by a constant A in the range 0 < A < 1 and extract the fractional part of kA. Then we multiply this value by m and take the floor of the result. In short, the hash function is:

$$h(k) = \lfloor m (k A \bmod 1) \rfloor$$

Where "k A mod 1" means the fractional part of KA, that is, $k A - \lfloor kA \rfloor$

3. Mid square Method

We consider a hashing method which avoids the use of division. Since integer division is usually slower than integer multiplication, by avoiding division we can potentially improve the running time of the hashing algorithm. We can avoid division by making use of the fact that a computer does finite-precision integer arithmetic. *e.g.*, all arithmetic is done by modulo W where $W = 2^x$, a power of two such that w is the *word size* of the computer.

The *middle-square hashing method* works as follows. First, we assume that M is a power of two, say $M = 2^k$ for some K>=1. Then, to hash an integer x, we use the following hash function:

$$h(x) = \left\lfloor \frac{M}{W}(x^2 \bmod W) \right\rfloor.$$

Notice that since M and W are both powers of two, the ratio $W/M = 2^{x-k}$ is also a power of two. Therefore, in order to multiply the term (x^2 mod W) by M/W we simply shift it to the right by w-k bits! In effect, we are extracting k bits from the middle of the square of the key--hence the name of the method.

The middle-square method does a pretty good job when the integer-valued keys are equiprobable. The middle-square method also has the characteristic that it scatters consecutive keys nicely. However, since the middle-square method only considers a subset of the bits in the middle of x^2, keys which have a large number of leading zeroes will collide. *e.g.*, consider the following set of keys:

$$\left\{x \varepsilon Z^+ : x < \sqrt{W/M}\right\}.$$

This set contains all keys x such that $x < 2^{(x-K)/2}$. For all of these keys $h(x) = 0$.

A similar line of reasoning applies for keys which have a large number of trailing zeroes.

Let W be an even power of two. Consider the set of keys

$$\left\{x \varepsilon Z^+ : x = n\sqrt{W}: n \varepsilon Z+\right\}.$$

The least significant $w/2$ bits of the keys in this set are all zero. Therefore, the least significant w bits of x^2 are also zero and as a result $h(x)=0$ for all such keys.

In mid square method we square the key, after getting number we take some digits from the middle of that number as an address. Let us take some 4 digit number as a key:

1228 1384 1481 1024

Now square these keys:

1228	1384	1481	1024
15<u>79</u>84	19<u>54</u>56	21<u>93</u>361	104<u>85</u>76

Now take the 3rd and 4th digit from each number and that will be the hash address of these keys. Let us assume here table size is 1000. So the hash address for keys will be 79, 54, 33 and 85

4. Folding Method

In this method the key is interpreted as an integer using some radix (say 10). The integer is divided into segments, each segment except possibly the last having the same number of digits. These segments are then added to obtain the home address.

As an example, consider the key **76123451001214**. Assume we are dividing keys into segments of size 3 digits. The segments for our key are 761, 234, 510, 012, and 14. The home bucket is 761 + 234 + 510 + 012 + 14 = 1531.

In a variant of this scheme, the digits in alternate segments are reversed before adding. This variant is called **folding at the boundaries** and the original version is called **shift folding**. Applying the folding at the boundaries method to the above example, the segments after digit reversal are 761, 432, 510, 210, and 14; the home bucket is 761 + 432 + 510 + 210 + 14 = 1927.

Hash Function for strings

Most of the places strings are used as keys. It can be alphabetic or alphanumeric. Best example is the English word dictionary. Every character has some ASCII value that can be used for calculation in generating hash key value and that value can be used with modulus operation for mapping with hash table. Suppose key has alphabetic character. Let us take table size is M (95) and keys is "arham". We can add the ASCII value of each character and then we can apply modulus operation on this value as:

arham = a + r + h + a + m

= 97+114+104+97+109

= 521

H(arham) = 521% 95 = 46

So the key "arham" can be mapped on the 46th position in the hash table.

Second method we can apply is, multiply each character ASCII value by 127 and add all the values then do the modulus operation. Let us take the key "arham" and table size 995.

arham = a x 127 + r x 127 + h x 127 + a x 127 + m x 127

= 97 x 127 + 114 x 127 + 104 x 127 + 97 x 127 + 109 x 127

= 12319 + 14478 + 13208 + 12319 + 13843

= 66167

After modulus operations:

H(arham) = 66167% 995

= 497

We use the value 127 for multiplication because ASCII character has maximum value 127. The key "arham" can be mapped on the 497th position in the table.

9.7 COLLISION RESOLUTION TECHNIQUES

Suppose we want to add a new record R with key k to our file F, but suppose the memory location address H (k) is already occupied. This situation is called collision. That is a collision occurs when more than one keys map to same hash value in the hash table.

Types of Collision Resolution Techniques:

1. Collision resolution by open addressing.
2. Collision resolution by separate chaining.

The performance of these methods depends on load factor *i.e.*, ratio $\lambda = n/m$. This is the ratio of the number n of keys in k to the number m of hash addresses. The efficiency of a hash function with a collision resolution is measured by the average number of **probes** needed to find the location of the record with a given key k.

9.8 HASHING WITH OPEN ADDRESSING

In open addressing, all elements are stored in the hash table itself. That is, each table entry contains either an element of the dynamic set or NIL. When searching for an element, we systematically examine table slots until the desired element is found or it is clear that the element is not in the table. Thus, in open addressing, the load factor can never exceed 1. The advantage of open addressing is that it avoids pointers altogether. Instead of following pointers, we compute the sequence of slots to be examined. The extra memory freed by not storing pointers provides the hash table with a larger number of slots for the same amount of memory, potentially yielding fewer collisions and faster retrieval. The process of examining the locations in the hash table is called a **'Probing'.** To perform insertion using open addressing, we successively examine, or probe, the hash table until we find an empty slot in which to put the key.

Three techniques are commonly used to compute the probe sequences required for open addressing: **Linear probing, quadratic probing and double hashing.**

1. Linear Probing

Suppose that a key hashes into a position that is already occupied. The simplest strategy is to look for the next available position to place the item. Suppose, we have a set of hash codes consisting of {89, 18, 49, 58, and 9} and we need to place them into a table of size 10. The following table demonstrates this process.

hash (89, 10) = 9

hash (18, 10) = 8

hash (49, 10) = 9

hash (58, 10) = 8

hash (9, 10) = 9

	After insert 89	After insert 18	After insert 49	After insert 58	After insert 9
0			49	49	49
1				58	58
2					9
3					
4					
5					
6					
7					
8		18	18	18	18
9	89	89	89	89	89

The first collision occurs when 49 hashes to the same location with index 9. Since 89 occupies the A[9], we need to place 49 to the next available position. Considering the array as circular, the next available position is 0. That is (9+1) mod 10. So we place 49 in A[0]. Several more collisions occur in this simple example and in each case we keep looking to find the next available location in the array to place the element. Now, if we need to find the element, say for example, 49, we first compute the hash code (9), and look in A[9]. Since, we do not find it there, we look in A[(9+1) % 10] = A[0], we find it there and we are done. So what if we are looking for 79? First we compute hashcode of 79 = 9. We probe in A[9], A[(9+1)%10]=A[0], A[(9+2)%10]=A[1], A[(9+3)%10]=A[2], A[(9+4)%10]=A[3] etc. Since A[3] = null, we do know that 79 could not exists in the set.

2. Quadratic probing

Although linear probing is a simple process where it is easy to compute the next available location, linear probing also leads to some clustering when keys are computed to closer values. Therefore, we define a new process of Quadratic probing that provides a better distribution of keys when collisions occur. In quadratic probing, if the hash value is K, then the next location is computed using the sequence K + 1, K + 4, K + 9 etc..

The following table shows the collision resolution using quadratic probing.

hash (89, 10) = 9

hash (18, 10) = 8

hash (49, 10) = 9

hash (58, 10) = 8

hash (9, 10) = 9

	After insert 89	After insert 18	After insert 49	After insert 58	After insert 9
0			49	49	49
1					
2				58	58
3					9
4					
5					
6					
7					
8		18	18	18	18
9	89	89	89	89	89

3. Double Hashing

Double hashing uses the idea of applying a second hash function to the key when a collision occurs. The result of the second hash function will be the numbers of positions from the point of collision to insert.

There are a couple of requirements for the second function:

- it must never evaluate to 0
- must make sure that all cells can be probed

A popular second hash function is: $Hash_2(key) = R - (key \% R)$ where R is a prime number that is smaller than the size of the table.

Table Size = 10 elements
$Hash_1$ (key) = key % 10
$Hash_2$ (key) = 7 – (k % 7)

Insert keys:89, 18, 49, 58, 69

Hash(89) = 89%10 = 9

Hash(18) = 18%10 = 8

Hash(49) = 49%10 = 9 a collision!
= 7– (49 % 7)
= 7 position from [9]

Hash(58) = 58%10 = 8
= 7– (58 % 7)
= 5 position from [8]

Hash(69) = 69%10 = 9
= 7– (69 % 7)
= 1 position from [9]

[0]	49
[1]	
[2]	
[3]	69
[4]	
[5]	
[6]	
[7]	58
[8]	18
[9]	89

Hashing with Rehashing

Once the hash table gets too full, the running time for operations will start to take too long and may fail. To solve this problem, a table at least twice the size of the original will be built and the elements will be transferred to the new table.

The new size of the hash table:

- should also be prime
- will be used to calculate the new insertion spot (hence the name **rehashing**)

This is a very expensive operation! O(N) since there are N elements to rehash and the table size is roughly 2N. This is ok though since it doesn't happen that often.

The question arises when should the rehashing be applied?

Some possible answers:

- once the table becomes half full
- once an insertion fails
- once a specific load factor has been reached, where load factor is the ratio of the number of elements in the hash table to the table size

More Examples for Hashing Concept

Hashing

Hashing can be used to build, search, or delete from a table. The basic idea behind hashing is to take a field in a record, known as the **key**, and convert it through some fixed process to a numeric value, known as the **hash key**, which represents the position to either store or find an item in the table. The numeric value will be in the range of 0 to n-1, where n is the maximum number of slots (or **buckets**) in the table.

The fixed process to convert a key to a hash key is known as a **hash function**. This function will be used whenever access to the table is needed.

One common method of determining a hash key is the **division method** of hashing. The formula that will be used is:

hash key = key % number of slots in the table

Assume a table with 8 slots:

Hash key = key% table size

4 = 36% 8

2 = 18% 8

0 = 72% 8

3 = 43% 8

6 = 6% 8

[0]	72
[1]	
[2]	18
[3]	43
[4]	36
[5]	
[6]	6
[7]	

The division method is generally a reasonable strategy, unless the key happens to have some undesirable properties. For example, if the table size is 10 and all of the keys end in zero.

In this case, the choice of hash function and table size needs to be carefully considered. The best table sizes are prime numbers.

One problem though is that keys are not always numeric. In fact, it's common for them to be strings.

One possible solution: add up the ASCII values of the characters in the string to get a numeric value and then perform the division method.

```
Int hashValue = 0;
for ( int j = 0; j < stringKey.length(); j++ )
hashValue += stringKey[j];
int hashKey = hashValue % tableSize;
```

The previous method is simple, but it is flawed if the table size is large. For example, assume a table size of 10007 and that all keys are eight or fewer characters long.

No matter what the hash function, there is the possibility that two keys could resolve to the same hash key. This situation is known as a **collision**.

When this occurs, there are two simple solutions:

1. chaining
2. linear probe (aka linear open addressing)

And two slightly more difficult solutions

3. Quadratic Probe
4. Double Hashing

9.9 HASHING WITH CHAINS

When a collision occurs, elements with the same hash key will be **chained** together. A **chain** is simply a linked list of all the elements with the same hash key.

The hash table slots will no longer hold a table element. They will now hold the address of a table element.

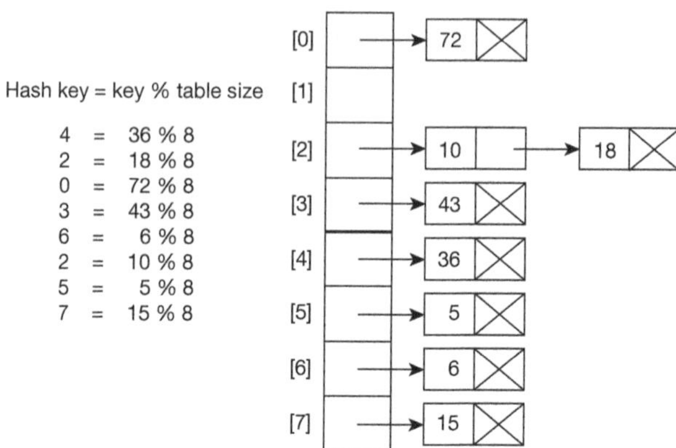

Searching a hash table with chains

Compute the hash key
If slot at hash key is null
Key not found
Else
Search the chain at hash key for the desired key
Endif

Inserting into a hash table with chains

Compute the hash key
If slot at hash key is null
Insert as first node of chain
Else
Search the chain for a duplicate key
If duplicate key
Don't insert
Else
Insert into chain
Endif
Endif

Deleting from a hash table with chains

Compute the hash key
If slot at hash key is null
Nothing to delete
Else
Search the chain for the desired key
If key is not found
Nothing to delete
Else
Remove node from the chain
Endif
Endif

Hashing with Linear Probe

When using a linear probe, the item will be stored in the next available slot in the table, assuming that the table is not already full.

This is implemented via a linear search for an empty slot, from the point of collision. If the physical end of table is reached during the linear search, the search will wrap around to the beginning of the table and continue from there.

If an empty slot is not found before reaching the point of collision, the table is full.

[0]	72
[1]	
[2]	18
[3]	43
[4]	36
[5]	
[6]	6
[7]	

Add the keys 10, 5, and 15 to the previous table.

Hash key = key % table size

2 = 10 % 8

5 = 5 % 8

7 = 15 % 8

[0]	72
[1]	15
[2]	18
[3]	43
[4]	36
[5]	10
[6]	6
[7]	5

A problem with the linear probe method is that it is possible for blocks of data to form when collisions are resolved. This is known as **primary clustering**.

This means that any key that hashes into the cluster will require several attempts to resolve the collision.

For example, insert the nodes 89, 18, 49, 58, and 69 into a hash table that holds 10 items using the division method:

[0]	49
[1]	58
[2]	69
[3]	
[4]	
[5]	
[6]	
[7]	
[8]	18
[9]	89

Hashing with Quadratic Probe

To resolve the primary clustering problem, **quadratic probing** can be used. With quadratic probing, rather than always moving one spot, move i^2 spots from the point of collision, where i is the number of attempts to resolve the collision.

89 % 10 = 9

10 % 10 = 9

49 % 10 = 9 – 1 attempts needed – 1^2 = 1 spot

58 % 10 = 8 – 3 attempts needed – 3^2 = 9 spot

69 % 10 = 9 – 2 attempts – 2^2 = 4 spot

[0]	49
[1]	
[2]	
[3]	69
[4]	
[5]	
[6]	
[7]	58
[8]	18
[9]	89

Limitation: atmost half of the table can be used as alternative locations to resolve collisions.

This means that once the table is more than half full, it's difficult to find an empty spot. This new problem is known as **secondary clustering** because elements that hash to the same hash key will always probe the same alternative cells.

Hashing with Double Hashing

Double hashing uses the idea of applying a second hash function to the key when a collision occurs. The result of the second hash function will be the number of positions from the point of collision to insert.

There are a couple of requirements for the second function:

- it must never evaluate to 0
- must make sure that all cells can be probed

A popular second hash function is: $Hash_2(key) = R - (key \% R)$ where R is a prime number that is smaller than the size of the table.

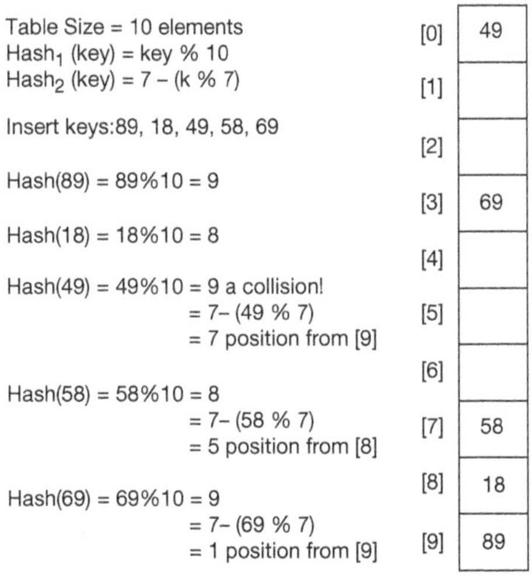

Table Size = 10 elements
$Hash_1$ (key) = key % 10
$Hash_2$ (key) = 7 – (k % 7)

Insert keys:89, 18, 49, 58, 69

Hash(89) = 89%10 = 9

Hash(18) = 18%10 = 8

Hash(49) = 49%10 = 9 a collision!
= 7– (49 % 7)
= 7 position from [9]

Hash(58) = 58%10 = 8
= 7– (58 % 7)
= 5 position from [8]

Hash(69) = 69%10 = 9
= 7– (69 % 7)
= 1 position from [9]

[0]	49
[1]	
[2]	
[3]	69
[4]	
[5]	
[6]	
[7]	58
[8]	18
[9]	89

9.10 HASHING WITH REHASHING

Once the hash table gets too full, the running time for operations will start to take too long and may fail. To solve this problem, a table at least twice the size of the original will be built and the elements will be transferred to the new table.

The new size of the hash table:

- should also be prime
- will be used to calculate the new insertion spot (hence the name **rehashing**)

This is a very expensive operation! O (N) since there are N elements to rehash and the table size is roughly 2N. This is ok though since it doesn't happen that often.

The question arises when should the rehashing be applied?

Some possible answers:

- once the table becomes half full
- once an insertion fails
- once a specific load factor has been reached, where load factor is the ratio of the number of elements in the hash table to the table size

Deletion from a Hash Table

The method of deletion depends on the method of insertion. In any of the cases, the same hash function(s) will be used to find the location of the element in the hash table.

There is a major problem that can arise if a collision occurred when inserting -- it's possible to "lose" an element.

9.11 INDEXED SEARCH TECHNIQUES

This searching technique is useful in searching direct access secondary storage devices. The general strategy of an indexed search is that the key is used to search the index, find the relative record position of the associated data and from there only one access is made to find the data.

Indexed Sequential Search Techniques

The Indexed Sequential Access Method (ISAM) involves considering the disk dependent factors of blocking and track size to build a partial index. ISAM first identifies the region and then within that region, a sequential search is made.

The strategy used to conduct an ISAM search is as follows:

(*a*) Search the main memory directory for a key that is greater than or equal to the target.

(*b*) Follow the corresponding pointer out to the disk and then sequentially search until we find a match (success) or the key that the directory maintains as the high key within that particular region failure.

For larger files, it may be advantageous to have more than level of this directory, structures. In this case, a two level directory structure may be used. In a two-level directory structure the entire primary directory should be kept in the main memory. The secondary directory should be brought as a single block of the disk file and the data records are stored as some n number of records per track. The primary directory divides the file into some m regions of records each. The pointer field in the primary directory points a record in the sub-directory instead of the actual file. Here, the search operation is done as follows:

(*a*) The search operation in a primary directory is done in a way to find a key which is greater than or equal to the target. Using the corresponding pointer field, the sub–directory is searched.

(*b*) In the sub–directory also, the search is made such that the key is greater than or equal to the target. The corresponding pointer filed is used to address a particular record in the actual file.

The search efficiency of the indexed sequential file is based on many factors. Some of them are:

1. To what degree the directory structures are able to subdivide the actual file.
2. To what degree the directory structure are able to reside in main memory.
3. The relationship of data records to physical characteristics of the disk such as blocking factors, track size and cylinder size.

This searching method is not suitable for a highly volatile file. It requires that the data records must be stored in a physically increasing or decreasing key order. If there are more records in the overflow area, the search efficiency tends to deteriorate. In that case, ISAM is called Intrinsically Slow Access Method. To avoid the deterioration problem, the actual file should be reorganized into a new file with no overflow. This organization operation cannot be done dynamically. It is a time–consuming task. The maintenance problems involved with the ISAM structures lead to the development of several dynamic indexing schemes.

POINTS TO REMEMBER

1. Hash table is a data structure in which keys are mapped to array positions by a hash function.
2. Popular hash function which use numeric keys are division method, multiplication method, mid-square method and folding method.
3. Division method divides x by M and then uses the remainder obtained.
4. Multiplication method applies the hash function given as h (x) = [m (ka mod 1)]
5. Collision occur when a hash function maps two different keys to the same location. Therefore, a method used to solve the problem of collisions, also called collision resolution techniques is applied.
6. Open addressing technique can be implemented using linear probing, quadratic probing, double hashing and rehashing.
7. The storage requirement for a hash table is o (k), where k is the number of keys actually used.

MULTIPLE CHOICE QUESTIONS

1. In a hash table, an element with key k is stored at index

(*a*) k (*b*) log k
(*c*) h (k) (*d*) k^2

2. In any hash function, m should be a
(*a*) prime number (*b*) composite number
(*c*) even number (*d*) odd number

3. In which of the following hash functions, do consecutive keys map to consecutive hash value?
(*a*) division method (*b*) multiplication method
(*c*) folding method (*d*) mid-square method

4. The process of examining memory locations in a hash table is called.
(*a*) hashing (*b*) collision
(*c*) probing (*d*) addressing

5. Which of the following methods is applied in the Berkeley fast file system to allocate free blocks?
(*a*) linear probing (*b*) quadratic probing
(*c*) double hashing (*d*) rehashing

6. Which open addressing technique is free from clustering problems?
(*a*) linear probing (*b*) quadratic probing
(*c*) double hashing (*d*) rehashing

TRUE OR FALSE

1. Hash table is based on the p of locality of reference.
2. Binary search takes o (n log n) time to execute.
3. The storage requirement for a hash table is o (k^2), where k is the number of keys.
4. Hashing takes place when two or more keys map to the same memory location.
5. A good hash function completely eliminates collision.
6. M should be too close to exact power of 2.
7. A sentinel value indicates that the location contains valid data.
8. Linear probing is sensitive to the distribution of input values.
9. A chained hash table is faster than a simple hash table.

FILL IN THE BLANKS

1. In a hash table, keys are mapped to array positions by a ________.
2. __________ is the process of mapping keys to appropriate locations in a hash table.

3. In open addressing, hash table stores either of two values ______ and ________.
4. When there is no free location in the hash table then _____ occurs.
5. More the number of collisions, higher is the number of ______ to find free location ________ which eliminates primary clustering but not secondary clustering.
6. _______ eliminates primary clustering but not secondary clustering.

EXERCISES

1. Discuss how one can handle overflow in hashing?
2. Write short notes on Hash Functions?
3. Define Hashing? Explain with example?
4. What is Collision? Explain any one collision resolution techniques with example?
5. What do you understand by hashing? Name two hashing techniques and explain them?
6. Define Hash Function? State different types of hash function, explain them with suitable example?
7. What is clustering in a Hash Table? Describe two methods for collision resolution?
8. Explain open addressing techniques?
9. Define the following:
   (*a*) Hash Table
   (*b*) Re-hashing
   (*c*) Hash Function
   (*d*) Hash Table Implementation

REFERENCES

1. Bell, J., A Hash code eliminating secondary clustering, the quadric quotient method, communication of the ACM, 13, 1970.
2. Enbody, R.J and H.C. Du, Dynamic Hashing schemes, computer surveys, 20, 1988.
3. Gonnet, G.H. and R. Baeza Yates, handbook of algorithms and data structures, Addison-Wesley, Reading, Massachusetts, 1988.
4. Gotlieb, C.C. and L.R. Gotlieb, Data types and structures, Prentice-Hall, Englewood Cliffs, New Jersey, 1986.
5. Guibas, L.J. and E. Szemerdi, the analysis of double hashing, sciences, 16, 1978.
6. Knuth, D.E., sorting and searching, the art of computer programming, 3 Addison-Wesley, Reading, Massachusetts, 1984.
7. Maurrer, W.D. and T.G. Lewis, Hash Table Methods, Computing Surveys, 7, 1995.
8. McKenzie, B.J., R. Harries and T. Bell, selecting a hashing algorithm, software practice and experience, 20, 1990.
9. Morris, R., Scatter storage techniques, Communication of the ACM, 11, 1998.